In this brilliant, definitive study, Père de Vaux has collected, sifted and organized a tremendous amount of information about the society and institutions of ancient Israel. His work is vast in scope, covering every aspect of Israelite life in Old Testament times, and will be an indispensable reference book for scholars. But it was primarily written for the non-specialist, giving him a fascinating and readable account of the society that was ancient Israel.

Father Roland de Vaux, O.P., is the director of the renowned Ecole Biblique in Jerusalem (Jordan) and was for fifteen years editor of its famous Revue Biblique. He is also a distinguished field archaeologist and a specialist in Biblical scripts and languages. In 1964-65 he was guest professor at Harvard Divinity School.

Volume 1: Social Institutions contains the Introduction and Parts I through III of the original one-volume edition.

Volume 2: Religious Institutions contains Part IV of the original edition.

Cyprus

THE GREAT SEA

○Hamath

▲Arvad

●Kadesh

Tadmor○

Riblah
Chun Zedad○
Berothai ZOBAH ►Hazar-enan?

Byblos
Gebal

○Helbon

Sidon Ijon? MT.HERMON ○Damascus
PHOENICIA MT.LEBANON

Tyre ○Dan
Abel MAACHAH ○Ashtaroth Nobah
IX VIII GESHUR
Accho VI ○Edrei
Cabul X ○Ramoth- ○Saicah
Dor Megiddo gilead
IV V Manahaim?
III Shechem○ VII
I ○Adamah
Joppa II Bethel XII ○Rabbath-ammon
Ashdad XI Heshbon Rabbah
Ashkelon Gath Jerusalem
Gaza Lachish Hebron Medeba
Gerar Dibon
SALT SEA A B
Beer-sheba Ar?○
●Kir-hareseth MOAB

ISRAEL JUDAH PHILISTIA AMMON

ARABIAN DESERT)

○Bozrah
○Punon
○Kadesh-barnea? EDOM
Sela ∞Teman?

River of Egypt

Ezion-geber●

┌─────────────────────────┐
│ The EMPIRE of DAVID   │
│ and SOLOMON   │
│ (c.1000–930 B.C.)   │
└─────────────────────────┘

Outline based on Plate V of *A History of Israel.* © W. L. Jenkins, 1959,
The Westminster Press. Used by permission.

Ancient Israel

Roland de Vaux

Volume 1

Social Institutions

McGraw-Hill Book Company
New York Toronto

First McGraw-Hill Paperback Edition, 1965

13141516171   MUMU   8987654321
ISBN 07-016599-8

Library of Congress Catalog Card No: 61-12360
Originally published in France under the title of
Les Institutions de L'Ancien Testament
by Les Editions du Cerf

English translation © Darton, Longman & Todd Ltd., 1961

First published in the United States by McGraw-Hill, Inc. in 1961

McGraw-Hill Paperbacks

Printed in the United States of America

TO THE STUDENTS OF THE ÉCOLE BIBLIQUE

WITH WHOM I HAVE LEARNED

WHAT THIS BOOK CONTAINS

PREFACE

INSTITUTIONS are the various forms in which the social life of a people finds expression. Some it will take for granted as a matter of custom; others it will adopt of its own choice; and yet others will be imposed upon it by an authority. Individuals are subject to the nation's institutions, but the institutions themselves exist, ultimately, for the sake of the society whose welfare they promote, whether the society be small as a family, or large as a state or religious community. Again, the institutions of a society will vary with time and place, and will depend, to some extent, on natural conditions such as geography and climate, but their distinguishing characteristic is that they all proceed, in the end, from the human will.

The institutions of a people with a long past are therefore closely bound up not only with the territory in which it has lived but with history. They will be made to suit that people, and will bear the mark of its psychology, of its ideas on man, the world and God. Like its literature, its art, its science and religion, its institutions too are an element in, and an expression of, its civilization. In order to understand and describe these ancient witnesses to the life of a people, the historian has to take into account all the traces of the past. Clearly, written documents have pride of place, but the things which survive, even the humblest remains of man's labour, cannot be passed over. Everything is grist which will enable us to reconstruct the conditions and the setting of the people's social life.

Because of these various relations with other sciences, the institutions of Israel have usually been studied as part of a larger whole. Long treatises have been devoted to them in the classic historical works, the *Geschichte des Volkes Israel* by Rudolf Kittel, and especially in Schürer's *Geschichte des jüdischen Volkes* for the last period of the Old Testament. Conversely, the recent studies by J. Pirenne on *Les Institutions des Hébreux*[1] follow the historical development. Formerly, institutions were treated under the heading of *Antiquitates Hebraicae*, but nowadays they are associated with archaeology, and are thus presented by I. Benziger in *Hebräische Archäologie*, 3rd edition, 1927, by F. Nötscher in *Biblische Altertumskunde*, 1940, and by A. G. Barrois in *Manuel d'Archéologie Biblique*, I, 1939; II, 1953. Ample space is devoted to them in histories of civilization, such as A. Bertholet, *Kulturgeschichte Israels*, 1919, and J. Pedersen, *Israel, its Life and Culture*, I-II, 1926; III-IV, 1940.

1. *Archives d'Histoire du Droit Oriental*, IV, 1949, pp. 51-76; V, 1950, pp. 99-132; *Revue Internationale des Droits de l'Antiquité*, I, 1952, pp. 33-86; II, 1953, pp. 109-149; III, 1954, pp. 195-255.

All these works are excellent and have constantly been used in the prepara-
tion of this book, but it has been felt that Old Testament institutions could
well form the subject of a special study. For this the main source is evidently
the Bible itself. Except in the legislative and ritual sections, the Bible does not
treat directly of these questions, but the historical, prophetical and wisdom
books contain much information, all the more interesting because it tells us
what actually did happen and not what ought to have happened. To make
use of all these texts calls for accurate exegesis, and before we can draw conclusions, literary criticism must assign dates to the various passages, for the
development of institutions followed the course of history. Archaeology, in
the strict sense, *i.e.* the study of the material remains of the past, is only an
auxiliary science, which helps us to reconstruct the actual setting in which the
institutions functioned: but it reveals to us the houses in which families lived,
the towns administered by the elders of the people or the king's officials, the
capitals where the court resided, the gates where justice was administered and
the merchants set up their stalls, with their scales and the weights they kept in
their purses. It shows us the ramparts which armies defended, the tombs at
which the funeral rites were performed, and the sanctuaries where the priests
directed worship. Finally, if we wish to have a real understanding of the
institutions of Israel, we must compare them with those of its neighbours,
with Mesopotamia, Egypt and Asia Minor, where information is plentiful,
and with the little states of Syria and Palestine, where it is scanty. But it was
among the latter that Israel carved out for itself a homeland; many of them
were founded about the same time, and Israel had constant contact with them
throughout its long history.

The present book offers only the conclusions of all this research. Nomadic
customs and tribal organization left traces on the life of Israel long after the
settlement in Canaan; hence the book begins with an introductory study of
nomadism. Next come family institutions, then civil and political institutions. The second volume[1] will deal with military and religious institutions.
This book, however, is not intended for specialists in biblical studies; rather,
it is meant to help towards an intelligent reading of the Bible. Consequently,
there are many references to biblical texts, but the author has deliberately
refrained from over-technical discussions and from loading the pages with
erudite footnotes. Many of the suggestions or statements advanced here need
to be more fully supported and are based on findings of textual, literary or
historical criticism which are open to debate. He can only hope that his
readers will have confidence in him. Those who wish to check his statements
and to form their own judgment will find the necessary material in the
bibliographical notes which are grouped according to the chapters. This
bibliography, however, is not meant to be complete; it contains only such
older works as have not been superseded, and those more recent studies

1. This English edition contains both volumes together.

which seem most useful and from which the author has drawn his information. In quoting them, he wishes to acknowledge his debt to those who have studied these questions before him, but he is also providing weapons against himself, for many of these works put forward solutions very different from those he has finally adopted. The inquiring reader may look and choose for himself.

The subject-matter of the book is restricted by its title to the Old Testament period, and the New Testament period is called as witness only by way of clarification or addition. In the study of the Old Testament itself, institutions occupy a subordinate place, and the reader may sometimes feel that he is very far from the spiritual and doctrinal message he seeks for in the Bible. Nevertheless, he is always on the border-land of biblical religion, and often in direct contact with the message it enshrines. Family customs, funeral rites, the status of foreigners, of slaves, the notions of personality and the rôle of the king, the connection between the law—even profane law—and the Covenant with God, the manner of waging war—all these reflect religious ideas, and these same ideas find conscious expression in worship and liturgy. The institutions of the Chosen People prepare the way for, and indeed foreshadow, the institutions of the community of the elect. Everything in this sacred past matters to us, for the Word of God is a living thing, and a man is better able to hear its tones if he listens to it in the actual surroundings in which it was first given to mankind.

Jerusalem, June, 1957.

TRANSLATOR'S NOTE

THIS book is a translation of *Les Institutions de l'Ancien Testament*, published in two volumes by *Les Editions du Cerf*, Paris; the first volume was published in 1958, the second in 1960. The translation has been made from this first edition of the French original, but it incorporates a number of additions and corrections which Fr de Vaux wishes to see inserted in the text; he has also brought the entire bibliography up to date to the beginning of 1961. The principal additions will be found on pp. 37, 58, 82, 130 and 208, and the main corrections on pp. 147, 183 and 203.

The spelling of proper names follows that to be adopted in the forthcoming *Jerusalem Bible*,[1] the English edition of the *Bible de Jérusalem*,[2] but biblical names have been registered in the index under the spelling given in the Authorized Version as well. Biblical references are in every instance to the original text (Hebrew, Greek or Aramaic); where the numeration of verses differs among the various translations, it would have been cumbersome to refer to all the numerations in both Catholic and non-Catholic versions. The references have therefore been left as they stand, but they can always be found by referring to the *Bible de Jérusalem*. The index has been rearranged and expanded; in particular, the longer entries (*e.g.* Abraham) have been broken down into sub-headings, and the main references have been given first.

It only remains for me to thank Fr de Vaux for the interest he has taken in this translation, for the promptness with which he has answered all my queries, and for enabling us to include so much new material, especially in the Bibliography.

Ushaw College, Durham
Easter, 1961

---

1. London: Darton, Longman & Todd Ltd; New York: Doubleday & Co. Inc.
2. Paris: Les Editions du Cerf.

NOTE ON NOMENCLATURE OF SOME
BOOKS OF THE BIBLE AND APOCRYPHA

FOR the convenience of readers who are not familiar with the nomenclature adopted in this book, the lists below show the equivalents in the Authorized/King James Version, and in Douai-Challoner and Knox, where differences occur.

A.V./K.J.	In this book	D-C., Knox
Joshua	Josue	Josue
1 Samuel	1 Samuel (1 S)	1 Kings
2 Samuel	2 Samuel (2 S)	2 Kings
1 Kings	1 Kings (1 K)	3 Kings
2 Kings	2 Kings (2 K)	4 Kings
1 Chronicles	1 Chronicles (1 Ch)	1 Paralipomena
2 Chronicles	2 Chronicles (2 Ch)	2 Paralipomena
Ezra	Esdras (Esd)	1 Esdras
Nehemiah	Nehemias (Ne)	2 Esdras
1 Esdras	3 Esdras	——
2 Esdras	4 Esdras	——
Tobit	Tobias	Tobias
Ecclesiastes	Qoheleth (Qo)	Ecclesiastes
Ecclesiastes	Sirach (Si)	Ecclesiasticus
Solomon	Canticle (Ct)	Canticle of Canticles (D-C.)
		Song of Songs (Knox)
Hosea	Osee (Os)	Osee
Obadiah	Abdias (Abd)	Abdias
Micah	Michaeas	Michaeas
Zephaniah	Sophonias (So)	Sophonias
Haggai	Aggaeus	Aggaeus
Revelation	Apocalypse (Ap)	Apocalypse

CONTENTS VOLUME I

Chapter   *Page*

    7. *Runaway slaves*   87
    8. *The emancipation of slaves*   87
    9. *State slaves*   88

4. THE ISRAELITE CONCEPT OF THE STATE   91
    1. *Israel and the various Eastern notions of the State* 91
    2. *The Twelve Tribes of Israel*   92
    3. *The institution of the monarchy*   94
    4. *The Dual Monarchy*   95
    5. *The kingdoms of Israel and Judah*   96
    6. *The post-exilic community*   98
    7. *Was there an Israelite idea of the State?*   98

5. THE PERSON OF THE KING   100
    1. *Accession to the throne*   100
    2. *The coronation rites*   102
        (a) *The setting: the sanctuary*   102
        (b) *The investiture with the insignia*   103
        (c) *The anointing*   103
        (d) *The acclamation*   106
        (e) *The enthronement*   106
        (f) *The homage*   107
    3. *The coronation name*   107
    4. *The enthronement psalms*   108
    5. *The king as saviour*   110
    6. *Divine adoption*   111
    7. *The king and worship*   113

6. THE ROYAL HOUSEHOLD   115
    1. *The harem*   115
    2. *The Great Lady*   117
    3. *The royal children*   119
    4. *The king's attendants*   120
    5. *The royal guard*   123
    6. *The royal estate*   124

7. THE PRINCIPAL OFFICIALS OF THE KING   127
    1. *The ministers of David and Solomon*   127
    2. *The master of the palace*   129
    3. *The royal secretary*   131
    4. *The royal herald*   132

PART III

MILITARY INSTITUTIONS

CONTENTS VOLUME II

PART IV

RELIGIOUS INSTITUTIONS

INTRODUCTION

Nomadism and its Survival

AT the beginning of their history the Israelites, like their ancestors before them, lived as nomads or semi-nomads, and when they came to settle down as a nation, they still retained some characteristics of that earlier way of life. Consequently, any study of Old Testament institutions must begin with an investigation into nomadism. The biblical records preserve many ancient traditions about the early life of the Israelites, and these are of first importance in our study; but since this evidence has been to some extent systematized by later editors of the books, great care is needed in interpreting these records. We have other sources of information too: texts about the Arabs in pre-Islamic times, and ethnographical studies about the Arabs of to-day. These nomad Arabs, by race and country, are closely related to the Israelites, and what we know of pre-Islamic, modern and contemporary Arab life can help us to understand more clearly the primitive organization of Israel. On the other hand, one must beware of hasty comparisons which may overlook essential differences.

The fact is, that even in the comparatively small area of the Middle East, there have always been different types of nomads, and what is true of one type is not necessarily true of another. Even to-day, these differences persist (though one wonders how much longer any form of nomadism can survive).

(1) The real nomad, or true Bedouin (the word means 'man of the desert') is a camel-breeder. He can live in, or at least traverse, regions which are strictly desert, *i.e.* where the annual rainfall is less than 4 inches. He travels enormous distances with his herds in search of grazing, and has very little contact with settled people.

(2) A nomad, however, may breed only sheep and goats, and these flocks are not so hardy; they need to drink more often and cannot survive on the rough pastures which are sufficient for camels. This type of Bedouin lives mainly in the half-desert region (where the rainfall is 4-10 inches), and the distances he travels from one grazing ground to the next are necessarily shorter. Sometimes he does cover considerable ground, but then he must follow a route where the watering-places are not too distant from one another. He has far more contact with the settled regions, for his grazing lies along their borders.

(3) Once he begins to raise cattle as well as flocks, the shepherd ceases to be a true nomad. He settles in one place, begins to cultivate the land and to build houses. Among the group, however, some will continue to live in tents with the flocks, at least during the winter and the spring. Depending on the extent to which he is tied to the land, such a man is either half a nomad or half a settler.

In and between these main types of society there are of course intermediate stages and hybrid forms. A camel-breeding tribe may possess flocks of sheep also, or even land at the far ends of the track of its migration, or oases cultivated by serf-labour.

Neither the Israelites nor their ancestors were ever true Bedouin, that is, camel-breeders. Their fathers kept sheep and goats, and when we first meet them in history, the Patriarchs are already becoming a settled people. This is one factor which puts limits on the comparisons which can be drawn from the Bedouin whom ethnographers have studied.

These modern writers have also studied sheep-breeding tribes who are beginning to settle down. The latter represent the same social type as the earliest Israelite groups, and here the comparison has greater truth in it. But again there is a difference. The sheep-breeders of to-day, half nomad or half settler, were formerly camel-breeders. They no longer wander so far afield for pasture, and are now gradually settling down, but they retain the memory and some of the customs of that life of liberty in the open desert. The Israelites had no such memories, because neither they nor their ancestors had ever known this life. Besides, in their time, there was no real 'desert civilization' to lay down codes of behaviour; in their eyes the desert was the refuge of outlaws, the haunt of brigands, the home of demons and wild beasts. We shall return to this subject when discussing what has been called the 'nomadic ideal' of the Old Testament.

Nevertheless, the fact remains that the Israelites or their ancestors did live for a time in the desert as nomads or semi-nomads. Naturally, such a life entails a distinct pattern of society, and enjoins a code of behaviour all of its own; we are therefore justified in using, with due reservation, the organization and customs of the Arabs for comparison.

In the desert, the unit of society must be compact enough to remain mobile, yet strong enough to ensure its own safety; this unit is the tribe. In the desert, an individual who is separated from his own group must be able to count without question on a welcome from the groups through which he passes or which he joins. Anyone may have need of this help, and therefore everyone must give it; this is the basis of the law of hospitality and asylum. Finally, in the desert there is no police force or court of justice with authority over the tribes; consequently, the group as a whole is held responsible for crime, and liable for its punishment—the law of blood-vengeance. These three sociological facts, which are the most obvious characteristics of nomadism, must now claim our attention for a time.

2. Tribal Organization

(a) The constitution of a tribe

A tribe is an autonomous group of families who believe they are descended from a common ancestor. Each tribe is called by the name or surname of that ancestor, sometimes, but not always, preceded by 'sons of'. Arab examples are innumerable. In the Bible, the descendants of Amalek, Edom and Moab are called Amalek, Edom and Moab without the addition of 'sons of'. On the other hand, we find both 'Israel' and 'sons of Israel', both 'Judah' and 'sons of Judah' and so on, but always 'sons of Ammon' (except in two instances, one of which is textually uncertain). Instead of 'sons' we may find 'house', in the sense of family or descendants: 'the house of Israel', for example, and especially 'the house of Joseph'. Assyrian texts follow the same usage in references to Aramaean groups who lived in conditions similar to those of the first Israelites: *bit* (house of) *Yakin* and *mar* (sons of) *Yakin*, or *bit Adini* and *mar Adini*; the terms are even used, long after the settlement, for Israelites in the northern kingdom after Omri: *bit Ḥumri* and *mar Ḥumri*.

What unites all the tribesmen, then, is this blood-relationship, real or supposed; they all consider themselves 'brothers' in a wide sense. Abimelek says to the entire clan of his mother, 'Remember that I am of your bones and of your flesh' (Jg 9: 2). All the members of David's clan are, in his eyes, his 'brothers' (1 S 20: 29), and he goes so far as to tell all the elders of Judah, 'You are my brothers, you are of my flesh and of my bones' (2 S 19: 13). Every tribe has its traditions, too, about the ancestor from whom it claims descent. These traditions are not always historically true, but whatever their value, the important fact is that the nomad believes he is of the same blood as the rest of his tribe, and that the relationship between different tribes is also explained in terms of kinship. In his eyes, the whole social organization of the desert is summed up in a genealogy.

It was this idea which, in the early days of Islam, led to the composition of those great genealogies catalogued by Wüstenfeld. Each tribe descends from a single ancestor, and two allied tribes descend from two ancestors who were brothers in the strict sense. These genealogies, however, though they may be accurate for a small group, inevitably become arbitrary and artificial once an attempt is made to extend them in space and time. In the Mid-Euphrates region there is a group of small sheep-breeding tribes called the 'Agêdât, *i.e.* 'Confederates', whose name signifies clearly enough just how the group was formed; but this political and economic union has since been expressed in a genealogical table. This procedure leads to the invention of eponymous ancestors. We know of a tribe called the Khoza'a ('Separated'), because it separated from the Azd at the time of the great Yemenite dispersion, but the genealogists have assigned it a personal ancestor, whom they call Khoza'a. Similarly the Kholoj ('Transported') are so called because Omar I transferred them from the 'Adwan to the Al-Harith, whereas, according to the genealogists, Kholoj is a surname of Qais, the son of Al-Ḥarith.

In practice, other factors besides common descent may help to constitute a tribe. The mere fact of living in the same region leads groups of families to join together. Weak elements are absorbed by stronger neighbours;

alternatively, several weak groups combine to form a body capable of remaining autonomous, that is, of standing up to attack. Individuals, too, can be incorporated into a tribe either by adoption into a family (as often happens with freed slaves), or through acceptance by the sheikh or the elders.

But even here the principle is safeguarded, for the newcomer is attached 'in name and in blood' to the tribe; this means that he acknowledges the tribe's ancestor as his own, that he will marry within the tribe and raise up his family inside it. The Arabs say that he is 'genealogized' (root: *nasaba*). With a whole clan the fusion takes longer, but the result is the same, and the new-comers are finally considered as being of the same blood. A text of Al-Bakri puts it neatly: 'And the Nahd ben Zaïd joined the Bené al-Harith, became confederate with them and completely united with them; and the Jarm ben Rabbân joined the Bené Zubaïd, attached themselves to them and lived together, and the whole tribe with its confederates was attached to the same ancestor (*nusibat*).'

The tribes of Israel were not exempt from such changes, and they absorbed groups of different origin. Thus the tribe of Judah eventually welcomed to its own ranks the remnants of the tribe of Simeon, and incorporated foreign groups like the Calebites and Yerahmeelites. The Bible gives a clear picture of the process in its references to the Calebites. They were originally outside the Israelite confederation, for Caleb was the son of Yephunneh the Qeniz-ite (Nb 32: 12; Jos 14: 6, 14; comp. Gn 15: 19; 36: 11), but they had contact with Israel from the time of the sojourn at Qadesh, where Caleb was named as Judah's representative for the exploration of Canaan (Nb 13: 6). Their integration into this tribe is recorded in Jos 15: 13; cf. Jos 14: 6-15, and in the end Caleb is genealogically attached to Judah. The son of Yephunneh becomes the son of Hesron, son of Peres, son of Judah (1 Ch 2: 9, 18, 24) and brother of Yerahmeel (1 Ch 2: 42), another foreign group (1 S 27: 10) also attached to the line of Judah (1 Ch 2: 9). There can be no doubt that simi-lar fusions took place frequently, especially in early days, and that the very concept of the 'Twelve Tribes' contains some elements of systematic arrange-ment, though one cannot say precisely how far this system is artificial. In any case, the number and order of the tribes, sometimes even their names, vary from text to text, and these variations prove that the system which finally prevailed was not reached straightaway.

(b) The union, division and disappearance of tribes

The Twelve Tribes of Israel were a federation, and parallel examples are found among Arab tribes. Sometimes it is merely an association of small tribes which unite to present a common front against powerful neighbours, like the 'Agêdât, the 'Confederates' of the Mid-Euphrates, mentioned above. At other times, a tribe may be compelled to split up when its numbers become too great; these new groups, all originating from the common stock, then become autonomous, though the extent of their independence may vary. Nevertheless, they do retain a feeling of family solidarity; when they unite for common enterprises, such as migrations or wars, they recognize a chief to be obeyed by some or all of the groups. These patterns of society can be studied in our own day in the two great rival federations of the Syrian desert, the 'Anezeh and the Shammar. During its years of wandering in the desert and its struggle for the conquest of Canaan, Israel lived in similar conditions, conditions which persisted after the settlement, in the period of the Judges. The system of the Twelve Tribes has been compared with the amphictyonies which united a number of Greek cities round a sanctuary. The comparison, though interesting, should not be pressed too far, for, unlike the amphictyonies, the Twelve Tribes were not ruled by a permanent body, and, in their system, were not subject to the same measure of effective political control. The importance of the Israelite confederation was primarily religious; it was not only the feeling of kinship, but also their common faith in Yahweh, whom they had all agreed to follow (Jos 24), which united the tribes around the sanctuary of the Ark, where they assembled for the great feasts.

On the other hand, when a nomad group becomes too numerous to continue living together on the same grazing grounds, it sometimes divides into two groups which then live quite independently of one another. This was the reason why Abraham and Lot separated (Gn 13: 5-13). But the claims of kinship still hold good, and when Lot was carried off a prisoner by the four victorious kings, Abraham went to his help (Gn 14: 12-16).

The numbers of a tribe may, however, diminish instead of increasing until it finally disappears. Thus Reuben grows weaker (cf. Gn 49: 3-4 and Dt 33: 6), and the civil tribe of Levi disappears (Gn 34: 25-30; 49: 5-7), to be replaced by the priestly tribe 'dispersed throughout Israel' (cf. Gn 49: 7). Simeon disappears, and at an early date the remnants were absorbed by Judah (Jos 19: 1-9; Jg 1: 3f.); it is no longer mentioned in the Blessings of Moses (Dt 33), which may perhaps be earlier than the reign of David.

(c) The organization and government of a tribe

A tribe, though it forms a single unit, has an internal organization which is also founded on blood-ties. Among nomadic Arabs, the limits and names of these sub-divisions fluctuate somewhat. The basic unit is naturally the family ('ahel), a concept which has a fairly wide meaning. Several related families constitute a clan, or fraction of a tribe, called, according to the locality, either ḥamûleh or 'ashireh. The tribe itself is called a qabileh, but formerly it was called a baṭn or a ḥayy, two words expressing that unity of blood on which the tribe is founded.

The Israelites had a very similar organization. The bêth 'ab, the 'house of one's father', was the family, which comprised not only the father, his wife or wives and their unmarried children but also their married sons with their wives and children, and the servants. Several families composed a clan, the *mishpahah*. The latter usually lived in the same place, and its members always met for common religious feasts and sacrificial meals (1 S 20: 6, 29). In particular, the clan assumed the responsibility for blood-vengeance. Each clan was ruled by the heads of its families, the *z'qenîm* or 'elders', and in time of war it furnished a contingent, theoretically a thousand strong, commanded by a chief, *śar*. In Jg 8: 14 the 'chiefs' of Sukkoth are distinguished from the 'elders'. In Gn 36: 40-43 there is a list of the chiefs of the clans of Edom, who bore the special name of *'allûph*, perhaps etymologically connected with *'eleph* ('a thousand'), A group of clans, of *mishpaḥôth*, formed a tribe, *shebeṭ* or *maṭṭeh*, two words with the same meaning, which also denote the commander's staff and the royal sceptre. The tribe therefore embraced all those who obeyed the same chief.

The hierarchy of the three terms, *bêth 'ab*, *mishpahah* and *shebeṭ*, is clearly expressed in Jos. 7: 14-18, but one term may sometimes be used for another, as in Nb 4: 18 and Jg 20: 12 (Hebrew text). Similarly, Makir and Gilead, which are clans of Ephraim, are mentioned in the Song of Deborah on a par with the other tribes (Jg 5: 14-17).

Among the Arabs a tribe is governed by a sheikh, who acts in conjunction with the principal heads of its families. This authority generally stays in the same family, but does not always pass to the eldest son, for the Arabs set great store by personality and character, and expect their sheikh to be prudent, courageous, noble-hearted . . . and rich.

It is difficult to say who, among the Israelites, corresponded to the sheikh, or what title he bore. Possibly it was the *nasî'*. This is the name given to the leaders of the Twelve Tribes during the time in the desert (Nb 7: 2), with the further detail that they were 'the chiefs of their fathers' houses, the leaders of the tribes' (cf. Nb 1: 16, etc.). The same word denotes the chieftains of Ishmael (Gn 17: 20; 25: 16), and the Ishmaelites had twelve *nasî'* for as many tribes (the parallel with Israel is obvious). The same word is used of Midianite leaders in Nb 25: 18 and Jos 13: 21. One could object that these texts belong to the Priestly tradition, which is generally held to be the most recent of all, and that the same word frequently recurs in Ezechiel; but it is also found in texts which are certainly ancient (Gn 34: 2; Ex 22: 27). It has also been suggested that the word denoted the deputy of a tribe to the Israelite amphictyony, but that is assigning to it a religious sense which is not apparent in the passages just referred to. On the other hand, if such an organization existed and was ruled by some kind of council, the tribes would naturally have been represented in it by their chiefs. One should note, however, that the word was not employed exclusively for the chief of a tribe, but was used for the leaders of smaller sections too. The Arabs use the word 'sheikh' with the same freedom.

(d) Tribal territory. War and raiding

Each tribe has a territory recognized as its own, inside which the cultivated land is generally privately owned, and pasture land is held in common. Boundaries are sometimes ill defined, and groups belonging to different tribes sometimes live side by side in very fertile regions, if their tribes are on friendly terms. But the tribe which has the primary right of possession can lay down conditions and demand some form of payment for grazing rights.

This lack of precise law easily gives rise to disputes, especially over the use of wells or cisterns. Everyone in the desert is bound to know that such and such a watering-place belongs to such and such a group, but from time to time a title may be disputed and quarrels break out between shepherds. It has always been so: Abraham's herdsmen quarrel with Lot's (Gn 13: 7); Abimelek's servants seize a well dug by Abraham (Gn 21: 25); Isaac is hard put to it to maintain his rights over the wells he himself had dug between Gerar and Beersheba (Gn 26: 19-22).

If quarrels about routes of migration, grazing lands and watering-places are not settled amicably, as in the biblical examples just mentioned, they lead to war. The sheikh takes the decision, and all the men must follow him. As a rule, the booty is shared between the fighting men, but the chief has a right to a special share, which was originally fixed at one-quarter of the total captured, but later was left to the chief's discretion. In Israel, in the time of David, the booty was divided equally between the combatants and those who stayed at the rear, one portion being reserved for the chief (1 S 30: 20-25). Nb 31: 25-30 dates this institution back to the period in the desert, and the chief's portion is there considered as a tribute for Yahweh and the Levites.

Every Arab tribe has its war-cry and its standard. In addition, it carries into battle a decorated litter, called *'utfa*, or, more recently, *merkab* or *abu-Dhur*. Nowadays, the litter is empty, but in days gone by the most beautiful girl in the tribe rode in it to spur on the fighting men. Israel, too, had its war-cry, the *t'rû'ah* (Nb 10: 5, 9; 31: 6; Jos 6: 5, 20; Jg 7: 20-21; 1 S 17: 20, 52; cf. Am 1: 14; 2: 2; So 1: 14, 16, etc.). This war-cry formed part of the ritual of the Ark of the Covenant (1 S 4: 5; 2 S 6: 15), which was the palladium of Israel; its presence in battle (1 S 4: 3-11; 2 S 11: 11) reminds us of the sacred litter of the Arabs. Perhaps, too, the tribes in the desert grouped themselves, in camp and on the march, under standards, *'ôth* (Nb 2: 2).

When several tribes join together to form a confederation, they adopt a common standard, like the flag of the Prophet unfurled at Mecca and Medina. Here again we may find a parallel with the Ark of the Covenant and the name 'Yahweh-Nissi' ('Yahweh is my banner') given to the altar which Moses erected after his victory over the Amalekites (Ex 17: 15).

Raiding is different from war, for its object is not to kill but to carry off plunder and to escape unharmed. It is the desert's 'sport of kings'; it involves the use of racing camels and of thoroughbred mares, and has its own clearly-defined rules. Ancient Israel knew nothing quite like this. The nearest approach is to be found in those incursions of the Midianites and 'sons of the East' in the days of the Judges: these invaders were mounted on camels (Jg 6: 3-6). On a smaller scale, one might point to David's expeditions into the Negeb during his stay with the Philistines (1 S 27: 8-11).

3. *The Law of Hospitality and Asylum*

Hospitality, we have said, is a necessity of life in the desert, but among the nomads this necessity has become a virtue, and a most highly esteemed one. The guest is sacred: the honour of providing for him is disputed, but generally falls to the sheikh. The stranger can avail himself of this hospitality for three days, and even after leaving he has a right to protection for a given time. This time varies from tribe to tribe: among some it is 'until the salt he has eaten has left his stomach'; in big tribes like the Ruwalla of Syria it is for three more days and within a radius of 100 miles.

Old Testament parallels spring to mind. Abraham gives a lavish reception to the three 'men' at Mambre (Gn 18: 1-8), and Laban is eager to welcome Abraham's servant (Gn 24: 28-32). Two stories show to what excesses the sentiment of hospitality could lead: that of the angels who stayed in Lot's house at Sodom (Gn 19:1-8), and the story of the crime at Gibeah (Jg 19: 16-24). Both Lot and the old man of Gibeah are ready to sacrifice the honour of their daughters in order to protect their guests, and the reason is stated in both cases: it is simply because the latter have come under their roof (Gn 19: 8; Jg 19: 23).

Nomad life also gives rise, invariably, to a law of asylum. In this type of society is is impossible and inconceivable that an individual could live isolated, unattached to any tribe. Hence, if a man is expelled from his tribe after a murder or some serious offence, or if, for any reason whatever, he leaves it of his own free will, he has to seek the protection of another tribe. There he becomes what modern Arabs call a *daḥil*, 'he who has come in', and what their forefathers called a *jâr*. The tribe undertakes to protect him, to defend him against his enemies and to avenge his blood, if necessary. These customs are reflected in two Old Testament institutions, that of the *ger* (which is the same word as the Arabic *jâr*) and that of cities of refuge.[1]

4. *Tribal Solidarity and Blood-Vengeance*

The bond of blood, real or supposed, creates a certain solidarity among all the members of a tribe. It is a very deep-rooted feeling, and persists long after the settlement in Canaan. The honour or dishonour of every member affects

1. Cf. pp. 74-76 and 160-163.

the entire group. A curse extends to the whole race, and God visits the sins of the fathers on the children to the fourth generation (Ex 20: 5). A whole family is honoured if its head is brave, while the group is punished for a fault of its leader (2 S 21: 1).

This solidarity is seen above all in the group's duty to protect its weak and oppressed members. This is the obligation which lies behind the institution of the *go'el,* but as this is not confined to the nomadic state it will be treated along with family institutions.[1]

The most solemn responsibility of the Israelite *gò'el* was to enforce blood-vengeance, and here we encounter another law of the desert, the *tàr* of the Arabs. The blood of a kinsman must be avenged by the death of the one who shed it, or, failing him, by the blood of one of his family. Blood-vengeance does not operate within the group, but the guilty man is punished by his group or expelled from it. The Arabs say, 'Our blood has been shed.' In primitive times this duty devolved on all the members of the tribe, and the extent of it served to determine the limits of the tribal group. In recent times, however, the obligation has become more restricted and does not extend beyond the family circle, taken in a fairly wide sense. Moreover, to avoid a series of assassinations, they try to substitute for the *tàr* some compensation which the victim's family are compelled to accept, whatever their feelings about blood-vengeance.

The same law existed in Israel. It is expressed with savage ferocity in the song of Lamek (Gn 4: 23-24):

> 'I have killed a man for a wound,
> A child for a bruise.
> The vengeance for Cain may be sevenfold,
> But for Lamek, seventy-sevenfold!'

Lamek is the descendant of Cain, who was condemned to live in the desert. And Cain bears a 'sign', which is not a stigma of condemnation, but a mark which shows he belongs to a group in which blood-vengeance is ruthlessly exacted. This story (Gn 4: 13-16) states clearly the social basis for the institution. It is not simply to obtain compensation, 'man for man, woman for woman', as the Koran puts it; rather, it is a safeguard. Where society is not centralized, the prospect of the blood-debt which will have to be paid is a deterrent which restrains both individuals and the group.

The custom persisted after the tribes had settled in Canaan. Thus Joab kills Abner (2 S 3: 22-27 and 30) to avenge the death of his brother (2 S 2: 22-23). Legislation, however, endeavoured to mitigate this vengeance by the introduction of a system of justice. Though the laws about cities of refuge (Nb 35: 9-34; Dt 19: 1-13) sanction blood-vengeance, they hold it in check to some extent by requiring a preliminary judgment on the guilt of the accused and

1. Pp. 21-22.

by excluding cases of involuntary manslaughter.[1] In contrast with Bedouin law, however, Israelite legislation does not allow compensation in money, alleging for this a religious motive: blood which is shed defiles the land in which Yahweh dwells, and must be expiated by the blood of him who shed it (Nb 35: 31-34).

The law of blood-vengeance, we have said, does not operate inside the group itself. There appears to be a single exception, in 2 S 14: 4-11. To obtain the recall of Absalom, banished after the murder of Amnon, the woman of Teqoa pretends that one of her sons has been killed by his brother, and that her clansmen want to put the latter to death; the woman begs David to intervene so that the 'avenger of blood' may not slay her son. But the decision of the clan is normal if we understand it as the punishment of the guilty, just as the banishment of Absalom was normal: it is the exclusion of the guilty from the family. In this passage only the term 'avenger of blood' is abnormal, and it may be used here in a loose sense.

5. The Later Development of Tribal Organization in Israel

Though analogies from the life of Arab nomads may throw useful light on the primitive organization of Israel, it is important to realize that nowhere in the Bible are we given a perfect picture of tribal life on the full scale. The traditions about the Patriarchs concern families, or, at the most, clans; and no one can deny that in the accounts of the desert wanderings and of the conquest the characteristic profile of each tribe has been to some extent subordinated to the wider interest of 'all Israel'. Quite the most rewarding period to investigate is that of the Judges, where we read of tribes living, and taking action, sometimes independently of one another, and sometimes in association with one another. But this is precisely the time when the tribes have no individual chiefs; it is the elders who wield authority, and one senses that the clan, the *mishpaḥah*, is becoming the most stable unit of society. In short, tribal organization is beginning to crumble. It is the price to be paid for becoming a settled people; a tribe gradually turns into a territorial group, which itself continues to sub-divide.

Such an evolution is in fact commonplace. The Caliph Omar I complained that the Arabs who had settled in Iraq had begun to call themselves by the names of their villages instead of their ancestors. In our own day, certain half-settled Bedouin in Palestine are called after their present homes, *e.g.* the Belqaniyeh of the Belqa, the Ghoraniyeh of the Ghôr, etc.; or after their place of origin, like the Ḥaddadin of Ma'în, who come from Kh. Ḥaddad. Similarly, in the Song of Deborah (Jg 5: 17), the 'tribe' of Gilead takes its name from its homeland, and some authors ascribe a geographical meaning to the names of other Israelite tribes. We may note, too, that the Blessings of

---

1. Cf. pp. 160f.

Jacob (Gn 49) and of Moses (Dt 33) frequently allude to the territory occupied by the tribes.

This territorial disposition of the tribes was itself modified by the administrative organization under the monarchy. True, everyone remembered to which tribe he belonged, but the unit of society which survived, and which to some extent retained the ancient customs, was the clan. In practice, after the settlement, the village stood for the clan, and in many of the genealogies of Chronicles, names of villages replace names of ancestors.

6. Relics of Nomadism

Amid these new surroundings, certain ancient customs survived, and the comparisons we have drawn with Arab nomadism often held good long after the settlement. Blood-vengeance is a desert law, but it became a permanent institution, and the solidarity of the clan never disappeared.

Language is more conservative than custom, and Hebrew retained several traces of that life of years gone by. For example, generations after the conquest, a house was called a 'tent', and not only in poetry (where it is frequent) but also in everyday speech (Jg 19: 9; 20: 8; 1 S 13: 2; 1 K 8: 66). Disbanded soldiers return 'every man to his own tent' (1 S 4: 10; 2 S 18: 17). 'To your tents, Israel' was the cry of revolt under David (2 S 20: 1) and after the death of Solomon (1 K 12:16). On the other hand, this expression did not last, for shortly afterwards we read how every man returned 'to his house' (1 K 22: 17) or 'his town' (1 K 22: 36). Again, to express 'leaving early in the morning', a verb is often used which means 'to load the beasts of burden' (Jg 19: 9; 1 S 17: 20, etc.); nomads use the word to say 'striking camp at dawn'. These expressions continued in use long after Israel had settled in Canaan, and when their ideal was to live a quiet life 'every man under his vine and his fig-tree'.

Though it is less significant, the frequent use, in Old Testament poetry, of metaphors borrowed from nomadic life should not pass unnoticed. Death, for example, is the cut tent-rope, or the peg which is pulled out (Jb 4: 21), or the tent itself which is carried off (Is 38: 12). Desolation is represented by the broken ropes, the tent blown down (Jr 10: 20), whereas security is the tent with tight ropes and firm pegs (Is 33: 20). A nation whose numbers are increasing is a tent being extended (Is 54: 2). Lastly, there are countless allusions to the pastoral life, and Yahweh or his Messiah are frequently represented as the Good Shepherd (Ps 23; Is 40: 11; Jr 23: 1-6; Ez 34, etc.).

7. The 'Nomadic Ideal' of the Prophets

In spite of these surviving traces, our oldest biblical texts show little admiration for the nomadic life. The story of Cain (Gn 4: 11-16) is a condemnation of outright nomadism. Cain is driven into the desert in punishment for the murder of Abel; he will be a wanderer and a vagabond, marked with a sign, the *wasm* of the desert nomad. Doubtless, Abel was a herdsman (Gn 4: 2), and has all the narrator's sympathy, but the text makes it clear that it was sheep and goats that he looked after; in other words, he is supposed to have led the same sort of life as the Hebrew Patriarchs, on the border of the real desert. Before his crime Cain was a farmer (Gn 4: 2). So, in this story, the desert is presented as the refuge of disgraced settlers and outlaws, as in fact it was before the rise of the large camel-breeding tribes who founded a desert civilization, one which had its greatness indeed, but which the Israelites never knew.

The same unfavourable tone recurs in the story of Ishmael: 'His hand will be against everyone, everyone's hand will be against him; he will settle down away from his brethren' (Gn 16: 12). The desert is the home of wild beasts, monsters and demons (Is 13: 21-22; 34: 11-15), and the scapegoat is driven out there, loaded with all the sins of the people (Lv 16).

On the other hand, we do encounter what has been called the 'nomadic ideal' of the Old Testament. The Prophets look back to the past, the time of Israel's youth in the desert, when she was betrothed to Yahweh (Jr 2: 2; Os 13: 5; Am 2: 10). They condemn the comfort and luxury of urban life in their own day (Am 3: 15; 6: 8, etc.), and see salvation in a return, at some future date, to the life of the desert, envisaged as a golden age (Os 2: 16-17; 12: 10).

There is, in this attitude, a reaction against the sedentary civilization of Canaan, with all its risks of moral and religious perversion. There is also a memory of, and a nostalgia for, the time when God made a Covenant with Israel in the desert, when Israel was faithful to its God. But nomadism itself is not the ideal; rather, it is that purity of religious life and that faithfulness to the Covenant, which was associated in Israel's mind with its former life in the desert. If the Prophets speak of a return to the desert, it is not because they recall any glory in the nomadic life of their ancestors, but as a means of escape from the corrupting influence of their own urban civilization. We shall encounter this mystique of the desert again in the last days of Judaism, among the sectaries of Qumran, when Christian monasticism still lies in the future.

8. *The Rekabites*

The ideal which the Prophets exalted, but never tried to put into practice, was actually carried out by a group of extremists, the Rekabites. We know of them chiefly through Jeremias. To give an object lesson to the people, the prophet invited the members of Rekab's family to the Temple, and offered them a drink of wine. They refused it, saying that their ancestor Yonadab, son of Rekab, had given them this command: 'Neither you nor your sons shall ever drink wine, and you must not build houses, or sow seed, or plant vines, or own property. On the contrary, you are to dwell in tents all your life, so that your days may be long in the land where you live as aliens (*gerîm*).' This age-old fidelity to the commands of their ancestor is held up as an example to the Jews who do not obey the word of Yahweh (Jr 35).

It is interesting to compare this passage with a remark of Jerome of Cardia about the Nabateans at the close of the fourth century B.C. 'It is a law among them not to sow corn or to plant fruit-trees, not to drink wine or to build a house; whoever does so is punished with death' (cited in Diodorus Siculus XIX, 94). In these two passages, so curiously alike, we have the essential contrast between nomadic life and the life of a settled farmer. The Rekabites had chosen to live far away from urban civilization, and only exceptional circumstances account for their presence in Jerusalem; they had taken refuge there to escape from the Chaldeans (Jr 35: 11).

Normally they lived as nomads, unattached to the land. But at the same time they were fervent worshippers of Yahweh: all the Rekabite names we know are Yahwistic names (Jr 35: 3). Jeremias holds them up as examples, and Yahweh promises them his blessing (Jr 35: 19). Like nomads, they are organized as a clan; they are the *b'nê Rekab* and form the *bêth Rekab*, but they also constitute a religious sect, and their ancestor Yonadab is a religious legislator.

This Yonadab ben Rekab is known to us for his part in Jehu's revolution (2 K 10: 15-24). Jehu, on his way to exterminate the cult of Baal at Samaria, takes Yonadab with him to witness his 'zeal for Yahweh' (v. 16). Yonadab, then, must have been a convinced Yahwist, and his uncompromising faith must have been known to all. This incident allows us to date the origin of the Rekabites about 840 B.C., and, according to Jeremias, they were still faithful to the same way of life 250 years later.

Some would go even further, and connect the Rekabites with the Qenites, that group of non-Israelite origin which lived a semi-nomadic life on the borders of Israel, or in its midst (Jg 1: 16; 4: 11; 5: 24; 1 S 15: 4-6; 27: 10), and from whom, according to some authors, the Israelites first learned the name of Yahweh. This connection between the Rekabites and the Qenites depends on two texts in Chronicles (1 Ch 2: 55 and 4: 12). From the critical point of view, these texts are uncertain, yet it is strange that they mention Rekab or the *bêth Rekab* but not Yonadab. At the best, they mean that the Chronicler has used the fiction of a genealogical link to connect two communities who lived more or less the same kind of life.

Our history of the Rekabites begins under Jehu and ends in the time of Jeremias. We are not justified in regarding them as survivors of an age when Israel led a nomadic life, and the Bible states explicitly that their rule was established by Yonadab only in the ninth century B.C. It was not a survival of earlier days but a reactionary movement.

PART I

FAMILY INSTITUTIONS

CHAPTER ONE

THE FAMILY

1. *Of what type was the Israelite family?*

ETHNOGRAPHERS distinguish several types of family. In a *fratriarchate*, for example, the eldest brother is the head of the family, and this authority is handed on, along with the property, from brother to brother. Evidence of this type of society has been found among the Hittites and Hurrites in Assyria and Elam. It has been claimed that there are traces of it in the Old Testament, *e.g.* in the institution of the levirate (which will be discussed under marriage[1]), in the action of Jacob's sons to avenge the rape of their sister Dinah (Gn 34), and in the part Laban plays in the arrangement of the marriage of his sister Rebecca (Gn 24). Though none of these examples seems conclusive, we must admit the possibility of Assyrian and Hurrite influence on the customs of Aram Naharaim; and among these two peoples the existence of a fratriarchate, in early times, is now admitted, at least as a hypothesis. We cannot, therefore, exclude the possibility of its influence on the levirate institution, and there may be traces of it in the story of Rebecca.

As a type of family, *matriarchate* is much more common in primitive societies. The characteristic mark of this type of society is not that the mother exercises authority (this is rare), but that a child's lineage is traced through the mother. The child belongs to the mother's family and social group, and is not considered as related to its father's connections; even rights of inheritance are fixed by maternal descent. According to the ethnographical school of Graebner and Schmidt, a matriarchate is associated with small-scale cultivation, while pastoral civilization is patriarchal.

Many authors, however, following Robertson Smith, believe that a matriarchal regime was the original form of the family among the Semites. Certain Old Testament customs and stories, they hold, indicate the presence of this regime among the Israelites. In Gn 20: 12 Abraham is excused for passing off Sarah as his sister, because she was in fact his half-sister, whom he had married. Similarly, 2 S 13: 13 gives us to understand that Amnon and Tamar could have been married, because, though both were David's children, they were born of different mothers. Marriage with one's step-sister, either on the father's or mother's side, is forbidden by the laws of

1. Pp. 37-38.

Lv 18: 9; 20: 17; Dt 27: 22; cf. Ez 22: 11, but the last two texts indicate that this had not always been so; and from this the above-mentioned authors conclude that consanguinity was originally reckoned only through the mother. They point out, too, that the name of a baby was generally decided by the mother,[1] and that the two sons of Joseph, who were born of Egyptian wives, were not acknowledged as children of Israel until they had been adopted by Jacob (Gn 48: 5).

These arguments do not prove the point at issue. The passage about Joseph's children has not the meaning they attribute to it, as the next verse shows (Gn 48: 6). The texts about Sarah and Tamar prove only that marriage with a half-sister was not yet forbidden. Thirdly, it was not always the mother who gave the child its name (Gn 16: 15; 17: 19; 38: 29-30).

Some would also see in the Bible, especially in the marriage of Samson to Timna (Jg 14), a rare type of marriage in which the wife does not leave her clan but brings her husband into it; this, too, would be a relic of a matriarchate. The question will be treated under marriage.[2]

Prehistoric Israel is to us a closed book; but whatever may be true of that epoch, there is no doubt that from the time of our oldest documents, at any rate, the Israelite family is patriarchal. The proper word to describe it is bêth 'ab, the 'house of one's father'; the genealogies are always given in the father's line, and women are rarely mentioned; and the nearest relation in the collateral line is the paternal uncle (cf. Lv 25: 49). In the normal type of Israelite marriage the husband is the 'master', the ba'al, of his wife. The father had absolute authority over his children, even over his married sons if they lived with him, and over their wives. In early times this authority included even the power over life and death: thus Judah condemned to death his daughter-in-law Tamar when she was accused of misconduct (Gn 38: 24).

The family consists of those who are united by common blood and common dwelling-place. The 'family' is a 'house'; to found a family is 'to build a house' (Ne 7: 4). Noah's family includes his wife, his sons and their wives (Gn 7: 1 and 7); Jacob's family comprises three generations (Gn 46: 8-26). The family included the servants, the resident aliens or gerîm[3] and the 'stateless persons', widows and orphans, who lived under the protection of the head of the family. Jephthah, an illegitimate son expelled by his brothers, still claimed to belong to his 'father's house' (Jg 11: 1-7).

Again, the term bêth or 'house', like the word 'family' in modern languages, is very flexible and may even include the entire nation (the 'house of Jacob' or the 'house of Israel'), or a considerable section of the people (the 'house of Joseph' or the 'house of Judah'). It may denote kinship in the wide sense: Yaazanyah, the descendant of Rekab, his brothers and all his sons form the bêth Rekab (Jr 35: 3); the heads of 'families' in the Chronicler's lists some-

---

1. P. 43.   2. Pp. 28-29.
3. On the gerîm, cf. pp. 74-76.

times stand as the heads of very numerous groups (1 Ch 5: 15, 24; 7: 7, 40;
8: 6, 10, 13; 9: 9; 23: 24; 24, 6, etc.); and the heads of 'families' who return
from Babylon with Esdras are each accompanied by anything from twenty-
eight to three hundred men (Esd 8: 1-14).

In this wide sense, the family was the same group as the clan, the *mishpahah*.
The latter concentrated in one area, occupying one or more villages according to its size, like the *mishpahah* of the Danites at Soreah and Eshtaol (Jg 18:
11); alternatively, several *mishpahôth* might live together within a city, like
the groups from Judah and Benjamin listed in the census of Jerusalem by
Nehemias (Ne 11: 4-8) and by the Chronicler (1 Ch 9: 4-9). The clan had
common interests and duties, and its members were conscious of the blood-
bond which united them: they called each other 'brothers' (1 S 20: 29).

On the religious level, too, the family played its part as a unit of society.
The Passover was a family festival kept in every home (Ex 12: 3-4, 46),
and year by year Samuel's father took the whole family on pilgrimage to
Shiloh (1 S 1: 3f.).

2. *Family solidarity.* The go'el

The members of the family in this wider sense had an obligation to help
and to protect one another. There was in Israel an institution which defined
the occasions when this obligation called for action; it is the institution of the
go'el, from a root which means 'to buy back or to redeem', 'to lay claim to',
but fundamentally its meaning is 'to protect'. The institution has analogies
among other peoples (for example, the Arabs), but in Israel it took a special
form, with its own terminology.

The *go'el* was a redeemer, a protector, a defender of the interests of the
individual and of the group. If an Israelite had to sell himself into slavery in
order to repay a debt, he would be 'redeemed' by one of his near relations
(Lv 25: 47-49). If an Israelite had to sell his patrimony, the *go'el* had priority
over all other purchasers; it was his right and duty to buy it himself, to prevent the family property from being alienated. This law is codified in
Lv 25: 25, and it was in his capacity as *go'el* that Jeremias bought the field of
his cousin Hanameel (Jr 32: 6f.).

The story of Ruth is yet another illustration of this custom, but here the
purchase of the land is rendered more complicated by a case of levirate.
Naomi had some property which, because of her poverty, she was forced to
sell; and her daughter-in-law Ruth was a childless widow. Boaz was a *go'el*
of Naomi and Ruth (Rt 2: 20), but there was a closer relative who could
exercise this right before him (Rt 3: 12; 4: 4). This first *go'el* would have
bought the land, but he would not accept the double obligation of buying
the land and marrying Ruth, because the child of this union would bear the
name of the deceased husband and inherit the land (Rt 4: 4-6). So Boaz
bought the family property and married Ruth (Rt 4: 9-10).

This story shows that the right of the *go'el* followed a certain order of kinship, an order which is specified in Lv 25: 49: first, the paternal uncle, then his son, then other relations. Further, the *go'el* could renounce his right or decline his duty without blame. By taking off one shoe (Rt 4: 7-8) a man proclaimed that he was forgoing his right; Dt 25: 9 describes a similar action in the law of levirate, but there the procedure is meant to bring the brother-in-law into disgrace. Comparison of this law with the story of Ruth seems to indicate that the obligation of the levirate was at first undertaken by the clan, like the redemption of the patrimony, but was later restricted to the brother-in-law.[1]

One of the gravest obligations of the *go'el* was blood-vengeance, but we have already examined this in connection with tribal organization, because it is rooted in desert custom.[2]

The term *go'el* passed into religious usage. Thus Yahweh, avenger of the oppressed, and saviour of his people, is called a *go'el* in Jb 19: 25; Ps 19: 15; 78: 35; Jr 50: 34, etc., and frequently in the second part of Isaias (Is 41: 14; 43: 14; 44: 6, 24; 49: 7; 59: 20, etc.).

3. *The later development of family customs*

The firmness of these family ties was an inheritance from tribal organization. The transition to settled life, and still more the development of town life, brought about social changes which affected family customs.

The family ceased to be self-sufficient, because the standard of material welfare rose, and the development of industries led to a specialization of activities. Still, blood will have its say, and crafts were probably handed on, just as in Egypt, from father to son; the reservation of the priesthood to families of the tribe of Levi was, no doubt, only an extreme instance of a general practice. There can be no doubt, also, that certain villages were composed of woodworkers or ironfounders (1 Ch 4: 14; cf. Ne 11: 35), while other villages specialized in linen (1 Ch 4: 21) or pottery (1 Ch 4: 23). These guilds of artisans were ruled by a 'father', and were called *mishpaḥôth*, implying that their members were united by kinship, or at least that they were grouped like families.[3]

Of those great patriarchal families which united several generations around one head, few, if any, remained. Living conditions in the towns set a limit to the numbers who could be housed under one roof: the houses discovered by excavation are small. We rarely hear of a father surrounded by more than his unmarried children, and, when a son married and founded a new family, he was said to 'build a house' (Ne 7: 4). The prologue to the book of Job is a pastiche of a patriarchal story, but it betrays its period when it describes Job's

---

1. On the levirate, cf. p. 37.
2. P. 11.
3. Cf. p. 77.

sons as attending feasts by turns in one another's houses (Jb 1: 4, 13, 18). Amnon and Absalom, too, had their own homes, away from the palace where David lived with their unmarried sister Tamar (2 S 13: 7, 8, 20).

Slaves were still counted as members of the family, but they were not so numerous; instead, another social class made its appearance—that of wage-earners. A world which consisted merely of family groups, where the servants lived with the master of the house, passed away, and in its place there arose a society divided into king and subjects, employers and workmen, rich and poor. This transformation was complete, both in Israel and Judah, by the eighth century B.C.

By then the authority of the head of the family was no longer unlimited. A father could no longer put his son to death, and judgment—even on offences against a father or mother—was reserved to the elders of the town (Dt 21: 18-21). Even in David's day, a member of a clan had a right of appeal from the judgment of his clan to the king himself (2 S 14: 4-11).

So, as the feeling of solidarity grew weaker, the individual person began to emerge from the family group. The principle of individual responsibility is stated in Dt 24: 16 and applied in 2 K 14: 6; it is confirmed in Jr 31: 29-30 and developed in Ez 14: 12-20; 18: 10-20. At the same time, however, the duty of mutual assistance was neglected by relatives, and the prophets had to plead the case of the widow and orphan (Is 1: 17; Jr 7: 6; 22: 3). The obligation of the levirate was no longer as binding as it appears in the story of Judah and Tamar (Gn 38), and the law of Dt 25: 5-10 shows that this obligation could be rejected. Even the practice of blood-vengeance was circumscribed by the advent of forensic justice and by the legislation on cities of refuge (Nb 35: 9-29; Dt 19: 1-13).

CHAPTER TWO

MARRIAGE

1. *Polygamy and monogamy*

THE story of the creation of the first two human beings (Gn 2: 21-24) presents monogamous marriage as the will of God. The patriarchs of Seth's line (*e.g.* Noah in Gn 7: 7) are said to be monogamous, and polygamy first appears in the reprobate line of Cain, when Lamek takes two wives (Gn 4: 19). Such was the traditional story of the origins of man.

In the patriarchal age, Abraham had at first only one wife, Sarah, and it was because she was barren that he took her handmaid Hagar, at Sarah's own suggestion (Gn 16: 1-2). Abraham also married Qeturah (Gn 25: 1), but since this is related after the death of Sarah (Gn 23: 1-2), Qeturah could have been his lawful, wedded wife. (Against this view, however, Gn 25: 6, which speaks of Abraham's concubines in the plural, seems to refer to Hagar and Qeturah.) Similarly, Nahor, who had children by his wife Milkah, also had a concubine, Reumah (Gn 22: 20-24); and Eliphaz, son of Esau, had both a wife and a concubine (Gn 36: 11-12).

In all this the patriarchs are following the customs of the time. According to the Code of Hammurabi (about 1700 B.C.), the husband may not take a second wife unless the first is barren, and he loses this right if the wife herself gives him a slave as concubine. The husband can, however, himself take a concubine, even if his wife has borne him children; but the concubine never has the same rights as the wife, and he may not take another concubine unless the first is barren. In the region of Kirkuk, in the fifteenth century B.C., the same customs obtained, but it seems that there the barren wife was under an obligation to provide a concubine for her husband.

In all these instances there is relative monogamy, for there is never more than one lawful, wedded wife. But other examples show that these restrictions were not always observed. Jacob married the two sisters Leah and Rachel, each of whom gave him her maid (Gn 29: 15-30; 30: 1-9), and Esau had three wives who were of equal rank (Gn 26: 34; 28: 9; 36: 1-5). It would seem that the patriarchs followed a less stringent code of conduct than that which prevailed in Mesopotamia at the same time, but the latter too was soon relaxed. At the end of the second millennium B.C., the Assyrian Code of Law assigns an intermediary place, between the wife and the concubine who is a slave, to the *esirtu*, or 'woman of the harem'; a man may have several *esirtu*, and an *esirtu* may be raised to the rank of wife.

In Israel, under the Judges and the monarchy, the old restrictions fell into disuse. Gideon had 'many wives' and at least one concubine (Jg 8: 30-31). Bigamy is recognized as a legal fact by Dt 21: 15-17, and the kings sometimes kept a large harem.[1]

There was, it seems, no limit to the number of wives and concubines a man might have. Much later, the Talmud fixed the number of wives at four for a subject and eighteen for a king. In practice, however, only royalty could afford the luxury of a large harem, and commoners had to be content with one wife, or two at the most. Samuel's father had two wives, one of whom was barren (1 S 1: 2); and, according to 2 Ch 24: 3, the priest Yehoyada had chosen two wives for King Joas. It is hard to say whether bigamy of this kind, referred to in Dt 21: 15-17 also, was very common, but it was probably no more frequent than with the Bedouin and fellahs of modern Palestine, who, for all the liberty allowed by Moslem law, are rarely polygamous. Sometimes self-interest leads a man to take a second wife, for he thus acquires another servant; more often, it is the desire for many children, especially when the first wife is barren, or has borne only daughters. There is also the fact that the Eastern woman, being married very young, ages quickly. The same motives played their part, no doubt, in ancient Israel.

The presence of several wives did not make for peace in the home. A barren wife would be despised by her companion (*e.g.* Anna and Peninnah, in 1 S 1: 6), even if the latter were a slave (cf. Sarah and Hagar, in Gn 16: 4-5); and the barren wife could be jealous of one with children (as Rachel was of Leah, Gn 30: 1). The husband's preference for one of his wives could make this rivalry more bitter (Gn 29: 30-31; 1 S 1: 5), until eventually the law (Dt 21: 15-17) had to intervene to prevent the children of his favourite from receiving more than their fair share of the inheritance. The attitude has left its mark on the language, which calls the wives of one man 'rivals' (1 S 1: 6; cf. Si 37: 12).

It is clear, however, that the most common form of marriage in Israel was monogamy. It is noteworthy that the books of Samuel and Kings, which cover the entire period of the monarchy, do not record a single case of bigamy among commoners (except that of Samuel's father, at the very beginning of the period). The Wisdom books, too, which provide a picture of society in their age, never mention polygamy. Except for the text of Si 37: 11, just cited, which might be interpreted in a wider sense, the many passages in these books which speak of a wife in her home all yield a better meaning against the background of a strictly monogamous family (cf., for example, Pr 5: 15-19; Qo 9: 9; Si 26: 1-4 and the eulogy of a perfect wife which closes the book of Proverbs, Pr 31: 10-31). The book of Tobias, a family

1. Cf. p. 115.

tale, never refers to any but monogamous families, that of the elder Tobias, that of Raguel, and that founded by the younger Tobias and Sarra. The image of a monogamous marriage is before the eyes of those prophets who represent Israel as the one wife chosen by the one and only God (Os 2: 4f.; Jr 2: 2; Is 50: 1; 54: 6-7; 62: 4-5), and Ezechiel develops the same metaphor into an allegory (Ez 16). It is true that the same prophet compares Yahweh's dealings with Samaria and Jerusalem to a marriage with two sisters (Ez 23; cf. also Jr 3: 6-11), but this is merely to adapt the allegory of chapter 16 to the historical conditions which prevailed after the political schism.

2. *The typical Israelite marriage*

Just as the unmarried woman was under the authority of her father, so the married woman was under the authority of her husband. The Decalogue (Ex 20: 17) lists a wife among a man's possessions, along with his servants and maids, his ox and his ass. The husband is called the *ba'al* or 'master' of his wife, just as he is the *ba'al* of a house or field (Ex 21: 3, 22; 2 S 11: 26; Pr 12: 4, etc.); a married woman is therefore the 'possession' of her *ba'al* (Gn 20: 3; Dt 22: 22). Indeed, 'to marry a wife' is expressed by the verb *bâ'al*, the root meaning of which is 'to become master' (Dt 21: 13; 24: 1).

The question immediately arises, whether this usage indicates that the wife was really considered as her husband's property; in other words, had she been bought by him? It has often been suggested that the Israelites practised a form of 'marriage by purchase' (ethnographers have certainly shown its existence among other peoples). The argument is based partly on the vocabulary employed, and partly on the story of Rachel and Leah (who complain that their father has sold them, Gn 31: 15). But one need not give a formal, juridical sense to words spoken by women in a moment of anger. However, the supporters of the purchase-theory appeal above all, and with more reason, to the custom of the *mohar*.

The *mohar* was a sum of money which the fiancé was bound to pay to the girl's father. The word occurs only three times in the Bible (Gn 34: 12; Ex 22: 16; 1 S 18: 25). The amount could vary; it depended on the girl's father (Gn 34: 12), and on the social standing of the family (1 S 18: 23). For a compulsory marriage after a virgin had been raped, the law prescribed the payment of fifty shekels of silver (Dt 22: 29). But, since this was a penalty, the ordinary *mohar* must have been less. Besides, fifty shekels is roughly the sum paid by the Pharaoh Amenophis III for the women of Gezer destined for his harem. According to Ex 21: 32, thirty shekels was the indemnity due for the death of a female servant, but this too was a penalty. The law on the fulfilment of vows (Lv 27: 4-5) valued a woman at thirty shekels, and a girl under twenty years of age at ten shekels.

A fiancé could compound for the payment of the *mohar* by service, as

Jacob did for both his marriages (Gn 29: 15-30), or by accomplishing an appointed task, as David did for Mikal (1 S 18: 25-27) and Othniel for Caleb's daughter (Jos 15: 16=Jg 1: 12).

This obligation to pay a sum of money, or its equivalent, to the girl's family obviously gives the Israelite marriage the outward appearance of a purchase. But the *mohar* seems to be not so much the price paid for the woman as a compensation given to the family, and, in spite of the apparent resemblance, in law this is a different consideration. The future husband thereby acquires a right over the woman, but the woman herself is not bought and sold. The difference becomes clear if we compare the *mohar* marriage with another type of union, which really was a purchase: a girl could be sold by her father to another man who intended her to be his own, or his son's, concubine; she was a slave, and could be re-sold, though not to an alien (Ex 21: 7-11). Furthermore, it is probable that the father enjoyed only the usufruct of the *mohar*, and that the latter reverted to the daughter at the time of succession, or if her husband's death reduced her to penury. This would explain the complaint of Rachel and Leah against their father, that he had 'devoured their money' after having 'sold' them (Gn 31: 15).

A similar custom, with the same name (*mahr*), is found among the Palestinian Arabs of to-day. The *mahr* is a sum of money paid by the fiancé to the girl's parents. Its amount varies from village to village, and according to the family's income; the amount depends, too, on whether the girl is marrying within her kin or outside the clan, whether she is of the same village or from some other place. Those concerned do not regard this payment as a real purchase, and part of the sum goes towards the bride's trousseau.

A parallel, though not identical, custom existed in ancient Babylonian law: the *tirḫatu*, though not a necessary condition of the marriage, was usually paid over to the girl's father, and sometimes to the girl herself. The amount varied greatly, from one to fifty shekels of silver. This sum was administered by the father, who enjoyed the usufruct of it; but he could not alienate it, and it reverted to the wife if she was widowed, or to her children after their mother's death. In Assyrian law, the *tirḫatu* was given to the girl herself. It was not a purchase price, but, according to two very probable theories, either a compensation to the girl for the loss of her virginity, or a dowry intended to assist the wife if she lost her husband. There is a close parallel in the marriage-contracts found in the Jewish colony at Elephantine; there the *mohar* is counted among the wife's possessions, though it had been paid to the father.

The gifts presented by the bridegroom on the occasion of the wedding are quite different from the *mohar*: the two things are clearly distinguished in Gn 34: 12. These presents offered to the girl and her family were a reward for their accepting the proposal of marriage. So, as soon as Rebecca's marriage had been agreed on, Abraham's servant brought out jewels and dresses for the girl, and rich presents for her father and mother (Gn 24: 53).

The same custom is found in Mesopotamia. According to the Code of Hammurabi, the bridegroom distributed presents to the girl's parents, and if they broke off the engagement, they had to restore twice what they had received. By Assyrian law, where the *tirḥatu* was a gift of money made previously to the bride, the man gave her ornaments also and made a present to her father.

Was there, in addition, a dowry, a contribution on the part of the bride at the time of the marriage? It is difficult to reconcile any such custom with the payment of the *mohar* by the bridegroom. In fact, there is no mention of any *mohar* in those texts which mention what seems like a dowry: the Pharaoh gave Gezer as a wedding gift to his daughter when Solomon married her (1 K 9: 16); and when Tobias married Sarra, her father gave Tobias half of his fortune (Tb 8: 21). Solomon's marriage, however, follows Egyptian custom, and he is above convention, while the story of Tobias is set in a foreign land. Besides, since Sarra was an only child, this grant appears to be an advance of the inheritance. In Israel, parents might give presents to their daughter at her wedding—a slave, for example (Gn 24: 59; 29: 24, 29), or a piece of land (Jos 15: 18-19), though the latter present was made after the wedding. In general, the custom of providing a dowry never took root in Jewish territory, and Si 25: 22 seems even to repudiate it: 'A woman who maintains her husband is an object of anger, of reproach and of shame.'

In Babylonian law, however, the father gave the young bride certain possessions, which belonged to her in her own right, the husband having only the use of them. They reverted to the wife if she were widowed or divorced without fault on her part. Assyrian law seems to contain similar provisions.

By marriage a woman left her parents, went to live with her husband, and joined his clan, to which her children would belong. Rebecca left her father and mother (Gn 24: 58-59), and Abraham would not allow Isaac to go to Mesopotamia unless the wife chosen for him agreed to come to Canaan (Gn 24: 5-8). A few marriages mentioned in the Bible seem, however, to be exceptions to this general rule. Jacob, after marrying Leah and Rachel, continued to live with his father-in-law, Laban; when he stole away, Laban reproached him for taking away Leah and Rachel, protesting that they were 'his' daughters and their children 'his' children (Gn 31: 26, 43). Gideon had a concubine who continued to live with her family at Shechem (Jg 8: 31), and her son Abimelek asserted the relationship which united him to his mother's clan (Jg 9: 1-2). When Samson married a Philistine woman of Timnah, the woman continued to live with her parents, where Samson visited her (Jg 14: 8f.; 15: 1-2).

Some think these marriages are a type of union in which the wife does not leave her father's house; instead, the husband takes up residence in her home, and severs his connections with his own clan. Ethnographers call it a *beena* marriage, from its name in Ceylon, where their research has been principally centred. But the comparison is not exact. Jacob's fourteen years of service were equivalent to the *mohar*. He stayed a further six years with his father-in-law (Gn 31: 41) simply because he was afraid of Esau's vengeance (Gn 27: 42-45) and because he had a contract with Laban (Gn 30: 25-31). It was not, in fact, on the plea of matrimonial law that Laban opposed Jacob's departure with his wives (Gn 30: 25f.); he merely blamed him for running away secretly (Gn 31: 26-28). He would have spoken differently if Jacob, by his marriage, had become a member of his own clan. As for Gideon, the text stresses that the woman was a concubine. The story of Samson's marriage is more to the point, but it must be noted that Samson did not stay at Timnah with his wife; he only came to visit her, and he was not incorporated into her clan, so that this too is not a *beena* marriage.

Gideon's marriage should be compared, rather, with the *ṣadiqa* union of the ancient Arabs. It is not so much a marriage as a liaison sanctioned by custom: *ṣadiqa* means 'lover' or 'mistress'. Samson's marriage has close similarities with a form found among Palestinian Arabs, in that it is a true marriage but without permanent cohabitation. The woman is mistress of her own house, and the husband, known as *joz musarrib*, 'a visiting husband', comes as a guest and brings presents. Ancient Assyrian law also provided for the case where a married woman continued to live with her father, but it has not been proved that this kind of marriage (called *erebu*) constitutes a special type of marriage.

3. Choosing the bride

The Bible gives no information about the age at which girls were married. The practice of marrying the eldest first was not universal (Gn 29: 26). On the other hand, it seems certain that girls, and therefore presumably boys too, were married very young; for centuries this has been the custom of the East, and in many places it still obtains to-day. The books of Kings, however, usually give the age of each king of Judah at his accession, followed by the length of his reign and the age of his son (normally the eldest) who succeeded him. From these figures we can deduce that Joiakin married at sixteen, Amon and Josias at fourteen; but the calculations are based on figures which are not all reliable. In later days the Rabbis fixed the minimum age for marriage at twelve years for girls and thirteen for boys.

Under these circumstances it is understandable that the parents took all the decisions when a marriage was being arranged. Neither the girl nor, often, the youth was consulted. Abraham sent his servant to choose a wife for Isaac, and the servant arranged the contract with Rebecca's brother, Laban (Gn 24: 33-53).[1] Her own consent was asked only afterwards (vv. 57-58), and, if

---

1. The mention of Bethuel, Rebecca's father, in v. 50, is an addition. Bethuel was dead, and Laban was the head of the family (cf. vv. 33, 53, 55, 59).

we interpret this by analogy with certain Mesopotamian texts, her consent was asked only because her father was dead, and because her brother, not her father, had authority over her. When Abraham expelled Hagar from his camp, she took a wife for Ishmael (Gn 21: 21), and Judah arranged the marriage of his first-born (Gn 38: 6). Alternatively, the father might guide his son's choice, as, for example, when Isaac sent Jacob to marry one of his cousins (Gn 28: 1-2). Hamor asked for Dinah as a wife for his son Shechem (Gn 34: 4-6), and Samson, when he fell in love with a Philistine woman, asked her parents for her (Jg 14: 2-3). Even the independent-minded Esau took his father's wishes into account (Gn 28: 8-9). Caleb decided on his daughter's marriage (Jos 15: 16), as did Saul (1 S 18: 17, 19, 21, 27; 25: 44). At the end of the Old Testament, the elder Tobias advised his son on the choice of a wife (Tb 4: 12-13), and the marriage of young Tobias with Sarra was agreed on with the father of Sarra, in her absence (Tb 7: 9-12).

Once the proposal of marriage had been put to the girl's parents, they discussed the conditions, especially the amount of the *mohar* (Gn 29: 15f.; 34: 12). In short, even in those days marriageable daughters caused as much anxiety to their parents as to-day (Si 42: 9).

Nevertheless, parental authority was not such as to leave no room for the feelings of the young couple. There were love marriages in Israel. The young man could make his preferences known (Gn 34: 4; Jg 14: 2), or take his own decision without consulting his parents, and even against their wishes (Gn 26: 34-35). It was rarer for the girl to take the initiative, but we do read of Saul's daughter Mikal falling in love with David (1 S 18: 20).

Actually, young people had ample opportunity for falling in love, and for expressing their feelings, for they were very free. 2 M 3: 19, it is true, speaks of the young girls of Jerusalem being confined to the house, but this text refers to the Greek period and to an exceptional state of affairs. The veiling of women came even later. In ancient times young girls were not secluded and went out unveiled. They looked after the sheep (Gn 29: 6), drew the water (Gn 24: 13; 1 S 9: 11), went gleaning in the fields behind the reapers (Rt 2: 2f.) and visited other people's houses (Gn 34: 1). They could talk with men without any embarrassment (Gn 24: 15-21; 29: 11-12; 1 S 9: 11-13).

This freedom sometimes exposed girls to the violence of young men (Gn 34: 1-2), but the man who seduced a virgin was bound to marry his victim and to pay an enhanced *mohar*; and he forfeited the right to divorce her (Ex 22: 15; Dt 22: 28-29).

It was the custom to take a wife from among one's own kith and kin; the custom was a relic of tribal life. So Abraham sent his servant to find Isaac a wife among his own family in Mesopotamia (Gn 24: 4), and Isaac in turn sent Jacob there to find a wife (Gn 28: 2). Laban declared that he would rather give his daughter to Jacob than to a stranger (Gn 29: 19), and Samson's father was saddened because his son did not choose a wife from his own clan

(Jg 14:3) ; Tobias, too, advised his son to choose a wife within his tribe (Tb 4:12).

Marriages between first cousins were common, *e.g.* the marriage between Isaac and Rebecca, and those of Jacob with Rachel and Leah. Even to-day such marriages are common among the Arabs of Palestine, where a young man has a strict right to the hand of his cousin. According to Tb 6:12-13 and 7:10, Tobias' request for Sarra's hand could not be refused, because he was her nearest kinsman; it is 'a law of Moses' (Tb 6:13; 7:11-12). The Pentateuch, however, contains no such prescription. The text in Tobias must refer either to the accounts of the marriages of Isaac and Jacob (cf. especially Gn 24:50-51), or perhaps to the law requiring heiresses to marry within their father's clan, to preclude the alienation of family property (Nb 36:5-9), for Sarra was Raguel's only daughter (Tb 6:12). The same considerations of patrimony and blood-relationship were the basis of the obligation of the *levir* towards his widowed sister-in-law.[1]

Marriages did take place, however, between persons of different families, and even with foreign women. Esau married two Hittite women (Gn 26:34), Joseph an Egyptian (Gn 41:45) and Moses a Midianite (Ex 2:21). Naomi's two daughters-in-law were Moabites (Rt 1:4); David had a Calebite and an Aramaean among his wives (2 S 3:3), and Solomon's harem included, 'besides the pharaoh's daughter, Moabites, Ammonites, Edomites, Sidonians and Hittites' (1 K 11:1; cf. 14:21). Achab married Jezabel, a Sidonian (1 K 16:31). Israelite women, too, were married to foreigners, Bathsheba to a Hittite (2 S 11:3), and the mother of Hiram the bronze-worker to a Tyrian (1 K 7:13-14).

These mixed marriages, made by kings for political reasons, became common among subjects also, after the settlement in Canaan (Jg 3:6). They not only tainted the purity of Israel's blood, but also endangered its religious faith (1 K 11:4), and were therefore forbidden by law (Ex 34:15-16; Dt 7:3-4). An exception was made for women captured in war, whom Israelites could marry after a ceremony symbolizing the abandonment of their country of origin (Dt 21:10-14). Scant respect was paid to these prohibitions, however, and the community which returned from the Exile continued to contract mixed marriages (Ml 2:11-12); Esdras and Nehemias both had to take strict measures, which, it seems, were not always very effective (Esd 9-10; Ne 10:31; 13:23-27).

Within the family, marriages with very close relations were forbidden, because one does not unite with 'the flesh of one's body' (Lv 18:6), affinity being held to create the same bond as consanguinity (Lv 18:17). These bans amount to the prohibition of incest. Some are primitive, others represent later additions to the law; the main collection of precepts is found in Lv 18. An impediment of consanguinity exists in the direct line between father and

1. See p. 38.

daughter, mother and son (Lv 18: 7), father and granddaughter (Lv 18: 10), and in the collateral line between brother and sister (Lv 18: 9; Dt 27: 22). Marriage with a half-sister, which was permitted in the patriarchal age (Gn 20: 12) and even under David (2 S 13: 13), is forbidden by the laws of Lv 18: 11; 20: 17; marriage between a nephew and aunt, like that from which Moses was born (Ex 6: 20; Nb 26: 59), is prohibited by Lv 18: 12-13; 20: 19. The impediment of affinity exists between a son and his step-mother (Lv 18: 8), between father-in-law and daughter-in-law (Lv 18: 15; 20: 12; cf. Gn 38: 26), between mother-in-law and son-in-law (Lv 20: 14; Dt 27: 23), between a man and the daughter or granddaughter of a woman he has married (Lv 18: 17), between a man and his uncle's wife (Lv 18: 14; 20: 20), between brother-in-law and sister-in-law (Lv 18: 16; 20: 21). Marriage with two sisters, which might seem to be authorized by the example of Jacob, is forbidden by Lv 18: 18.

Members of the priestly line were subject to special restrictions. According to Lv 21: 7, they could not take a wife who had been a prostitute, or divorced by her husband. Ez 44: 22 adds also widows, unless they were widows of a priest. The rule was even stricter for the high priest: he could marry only a virgin of Israel.

4. Engagements

Engagement, or betrothal, is a promise of marriage made some time before the celebration of the wedding. The custom existed in Israel, and Hebrew has a special word for it, 'araś, which occurs eleven times in the Bible.

The historical books provide little information. The engagements of Isaac and Jacob are rather peculiar. Though Rebecca was promised to Isaac in Mesopotamia, the wedding took place only when she joined him in Canaan (Gn 24: 67); Jacob waited seven years before marrying, but he had a special contract with Laban (Gn 29: 15-21). The story of David and Saul's two daughters is clearer. Merab had been promised to him, but 'when the time came' she was given to another man (1 S 18: 17-19); Mikal was promised to David on payment of a hundred foreskins from the Philistines, which he brought 'before the time had passed' (1 S 18: 26-27). On the other hand, Tobias married Sarra as soon as the terms of the marriage contract were agreed (Tb 7: 9-16).

Legal texts, however, show that engagement was a recognized custom with juridical consequences. According to Dt 20: 7, a man who is engaged, though not yet married to a girl, is excused from going to war. The law of Dt 22: 23-27 makes provision for the case in which a betrothed virgin is violated by a man other than her fiancé. If the crime was committed in a town, the girl is stoned along with her seducer, because she should have cried for help; if she was assaulted in the country, only the man is put to death, because the woman might have cried without being heard.

The gloss in 1 S 18: 21 probably preserves the formula spoken by the girl's father to make the engagement valid: 'To-day you shall be my son-in-law.' The amount of the *mohar* was discussed with the girl's parents at the time of the engagement, and was no doubt paid over at once if, as usually happened, it was paid in money.

The custom existed in Mesopotamia also. An engagement was concluded by the payment of the *tirḥatu*, the equivalent of the *mohar*, and it entailed juridical consequences. A certain interval elapsed between the engagement and the marriage, during which either party could withdraw, but at the price of a forfeit. Hittite law contained similar provisions.

5. *Marriage ceremonies*

It is interesting to note that both in Israel and in Mesopotamia, marriage was a purely civil contract, not sanctioned by any religious rite. Malachy, it is true, calls the bride 'the wife of thy covenant' (*b'rîth*: Ml 2: 14), and *b'rîth* is often used for a religious pact; but here the pact is simply the contract of marriage. In Pr 2: 17 marriage is called 'the covenant of God', and in the allegory of Ez 16: 8 the covenant of Sinai becomes the contract of marriage between Yahweh and Israel.

The texts just cited may well allude to a written contract; apart from these references, the Old Testament mentions a written marriage contract only in the story of Tobias (Tb 7: 13). We possess several marriage contracts originating from the Jewish colony at Elephantine in the fifth century B.C., and the custom was firmly established among the Jews in the Graeco-Roman era. How far back it dates is hard to say. The custom existed in very early times in Mesopotamia, and the Code of Hammurabi declares that a marriage concluded without a formal contract is invalid. In Israel, acts of divorce were drawn up before the Exile (Dt 24: 1-3; Jr 3: 8), and it would be surprising if contracts of marriage did not exist at the same time. Perhaps it is merely by accident that they are never mentioned in the Bible.

The formula pronounced at marriage is given in the Elephantine contracts, which are made out in the name of the husband: 'She is my wife and I am her husband, from this day for ever.' The woman made no declaration. An equivalent formula is found in Tb 7: 11, where Sarra's father says to Tobias: 'Henceforth thou art her brother and she is thy sister.' In a contract of the second century after Christ, found in the desert of Judah, the formula is: 'Thou shalt be my wife.'

Marriage was, of course, an occasion for rejoicing. The chief ceremony was the entry of the bride into the bridegroom's house. The bridegroom, wearing a diadem (Ct 3: 11; Is 61: 10) and accompanied by his friends with tambourines and a band (1 M 9: 39), proceeded to the bride's house. She was richly dressed and adorned with jewels (Ps 45: 14-15; Is 61: 10), but she wore a veil (Ct 4: 1, 3; 6: 7), which she took off only in the bridal chamber. This explains why Rebecca veiled herself on seeing Isaac, her fiancé (Gn 24: 65), and how Laban was able to substitute Leah for Rachel at Jacob's first marriage (Gn 29: 23-25). The bride, escorted by her companions (Ps 45: 15), was conducted to the home of the bridegroom (Ps 45: 16; cf. Gn 24: 67). Love songs were sung in praise of the bridal pair (Jr 16: 9), examples of which survive in Ps 45 and in the Song of Songs, whether we interpret them literally or allegorically.

The Arabs of Palestine and Syria have preserved similar customs—the procession, the wedding songs and the veiling of the bride. Sometimes, during the procession, a sword is carried by the bride or in front of her, and sometimes she performs the dance of the sabre, advancing and retiring before it. Some have compared this with the dance of the Shulamite in Ct 7: 1. In some tribes the bride pretends to escape from the bridegroom, and he has to make a show of capturing her by force. It has been suggested that these games are a survival of marriage by abduction; the story of the men of Benjamin and the girls who danced in the vineyards of Shiloh would be an example from the Old Testament (Jg 21: 19-23). There seems to be little foundation for these comparisons. The brandishing of the sword is symbolic: it cuts away bad luck and drives off evil spirits. There is nothing to suggest that the Shulamite's dance was a sabre-dance, and the incident at Shiloh is explained by exceptional circumstances which are recorded in the story.

Next came a great feast (Gn 29: 22; Jg 14: 10; Tb 7: 14). In these three passages the feast took place at the home of the bride's parents, but the circumstances were exceptional. As a general rule it was certainly given at the bridegroom's house (cf. Mt 22: 2). The feast normally lasted seven days (Gn 29: 27; Jg 14: 12), and could even be prolonged for two weeks (Tb 8: 20; 10: 7). But the marriage was consummated on the first night (Gn 29: 23; Tb 8: 1). The blood-stained linen of this nuptial night was preserved; it proved the bride's virginity and would be evidence if she were slandered by her husband (Dt 22: 13-21). The same naïve custom still obtains in Palestine and other Moslem countries.

6. Repudiation and divorce

A husband could divorce his wife. The motive accepted by Dt 24: 1 is 'that he has found a fault to impute to her'. The expression is very vague, and in the Rabbinical age there was keen discussion on the meaning of this text. The rigorist school of Shammai admitted only adultery and misconduct as grounds for divorce, but the more liberal school of Hillel would accept any reason, however trivial, such as the charge that a wife had cooked a dish badly, or merely that the husband preferred another woman. Even before this age, Si 25: 26 had told the husband: 'If thy wife does not obey thee at a signal and a glance, separate from her.'

The form of divorce was simple: the husband made out a declaration contradicting that which had sealed the marriage contract: 'She is no longer my wife and I am no longer her husband' (Os 2: 4). In the colony at Elephantine he pronounced in front of witnesses the words: 'I divorce my wife' (literally: 'I hate my wife'). In Assyria he said: 'I repudiate her' or 'You are no more my wife.' But in Israel, Mesopotamia and Elephantine, the husband had to draw up a writ of divorce (Dt 24: 1, 3; Is 50: 1; Jr 3: 8) which allowed the woman to remarry (Dt 24: 2). A writ of divorce dating from the beginning of the second century of our era has been found in the caves of Murabba'at.

The law laid few restrictions on the husband's right. A man who had falsely accused his wife of not being a virgin when he married her could never divorce her (Dt 22: 13-19), nor could a man who had been compelled to marry a girl he had violated (Dt 22: 28-29). If a divorced wife remarried, and later regained her liberty by the death of her second husband or by divorce from him, the first husband could not take her back (Dt 24: 3-4; cf. Jr 3: 1). Osee's double marriage (Os 2-3)—if, as it seems, he did take back a wife he had divorced—is not forbidden by this law, for in the meantime she had not remarried, but had become a prostitute. Nor did the law apply to Mikal, first married to David, then given to another man and finally taken back by David (1 S 18: 20-27; 25: 44; 2 S 3: 13-16), because David had never divorced her.

We do not know whether Israelite husbands made much use of this right, which seems to have been very far-reaching. The Wisdom books praise conjugal fidelity (Pr 5: 15-19; Qo 9: 9), and Malachy teaches that marriage makes the two partners one person, and that the husband must keep the oath sworn to his partner: 'I hate divorce, says Yahweh, the God of Israel' (Ml 2: 14-16). But not until New Testament times do we find the proclamation, by Jesus, of the indissolubility of marriage. He uses the same argument as Malachy: 'what God has joined together, let no man separate' (Mt 5: 31-32; 19: 1-9 and parallels).

Women, on the other hand, could not ask for a divorce. Even at the beginning of the Christian era, when Salome, the sister of Herod, sent her husband Kostabar a letter of divorce, her action was held to be against Jewish law. If the Gospel envisages the possibility of a woman divorcing her husband (Mk 10: 12, but not in the parallels), it is certainly with reference to Gentile customs. The Jewish colony of Elephantine, which was subject to foreign influence, did allow a woman to divorce her husband. In Palestine itself the custom is attested in the second century of our era by a document from the desert of Judah.

In Mesopotamia, according to the Code of Hammurabi, the husband could divorce his wife by pronouncing the appropriate formula, but he had to pay her compensation, varying according to the circumstances. The wife could obtain a divorce only after a judicial decision recognizing the husband's guilt. In Assyrian law the husband could repudiate his wife without any compensation, but the wife could not obtain a divorce at all. The situation revealed by Assyrian marriage contracts is still more complicated, for they often stipulate still more onerous conditions for the husband: when arranging the marriage, the wife's parents might protect her interests by special clauses.

Though the Old Testament makes no mention of them, it is likely that in Israel too, certain financial conditions were attached to divorce. According to the marriage contracts of Elephantine, the husband who repudiated his wife could not reclaim the *mohar*; he paid the 'price of divorce'. Similarly, the wife who separated from her husband paid the same 'price of divorce', but took away her personal property, which presumably included the *mohar*.

7. Adultery and fornication

The condemnation of adultery in the Decalogue (Ex 20: 14; Dt 5: 18) is placed between the prohibitions of murder and stealing, among acts which injure one's neighbour. In Lv 18: 20 it is ranked among sins against marriage: it makes a person 'unclean'. In Israel, then, as everywhere in the ancient East, adultery was a sin against one's neighbour, but the text of Lv 18: 20 adds a religious consideration, and the stories of Gn 20: 1-13; 26: 7-11 represent adultery as a sin against God.

If a man commits adultery with a married woman, both the partners in crime are put to death (Lv 20: 10; Dt 22: 22), and, on this count, a girl engaged to be married is treated exactly like a woman already married (Dt 22: 23f.), for she belongs to her fiancé in exactly the same way as a married woman belongs to her husband. According to Dt 22: 23f.; Ez 16: 40 (cf. Jn 8: 5), the penalty was death by stoning, but it is possible that in ancient times it was death by burning. Judah condemned his daughter-in-law Tamar to be burned alive (Gn 38: 24), because he suspected she had given herself to a man at a time when she was the widow of his son Er, and, by the law of levirate, promised to his other son Shelah.

The latest collection of Proverbs (Pr 1-9) often puts young men on their guard against the seductions of a woman who is unfaithful to her husband. She is called the 'strange woman', meaning simply the wife of another man (Pr 2: 16-19; 5: 2-14; 6: 23-7: 27). Such love leads to death (2: 18; 5: 5; 7: 26-27), but this 'death' is generally synonymous with moral perdition: it appears once as the revenge of the injured husband (6: 34), never as the legal punishment of adultery.

The older parts of Proverbs rarely refer to adultery (Pr 30: 18-20) but they rank it side by side with prostitution (23: 27). The man who goes after prostitutes dissipates his wealth and loses his strength (Pr 29: 3; 31: 3), but he commits no crime in the eyes of the law. Judah, for example, is not blamed for taking his pleasure with one whom he thinks is a prostitute (Gn 38: 15-19); his only fault is in not observing the law of levirate towards his daughter-in-law (Gn 38: 26).

The husband is exhorted to be faithful to his wife in Pr 5: 15-19, but his infidelity is punished only if he violates the rights of another man by taking a married woman as his accomplice.

In contrast with the licence which the husband enjoyed, the wife's mis-conduct was punished severely: it is the 'great sin' mentioned in certain Egyptian and Ugaritic texts, the 'great sin' which the king of Gerar almost committed with Sarah (Gn 20: 9; cf. the metaphorical use of the same term with reference to idolatry, in Ex 32: 21, 30, 31; 2 K 17: 21). Her husband could, indeed, pardon her, but he could also divorce her, and her punishment entailed disgrace (Os 2: 5, 11-12; Ez 16: 37-38; 23: 29). We have no informa-tion about unmarried women, except that a priest's daughter who turned to prostitution was to be burned alive (Lv 21: 9).

8. *The levirate*

According to a law of Dt 25: 5-10, if brothers live together and one of them dies without issue, one of the surviving brothers takes his widow to wife, and the first-born of this new marriage is regarded in law as the son of the deceased. The brother-in-law can, however, decline this obligation, by making a declaration before the elders of the town; but it is a dishonourable action. The widow takes off his shoe and spits in his face, because 'he does not raise up his brother's house'.

This institution is called levirate, from the Latin *levir*, translating the Hebrew *yabam* ('brother-in-law'). Only two examples of it occur in the Old Testament, both of them difficult to interpret and only imperfectly corres-ponding to the law in Deuteronomy: the stories of Tamar and Ruth.

Judah's first-born son, Er, dies without having a child by his wife Tamar (Gn 38: 6-7). It is the duty of his brother Onan to marry the widow, but Onan does not want to have a child who would not be, in law, his own son, so he frustrates his union with Tamar; for this sin, Yahweh brings about his death (Gn 38: 8-10). Judah ought now to give Tamar his youngest son Shelah, but he shirks this duty (38: 11); so Tamar tricks her father-in-law into having intercourse with her (38: 15-19). This story of ancient times presents the obligation of the levirate as much stricter than in the law of Deuter-onomy; the brother-in-law may not decline the duty, and it passes to all the surviving brothers in turn (cf. Mt 22: 24-27). Tamar's intercourse with Judah may be a relic of a time when the duty of levirate fell on the father-in-law if he had no other sons, a practice which is found among some peoples.

More probably, it is the desperate act of a woman who desires children of the same stock as her husband.

The story of Ruth combines the custom of the levirate with the duty of redemption which fell on the *go'el*.[1] The law of Dt 25 does not apply, for Ruth had no more brothers-in-law (Rt 1: 11-12). The fact that some near relative must marry her, and that this obligation proceeds in a certain order Rt. 2: 20; 3: 12), no doubt indicates a period or a *milieu* in which the law of levirate was a matter for the clan rather than for the family in the strict sense. In any case, the intentions and effects of the marriage were those of a levirate marriage, for it was made 'to perpetuate the name of the dead' (Rt 4: 5, 10; cf. 2: 20), and the child born of it was considered the son of the deceased (Rt 4: 6; cf. 4: 17).

There are parallels to this custom among other peoples, and especially among Israel's neighbours. Though the Code of Hammurabi does not mention it, the Assyrian laws devote several articles to it. Though they do not expressly state that the widow had to be childless, this may be due to a gap in the text. On the other hand, they treat engagement, for this purpose, in just the same way as a consummated marriage; if a betrothed man dies, his fiancée must marry the dead man's brother. Some of the Hittite laws also mention the levirate, but they are less detailed. The custom also existed among the Hurrites of Nuzu and perhaps in Elam, and there is evidence of it at Ugarit also.

Discussion about the purpose of the levirate seems to be endless. Some have regarded it as a means of perpetuating ancestor-worship, others as an indication of a fratriarchal society. But, whatever may be true of other nations, the Old Testament gives its own explanation, which seems sufficient. The essential purpose is to perpetuate male descent, the 'name', the 'house', and therefore the child (probably only the first child) of a levirate marriage was considered the child of the deceased man. It was not mere sentiment, but an expression of the importance attached to blood-ties. A secondary, but similar, purpose was to prevent the alienation of family property. This consideration appears in Dt 25: 5, which makes it a condition of the levirate that the brothers should be living together, and it explains why, in the story of Ruth, the right of redeeming the land is linked with the duty of marrying the widow. The same motive is found in the legislation about the Jubilee (Lv 25), and in the law about daughters who are heiresses (Nb 36: 2-9).

1. See p. 21.

CHAPTER THREE

THE POSITION OF WOMEN: WIDOWS

IT has already been said that the wife called her husband *ba'al* or 'master'; she also called him *'adôn* or 'lord' (Gn 18: 12; Jg 19: 26; Am 4: 1); she addressed him, in fact, as a slave addressed his master, or a subject his king. The Decalogue includes a man's wife among his possessions, along with his house and land, his male and female slaves, his ox and his ass (Ex 20: 17; Dt 5: 21). Her husband can repudiate her, but she cannot claim a divorce; all her life she remains a minor. The wife does not inherit from her husband, nor daughters from their father, except when there is no male heir (Nb 27: 8). A vow made by a girl or married woman needs, to be valid, the consent of father or husband and if this consent is withheld, the vow is null and void (Nb 30: 4-17).

For all this, the wife of an Israelite was by no means on the level of a slave. A man could sell his slaves, or even his daughter (Ex 21: 7), but he could never sell his wife, even though he had acquired her as a captive in war (Dt 21: 14). The husband could divorce his wife, but she was protected by the letter of repudiation, which restored her freedom. Most probably, the married woman kept, if not the use, at least the ownership, of part of the *mohar* and of whatever she received from her parents (cf. Jos 15: 19; Jg 1: 15).

All the hard work at home certainly fell to her; she looked after the flocks, worked in the fields, cooked the food, did the spinning, and so on. All this apparent drudgery, however, far from lowering her status, earned her consideration. Sometimes, in exceptional circumstances, a woman could even take part in public affairs. Israel honoured Deborah and Jael as heroines (Jg 4-5), Athaliah reigned over Judah for several years (2 K 11); Huldah the prophetess was consulted by the king's ministers (2 K 22: 14f.); and the books of Judith and Esther tell how the nation was saved by a woman.

Within the family, respect for a wife increased on the birth of her first child, especially if the child were a boy (Gn 16: 4 and Gn 29: 31—30: 24; note the explanation of the names which Leah and Rachel gave to their children). Her husband became more attached to her, and her children owed her obedience and respect. The law condemned the faults of children against their mother as much as offences against their father (Ex 21: 17; Lv 20: 9; Dt 21: 18-21; 27: 16), and the Decalogue (Ex 20: 12) commanded equal honour to be given to father and mother (cf. Lv 19: 3). The Wisdom books insist on the respect due to one's mother (Pr 19: 26; 20: 20; 23: 22; 30: 17; Si 3: 1-16). And those rare passages which give us a glimpse into the intimacy of family life show that an Israelite wife was loved and listened to by her husband, and treated by him as an equal: Samuel's mother, for example (1 S 1: 4-8, 22-23), and the woman of Shunem (2 K 4: 8-24), or the two aged couples in the book of Tobias. And there is no doubt that this was the normal picture. It was a faithful reflection of the teaching enshrined in Genesis, where God is said to have created woman as a helpmate for man, to whom he was to cling (Gn 2: 18, 24); and the last chapter of Proverbs sings the praises of a good housewife, blessed by her children, and the pride of her husband (Pr 31: 10-31).

The social and legal position of an Israelite wife was, however, inferior to the position a wife occupied in the great countries round about. In Egypt the wife was often the head of the family, with all the rights such a position entailed. In Babylon she could acquire property, take legal action, be a party to contracts, and she even had a certain share in her husband's inheritance.

In the colony at Elephantine, under such foreign influence, the Jewish wife acquired certain civil rights. We have already said that she could obtain a divorce. She could also own property, and thereby became liable to taxation (in a long list of taxpayers, there are thirty-two names of women). Deeds of exchange and donations, etc., also survive, in which the contracting parties were women.

The position of widows calls for some special remarks. A vow made by a wife continued to bind her after her husband's death (Nb 30: 10). By the levirate law, a childless widow could continue as part of her husband's family. If there were no levir, she could re-marry outside the family (Rt 1: 9), spending the interval before her second marriage with her own father and mother (Rt 1: 8; Gn 38: 11; cf. Lv 22: 13). The story of Tamar, however, shows that even during this period her father-in-law retained authority over her (Gn 38: 24). The widow wore mourning, at least for a time (Gn 38: 14; 2 S 14: 2; Jdt 8: 5; 10: 3). How long the period of mourning lasted is not known, but to spend more than three years mourning, as Judith did, seems exceptional (Jdt 8: 4).

Judith was a rich widow. More commonly widows, especially those with children to support, were in a piteous condition (1 K 17: 8-15; 2 K 4: 1-7; cf. the widow in the Gospel, Mk 12: 41-44; Lk 21: 1-4). They were therefore protected by religious law and commended to the charity of the people, together with orphans and resident aliens—all those, in fact, who no longer had a family to assist them (Ex 22: 21, and emphatically in Deuteronomy 10: 18; 24: 17-21; 26: 12-13; 27: 19; cf. Is 1: 17; Jr 22: 3; note in contrast Is 1: 23; Jr 7: 6; cf. also Jb 29: 13). God himself is their protector, according to Ps 146: 9.

CHAPTER FOUR

CHILDREN

1. *Attitude to children*

AT a peasant or Bedouin wedding in modern Palestine, a pomegran-
ate is sometimes split open on the threshold of the house or at the
opening of the tent: its grains symbolize the many children their
friends wish them.

In ancient Israel, to have many children was a coveted honour, and the
wedding guests often expressed the wish that the couple would be blessed
with a large family. As Rebecca leaves her family, she is blessed with the
words: 'O sister of ours, become the mother of thousands of ten thousands'
(Gn 24: 60). When Boaz marries Ruth, the wish is expressed that his young
wife may be 'like Rachel and Leah, the two who built up the house of
Israel' (Rt 4: 11-12). First Abraham and then Isaac received the promise that
their posterity would be countless as the stars in the sky (Gn 15: 5; 22: 17;
26: 4). God promised Hagar, too, that her posterity would be past counting
(Gn 16: 10). Children are 'the crown of man' (Pr 17: 6), and sons are 'olive
plants around the table' (Ps 128: 3), 'a reward, like arrows in the hand of a
hero; happy the man who has his quiver full of them' (Ps 127: 3-5).

Sterility, on the other hand, was considered a trial (Gn 16: 2; 30: 2; 1 S 1:
5) or a chastisement from God (Gn 20: 18), or a disgrace, from which Sarah,
Rachel and Leah all tried to clear themselves by adopting the child which
their maids bore to their husbands (Gn 16: 2; 30: 3, 9).

All these texts show that the Israelites wanted mainly sons, to perpetuate
the family line and fortune, and to preserve the ancestral inheritance.
Daughters were held in less regard; they would leave the family when they
married, and so the strength of a house was not measured by the number of
its daughters.

Among the sons, the eldest enjoyed certain privileges. During his father's
lifetime, he took precedence of his brothers (Gn 43: 33). On his father's death
he received a double share of the inheritance (Dt 21: 17) and became the head
of the family. With twins, the first to see the light was reckoned the elder
(Gn 25: 24-26; 38: 27-30; although Zerah's hand was seen first. Peres was the
elder—cf. 1 Ch 2: 4—because he was the first to emerge from his mother's
womb). The eldest could lose his right of primogeniture for a grave offence,

as Reuben did by his incest (Gn 35: 22; cf. 49: 3-4 and 1 Ch 5: 1), or he could surrender it, as Esau did by selling his birth-right to Jacob (Gn 25: 29-34). But the eldest son was protected by law against favouritism on the part of his father (Dt 21: 15-17).

Nevertheless, the displacing of the elder son by a younger one is a theme which often recurs in the Old Testament. Apart from Jacob and Esau, Peres and Zerah, many other examples could be quoted. Isaac inherits, not Ishmael; Joseph is his father's favourite, then Benjamin; Ephraim is preferred to Manasseh; David, the youngest in his family, is chosen from among all his brothers and leaves his kingdom to Solomon, his youngest son. Some would treat these instances as signs of a custom opposed to the right of the firstborn; such a custom does exist among some peoples, and is known as ultimogeniture, because the inheritance and the father's rights pass to the youngest son. But the examples quoted from Israelite history are exceptions to the ordinary law, and merely emphasize the tension between juridical custom and the love which tended to make a father most fond of a son born in his old age (cf. Gn 37: 3; 44: 20). Moreover, the Bible states explicitly that these stories stress the fact that God's choice is absolutely unmerited and quite gratuitous: he accepted Abel's offering and rejected that of his elder brother Cain (Gn 4: 4-5); he 'loved Jacob and hated Esau' (Ml 1: 2-3; Rom 9: 13; cf. Gn 25: 23); he pointed out David (1 S 16: 12) and gave the kingdom to Solomon (1 K 2: 15).

The firstborn, because he was the first-fruits of marriage, belonged to God. The firstborn of a flock were sacrificed, but those of mankind were redeemed (Ex 13: 11-15; 22: 28; 34: 20), for the God of Israel abhorred the sacrifice of children (Lv 20: 2-5, etc., and cf. the sacrifice of Isaac in Gn 22). Instead, the Levites were consecrated to God as substitutes for the firstborn of the people (Nb 3: 12-13; 8: 16-18).

2. Birth

According to a rather obscure text in Ex 1: 16, a woman in labour perhaps sat on two stones placed at a slight distance from each other; these stones would be the equivalent of the chair of childbirth, mentioned in Rabbinical times and still used in some parts of the East. In Gn 30: 3, Rachel asks Bilhah to give birth on her knees; Gn 50: 23 says that 'the children of Makir, son of Manasseh, were born on the knees of Joseph'; and Job, cursing the day of his birth, bewails the fact that he found two knees to receive him (Jb 3: 12). From this some authors have concluded that childbirth sometimes took place on the knees of another person, a midwife or a relative, and this custom is in fact found outside Israel. But there is probably a simpler explanation: the texts about Rachel and Joseph must be referring to adoption (cf. Gn 48: 12¹), and Job 3: 12 refers to the knees of a mother who is suckling her child.

From Ex 1: 19 we might deduce that the women of Israel had easy

1. Cf. p. 51.

delivery, as so often occurs among the peasants and Bedouin of Palestine to-day. But this isolated text carries little weight when set side by side with the curse pronounced against woman in Gn 3: 16: 'I will multiply thy sorrows when thou art with child; in sorrow thou shalt bring forth children.' This was the common experience, and the pains of childbirth are frequently used, in a metaphorical sense, by the prophets (Is 13: 8; 21: 3; 26: 17; Jr 4: 31; 6: 24; 13: 21; 22: 23; 50: 43; cf. also Ex 15: 14; Is 37: 3; 2 K 19: 3; Os 13: 13; Ps 48: 7). The mother was assisted by a midwife (Gn 35: 17; 38: 28) and Ex 1: 15 shows that there were professional midwives. According to Jr 20: 15 (cf. Jb 3: 3), the father was not present at the birth.

The baby was washed, rubbed with salt—Palestinian peasants still say 'it makes them strong'—and wrapped in swathing cloths (Ez 16: 4; cf. Jb 38: 8-9). As a general rule, it was suckled by its mother (Gn 21: 7; 1 S 1: 21-23; 1 K 3: 21; 2 M 7: 27), but sometimes a child would be entrusted to a nurse (Gn 24: 59; 35: 8; Ex 2: 7-9; Nb 11: 12; 2 S 4: 4; 2 K 11: 2), as was the custom in Mesopotamia and Egypt.

The child was weaned much later than nowadays (cf. for Samuel 1 S 1: 20-23); according to 2 M 7: 27 a child was weaned at the age of three; this was the custom in ancient Babylon also. Isaac's weaning was celebrated by a feast (Gn 21: 8).

3. The name

The child was given a name immediately after birth. This name was usually chosen by the mother (Gn 29: 31—30: 24; 35: 18; 1 S 1: 20), but sometimes by the father (Gn 16: 15; 17: 19; Ex 2: 22; cf. Gn 35: 18). The custom of postponing the naming until circumcision, eight days later, is not recorded until New Testament times (Lk 1: 59; 2: 21).

Among primitive peoples, and throughout the ancient East, the name denotes the essence of a thing: to name it is to know it, and, consequently, to have power over it. In the earthly paradise, when God allowed men to name the animals (Gn 2: 19-20), it was a sign that he was putting them under man's power (cf. the parallel story in Gn 1: 28). To know the name of a person is to be able to hurt him (hence 'taboo names' among primitive peoples, and secret names among the Egyptians), or to be able to do him good (e.g. Moses, whom God knew by name, Ex 33: 12, 17). This is the reason why it is so important for the believer to know the true name of his God (Ex 3: 13-15; cf. Gn 32: 30), and this is a feature found in all Eastern religions. Finally, since the name defines the essence, it reveals the character and destiny of the bearer. The name becomes the expression of a hope, or a symbol which men try to decipher by rough etymologies.

Sometimes a particular circumstance of the birth provided the inspiration for a child's name. It might concern the mother who bore the child: Eve called her firstborn Cain (Qaïn) because she had 'acquired' (qanah) a man

(Gn 4: 1). The names of Jacob's sons tell a similar story (Gn 29: 31—30: 24):
Rachel, dying in childbirth, called her son Ben-Oni, 'son of my sorrow', but
Jacob changed this name of ill omen to Benjamin, 'son of the right hand'
(Gn 35: 18). Less often, the name concerns the father: Moses called his son
Gershom, because he was born when Moses was a *ger*, living in a foreign
land (Ex 2: 22). The child himself might provide the occasion: Jacob was so
called because, while still in his mother's womb, he grasped the heel, *'aqeb*, of
his twin (Gn 25: 26), whom he displaced, *'aqab* (Gn 27: 36; Os 12: 4); Peres
was born by opening a breach, *peres* (Gn 38: 29). Finally, the circumstance
may be an event contemporary with the birth: the wife of Phinehas, hearing
that the Philistines have captured the Ark, brings to birth a son whom she
calls Ikabod, meaning 'Where is the glory?' (1 S 4: 21). We may compare
with the last example the symbolic names which Osee and Isaias gave to
their children (Os 1: 4, 6, 9; Is 7: 3; 8: 3).

In the explanation of these names, the Bible often gives a popular etymology, made up after the event and justified by some imaginary feature of
the person named. This is certainly true of a number of examples, but it is not
always and necessarily so. The same custom of calling a child after the circumstances of its birth obtains among many peoples, including present-day Arabs.
Thus a woman who had borne only daughters called the fourth Za'uleh
('Irritating'), and the eighth Tamâm ('Enough!'), and a man whose daughter
was born on a morning of heavy dew called her Endeyeh ('Full of dew').
Names taken from a child's physical appearance are quite rare: Nahor means
'the snorer', Qareah 'the bald' and Paseah 'the lame'. With these we may
compare a modern example: a woman from the district of Jerusalem exclaimed, on seeing her son, 'But this child's a negro (*habash*)!' So they called
him Habash.

Names of animals were commonly used, especially in the early ages:
Rachel means 'sheep', Deborah 'bee', Yona 'dove', Aiiah 'vulture',
Shephuphan 'viper', Caleb 'dog', Nahash 'serpent', Eglah 'heifer', Akbor
'mouse' and so on. Some authors have maintained that these were originally
names of clans, and that the names are evidence of primitive totemism. In fact,
however, they are names of individuals, not of clans, and date from an epoch
when no other trace of totemism is found. Moreover, similar names were
known among the ancient Arabs and are found among the Bedouin to-day.
Some are descriptive, or expressive of a wish: a girl called Deborah will be as
busy as a bee, a boy called Caleb, Shephuphan or Aiiah will be strong or
terrible to his enemies, like a dog, a viper or a vulture. Again, a child may be
called after the first animal seen at the time of its birth; the custom still
obtains with modern Bedouin.

Names taken from plants are much rarer: Elôn means 'oak-tree', Zeitan
'olive', Qôs 'thorn' and Tamar 'palm-tree'. These names are to be explained in the same way as names of animals.

The most important category of names is the 'theophoric', *i.e.* those which contain some divine name or title. Some are formed with 'Baal'; this may at times be an epithet of Yahweh, for *ba'al* means 'master', but it is often the name of the Canaanite God. The proportion of these names is especially high in the ostraka of Samaria, which date from a period when the religion of the northern kingdom was corrupted by syncretism. They disappear after the monarchical period. Under the influence of Yahwism, some of these names were altered in the texts, 'Baal' being replaced by 'El' or 'Yahweh'; alternatively, they might be emended for the purpose of public reading, as when Ishbaal was changed into Ishbosheth, Yerubbaal into Yerubbosheth, and Meribbaal into Mephibosheth.

But far more common than these are names derived from Israel's national God, denoted by his names of El or Yahweh (in shortened forms) or by some epithet or attribute. The names are composed of this divine word and a verb (or, less frequently, a noun or an adjective). They express a religious idea, the power or the mercy of God, the help expected from him, the feeling of kinship with him. No doubt the everyday use of these names tended to weaken their significance, but they became much more common in periods of religious revival, and some reflect the particular religious situation of an age, for example, that of the Exile or the Return. These facts prove that their real significance had not been forgotten.

Theophoric names could be abridged, the divine element being understood ('hypochoristic words'): *e.g.* Nathan, 'he has given', instead of 'Nathanyahu', 'Yahweh has given'; Mattan 'Gift', instead of Mattanyahu, 'Gift of Yahweh'.

At the close of biblical times there arose the custom of giving a patronymic name, *i.e.* the child was called after its grandfather (less often its father), greatgrandfather, or uncle. There is evidence of it first at Elephantine, then in Judaea in the third century B.C., and it seems to have been common at the beginning of the Christian era (cf. Lk 1: 59).

Occasionally, Israelites or Jews by birth have foreign names, not only in the colonies outside Palestine, but in Palestine itself. Aramaic names appear after the Exile and are very common in the New Testament period: Martha, Tabitha, Bar-Tolomai, etc.

In the Graeco-Roman period a person might have a Greek or Roman name in addition to a Jewish one: *e.g.* Salome Alexandra, John Mark. Sometimes the name was translated into Greek (Mattanyah became Theodotos), or the Semitic name given a Greek form (such as Jesus or Maria).

A person could change his name when he grew up. The Bible ascribes some of these changes to divine intervention. Jacob's name was changed to Israel for wrestling with God (Gn 32: 29; cf. 35: 10). The names of Abram and Sarai were changed into Abraham and Sarah (Gn 17: 5, 15); these are only dialect forms of the same names, but if one recalls the significance of names discussed above, a change of name would mark a change in the person's destiny (cf. Gn 17: 6, 16). We have also observed that to name a person is to assert one's authority over him, and this explains the changes of name imposed by a master. The pharaoh gave Joseph the name of Saphenath-Paneah (Gn 41: 45). The chief eunuch changed the names of Daniel, Ananias, Misael and Azarias into Baltassar, Shadrak, Meshak and Abed Nego (Dn 1: 6-7). When the pharaoh installed Elyaqim as king of Judah, he made him take the name of Joiaqim (2 K 23: 34), and similarly Nabuchodonosor changed the name of Mattanyah, whom he set on the throne, to Sedecias (2 K 24: 17). These last examples involve the problem of the coronation name in Israel, a subject which will be considered in connection with the king.[1]

4. *Circumcision*

Circumcision is the removal of the foreskin. The ceremony was to be performed on the eighth day after birth, according to the law of Lv 12: 3 and the Priestly account of the covenant with Abraham (Gn 17: 12). The same tradition says it was actually on the eighth day after his birth that Isaac was circumcised (Gn 21: 4). According to Ex 4: 25 and Jos 5: 2-3, flint knives were used, which shows how ancient the custom is; later, however, metal instruments came into use.

The operation was carried out by the father (Gn 21: 4), in the exceptional case of Ex 4: 25 by the mother, or, in later times, by a physician or a specialist (1 M 1: 61). There was no ruling about the place where it was to be performed, but it was never done in the sanctuary or by a priest. With adults, the wound healed only after several days of rest (Gn 34: 25; Jos 5: 8).

The Israelites were commanded to circumcise not only their children, but also their servants, both native and foreign (Gn 17: 12-13). Only circumcised foreigners, whether servants or resident aliens, could share in the Passover, the feast of the Israelite community (Ex 12: 43 :49). According to the biblical narrative, circumcision was first practised by Abraham's clan after its entry into Canaan; God ordered it as a sign of the covenant he had made with Abraham (Gn 17: 9-14, 23-27). The Patriarchs continued to observe the custom (Gn 34: 13-24), and Jos 5: 4-5 tells us that it was maintained throughout the sojourn in Egypt. On the other hand, Moses was not circumcised, according to the story of Ex 4: 24-26. The custom was forgotten in the desert, but resumed on entering the Promised Land (Jos 5: 4-9).

It is difficult to determine the extent of the practice of circumcision in the ancient East, for the available evidence is uncertain and contradictory. In Egypt, bas-reliefs bear witness to the custom from the third millennium B.C., texts mention it, Herodotus speaks of it, and yet some of the mummies are not circumcised. It certainly seems to have been obligatory for the priests.

1. Cf. pp. 107-108.

Yet Jos 5: 9 appears to describe uncircumcision as 'the disgrace of Egypt'. On the other hand, Jr 9: 24-25 mentions the Egyptians, along with Judah, Edom, Ammon, Moab and the Arabs as being circumcised in the flesh but uncircumcised in heart. Ez 32: 21-30 consigns Pharaoh and his army to Sheol with the uncircumcised, along with the Assyrians, the Elamites, the hordes of Meshek and Tubal, the Edomites, all the princes of the North and all the Sidonians. Flavius Josephus says that the Idumeans (Edomites) were compelled to accept circumcision by John Hyrcanus. But, if we are to believe Herodotus, all the Phoenicians and Syrians of Palestine were circumcised; Aristophanes asserts the same of the Phoenicians. According to the pre-Islamic poets, the ancient Arabs were circumcised, and the Pseudo-Bardesanus says that the Romans tried to forbid this practice in Arabia.

Among the peoples with whom the Israelites had direct contact in Palestine, the Philistines were uncircumcised (1 S 18: 25; cf. Jg 14: 3; 1 S 17: 26, 36) and the term 'uncircumcised' (without any addition) is sometimes enough to describe them (Jg 15: 18; 1 S 14: 6; 31: 4). This distinguishes them from the Canaanites, who are never so described, and must therefore have been circumcised. There is, of course, the episode of the Shechemites who were compelled to circumcise themselves in order to marry Israelite maidens (Gn 34: 13-24), but, according to Gn 34: 2, the Shechemites were 'Hivvites' ('Horites' in the Greek text); this implies that they constituted a non-Semitic enclave among the population.

It seems, then, that the Israelites were not distinguished from the Semitic population which they displaced, or with whom they mingled in Palestine, by the fact of their circumcision. On the contrary, they appear to have adopted this custom when they settled in Canaan (cf. Gn 17: 9-14, 23-27; Jos 5: 2-9), but with them the practice took on a particular religious significance.

Originally, and as a general rule, circumcision seems to have been an initiation-rite before marriage; consequently, it also initiated a man into the common life of the clan. This is certainly true of many African tribes which practise it to-day, and very probably true of ancient Egypt, where it was performed at the age of puberty. The custom must originally have had the same purpose in Israel: the story of the Shechemites expressly connects it with marriage (Gn 34); the obscure episode of Ex 4: 24-26 seems to refer to marriage also, for the pretence of circumcising Moses makes him a 'bridegroom of blood'. We may add that the Hebrew words for bridegroom, son-in-law and father-in-law are all derived from the same root, *hatan*, which means in Arabic 'to circumcise'.

The metaphorical uses of the word confirm this interpretation: the 'uncircumcised heart' (Jr 9: 25) is a heart which does not understand (contrast Dt 10: 16; 30: 6; Jr 4: 4). The 'uncircumcised ear' is an ear which does not listen (Jr 6: 10); 'uncircumcised lips' are those which cannot speak (Ex 6:

12, 30). Circumcision, therefore, is regarded as that which makes a man fit for normal sexual life; it is an initiation to marriage.

This significance must have died out when the operation was performed soon after birth. Above all, religion gave the rite a more lofty significance. It was a sign of incorporation into the life of the group, into the community of Israel (cf. Gn 34: 14-16; Ex 12: 47-48). Hence it is prescribed as an obligation, and as a sign of the covenant which God made with Abraham and his descendants (Gn 17: 9-14: from the Priestly tradition).

The religious importance of circumcision, however, gained ground only gradually. The laws of the Pentateuch make only passing references to it, in connection with the Passover (Ex 12: 44, 48), with the purification of women after childbirth (Lv 12: 3) and as a term of comparison with the first fruits of trees (Lv 19: 23). It was only during the Exile that circumcision became the distinctive mark of a man who belonged to Israel and to Yahweh. The explanation is not hard to find: the exiles lived among peoples who did not practise it, while, at the same time, apparently, the custom was being progressively abandoned among the nations surrounding Palestine. This would account for certain ancient references: Ez 32: 30 counts the Sidonians among the uncircumcised; so also were the Ammonites, according to Jdt 14: 10; and according to Josephus, John Hyrcanus compelled the Idumeans to circumcise themselves. The same author adds that in his time, the first century of our era, the Jews were the only inhabitants of Palestine who had themselves circumcised.

The importance of circumcision as a sign of the covenant with God was therefore all the more strongly emphasized. Proselytes were obliged to accept it (cf. the first Jewish-Christian controversies, Ac 15: 5f.; 16: 3; Gal 2: 3). The first references to pagans being circumcised when they accepted the Jewish faith are found in Jdt 14: 10 and Est 8: 17 (Greek), both late documents. In New Testament times the duty of circumcision took precedence of the law of the sabbath (Jn 7: 22, 23).

This custom aroused the scorn of the pagans (Martial, Persius, Horace) and had to contend with the invasion of Greek conventions, which did not accept it. Antiochus Epiphanes forbade it in Palestine, and inflicted cruel punishment on those who resisted his orders (1 M 1: 60-61; 2 M 6: 10). Indeed, Jews who followed Hellenistic fashions tried to hide the marks of their circumcision (1 M 1: 15; cf. 1 Cor 7: 18).

5. Education

During his early years a child was left to the care of his mother or nurse, even after he had been weaned (2 S 4: 4) and was learning to walk (Os 11: 3). The little Israelite spent most of his time playing in the streets or squares with boys and girls of his own age (Jr 6: 11; 9: 20; Za 8: 5; Mt 11: 16). They sang and danced, or played with little clay models, samples of which have been found in excavations; little girls, it would seem, have always played with dolls.

It was the mother who gave her children the first rudiments of education, especially of their moral formation (Pr 1: 8; 6: 20). She might continue to advise her children even in adolescence (cf. Pr 31: 1), but as the boys grew up to manhood, they were usually entrusted to their father. One of his most sacred duties was to teach his son the truths of religion (Ex 10: 2; 12: 26; 13: 8; Dt 4: 9; 6: 7, 20f.; 32: 7, 46) and to give him a general education (Pr 1: 8; 6: 20, and especially Si 30: 1-13). The whip and the rod played their part in this training (Pr 13: 24; 22: 15; 29: 15, 17; cf. Dt 8: 5; 2 S 7: 14; Pr 3: 12; Si 30: 1).

Writing was in common use at an early date. Besides the professional scribes, like those employed at the court for administration (2 S 8: 17; 20: 25; 1 K 4: 3, etc.), and private secretaries like Baruch (Jr 36: 4), members of the ruling class could write, judging by the stories of Jezabel (1 K 21: 8) and of Isaiah (Is 8: 1). But these were not the only ones: a young man of Sukkoth was able to give Gideon, in writing, the names of all the chiefs of his clan (Jg 8: 14), and the commandment of Dt 6: 9; 11: 20 presumed that every head of a family could write.

Most teaching, however, was done by word of mouth. The teacher told his story, gave explanations and asked questions; the pupil repeated the story, and asked or answered questions (Ex 13: 8; Dt 6: 7, 20f.; Ps 78: 3-4, etc.). This method of teaching continued under the Rabbis, and obtains even to-day in Koranic schools.

The content of the instruction was very general. The father handed on to his son the national traditions (which were also religious traditions), and the divine commands given to their forefathers (Ex 10: 2 and the other texts just quoted). Children were also taught literary passages, such as David's lament over Saul and Jonathan (2 S 1: 18), which was still being recited in the days of the Maccabees (1 M 9: 20-21).

The father also gave his son a professional education; in practice, trades were usually hereditary, and the crafts were handed down in the family workshop. A Rabbi was to say: 'He who does not teach his son a useful trade is bringing him up to be a thief.'

This educational rôle of the father explains why the priests, whose mission was to teach, are called 'father' (Jg 17: 10; 18: 19). It also explains how Joseph, who became the pharaoh's counsellor, was like a 'father' to him (Gn 45: 8), and how Aman, vizier to Assuerus, could be called his 'second father' (Est 3: 13 or 8: 12). Similarly, the relationship between teacher and pupil was expressed by the words 'father' and 'son' (2 K 2: 12, compared with 2 K 2: 3; cf. the frequent use of 'my son', 'my sons' and 'Hear, my son' in the book of Proverbs).

Apart from the education he received at home, the young Israelite had ample opportunity for learning. In the caravans and by the wells, he heard men sing of the 'justices of Yahweh' (Jg 5: 10-11). At the village gates he would listen to the palavers of the elders, to the settlement of lawsuits, and to the arrangement of commercial transactions. The child accompanied his parents to the sanctuaries (1 S 1: 4, 21) or to the temple at Jerusalem (cf. Lk 2: 41f.), where he would hear the chanting of the Psalms and the recounting of those historical episodes which were connected with each great festival. As in the Middle Ages, the liturgy was a powerful medium of religious instruction.

Certain men had a special mission to instruct the people. First of all came the priests, guardians and teachers of the Law, the *Tôrah*, which by etymology means 'directive', 'instruction'. Some didactic teaching was probably given at an early date in the centres of worship: the boy Samuel was entrusted to Eli the priest (1 S 2: 21, 26), and Joas was instructed by the priest Yehoyada (2 K 12: 3).

The prophets, too, had a mission to instruct the people; this was at least as much a part of their task as foretelling the future. And prophetic inspiration lent to their preaching the authority of a word of God. It is certain that under the monarchy the prophets were the religious and moral teachers of the people; and, we may add, the best of all their teachers, if not always the most heeded. Along with them 'wise men' taught men how to live a good life; their influence increased after the Exile, when wise men and scribes became identical terms, and moral education was combined with study of the Law. Their teaching was handed down in the gatherings of the elders (Si 6: 34), in the conversation at festive meals (Si 9: 16), in the open air, at the city gates, in the streets and at the cross-roads (Pr 1: 20f.; 8: 2 f.) They expressed their teachings in epigrams, which were preserved in oral tradition and later preserved in written collections (Pr 10: 1; 22: 17; 25: 1, etc.).

Apart from this teaching, given, as it were, when occasion offered, and from which anyone could benefit, the prophets and teachers of wisdom gathered pupils around them to whom they gave a more continuous training (Pr 8: 32; Is 8: 16; 50: 4). It is probable, too, that schools for scribes existed at an early date in the two capitals, where the civil servants were trained; similar training-schools existed in Mesopotamia, in Egypt and among the Hittites. There is, however, no proof of an organized system of schools until a late period. The word 'school' (*bêth-midrash*) occurs for the first time in the Hebrew text of Si 51: 23. According to a Jewish tradition, it was only in A.D. 63 that the high priest Joshua ben Gimla decreed that every town and village should have a school which all children would have to attend from the age of six or seven. This tradition is contested by some scholars who date the institution of public instruction from the time of John Hyrcanus, about 130 B.C.

The preceding paragraphs concern only the education of boys. Girls remained under the control of their mothers, who taught them what they needed to know for their duty as wives and housekeepers.

6. *Adoption*

Adoption is an act by which a man or woman acknowledges a person of different blood as his or her son or daughter, with the legal rights and duties of a true child. Adoption was practised in Mesopotamia from a very early time. Its object was to secure for barren couples the benefit of children, and thus to provide them with help and support in their old age. In the middle of the second millennium B.C., at Nuzu, in the region of Kirkuk, contracts of fictitious adoption were used to cover all manner of economic transactions.

The Old Testament laws contain no directives about adoption. The historical books record no example of adoption in the strict sense, *i.e.* the legal acknowledgement of one born outside the family as having the rights of a child born into the family. Thus we cannot regard as real adoptions the instances of Moses, who was treated as a son by Pharaoh's daughter (Ex 2: 10), or of Genubath, who was brought up among Pharaoh's children (1 K 11: 20), or of Esther, to whom Mardochai gave a home when she had no father or mother (Est 2: 7, 15). Moreover, these three examples all occur on foreign soil. The story of Abraham's planning to leave his goods to his servant because he had no child (Gn 15: 3) has been explained as the adoption of a slave, in conformity with a custom attested by the Nuzu texts; if this explanation is correct, it reveals the influences of a Mesopotamian custom in the patriarchal age, but it does not prove that the custom took root in Israel, and the Bible itself does not represent the act as an adoption.

Some other examples are clearer. Rachel gives Jacob her servant Bilhah, so that Bilhah may bear a child on her knees, and that Rachel may thus have a child, through Bilhah: Bilhah's two children are, in fact, named by Rachel and regarded as her sons (Gn 30: 3-8). Jacob considers Joseph's two sons, Ephraim and Manasseh, as his own (Gn 48: 5) and puts them 'between his knees' (Gn 48: 12). We are told, too, that the children of Makir, Manasseh's son, 'were born on Joseph's knees' (Gn 50: 23). Finally, Naomi takes Ruth's newborn child to her breast and says: 'A son is born to Naomi' (Rt 4: 16-17). We are almost bound to see in all these cases one and the same rite expressing adoption: the child was laid on or between the knees of the man or woman who adopted it. But these are not adoptions in the full sense, for they all take place within the family and in the direct line, the child being 'adopted' by its stepmother (cf. without any mention of the rite Gn 16: 2; 30: 1-13), its grandfather or its grandmother. The legal consequences of such an adoption are therefore not far-reaching.[1]

We might see a reflection of customs of adoption in those passages where the relations between Yahweh and Israel are expressed as those of father and son (Ex 4: 22; Dt 32: 6; Is 63: 16; 64: 7; Jr 3: 19; 31: 9; Os 11: 1, etc.), but these are hardly more than metaphors, in which the idea of divine fatherhood

1. But cf. p. 53.

fades into background before that of God as Master and Creator. Only in the New Testament will it be brought into full relief. More significant is Nathan's prophecy about the king of David's line: 'I shall be a father to him, and he shall be a son to me' (2 S 7: 14, with the other passages dependent on it, 1 Ch 17: 13; 22: 10; 28: 6; Ps 89: 27). Only one text is explicit, that of Ps 2: 7, 'Thou art my son; to-day I have begotten thee', which certainly seems to be using a formula of adoption.[1]

We may conclude that the notion of adoption, in the juridical sense, was known in Old Testament times, but had little influence on daily life; it was unknown in later Jewish law.

1. Cf. pp. 112-113.

Chapter Five

SUCCESSION AND INHERITANCE

IN ancient Israel there was no such thing as a written will or testament. But before he died, a father used to 'set his house in order' (2 S 17: 23; 2 K 20: 1; Is 38: 1), *i.e.* he gave verbal instructions about the distribution of his property (cf. Dt 21: 16; Si 14: 13; 33: 24). However, he had to conform to law and custom. Only two legislative texts refer to inheritance (Dt 21: 15-17 and Nb 27: 1-11, taken in conjunction with Nb 38: 6-9), and they concern particular cases. They need to be supplemented by incidental information from the biblical narratives, and these narratives are not always easy to interpret.

The fundamental rule is that sons alone have a right to the inheritance. Among the sons, the eldest had a privileged position[1] and received a double share of his father's goods (Dt 21: 17; cf. 2 K 2: 9, metaphorically). The same provision is made in the Assyrian laws, at Nuzu and at Mari. The law safeguards the right of the eldest by forbidding the father to show favour to the son of the wife he prefers at the expense of the eldest son (Dt 21: 15-17). (This law retrospectively condemns Abraham for expelling Ishmael [Gn 21: 10f.] and David for preferring Solomon to Adonias [1 K 1: 17, cf. 2: 15].) Probably only the movable chattels were shared, and the house, with the ancestral holdings, would be allotted to the eldest, or at least not divided. This would keep the family property intact, and might explain the text of Dt 25: 5 about brothers who 'live together'.

In the early days of Israel, and, indeed, as a general rule in Mesopotamian law-codes, the sons of concubines who were slaves had no share in the inheritance, unless their father had given them equal rank with the sons of free-born wives, by legal adoption. Sarah did not want Ishmael, the son of the slave-woman, to share the inheritance with her son Isaac (Gn 21: 10), and in the event Abraham left his goods to Isaac, and only made presents to the sons of his concubines (Gn 25: 5-6). But Sarah pretended she had forgotten her promise that Hagar's children should be recognized as her own (Gn 16: 2): Ishmael therefore, had a right to the inheritance, and Abraham was downhearted at sending him away (Gn 21: 11). The sons of the slave-women Bilhah and Zilpah were given equal rank with those of Rachel and Leah (Gn 49: 1-28) and had an equal share with them in the land of Canaan, which

---

1. On the rights of the eldest son, see pp. 41-42.

was Jacob's inheritance. But the reason is that they had been adopted by Rachel or by Leah (Gn 30: 3-13). Later usage seems to have been less strict. The case of Jephthah, excluded from his father's inheritance by his half-brothers, is sometimes quoted (Jg 11: 2), but Jephthah was an illegitimate son, born of a prostitute and not of a concubine (Jg 11: 1).

Daughters did not inherit, except when there were no male heirs. This precedent was established at the instance of the daughters of Selophehad (Nb 27: 1-8), but with the proviso that they were to find husbands from a clan of their father's tribe, and so prevent the family property from passing to another tribe (Nb 36: 1-9). Under this law the daughters of Eleazar married their cousins (1 Ch 23: 22), and this, too, is probably that 'law of Moses' to which Tb 7: 11 refers.

There is one notable exception. Job's three daughters received a share of the inheritance along with their seven brothers (Jb 42: 13-15). This may represent later custom, for the book of Job is post-Exilic, or perhaps it was then imagined that in patriarchal times, in which the story is set, the father had absolute freedom in the distribution of his property. Indeed, perhaps the purpose was to show the enormous wealth of Job and the ideal happiness of a family in which all the children were treated equally.

If a man died without issue, the property passed to his male kinsmen on his father's side, in the following order: his brothers, his father's brothers, his nearest relative in the clan (Nb 27: 9-11). His widow had no right to the inheritance. By contrast, Babylonian law and the usage of Nuzu both laid down that a widow did have a share in the inheritance, or at least that she was to keep what she had contributed to the marriage and the gifts she had received from her husband. The contracts of Elephantine allow a childless widow to inherit from her husband. In Israel, a childless widow either returned to her father (Gn 38: 11; Lv 22: 13; Rt 1: 8), or remained a member of her husband's family by a levirate marriage.[1] If a widow had grown-up children, they provided for her support. If the children were still young, she may have managed the property left to them as their trustee (this would explain 2 K 8: 3-6). The money owned by Mikayehu's mother (Jg 17: 1-4) was perhaps her own personal property, distinct from the legacy left by her husband. The case of Naomi, offering for sale a piece of land which had been the property of her deceased husband (Rt 4: 3, 9) is difficult to explain, but we should at least notice that in Rt 4: 9 the land is regarded as the joint property of her two sons, Kilyon and Mahlon. These two were also dead, and Naomi appears to be acting as the guardian of their rights. Judith had received from her husband quite a fortune, including both movable and immovable goods (Jdt 8: 7), and she disposed of it quite freely before her death (Jdt 16: 24); this story, however, dates from an age when custom had grown much more liberal, and when the way was already being prepared for

---

1. Cf. pp. 37-38 and 40.

that recognition of a widow's rights which was eventually sanctioned by Jewish law.

The episode of Naboth (1 K 21: 15) has led some writers to conclude that the property of men condemned to death reverted to the king; but it may simply be an instance of arbitrary confiscation. Some late passages show that the father could make advances of the inheritance long before his death (Tb 8: 21; Si 33: 20-24; cf. Lk 15: 12).

CHAPTER SIX

DEATH AND FUNERAL RITES

THE distinction between soul and body is something foreign to the Hebrew mentality, and death, therefore, is not regarded as the separation of these two elements. A live man is a living 'soul' (*nephesh*), and a dead man is a dead 'soul', a dead '*nephesh*' (Nb 6: 6; Lv 21: 11; cf. Nb 19: 13). Death is not annihilation. So long as the body exists and the bones at least remain, the soul exists, like a shade, in a condition of extreme weakness, in the subterranean abode of Sheol (Jb 26: 5-6; Is 14: 9-10; Ez 32: 17-32).

These ideas account for the care bestowed on the corpse and the importance of honourable burial, for the soul continued to feel what was done to the body. Hence to be left unburied, a prey to the birds and the wild beasts, was the worst of all curses (1 K 14: 11; Jr 16: 4; 22: 19; Ez 29: 5). Yet the corpse which was doomed to corruption, and the tomb which contained it, were both considered unclean, and conveyed uncleanness to those who touched them (Lv 21: 1-4; 22: 4; Nb 19: 11-16; Ag 2: 13; cf. Ez 43: 7).

1. *Treatment of the corpse*

In Gn 46: 4 there is an allusion to the custom of closing the eyes of the dead; this almost universal custom is perhaps simply explained by the resemblance of death to sleep. The nearest relatives embraced the body (Gn 50: 1). It is probable that it was then prepared for burial, but we have no information earlier than the New Testament (Mt 27: 59 and parallels; Jn 11: 44; 19: 39-40). The pins and other ornaments found in excavated tombs show that the dead were buried fully clothed. Samuel came up from Sheol with his cloak around him (1 S 28: 14), and Ez 32: 27 tells us that soldiers were laid to rest in their armour, with their swords under their heads and their shields under their bodies.

Embalming was never practised in Israel: the two examples known, those of Jacob and Joseph, are explicitly ascribed to Egyptian custom (Gn 50: 2-3). The corpse was not placed in a coffin (cf. 2 K 13: 21), but carried on a bier (2 S 3: 31; cf. Lk 7: 14). Joseph's body was placed in a coffin; but it is the only example recorded, and this also is to be explained by Egyptian custom (Gn 50: 26).

2. Burial

We do not know the interval which elapsed between death and burial. The seventy days' mourning before the transfer of Jacob's body is exceptional, for the Egyptians accorded the Patriarch a royal funeral. The precept of Dt 21: 22-23 concerns only the bodies of those who had been executed: they had to be removed before nightfall. The delay was probably very short, as it still is in the East; it is probable that, as a general rule, burial took place on the day of death.

There is no evidence that corpses were cremated in Palestine, except in days long before the coming of the Israelites, or among groups of foreigners; the Israelites never practised it. On the contrary, to burn a body was an outrage, inflicted only on notorious criminals (Gn 38: 24; Lv 20: 14; 21: 9), or upon enemies a man wanted to annihilate for ever (Am 2: 1). There remains one difficult instance: the people of Yabesh in Gilead burnt the bodies of Saul and his sons before burying their bones (1 S 31: 12); it seems to have been a departure from traditional usage, and the parallel passage in 1 Ch 10: 12 omits this point. In addition we must not confuse with cremation the references given in Jr 34: 5; 2 Ch 16: 14; 21: 19, which speak of a fire being lit at the death of a king who died in peace with God: this is certainly not cremation, but incense and perfumes were burned near the body.

The normal type of Israelite tomb is a burial chamber dug out of soft rock, or making use of a natural cave. The entry is a narrow passage opening on one of the sides: on the other three sides are ledges on which the bodies were laid. There is sometimes a cavity in which the bones of skeletons were placed, to make way for new burials. These tombs are, in fact, common tombs, used by a family or clan over a considerable period. There does not seem to have been any fixed rule about the position of the bodies. Some personal belongings and pottery were put beside the corpse. These funeral offerings, intended for the use of the dead, are not so numerous or rich as in the Canaanite period, and, at the end of the Israelite period, are confined to a few vases or lamps. Men's ideas on the fate of the dead had progressed, and their offerings had only symbolic value.

In the Hellenistic period a new type of tomb appears; instead of ledges, narrow niches are cut perpendicularly into the wall, and the corpses placed inside. For at least two hundred years, from 100 B.C. to A.D. 100, the bones were laid to rest in coffers of soft limestone: great numbers of these ossuaries have been discovered in the neighbourhood of Jerusalem. In Palestine, other methods of burial, such as shafts opened in the rock, stone sarcophagi and wooden or leaden coffins, are later than Old Testament times.

Not every family could afford the expense of owning and maintaining such tombs. The poor were simply laid to rest in the ground, and at Jerusalem, in the Kedron valley, there was a 'tomb of the sons of the people', a common trench, where the bodies cf 'stateless persons' and condemned criminals were thrown (Jr 26: 23; cf. 2 K 23: 6). The rich, on the other hand, provided themselves during life with burial-places worthy of their rank (Is 22: 16; cf. Jb 3: 14), and the remains of well-tended tombs, belonging to important persons in Jerusalem, can still be seen at Shiloah. The necropolis of the kings of Judah, where David and his successors until Achaz were buried, lay inside the ramparts, in the old city of David (1 K 2: 10; 11: 43; 14: 31, down to 2 K 16: 20, but cf. 2 Ch. 28: 27). Excavations have brought to light two galleries in the rock, which may be the remains of these tombs; they have been opened several times, and were later wrecked by quarrying.

The site of a tomb might be marked by a pillar: thus, Jacob set up a stele over Rachel's tomb (Gn 35: 20), and Absalom, who had no son 'to make his name remembered', had a stele prepared for himself near Jerusalem (2 S 18: 18). Some stelae were definitely funeral monuments, and stelae were also erected on the high places, the *bamôth*; this raises the question whether a cult of the dead was not practised on the high places. This suggestion can claim the support of a few biblical texts which have been corrupted or badly understood. Is 53: 9 should read, according to the Qumran manuscript: 'They set his grave among the wicked, and his bamah (here: the place of his tomb) with the rich (or: with evil-doers)'; Jb 27: 15, with a very simple change of vowels, reads: 'Their survivors will be buried in *bamôth*, and their widows will not weep for them'; Ez 43: 7 needs no correction: 'Never again will they defile my holy name with their prostitutions, and with the funeral stelae (*pégér*) of their kings in their *bamôth*.' But the construction of a monument over the tomb or in connection with it is a late practice. The first written mention of it occurs in connection with the tomb of the Maccabees at Modin (1 M 13: 27, 30). The tombs in the Kedron valley which have monuments over them (the so-called tombs of Absalom, Josaphat, St James and Zacharias) all date from the end of the Greek or the beginning of the Roman period, according to the experts.

Except for the kings of Judah, there is no evidence that the dead were buried inside the towns. The tombs were scattered over the surrounding slopes, or grouped in places where the nature of the soil was favourable. The tomb was family property, whether it stood on land belonging to the family (Jos 24: 30, 32; 1 S 25: 1; 1 K 2: 34), or in a piece of land bought as a burying place (Gn 23). It was thus that family tombs were established: the cave of Macpelah, which Abraham bought for the burial of Sarah (Gn 23) became in later days the tomb of Abraham himself (Gn 25: 9-10), of Isaac and Rebecca, of Jacob and Leah (Gn 49: 29-32; 50: 13). It was normal for a man to be buried 'in the tomb of his father' (Jg 8: 32; 16: 31; 2 S 2: 32; 17: 23); they hoped for it during life (2 S 19: 38), and David made this gesture as a last tribute to the bones of Saul and his descendants (2 S 21: 12-14). Conversely, to be excluded from the family tomb was a punishment from God

(1 K 13: 21-22). The expressions 'to sleep with one's fathers' and 'to be re-
united with one's own', which record the deaths of great Old Testament
figures, patriarchs and kings of Israel or Judah, perhaps referred originally to
this custom of a family tomb; but the original meaning later took on a
deeper sense, and the words became a solemn formula signifying death, and
at the same time emphasizing that the ties of blood reached beyond the grave.

3. Mourning rites

The deceased person's relatives, and those present at the death and funeral,
went through a certain ritual, many items of which were customary on
occasions of great sorrow, in public calamities and in seasons of penance.

At news of the death, the first action was to tear one's garments (Gn 37:
34; 2 S 1: 11; 3: 31; 13: 31; Jb 1: 20). Then 'sackcloth' was put on (Gn 37:
34; 2 S 3: 31); it was a coarse material, usually worn next to the skin, around
the waist and below the breast (cf. 2 K 6: 30; 2 M 3: 19). (The 'nakedness' of
Mi 1: 8 means this rudimentary garment, in spite of the parallel of Is 20: 2-4.)
The mourners took off their shoes (2 S 15: 30; Ez 24: 17, 23; Mi 1: 8) and
headdress (Ez 24: 17, 23). Yet, on the other hand, a man covered his beard
(Ez 24: 17, 23) or veiled his face (2 S 19: 5; cf. 15: 30). It is probable that to
put one's hands on one's head was a regular sign of mourning: the Bible
speaks of this gesture as an expression of sorrow or shame (2 S 13: 19; Jr 2:
37), and it is the pose of weeping women in certain Egyptian bas-reliefs and
on the sarcophagus of Ahiram, king of Byblos.

The mourner would put earth on his head (Jos 7: 6; 1 S 4: 12; Ne 9: 1;
2 M 10: 25; 14: 15; Jb 2: 12; Ez 27: 30); he would roll his head (Jb 16: 15), or
even his whole body (Mi 1: 10) in the dust, and lie or sit among a heap of
ashes (Est 4: 3; Is 58: 5; Jr 6: 26; Ez 27: 30).

Mourners would also shave their hair and beard, at least partly, and make
cuts on their bodies (Jb 1: 20; Is 22: 12; Jr 16: 6; 41: 5; 47: 5; 48: 37; Ez 7:
18; Am 8: 10). These rites, however, are condemned by Lv 19: 27-28; cf.
21: 5, and by Dt 14: 1, for the taint of heathenism they preserve. Lastly,
mourners refrained from washing and using perfumes (2 S 12: 20; 14: 2;
Jdt 10: 3).

4. Rites concerning food

David kept a day's fast for Saul and Jonathan (2 S 1: 12) and also for Abner
(2 S 3: 35), and people were surprised that he did not fast for his dead child
(2 S 12: 20-21). After burying the remains of Saul and his sons, the inhabitants of Yabesh fasted for seven days (1 S 31: 13), the usual period of strict
mourning (Gn 50: 10; Jdt 16: 24; Si 22: 12; but cf. 38: 17). The fact that Judith
continued to fast, except on feast days, throughout her widowhood, is noted
as something exceptional (Jdt 8: 5-6).

Neighbours or friends brought mourning bread and the 'cup of consola-tion' to the relatives of the deceased (Jr 16: 7; Ez 24: 17, 22; cf. Os 9: 4), for the uncleanness which was attached to the house of the dead prevented food from being prepared there.

On the other hand, some texts mention, though in mockery, the making of food-offerings to the dead person (Ba 6: 26), which might be placed on his tomb (Si 30: 18 [Greek: in Hebrew 'before an idol']). Excavations show that there was a time when the Israelites followed the Canaanite custom of depositing food in the tomb. In Tb 4: 17 the elder Tobias counsels his son to be lavish with bread and wine on the tomb of the just, but this precept is taken from the pagan book entitled *The Wisdom of Ahiqar*, and, in the imme-diate context of the book of Tobias, could be interpreted of alms given on the occasion of a funeral . Whatever be the true interpretation of this text, such and similar customs continued for a long time, and still do continue in parts of the Christian world; they indicate nothing more than a belief in survival after death and a feeling of affection towards the dead. They are not acts of worship directed towards the dead, for that attitude never existed in Israel. Prayer and sacrifice of expiation for the dead (both incompatible with a cult of the dead) appear at the very end of the Old Testament, in 2 M 12: 38-46.

Perhaps we should explain the very awkward text of Dt 26: 14 by refer-ence to the same customs. The Israelite there declares that he has taken noth-ing as mourning food, nor made any offering to the dead, out of the tithe, which is holy and reserved to the poor (v. 13); either use would have made the entire tithe unclean.

5. *The funeral lamentations*

The chief funeral ceremony was the lamentation for the dead. In its simplest form it was a sharp, repeated cry, compared in Mi 1: 8 to the call of the jackal or the ostrich. They cried, 'Alas, alas!' (Am 5: 16), 'Alas, my brother!' or, 'Alas, my sister!' (1 K 13: 30), or, if it were a member of the royal family, 'Alas, Lord! Alas, Majesty!' (Jr 22: 18; 34: 5). A father would call on his son by name (2 S 19: 1, 5). For the death of an only son, the lamentation was particularly heart-rending (Jr 6: 26; Am 8: 10; Za 12: 10). These cries were uttered by the men and women in separate groups (Za 12: 11-14); it was the duty of close relations (Gn 23: 2; 50: 10; 2 S 11: 26), though everyone present joined in (1 S 25: 1; 28: 3; 2 S 1: 11-12; 3: 31, etc., where to 'make mourning' means 'to perform the lamentation').

These exclamations of sorrow could be developed into a lament, a *qînah*, composed in a special rhythm (2 S 1: 17; Am 8: 10). The oldest and finest is that sung by David for the death of Saul and Jonathan (2 S 1: 19-27). David wrote one for Abner, too (2 S 3: 33-34). But these laments were usually com-posed and sung by professionals, men or women (2 Ch 35: 25; Am 5: 16), especially women (Jr 9: 16f.; cf. Ez 32: 16). It was a trade or profession which they taught their daughters (Jr 9: 19). There were fixed forms, and a stock number of themes, which the wailers then applied to the individual. Thus the lament over Judas Maccabee, the beginning of which is quoted in 1 M 9: 21, repeats the words of the lament over Saul and Jonathan. The mourners praised the qualities of the dead man and bewailed his fate, but it is a most striking fact that the examples preserved in the Bible never have a religious content. In the elegy on Saul and Jonathan, for example, there is deep human emotion, but not a word of religious feeling.

In the Prophets we find imitations of these funeral hymns, which they use to depict the misfortunes of Israel, of its kings and of its enemies (Jr 9: 9-11, 16-21; Ez 19: 1-14; 26: 17-18; 27: 2-9, 25-36; 28: 12-19; 32: 2-8; Am 5: 1-2). The best example of all is the book of *Lamentations*.

6. *Interpretation of these rites*

These funeral rites have sometimes been explained as evidence for a cult of the dead. Sometimes the argument is that the deceased person was feared, and that the living therefore wanted to protect themselves from him, or to secure his goodwill; at other times, it is argued that the living attributed a kind of divinity to the dead. There is no foundation for either opinion in the Old Testament.

At the other extreme, it has been held that these rites were merely the expression of sorrow at the loss of a dear one. It is true that many of these rites were used in times of great sorrow and national disaster; they were not, then, restricted to funeral services. But to say that the rites are merely the expression of sorrow is not sufficient, for some of them (wearing sackcloth, for example, or fasting) are found as penitential rites, and can therefore have a religious meaning. The self-mutilation and shaving of the head which the Law condemned (Lv 19: 27-28; Dt 14: 1) certainly had a religious significance, even though we cannot now define it. The food-offerings express, at the very least, belief in a life beyond the grave. Finally, these ceremonies were regarded as a duty which had to be paid to the dead, as an act of piety which was their due (1 S 31: 12; 2 S 21: 13-14; Tb 1: 17-19; Si 7: 33; 22: 11-12). For children, these rites formed part of that duty to their parents enjoined by the Decalogue. We conclude that the dead were honoured in a religious spirit, but that no cult was paid to them.

PART II

CIVIL INSTITUTIONS

POPULATION

IT would help to a better understanding of the institutions of Israel, if we could determine the size of its population. A demographic survey is essential for any sociological research, but, as usually happens when ancient civilizations are the subject, the lack of accurate statistics makes the problem complex.

There is, of course, some numerical information in the Bible, but it is not very helpful. According to Ex 12: 37-38, 600,000 foot-soldiers came out of Egypt, besides their families and a mixed multitude who went with them. Before the departure from Sinai (Nb 1: 20-46), a detailed count of the tribes gives 603,550 men over twenty years of age (cf. Ex 38: 26); the Levites are counted separately, and there are 22,000 over a month old (Nb 3: 39), and 8,580 between the ages of thirty and fifty years (Nb 4: 48). In the plains of Moab (Nb 26: 5-51), the total strength of the tribes is 601,730 men over twenty, and there are 23,000 Levites over a month old (Nb 26: 62). There is no great discrepancy between these various figures, but they presuppose a total population of several millions leaving Egypt and living in the desert, which is impossible. They are merely the expression of the way in which men of a much later age imagined the wonderful increase of the people, and the relative importance of the original tribes. In particular, Judah is the strongest and Simeon the smallest.

Another census is recorded, for the time of David (2 S 24: 1-9). This is a record of the kingdom at its widest extent, when it included Transjordan and stretched as far as Tyre and Sidon and the Orontes. It lists 800,000 men liable for military service in Israel, and 500,000 in Judah. In the parallel passage (1 Ch 21: 1-6) the Chronicler has put the figure for Israel even higher, though he excludes non-Israelite territories. The lower total, in 2 S, is still far too high: 1,300,000 men of military age would imply at least five million inhabitants, which, for Palestine, would mean nearly twice as many people to the square mile as in the most thickly populated countries of modern Europe. Moreover, to interpret these figures (or those of Numbers) as including the women and children is to go against the explicit statements of the text. We must simply acknowledge that these figures are artificial.

More reliable evidence is found in 2 K 15: 19-20. In 738 B.C. Tiglath-Pileser III imposed on Israel a tribute of a thousand talents of silver; in order to pay it, Menahem levied a tax of fifty shekels each from all the *gibbôrê haïl* of his kingdom. If we reckon three thousand shekels to the talent,[1] this means that there were in Israel, at that time, sixty thousand heads of families who enjoyed a certain prosperity.[2] This would give us, with their wives and children, between three and four hundred thousand souls. To them must be added the lower classes, the artisans and the poor (their number is uncertain, but they were fewer than the *gibbôrê haïl*), foreigners and slaves (also uncertain, but fewer still). The grand total, then, would not amount to 800,000 inhabitants for the whole kingdom of Israel, and would scarcely pass the million mark even with the addition of Judah, for the latter was only one-third as large as Israel, and much of it was more sparsely populated.

This estimate of the population of Judah may be confirmed by a non-biblical document from approximately the same date. The Annals of Sennacherib record that in the campaign of 701 against Ezechias, forty-six towns and innumerable villages were captured, and that 200,150 men, women and children were taken from them as prisoners of war. If this referred not to a deportation of captives, but to a census of the defeated enemy, the number would give us the total population of Judah except for Jerusalem, which was not captured. Unfortunately the text, as in parallel passages of the Annals, is clearly referring to captives carried off as prizes by the victors, and the number is then too high. The inscription is probably an error for 2,150.

The 'towns' of the Bible were not large. It is astonishing to see from excavations just how small they were. Most of them could easily be fitted into Trafalgar Square, and some would scarcely fill the courtyard of the National Gallery. The Annals of Tiglath-Pileser III give a list of the towns in Galilee conquered in 732; the number of captives varies between 400 and 650—and this king used to deport entire populations. They were, then, villages like those of to-day, and no bigger. Certain centres were larger, of course. According to the estimate of its excavator, Tell Beit-Mirsim, the ancient Debir, contained two or three thousand inhabitants during the time of its greatest prosperity, and it was a relatively important city.

For Samaria and Jerusalem other sources of information are available. Sargon II says that he carried off 27,290 persons from Samaria. This deportation affected mainly the capital, and was wholesale, but it must have included those who had taken refuge there during the siege. The archaeologists who have excavated it also assert that the town must have contained about thirty thousand inhabitants.

For Jerusalem, the figures of Nabuchodonosor's deportations are difficult; they are difficult to establish, and difficult to interpret, for the texts have preserved varying traditions. According to 2 K 24: 14, ten thousand men of rank and station, with all the blacksmiths and locksmiths, were exiled in 597, but

---

1. Cf. p. 204.
2. On the *gibbôrê haïl* cf. p. 70.

the doublet in 2 K 24: 16 reckons only seven thousand persons of quality and a thousand blacksmiths and locksmiths. Finally, according to Jr 52: 28-30, Nabuchodonosor deported 3,023 'Judeans' in 597 B.C., 832 citizens of Jerusalem in 587, and 745 'Judeans' in 583, making 4,600 in all. This last list, which is independent, no doubt concerns special classes of captives. The figures given in 2 K 24: 14 and 16 should not be added together, and are roughly equal: about ten thousand were deported. These represent only part of the population, but, on the other hand, they may include outsiders who had merely taken refuge inside the city walls. This makes all calculation precarious. Nor can we rely on 2 M 5: 14, according to which Antiochus Epiphanes put to death 40,000 in Jerusalem and sold as many again as slaves. The figures of the population of Jerusalem given by the Pseudo-Hecataeus and Josephus are still more exaggerated. At a reasonable estimate, in our Lord's time the city had about twenty-five or thirty thousand inhabitants. A few years ago this was just the population of the Old City within the walls, and in roughly the same space. The population cannot have been much bigger in Old Testament times.

The population of the country must have varied from time to time. It is certain that the territorial conquests and the assimilation of Canaanite enclaves which took place under David, and still more the economic prosperity of Solomon's reign, produced a sharp rise in population; this continued during the following two centuries, thanks to the progress of commerce, industry and agriculture. Even so, at the height of this prosperity, in the first half of the eighth century B.C., the total population of Israel and Judah cannot have been much more than one million. By way of comparison, we may note that at the British census of 1931, before the great Zionist immigration, Palestine had 1,014,000 inhabitants. It is questionable whether the country could ever have supported many more people in ancient times, without the assistance of those artificial resources which modern economy provides.

CHAPTER TWO

THE FREE POPULATION: ITS DIVISIONS

1. *Social evolution*

IN a nomad civilization there are simply families. They may be rich or poor, but the tribe is not divided into different social classes. Some tribes are 'nobler' than others, but all Bedouin regard themselves as 'noble' compared with the settled cultivators. Even slaves do not constitute a class apart: they form part of the family. From all that we can discover it was the same with Israel so long as it led a semi-nomad life.

Settlement on the land, however, brought about a profound social transformation. The unit was no longer the tribe but the clan, the *mishpaḥah*, settled in a town which was usually no more than a village. Social life became a life of small towns, and it is relevant to note that the old, and basic, framework of Deuteronomy is largely municipal law: *e.g.* the rules about the cities of refuge (Dt 19), unknown murderers (21: 1-9), rebellious sons (21: 18-21), adultery (22: 13-28), and the levirate (25: 5-10). This organization, based on the clan, survived to some extent under the monarchy,[1] and was still a living force at the return from the Exile (Ne 4: 7; Za 12: 12-14).

The centralization of the monarchy, however, brought about important changes.

The king's officials, civil or military, whether grouped in the two capitals or posted in the provinces as representatives of authority, formed a kind of caste, detached from, and sometimes opposed to, municipal interests. Above all, the play of economic life, business deals and the sale of land, destroyed the equality between families, some of whom became very rich while others sank into poverty. But it would be a mistake to see in ancient Israelite society the contrasts found in other societies, past or present, between 'nobles' and 'plebeians', 'capitalists' and 'proletariat'. In Israel, there never really existed social classes in the modern sense of groups conscious of their particular interests and opposed to one another. It is to avoid such misleading comparisons that we prefer to speak here of 'divisions of the population'. But it is not so easy to define them, owing to the variety and uncertainty of the vocabulary in use.

1. Cf. p. 138.

2. *The men of rank and influence*

In the texts from Deuteronomy quoted above, municipal affairs are in the hands of the *z'qenîm*. Some think this term means all the adult men—those who wore a beard, *zaqan*—gathered in popular assembly. It is much more likely that they are the 'elders' (the corresponding adjective means 'old'), the heads of families, who form a sort of council in every village (1 S 30: 26-31).

In Nb 22: 7 and 14 and in Jg 8: 6 and 16 they appear alternately with the *śarîm*, the 'chiefs'. The same two words appear side by side, as synonyms, in Jg 8: 14, where we learn that there were seventy-seven of them at Sukkoth. The two words appear to be synonyms in Is 3: 14 also. The same word *śarîm* denotes the heads of families, explicitly in Esd 8: 29 and probably in Esd. 8: 24f. In Jb 29: 9 the *śarîm* sit at the gate of the town, like the 'elders' of Pr 31: 23. The two terms are therefore to some extent equivalent.

Śarîm may have this meaning in some other texts too, but it often clashes with another sense. The *śarîm* are sometimes the officers or officials of the king, both in foreign kingdoms (Gn 12: 15; Jr 25: 19; 38: 17f.; Est 1: 3; 2: 18; Esd 7: 28) and in Israel. Often they are military officers, commanders of a unit or of the whole army (1 S 8: 12; 17: 18, 55; 2 S 24: 2, 4; 1 K 9: 22; 2 K 1: 14; 11: 4, etc.). Often too they are civil officials, such as Solomon's ministers (1 K 4: 2), governors (1 K 20: 14; 22: 26; 2 K 23: 8), or officials in general (Jr 24: 8; 26: 10f.; 34: 19, 21, etc.).

In relation to the king, these officers were merely 'servants' (2 K 19: 5; 22: 9, etc.).[1] But among the people they enjoyed a privileged position. The king sometimes gave them lands (1 S 8: 14; 22: 7).

They were specially numerous in the capitals, Samaria and Jerusalem, where they formed a powerful body with which the king had to reckon (Jr 38: 24-25), for they might even plot against their master (2 K 21: 23). They were men of influence, and in many cases are indistinguishable from the heads of the great families, from whose ranks they were often recruited.

In Nb 21: 18 and Pr 8: 16, *śarîm* alternates with *n'dîbîm*, the 'excellent' men. These had a seat of honour in the assemblies (1 S 2: 8; Ps 113: 8); they were rich and powerful (Ps 118: 9; 146: 3; Pr 19: 6).

In Is 34: 12 and Qo 10: 17 the *śarîm* are parallel with the *ḥorîm*, and in Jr 27: 20 *ḥorîm* takes the place of *śarîm* in the corresponding text of 2 K 24: 14. This word, always used in the plural, is quoted alongside *z'qenîm* in 1 K 21: 8, 11, and alongside *gibbôrê ḥaîl* (see below) in 2 K 24: 14. According to the root and its derivatives in languages related to Hebrew, these are 'free men', 'men of good birth'.

These words are therefore almost synonymous and denote the ruling class of the monarchical period, administrators and heads of influential families—in

---

1. Cf. p. 120.

short, the men of position. In other texts, they are simply called the 'great', the *g'dolîm* (2 K 10: 6, 11; Jr 5: 5; Jon 3: 7).

After the Exile other names appear, denoting the same group. In Jb 29: 9-10, the *n'gîdîm* are equated with the *śarîm*, and in 1 and 2 Ch the two are in practice equivalent. But the pre-exilic texts use only the singular, *nagîd*, and apply it to the king appointed by Yahweh (1 S 9: 16; 10: 1; 2 S 5: 2; 7: 8; 1 K 14: 7; 16: 2; 2 K 20: 5). On the other hand, we have the *s'ganîm* mentioned with the *horîm* in Ne 2: 16; 4: 8, 13, and with the *śarîm* in Esd 9: 2, and this word is frequently used in the Memoirs of Nehemias for the influential people. One feels that in his vocabulary this word replaces *z'qenîm*, 'the elders', which he does not use. But in the earlier texts the word means 'governor' and is borrowed from the Babylonian.

These men of influence and position can no doubt be called 'nobles' in a broad sense, but they do not form a nobility in the proper sense of a closed class to which one belongs by birth, which enjoys certain privileges and owns a large part of the land.

Some authors used to regard the *gibbôrê haïl* as a class of landed proprietors, a sort of squirearchy. They relied mainly on 2 K 15: 20, where Menahem taxes the *gibbôrê haïl* of his kingdom in order to pay tribute to the Assyrians. But it seems that this term meant originally (and often does mean in the Chronicles) the valiant men, the brave warriors, the gallant knights, like *gibbôrîm* on its own, even if they possess no property of their own (Jos 8: 3; Jg 11: 1).

The term was then applied to those who were bound to armed service and, having to provide their own equipment, enjoyed a certain standard of living. This is the sense which best answers the text of 2 K 15: 20, where there are sixty thousand of them, of 2 K 24: 14, where they are contrasted with the poorest people of the land, and of Rt 2: 1, where Boaz is simply a man of substance, like Saul's father in 1 S 9: 1.

3. *The 'people of the land'*

The texts often speak of the 'people of the land', *'am ha'ares*, an expression which has been interpreted in several ways. Many believe it means the lower social class, the common people, the plebs as opposed to the aristocracy, or the peasants as opposed to the townsfolk. Others, on the contrary, see them as the representatives of the people in the government, a sort of Parliament or House of Commons. Others, again, regard them as the body of free men, enjoying civic rights in a given territory.

Examination of the texts shows that the last explanation is the only one which can be accepted for the earliest period, but that the meaning of the term gradually changed.

First, let us consider the texts where it refers to non-Israelites. In Gn 23:

12-13, 'the people of the land' means the Hittites, the citizens of Hebron, by contrast with Abraham, who is only a resident stranger there.

In Gn 42: 6 it means the Egyptians, in contrast with the sons of Jacob; in Nb 14: 9 it means the Canaanites who are masters of the land, in contrast with the Israelites (cf. the parallel from Nb 13: 28, 'the people who dwell on the land'). Ex 5: 5 seems to contradict this interpretation, for in the Massoretic text the Pharaoh calls the Hebrews 'the people of the land'. This would justify translating it by 'the common people', but it is very tempting to adopt the Samaritan reading: 'they are more numerous than the people of the land'.

Turning now to Israel, three periods may be discerned in the use of this expression. Before the return from the Exile, it was used principally by 2 K, Jr and Ez. The 'people of the land' are distinguished from, or contrasted with, (a) the king or the prince, 2 K 16: 15; Ez 7: 27; 45: 22; (b) the king and his servants, Jr 37: 2; (c) the chiefs and the priests, Jr 1: 18; 34: 19; 44: 21; (d) the chiefs, the priests and the prophets, Ez 22: 24-29. They are never contrasted with another class of the people.

According to 2 K 24: 14, Nabuchodonosor left 'only the poorest of the people of the land' in Jerusalem, and the qualification inserted indicates that the term itself does not stand for the poorer classes (cf. also Es 22: 29). This emerges also from the texts just quoted, e.g. Jr 1: 18: '. . . against this whole land, against the kings of Judah, their chiefs (śarîm) their priests and all the people of the land'.

The law of Lv 4 distinguishes the sin-offerings which have to be offered: v. 3 for the high priest, v. 13 for the whole community of Israel, v. 22 for a chief, v. 27 for anyone of 'the people of the land'. The obligation of punishing certain offences rests upon all the 'people of the land' (Lv 20: 2-4).

The 'people of the land', then, stands for the whole body of citizens. That is why the expression, applied to the kingdom of Judah, is used as an alternative for the 'people of Judah': compare 2 K 14: 21, 'All the people of Judah chose Ozias' with 2 K 23: 30, 'The people of the land chose Joachaz.' In the same way, the 'people of the land' punished the murderers of Amon and proclaimed Josias king, 2 K 21: 24. In 2 K 11: 14, 18, 'all the people of the land' acclaimed Joas and destroyed the temple of Baal: this was a national revolution, directed against Athaliah and her foreign entourage. It is true that v. 20 contrasts the 'people of the land' with the city, that is, with Jerusalem. But the reason for the distinction is that the court resided in Jerusalem, with all the officials and supporters of the regime which had been overthrown. The contrast in v. 20, therefore, implies no more than the distinction between the people of Judah and the inhabitants of Jerusalem in Jr 25: 2. Nowhere does the expression mean a party or a social class.

At the return from the Exile it continued to be used in this general sense (Ag 2: 4; Za 7: 5), and it is found even in Dn 9: 6, where the enumeration of 'our kings, our princes, our fathers, all the people of the land' recalls those of Jeremiah and Ezechiel. But the meaning changes in Esd and Ne. The term is used in the plural, 'the peoples of the land' or 'of the lands', Esd 3: 3; 9: 1, 2, 11; 10: 2, 11; Ne 9: 30; 10: 29, 31, 32. Here it denotes the non-Jewish inhabitants of Palestine, who hinder the work of restoration, hinder the observance of the sabbath, and with whom mixed marriages are made. The 'peoples of the land' are contrasted with the 'people of Judah' in Esd 4: 4, and with the 'people of Israel' in Esd 9: 1. It is a complete reversal of the pre-exilic use, and again the explanation lies in the basic meaning of the expression: the community of the Return are *not* the 'people of the land' because they do not enjoy the political status accorded to the Samaritans, the Ammonites and the Moabites. It is these latter who are the 'people of the land' or of 'the lands'.

Thus the way was prepared for a third meaning. In the Rabbinical period the 'people of the land' are all those who are ignorant of the law or do not practise it.

4. Rich and poor

In the early days of the settlement, all the Israelites enjoyed more or less the same standard of living. Wealth came from the land, and the land had been shared out between the families, each of whom guarded its property jealously (cf. once more the story of Naboth in 1 K 21: 1-3). Commerce, and the buying and selling of real estate for profit, were as yet unimportant factors in economic life. There were, of course, exceptions: Nabal, for instance, was a rich stock-breeder in the highlands of Judah: he had 3,000 sheep and 1,000 goats and, in order to appease David, his wife Abigail could send 200 loaves, 100 bunches of dried grapes, 200 fig cakes, with skins of wine, bushels of parched grain and dressed mutton, 1 S 25: 2, 18. Job's wealth was even greater: 7,000 sheep, 3,000 camels, 500 pair of oxen, 500 she-asses, Jb 1: 3; but the story portrays Job after the manner of a great sheikh of the patriarchal age (cf. Abraham in Gn 12: 16; 13: 6; 24: 35). In contrast, the first two kings of Israel came from only moderately well-to-do families. Saul's father was a *gibbôr ḥaïl* (cf. above), but he sent his son to look for the lost she-asses, 1 S 9: 1f., and Saul ploughed the fields himself (1 S 11: 5). David looked after the flocks (1 S 16: 11, cf. 17: 20, 28, 34f.), and his father sent him off to his brothers in the army, with a measure of parched corn, ten loaves and ten cheeses (1 S 17: 17). According to another tradition, when David was called into the king's presence, he brought a present of five loaves, a skin of wine and a kid (1 S 16: 20). All this represents a very modest standard of living, and we do not hear of any other families in the same circles being any better off.

Excavations in Israelite towns bear witness to this equality in standards of living. At Tirsah, the modern Tell el-Farah near Nablus, the houses of the tenth century B.C. are all of the same size and arrangement. Each represents the dwelling of a family which lived in the same way as its neighbours. The contrast is striking when we pass to the eighth century houses on the same site: the rich houses are bigger and better built and in a different quarter from that where the poor houses are huddled together.

Between these two centuries, a social revolution had taken place. The monarchical institutions produced, as we saw, a class of officials who drew a profit from their posts and the favours granted them by the king. Others, by hard work or good luck, made vast profits from their lands. Prosperity was the order of the day. In Os 12: 9, Ephraim (Israel) says: 'Yes, I have become rich, I have amassed a fortune', and Is 2: 7 says: 'The land is full of silver and gold, and treasures past counting.' The prophets condemn their contemporaries for their luxury in building (Os 8: 14; Am 3: 15; 5: 11), in entertainment (Is 5: 11-12; Am 6: 4) and in dress (Is 3: 16-24). They condemn the buying up of the land by those 'who add house to house and join field to field till there is no room left' (Is 5: 8). The wealth of the day was in fact badly distributed and often ill-gotten: 'If they covet fields they seize them; if houses, they take them', Mi 2: 2. The rich landlords would speculate and defraud others (Os 12: 8; Am 8: 5; Mi 2: 1f.), the judges took bribes (Is 1: 23; Jr 5: 28; Mi 3: 11; 7: 3), and the creditors knew no pity (Am 2: 6-8; 8: 6).

On the other side we have the weak, the small men, the poor, who suffered from these burdens. The prophets took their cause in hand (Is 3: 14-15; 10: 2; 11: 4; Am 4: 1; 5: 12; cf. Ps 82: 3-4), and the law too protected them. In days gone by, there had been the precepts of Ex 22: 24-26; 23: 6, but Deuteronomy reflects the social conditions of its period. It promulgates the duty of almsgiving (Dt 15: 7-11), says that when a debtor is poor, his security must be given back to him before sunset (Dt 24: 12-13, supplementing the law of Ex 22: 25-26), and protects the hired labourer (Dt 24: 14-15).

It was well understood that the poor would always be with them (Dt 15: 11, cf. Mt 26: 11), but there were regulations which aimed at preventing pauperism and restoring a certain equality between Israelites, though it is hard to say how far they were actually put into practice.[1] In every sabbatical year, the produce of the land was left for the destitute (Ex 23: 11), and debts were cancelled (Dt 15: 1), 'so that there may no longer be any poor man among you' (Dt 15: 4). In the Jubilee year a general emancipation was to be proclaimed and every man was to have his ancestral land restored to him (Lv 25: 10, with the commentaries in the rest of the chapter).

The rich were found mostly among the influential people, and many passages in the Prophets condemn the two together. But the poor did not form a separate social class in contrast with them: the poor were individuals, and precisely because they were isolated, they were defenceless.

In themselves, the words 'rich' and 'poor' carry no moral or religious

1. Cf. pp. 173-177.

connotation. But they acquire moral overtones in two opposed lines of thought. On the theory of earthly rewards, wealth is a reward of virtue and poverty is a punishment; this we find in texts like Ps 1: 3; 112: 1-3; Pr 10: 15-16; 15: 6, a line against which Job protests. Another line of thought starts from the more common experience of life and from the facts denounced by the prophets: there are wicked, impious rich men who oppress the poor, but the poor are beloved by God (Dt 10: 18; Pr 22: 22-23), and his Anointed will do them justice (Is 11: 4). Thus the way was prepared for the spiritual transposition of vocabulary which begins in Sophonias: 'Seek Yahweh, all you humble of the earth' (So 2: 3, cf. 3: 12-13). The spirituality of the 'poor' was developed in the second part of Isaias and the post-exilic Psalter, but by then the terms for poverty had lost their sociological associations: neither before nor after the Exile were the poor a religious party or a social class.

5. Resident aliens

Besides the free citizens of Israel who formed the 'people of the land', and travelling foreigners who could count on the customs of hospitality but were not protected by law (Dt 15: 3; 23: 21), part of the population consisted of resident foreigners, the *gerîm*.

Among the ancient Arab nomads, the *jar* was the refugee or lone man who came seeking the protection of a tribe other than his own.[1] In the same way the *ger* is essentially a foreigner who lives more or less permanently in the midst of another community, where he is accepted and enjoys certain rights.

The word may be used of individuals or groups. Abraham was a *ger* at Hebron (Gn 23: 4), and Moses in Midian (Ex 2: 22; 18: 3). A man of Bethlehem went with his family to settle as a *ger* in Moab (Rt 1: 1). The Israelites were *gerîm* in Egypt (Ex 22: 20; 23: 9; Dt 10: 19; 23: 8). The people of Beeroth had taken refuge in Gittayim, where they lived as *gerîm* (2 S 4: 3).

When the Israelites had settled in Canaan, they considered themselves the legitimate owners of the land, the 'people of the land'; the former inhabitants, unless they were assimilated by marriage or reduced to slavery, became *gerîm*, and to these were added immigrants. The ancient texts considered an Israelite who went to live among another tribe as a *ger*: a man of Ephraim was a *ger* at Gibeah, where the Benjaminites live (Jg 19: 16).

Levites in general were in the same class, because they had no land of their own (Jg 17: 7-9; 19: 1), and the laws for the protection of society class Levites and *gerîm* together (Dt 12: 12; 14: 29; 26: 12).

From the social point of view these resident aliens were free men, not slaves, but they did not possess full civic rights, and so differed from Israelite citizens. They may be compared with the *perioikoi* of Sparta, the original inhabitants of the Peloponnese, who retained their freedom and could own

1. Cf. p. 10.

property, but had no political rights. The *gerîm* of Israel, however, were in the beginning less fortunate. Since all landed property was in Israelite hands, the *gerîm* were reduced to hiring out their services (Dt 24: 14), as the Levites did for their own profession (Jg 17: 8-10). As a rule they were poor, and are grouped with the poor, the widows and the orphans, all the 'economically weak' who were recommended to the Israelites' charity. The fallen fruit, the olives left behind on the tree, the leavings of the grapes, the gleanings after the harvest were to be left for them (Lv 19: 10; 23: 22; Dt 24: 19-21, etc., cf. Jr 7: 6; 22: 3; Ez 22: 7; Za 7: 10). Like the rest of the poor, they were under the protection of God (Dt 10: 18; Ps 146: 9; Ml 3: 5). The Israelites were to help them, remembering that they themselves had once been *gerîm* in Egypt (Ex 22: 20; 23: 9; Dt 24: 18, 22), and for the same reason they were charged to love these aliens as themselves (Lv 19: 34; Dt 10: 19).

They were to share in the tithe collected every third year (Dt 14: 29), and in the produce of the Sabbatical year (Lv 25: 6), and the cities of refuge were open to them (Nb 35: 15). In legal actions they were entitled to justice just like the Israelites (Dt 1: 16), but were liable to the same penalties (Lv 20: 2; 24: 16, 22). In everyday life there was no barrier between *gerîm* and Israelites. Some *gerîm* acquired a fortune (Lv 25: 47; cf. Dt 28: 43), and Ezechiel foretold that in the Israel of the future they would share the land with the citizens (Ez 47: 22).

From the religious point of view, though Dt 14: 21 says that a *ger* may eat a dead carcase, Lv 17: 15 forbids this to *gerîm* as well as to Israelites. Otherwise they are subject to the same laws of cleanness (Lv 17: 8-13; 18: 26; Nb 19: 10). They must observe the sabbath (Ex 20: 10; Dt 5: 14), and fast on the day of Atonement (Lv 16: 29). They can offer sacrifices (Lv 17: 8; 22: 18; Nb 15: 15, 16, 29), and they take part in religious festivals (Dt 16: 11, 14). They can even celebrate the Passover with the Israelites, provided that they are circumcised (Ex 12: 48-49; cf. Nb 9: 14).

It is noteworthy that nearly all these passages were written shortly before the Exile: Deuteronomy, Jeremias and the Law of Holiness in Leviticus. Thus it seems that at the end of the monarchy the number of *gerîm* in Judah had increased, and provision had to be made for them. There had probably been an influx of refugees from the former northern kingdom.

The assimilation of these *gerîm*, akin in race and of the same faith, was easy, and must have helped to hasten the assimilation of *gerîm* of foreign birth. This paved the way for the status of proselytes, and it was by this Greek word that the Septuagint translated the Hebrew word *ger*.

Sometimes the term *tôshab* occurs alongside that of *ger* (Gn 23: 4; Lv 25: 23, 25; 1 Ch 29: 15; Ps 39: 13). The *tôshab* appears also with the wage-earning workmen in Ex 12: 45; Lv 22: 10; 25: 40, with the slaves, the workmen and 'all those who dwell with you' in Lv 25: 6. From these texts it seems that the status of the *tôshab* was like that of the *ger*, though not exactly the same. He seems less assimilated, socially and religiously (Ex 12: 45; cf. Lv 22: 10), less firmly rooted in the land and also less independent: he has no house of his own, but is some man's *tôshab* (Lv 22: 10; 25: 6). It is a later word, appearing mostly in texts edited after the Exile.

6. *Wage-earners*

Besides the slaves, who will be the subject of the next chapter, there were paid workers, free men who hired themselves for a definite job, for a certain time, at an agreed wage. Resident or travelling foreigners also hired out their services in this way (Ex 12: 45; Lv 22: 10; Dt 24: 14), as Jacob had done with Laban (Gn 29: 15; 30: 28; 31: 7). As time went on, some families grew poorer and lost their lands, and so an increasing number of Israelites were obliged to work for wages (cf. Dt 24: 14). In early days it was mostly agricultural labourers who were hired in this way. They worked as herdsmen (Am 3: 12), as harvesters or grapepickers (perhaps Rt 2: 3f.; 2 K 4: 18; cf. Mt 20: 1f.). They could be hired by the day, like modern 'day-labourers' (Lv 19: 13; Dt 24: 15; cf. Mt 20: 8), or by the year (Lv 25: 50, 53; Is 16: 14; 21: 16; Si 37: 11).

The Old Testament gives no direct information on the amount of their wages. In Mesopotamia, workmen were paid either in money or in kind. According to the Code of Hammurabi they were paid one shekel of silver a month during the season of hard work, and rather less for the rest of the year; but some contracts fixed much smaller sums. The same code presumes that the yearly wage will amount to ten shekels or thereabouts, and perhaps this may explain Jg 17: 10 and the difficult text of Dt 15: 18. Its meaning would then be that a slave who has served for six years has repaid his master double his own worth, at the rate of a paid man, since the value of a slave was thirty shekels (Ex 21: 32). The labourers in the Gospel (Mt 20: 2) earn a denarius, which represents much more, but it would be pointless to compare values between two such distant periods.

The fact remains that the condition of the wage-labourers was far from enviable (Jb 7: 1-2; 14: 6), and unjust masters did not even give them their due (Jr 22: 3; Si 34: 22). Yet the law did make some effort to protect them. Lv 19: 13 and Dt 24: 14-15 lay down that workmen must be paid every evening (cf. Mt 20: 8), and the prophets were their champions against oppression (Jr 22: 13; Ml 3: 5; Si 7: 20).

7. *Craftsmen*

Apart from labourers, economic progress and the development of urban life multiplied the number of independent craftsmen. Many trades are mentioned in the Old Testament: millers, bakers, weavers, barbers, potters, fullers, locksmiths, jewellers, etc. A more general term, *ḥarash*, denotes a worker in wood or stone, and especially in metals, *i.e.* a smith, founder or carver. They worked on the system of the family workshop, where the father handed on the craft to his son, sometimes assisted by a handful of workmen, slaves or paid men.

The craftsmen of one trade lived and worked together in a certain quarter or street, as they do in Eastern towns to-day; again, a village would specialize in one industry. Geographical and economic circumstances accounted for these concentrations, *e.g.* the presence of the raw material, ore, clay or wool, or of the means of production, such as supplies of water or fuel, or good sites for ventilating the furnaces, etc. These groupings were also founded on tradition, for the crafts were, as a general rule, hereditary. Thus we learn that textiles were made at Beth-Ashbea in the south of Judaea (1 Ch 4: 21), and that the Benjaminites worked in wood and metal in the regions of Lod and Ono (Ne 11: 35). Excavations indicate that weaving and dyeing were flourishing industries at Debir, the modern Tell Beit-Mirsim. At Jerusalem there was a 'Bakers' Street' (Ne 3: 31-32), a 'Fuller's Field' (Is 7: 3), a 'Gate of the Potsherds' near which the potters worked (Jr 19: 1f.), and a 'Goldsmiths' Quarter' (Jr 37: 21). This specialization was carried still further in the Graeco-Roman and Rabbinical periods.

These craftsmen who worked side by side gradually organized themselves into guilds. There is clear evidence of this after the Exile, when the craft guilds, following the model of the family system from which they had sprung, called themselves families or clans, *mishpaḥoth*.[1] At Beth-Ashbea there are *mishpaḥoth* of linen-makers (1 Ch 4: 21). The head of the guild is called a 'father', *e.g.* Yoab, 'father' of the Valley of the Smiths, 1 Ch 4: 14, and the journeymen are called 'sons'. Uzziel is a 'son' of the goldsmiths (Ne 3: 8), that is, a journeyman goldsmith, like Malkiyyah of the same corporation (Ne 3: 31), and Hananyah, a perfumer by trade (Ne 3: 8). In Judaism these guilds were to be given legal status, and to make rules for the protection of their members. Sometimes they would even have their own places of worship: there was a weavers' synagogue in Jerusalem. The influence of the professional organizations in the Graeco-Roman world must have hastened this development, but the passages quoted, and the older parallels from Mesopotamia, show that these guilds originated long before. Perhaps they may date back to the monarchical period, if we admit that certain signs often engraved on the pottery, are, if not the owner's name, trade-marks of a corporation, not of a family workshop. It is difficult to decide, but in any case, during this pre-exilic period, all important enterprises were in the hands of the king. The foundry at Esyon Geber under Solomon, excavated some years ago, was a state factory. According to 1 Ch 4: 23, the potters of Netayim and Gedarah worked in the royal workshop. It was from these

1. Cf. pp. 8 and 21.

workshops that those jars with an official stamp came; the stamp was presumably meant as a guarantee of their capacity.[1]

8. *Merchants*

The Israelites did not take to commerce until late in their history. Foreign trade, or big business, was a royal monopoly. With the help of Hiram of Tyre, Solomon equipped a fleet on the Red Sea (1 K 9: 26-28; 10: 11, 22), which was to barter the products of the Esyon Geber foundry against the gold and wealth of Arabia. A similar enterprise was planned under Josaphat but did not succeed (1 K 22: 49-50). Solomon also traded with desert caravans (1 K 10: 15), and ran a forwarding agency; his agents bought horses in Cilicia and chariots in Egypt and then re-sold them both (1 K 10: 28-29)— but this interpretation of the text is not certain.

Achab signed a commercial agreement with Benhadad, by which he could set up bazaars in Damascus, as the Syrian king could in Samaria (1 K 20: 34); this is yet another royal concern. This kind of business went on all over the Near East in ancient times. Solomon's counterparts were the king of Tyre (1 K 5: 15-26; 9: 27; 10: 11-14), and the queen of Sheba (1 K 10: 1-13). And the tradition was of great antiquity. In the third millennium B.C. and again under Hammurabi, the kings of Mesopotamia owned caravans; in the Amarna period the kings of Babylon, Cyprus and other lands had merchants in their service; in the eleventh century B.C. the Egyptian story of Wen-Amon tells us that the prince of Tanis had a merchant navy and that the king of Byblos kept a register of the business he did with the pharaoh.

Private citizens in Israel did business only in their own locality. In the town or village square, where the market was held (2 K 7: 1), craftsmen sold their wares, and peasants the produce of their fields and herds. This business was on a very small scale and the producer sold direct to the consumer without any middleman; hence there was no merchant class. Real commerce was in the hands of foreigners, especially the Phoenicians, who were the universal agents of the East (cf. Is 23: 2, 8; Ez 27), and (according to Na 3: 16) the Assyrians also. Even after the Exile the Jews brought agricultural products to Jerusalem, but the Tyrians sold imported goods there (Ne 13: 15-16). Perhaps the first Israelite merchants we know of in Palestine itself are those who worked under Nehemias when he was restoring the ramparts (Ne 3: 32); on the other hand, these too may have been Tyrians, for, according to Ne 13: 16, some of them lived in the city.

This state of affairs is reflected in vocabulary; a 'Canaanite' means a 'merchant' in Jb 40: 30; Pr 31: 24; Za 14: 21. Other words describe the merchant as 'one who travels around', or by a root connected with the verb 'to walk'. They were foreigners, caravan drivers like the Midianites of

Gn 37: 28, or merchants on foot who toured the country, selling their imported rubbish and buying the local products for export.

It was in the Diaspora and by force of necessity that the Jews became merchants. In Babylonia the descendants of those exiles who did not take part in the Return are found as clients or agents of big commercial firms. In Egypt, in the Hellenistic period, we know from the papyri that some were traders, bankers or brokers. The Palestinian Jews gradually followed suit, but the wise men, and later the Rabbis, were far from approving of it. Though Ben-Sirach says that the profits of commerce are legitimate (Si 42; 5), he also observes that a merchant cannot live without sin (Si 26: 29; 27: 2).

Chapter Three

SLAVES

1. *The existence of slavery in Israel*

CERTAIN writers, and especially Jewish scholars, have denied that real slavery ever existed in Israel; at least, they maintain, Israelites were never reduced to slavery. There is a semblance of justification for this view if we compare Israel with classical antiquity; in Israel and the neighbouring countries, there never existed those enormous gangs of slaves which in Greece and Rome continually threatened the balance of social order. Nor was the position of the slave ever so low in Israel and the ancient East as in republican Rome, where Varro could define a slave as 'a sort of talking tool', '*instrumenti genus vocale*'. The flexibility of the vocabulary may also be deceptive. Strictly speaking '*ebed* means a slave, a man who is not his own master and is in the power of another. The king, however, had absolute power, and consequently the word '*ebed* also means the king's subjects, especially his mercenaries, officers and ministers; by joining his service they had broken off their other social bonds. By a fresh extension of meaning, the word became a term of courtesy. We may compare it with the development of its equivalents 'servant' in English or 'serviteur' in French, both derived from *servus*, a slave. Moreover, because a man's relations with God are often conceived on the model of his relations with his earthly sovereign, '*ebed* became a title for pious men, and was applied to Abraham, Moses, Josue or David, and finally to the mysterious Servant of Yahweh.

By 'slave' in the strict sense we mean a man who is deprived of his freedom, at least for a time, who is bought and sold, who is the property of a master, who makes use of him as he likes; in this sense there were slaves in Israel, and some were Israelites. The fact is proved by some early texts which speak of slaves in contrast with free men, wage-earners and resident foreigners, or which speak of their purchase for a sum of money; and the existence of slavery is presupposed also by the laws about emancipation.

2. *Slaves of foreign origin*

Throughout antiquity, war was one of the chief sources of supply for the slave-market, for captured prisoners were generally sold as slaves. The custom obtained in Palestine, too. In the days of the Judges, Sisera's army, had it been victorious, would have shared out the spoil: 'a damsel, two damsels, to every warrior' (Jg 5: 30). After the sack of Siqlag, the Amalekites carried off all the inhabitants into captivity (1 S 30: 2-3). Yahweh will judge the nations who 'have drawn lots for my people; they have traded boys against harlots; for wine they have sold the maidens' (Jl 4: 3). In the Hellenistic age, slave-traders followed the armies of Antiochus Epiphanes in order to buy the Jews whom they would take prisoner (1 M 3: 41; 2 M 8: 10-11). Later, Hadrian sold the prisoners taken in the Second Revolt.

All these are examples of Israelites enslaved by foreign enemies. But the Chronicler records that Peqah, king of Israel, in his war against Judah, took 200,000 prisoners, women, boys and girls, who were set free at the protest of a prophet (2 Ch 28: 8-15). It is uncertain what credence should be given to this story, which has no parallel in the Books of Kings; the figure, at least, is suspect. But it does show that the enslavement of prisoners of war who were brothers by race was not unheard of, though the custom was abhorred by right-thinking men. On the other hand, the presence in Israel of foreign prisoners as slaves is presumed by two laws of Deuteronomy. Dt 21: 10-14 considers the case of a female prisoner whom her captor takes as wife: he may later divorce her, but he may never sell her. This implies that he could have sold her, if he had not married her. The story of Nb 31: 26-47, which relates the sharing of the spoil after the war with Midian, is a parallel example: the virgins were shared among the combatants and the whole community, all the rest having been put to death to carry out the anathema (Nb 31: 15-18).

The law of Dt 20: 10-18 deals with the conquest of towns. If a town stands on the land assigned by God to Israel, it is to be totally destroyed and no living thing may be left in it. When a town outside the Holy Land is attacked, it must be given the chance to surrender. If it agrees, the whole population is condemned to forced labour; if it refuses and is captured, all the men are put to death and the women and children are reckoned as booty. In its present form, this law breathes the spirit of Deuteronomy (cf. the parallel in 7: 1-6), but it is unreal: the age of territorial conquest and foreign wars was long past. It reflects the memory of the ancient curses (Jos 6: 17-21; 8: 26; 10: 28f., etc.; 1 S 15: 3; cf. Dt 2: 34; 3: 6), of the obstacles to total conquest (Jos 17: 12-13; Jg 1: 28, 30, 33, 35), and of David's wars (2 S 8: 2; 12: 31), which provided the State with its first slaves.[1]

The slave traffic was general throughout the ancient East. In Am 1: 6 and 9, Gaza and Tyre are condemned for dealing in prisoners. According to Ez 27: 13, Tyre bought men in Asia Minor, and Jl 4: 6 says she sold Judaeans there. These Phoenicians, who were the chief traders in Israel, must also have been slave-dealers. The law allowed Israelites to buy slaves, men and women, of foreign birth, or born of resident aliens (Lv 25: 44-45; cf. Ex 12: 44; Lv 22: 11; Qo 2: 7).

1. Cf. pp. 88-90.

Slaves who had been bought for money are distinguished from those born in the house (Gn 17: 12, 23, 27; Lv 22: 11; cf. Jr 2: 14): *y'lîd bayth*. It is possible, however, that the expression does not refer only to those born in the house; it may include all those who are attached to a house as slaves, and who have certain obligations to the master of the house when it is necessary to take up arms. This would explain the 318 *y'lîdê bayth*, who were the 'partisans' of Abraham (Gn 14: 14), and the use of *yalîd* when referring to war (Nb 13: 28; 2 S 21: 16, 18). A master could buy married slaves, or marry off those he had; the children belonged to the master (cf. Ex 21: 4), and were a cheap addition to his domestic staff. If they had been brought up in the family, they would be more attached to it and would be better treated, but they had the same social status as those who had been bought.

3. Israelite slaves

We know for certain that there were slaves of foreign origin; but were Israelites ever reduced to slavery? We have just mentioned the text of 2 Ch 28: 8-15, which condemns this practice, and it is forbidden by Lv 25: 46 which, after speaking of foreigners, adds: 'You may have them as slaves, but none of you shall ever exercise such absolute power over your brethren, the children of Israel.' Yet Lv 25: 39-43 speaks of an Israelite who is 'sold' to another Israelite; he must be treated as a paid worker or a visitor, and not as a slave. On the other hand, Lv 25: 47-53 deals with the case of an Israelite who has 'sold' himself to a resident alien: he can be redeemed by his kin or can redeem himself, and must be treated with consideration. Whether their master is Israelite or foreign, these slaves are to be set free in the jubilee year (Lv 25: 40).

The Israelites, then, could not become slaves permanently; but the law does allow them to be 'sold' as real slaves, though only for a limited time, and under certain safeguards. It is difficult to say whether this law was ever applied. In Nehemias' time the Jews bewailed the fact that they had had to sell their sons and daughters as slaves, and Nehemias implored the people to cancel their debts and to free persons who had given themselves as security (Ne 5: 1-13). There is no allusion to the law of Lv 25.

It seems, then, that this law is later than the time of Nehemias, and even if this argument from silence is not pressed, the law must be late, since it is a substitute for earlier laws. In Dt 15: 12-18, if a 'Hebrew', man or woman, is sold to one of his brethren, he must serve him for six years and be set free in the seventh year. If he declines to be freed, he becomes a slave for life. This is the law referred to in Jr 34: 14, concerning the liberation of 'Hebrew' slaves under Sedecias.

The law of Ex 21: 2-11 is much older. A 'Hebrew' slave who has been 'bought' is to serve six years and to be freed in the seventh year; if he refuses his freedom he becomes a slave for life. These provisions are identical with those of Dt 15: 12-18, but they apply only to male slaves. Girls sold as slaves, to become concubines of their master or his son, are not freed, and their status is similar to that of female prisoners of war (Dt 21: 10-14, cf. above).

It is interesting that in the texts quoted from Ex, Dt and Jr, these slaves are called 'Hebrews', a term which, except in one late text (cf. Jon 1: 9), is applied to Israelites only in certain conditions. It has been suggested that the word means those Israelites who forfeited their freedom by a semi-voluntary slavery. The theory can be supported from 1 S 14: 21, where the Israelites who entered the service of the Philistines are called 'Hebrews', and by the analogy of documents from Nuzu, in which the ḫapiru sell themselves as slaves. The biblical texts would preserve traces of an archaic usage, but they certainly refer to Israelites.

The only reason why an Israelite was ever reduced to slavery was his own, or his relatives', poverty. Usually, if not always, they were defaulting debtors, or persons given as security for the repayment of a debt.[1] This is presumed in the laws of Lv 25 and Dt 15: 2-3, and confirmed by the other passages. Eliseus performs a miracle to help a woman whose two children are about to be taken as slaves by a money-lender (2 K 4: 1-7). In Is 50: 1, Yahweh asks the Israelites: 'To which of my creditors have I sold you?' Nehemias' contemporaries sell their sons and daughters into slavery as securities for the payment of debts (Ne 5: 1-5). This explains why such slavery was not permanent; it ended once the debt was paid or cancelled (Lv 25: 48; 2 K 4: 7; Ne 5: 8 and 11). The laws of Ex 21 and Dt 15 fixed a maximum duration of six years. (According to the Code of Hammurabi, certain slaves-for-debt could not be kept for more than three years.) But these laws were not obeyed, as Jr 34 shows. It is because of this difficulty that the ideal law of Lv 25 allows for an extension which may amount to fifty years, but puts the master under the obligation of treating his slave like a wage-earner or a guest.

There were, then, Israelite slaves under Israelite masters. In addition to those who had been reduced to this state by poverty or debt, there were thieves who could not clear themselves and were sold to repay the cost of their theft (Ex 22: 2). On the other hand, the laws of Ex 21: 16 and Dt 24: 7 prescribe the death penalty for abducting an Israelite in order to exploit or sell him as a slave. Possibly the prohibition in the Decalogue (Ex 20: 15; Dt 5: 19), which is clearly distinguished from the very detailed commandment about crimes against justice (Ex 20: 17; Dt 5: 21), condemns this particularly hateful seizure of a free person.

4. The number and value of slaves

We have very little information about the number of domestic slaves in Israel. Gideon took ten of his servants to demolish the sanctuary of Baal (Jg 6:

1. Cf. p. 172.

27). Abigail, wife of the wealthy Nabal, had an unstated number of slaves, and when she went to marry David, she took five maidservants with her (1 S 25: 19, 42). After Saul's death, the property of the royal family was valued by Siba, a steward, who had fifteen sons and twenty slaves of his own (2 S 9: 10). Some large landowners in the days of the monarchy may have had a comparatively large household, but they were exceptions. The census of the community on its return from the Exile (Esd 2: 64; Ne 7: 66), records 7,337 slaves of both sexes as compared with 42,360 free persons. The situation is therefore utterly different from that in Greece or Rome, but has its parallel in Mesopotamia, where a family of substance had one or two slaves in the earliest periods, and from two to five in the Neo-Babylonian era: in Assyria the figures were a little higher.

Evidence about the value of slaves is equally scanty. Joseph was sold by his brethren for twenty pieces of silver (Gn 37: 28), and that was also the average price of a slave in ancient Babylon. It was the same as the price of an ox. Prices doubled in the Neo-Babylonian age and rose even higher under the Persians. In the middle of the second millennium B.C. the market price of a slave was thirty shekels of silver at Nuzu, forty at Ugarit (Ras Shamra). In Israel a slave cost thirty shekels according to Ex 21: 32, and this is the sum given to Judas to betray Jesus (Mt 26: 15). But by the Greek period, prices had risen: when Nicanor promised the traders ninety captives for a talent, that is, about thirty-three shekels a head (2 M 8: 11), he was asking an absurdly low price, compared with those indicated in contemporary papyri, for he hoped to attract the traders by the prospect of an enormous profit.

5. The position of slaves

Strictly speaking, the slave is a chattel, belonging to his master by right of conquest, purchase or inheritance; the master makes use of him as he wills and can sell him again. The ancient laws of Mesopotamia presume that he is branded, like cattle, with tattoo marks or a brand made with hot iron or by some kind of label attached to his body. In practice, not all slaves bore these marks of identity, but they were commonly applied to runaway slaves who had been recaptured and to those who might be tempted to run away. The Rabbis allowed a slave to be marked in order to discourage him from running away, but the practice is not clearly attested in the Old Testament. A slave who declined to be freed had his ears pierced (Ex 21: 6; Dt 15: 17), but this was not a brand inflicted on him; it was a symbol of his attachment to the family. The nearest analogy to this is the name of Yahweh written on the hands of the faithful in Is 44: 5 to signify that they belong to God, like the name of the Beast marked on his followers in Ap 13: 16-17, or the tattoo marks of the Hellenistic cults.

Yet in the ancient East no one ever quite forgot that the slave was a human being: slaves had their rights. True, the Code of Hammurabi punished cruelty only against another man's slave, because the slave was his master's property; similarly, Ex 21: 32 states that if a slave is gored by a neighbour's bull, the owner of the bull owes compensation to the slave's master. Still, even in Mesopotamia slaves had legal remedy against unjust violence, and in Israel the laws protected them even more explicitly. A man who blinded his slave or broke his tooth was bound to set him free in compensation (Ex 21: 26-27). If a man should beat his slave to death, he was to be punished (Ex 21: 20), but if the slave survived for one or two days the master was exonerated, for 'it was his money' (Ex 21: 21). Obviously, they thought that the master had been sufficiently punished by the loss he had incurred, but this clause shows that even in Israel the slave was thought of as his master's chattel.

In Mesopotamia and in Rome the slave could save money of his own, carry on business and have his own slaves. We cannot be sure that this was so in Israel. Lv 25: 49 certainly allows a slave to redeem himself if he has the means, but the text does not give any more detail. Other cases are sometimes quoted: the servant who went with Saul had a quarter of a shekel in his pocket (1 S 9: 8). Gehazi, servant of Eliseus, persuaded Naaman to give him two talents of silver, with which, Eliseus says, he would be able 'to buy gardens, oliveyards and vineyards, flocks and herds, menservants and maidservants' (2 K 5: 20-26). Siba, steward to Saul's family, had twenty slaves (2 S 9: 10). But the master retained supreme control over his slave's property: 2 S 9: 12 states clearly that 'all who lived with Siba were in the service of Meribbaal'. But these cases do not afford conclusive proof, for here the Hebrew word is not 'ebed, 'slave', but na'ar, 'young man', and so 'servant', 'assistant', probably always a free man, attached to a master's service.

In everyday life the lot of a slave depended largely on the character of his master, but it was usually tolerable. In a community which attached such importance to the family, in which work was scarcely conceivable outside the framework of the family, a man on his own was without protection or means of support. The slave was at least assured of the necessities of life. More than that, he really formed part of the family, he was a 'domestic' in the original sense of the word. (That was why he had to be circumcised, Gn 17: 12-13.) He joined in the family worship, rested on the sabbath (Ex 20: 10; 23: 12), shared in the sacrificial meals (Dt 12: 12, 18), and in the celebration of religious feasts (Dt 16: 11, 14), including the Passover (Ex 12: 44), from which the visitor and the wage-earner were excluded. A priest's slave could eat the holy offerings (Lv 22: 11), which visitors and wage-earners could not (Lv 22: 10). Abraham's relations with his servant (Gn 24), show how intimate master and slave could be. Pr 17: 2 says: 'Better a shrewd servant than a degenerate son' (cf Si 10: 25). He could share in his master's inheritance (Pr 17: 2), and even succeed to it in the absence of heirs (Gn 15: 3). We know of one slave who married his master's daughter (1 Ch 2: 34-35). In these last two cases, obviously, the slave was *ipso facto* emancipated.

The slave had of course to obey and to work, and the wise men advised masters to treat them harshly (Pr 29: 19, 21). Firmness there had to be, but it was to the master's interest to combine with it justice and humanity (Si 33: 25-33). Devout men added a religious motive: Job protests that he has not neglected the rights of his servant and his handmaid, for, like him, they are God's creatures (Jb 31: 13-15).

Leviticus prescribes that a slave of Israelite birth is to be treated favourably: he is to be like a visitor or a wage-earner and is not to be made to do the work of a slave (Lv 25: 39-40). Commenting on this text, the Rabbis laid down that he should not be given tasks which were too exacting or too degrading, like turning the mill (cf. Jg 16: 21), or taking off his master's shoes or washing his feet (cf. 1 S 25: 41). Hence in the New Testament, when John the Baptist protests that he is not worthy to untie the sandals of the one he announces (Mt 3: 11 and parallels), he means he is less than a slave. Peter recoils when Jesus wants to wash his feet (Jn 13: 6-7), because that is a task only for a slave.

6. Female slaves

We have already had occasion to note that female slaves formed a special category. They attended to the personal needs of the mistress of the house (Gn 16: 1; 30: 3, 9; 1 S 25: 42; Jdt 10: 5, etc.), or nursed the children (Gn 25: 59; 2 S 4: 4; 2 K 11: 2). The master arranged their marriages at his discretion (Ex 21: 4). He might take a slave-woman as his concubine, and her lot was then improved. Abraham and Jacob, for example, took slaves as concubines, at the request of their childless wives. But they kept their status as slaves (cf. Gn 16: 6) unless their master freed them (cf. Lv 19: 20). The ancient law of Ex 21: 7-11 allows an Israelite father who is poor or in debt to sell his daughter to be the slave-concubine of a master or his son. She is not freed in the seventh year like the male slaves. If her master is not satisfied, he may re-sell her to her family, but may not sell her to a stranger. If he takes another wife, he must leave intact all the rights of the first. If he intends her to be his son's wife, he must treat her as a daughter of the family.

The Deuteronomic law makes similar provisions for female prisoners of war who are married by their captors (Dt 21: 10-14). But unlike Ex 21, Dt makes no distinction between men and women in the treatment of Israelite slaves: the woman is freed in the seventh year like the man, and like him she can refuse her freedom (Dt 15: 12 and 17). Similarly Jr 34 makes no distinction between male and female slaves. This seems to mean that by this period there were no slave-concubines. The later law of Lv 25 makes no mention of them, and Ne 5: 5 speaks of the violation of Israelite girls by their master, but does not mention their being taken as concubines.

7. *Runaway slaves*

As a rule, the slave's only way of escaping from his master's cruelty was flight (Si 33: 33), and even if he were well treated he might be tempted to run away, if only to enjoy that freedom to which every man has a right. Nabal was a man of wealth and selfishness and must have known something about this: 'There are too many slaves running away from their masters nowadays', he tells David's messengers (1 S 25: 10). Two of Shimei's slaves fled to Gath (1 K 2: 39). It was the same everywhere. The Code of Hammurabi prescribes the death penalty for aiding and abetting a runaway slave, refusing to give him up, or merely hiding him. Other Mesopotamian laws were less strict; at Nuzu anyone who harboured a fugitive slave paid a fine.

To deal with slaves who took refuge abroad, some treaties between states provided extradition clauses. Thus Shimei was able to recover his two slaves who fled to the king of Gath (1 K 2: 40, cf. also 1 S 30: 15).

Israelite law contains only one article on runaway slaves. Dt 23: 16-17 forbids anyone to hand over a slave who has escaped from his master and sought refuge; he is to be welcomed and well treated, in the town he has chosen. This provision has no parallel in ancient law and is difficult to interpret. It does not seem to apply to an Israelite slave deserting an Israelite master, for he would naturally return to his family or clan. For the same reason it does not apply to an Israelite slave fleeing from a foreign master. It seems then that the law must deal with a foreigner coming from abroad and admitted to Israel as a *ger* or a *tôshab*. Extradition would be refused and all the Holy Land would be considered a place of refuge, in the spirit of Is 16: 3-4.

8. *The emancipation of slaves*

The master obviously had the right to free his slave if he so willed, and further, certain cases are provided for by law. If a man took a female prisoner of war as his wife, she ceased to be a slave (Dt 21: 10-14). Liberation could also occur as compensation for a bodily injury (Ex 21: 26-27); note that the unconditional wording of this text does not allow us to restrict it to Israelite slaves. But, generally speaking, foreign slaves were bound to slavery for life, and were bequeathed with the rest of the inheritance (Lv 25: 46).

The enslavement of Israelites, however, was in theory temporary. Male slaves (according to Ex 21: 2-6) and female slaves as well (according to Dt 15: 12-17), had to be set free after six years of service. They could refuse this freedom, and no doubt often did so, for fear of falling into poverty once more: this, after all, was precisely what had led them to sell themselves. The present which they received from their master (Dt 15: 14) was only a meagre insurance for the future. They had still more cause to remain if their master had given them a wife, for the wife and children remained his property (Ex

21: 4). In such a case the slave had his ear pierced against the doorpost or lintel, as a symbol of his final attachment to the house, and he became a slave for life. These laws do not seem to have been strictly observed. According to Jr 34: 8-22, which is explicitly based on Deuteronomy, the people of Jerusalem had liberated their 'Hebrew' slaves, during the siege under Nabuchodonosor; but when the siege was raised for a while, they seized them again. The prophet denounces this as felony against their brethren and transgression of a law of God.

The provisions already quoted from Lv 25 concern the liberation of Israelite slaves, in connection with the jubilee year.[1] In this year both they and their children are to go free (Lv 25: 41, 54). Before this period they can be redeemed or can redeem themselves, counting the years left before the jubilee at the price of a hired man for each year (Lv 25: 48-53). These provisions seem somewhat Utopian: a slave who began his term of service soon after the beginning of a jubilee period might well die before seeing the end of it, or become too old to earn his living as a free man. The price of his freedom, unless the jubilee year was very near, would have cost him very dear, for three years' wage was enough to cover the price of a slave. We saw that a slave was valued at thirty shekels (according to Ex 21: 32), and that a workman earned about ten shekels a year, according to the Code of Hammurabi, and perhaps Dt 15: 18.[2] There is, however, no evidence that the law was ever applied, either before or after Nehemias, who makes no reference to it when he orders a remission of debts, involving the liberation of persons held as security (Ne 5: 1-13).

A freed slave is called *hofshi* in the laws of Ex 21 and Dt 15, and in Jr 34 (cf. also Lv 19: 20; Is 58: 6; Jb 3: 19). The word is never used in any context but that of the liberation of slaves, except, figuratively, in Jb 39: 5, and in 1 S 17: 25 (where it means exemption from taxes and forced labour). The only possible translation is, therefore, 'freed'. But there is nothing in the Old Testament to suggest that these freed persons formed a special class of society. This conclusion could only be derived from non-Biblical analogies: at Alalakh and Nuzu, in the Amarna letters and the Ras Shamra texts, in the Assyrian laws and the later Assyrian documents, *hupshu* denotes a class of the population, midway between the slaves and the landowners. They seem to have been serfs, farmers and sometimes craftsmen. In these different social backgrounds the same word has many different connotations, and it is unreasonable to apply one or other of these meanings to Israel, where there were no well-defined social classes. On his liberation the slave belonged once more to the 'people of the land'.

9. *State slaves*

Prisoners of war provided the states of the ancient East with the servile manpower they needed for the sanctuaries and the palace, for public works

1. Cf. p. 175.   2. Cf. pp. 76 and 84.

and the big commercial or industrial enterprises which were the monopoly of the king. Though the Old Testament laws deal only with domestic slaves, it seems that in Israel there were also State slaves.

After the capture of Rabbah, David 'set the population handling the saw, picks and iron axes, and employed it on the making of bricks, and so he did for all the towns of the Ammonites' (2 S 12: 31). For a long time it was thought that this text described a strange massacre of the inhabitants, carried out with workmen's tools; but the translation just given makes perfect sense, and there is no need to assume any such massacre. The only question is whether it means reduction to slavery for the service of the State, or simply subjection to forced labour. Under Solomon, the work in the mines of the Arabah and the foundry at Esyon Geber, in remote regions and under appalling conditions, must have caused fearful mortality, and it required a slave population in the king's service. It is unthinkable that free Israelites could have been conscripted for it, at least in any number. The Ophir fleet, which exported the half-finished products of the factory at Esyon Geber, had 'Solomon's slaves' for crews, working alongside the slaves of Hiram of Tyre (1 K 9: 27; cf. 2 Ch 8: 18; 9: 10). It is possible that these State slaves of foreign birth worked also on Solomon's large buildings (1 K 9: 15-21). The text uses the term *mas 'obed*, 'servile levy', to signify these labourers, who were recruited from the descendants of the Canaanites; the addition of 'servile' may be to distinguish this levy from that to which the Israelites were subjected.[1] We may question this distinction, by which the redactor tries to exempt the Israelites from a burden (cf. v. 22) to which they had in fact been subjected, according to the early documents of 1 K 5: 27; 11: 28. But the important point is that he adds (1 K 9: 21) that the Canaanites remained slaves 'until this day'. In his time, therefore, at the end of the monarchy, there were State slaves, whose institution was ascribed to Solomon.

Now after the Exile we find 'descendants of the slaves of Solomon' who had returned from Babylon and lived in Jerusalem and its suburbs (Esd 2: 55-58; Ne 7: 57-60; 11: 3). But their connections had changed. They are mentioned along with the *n'thinim*, the 'given', and counted with them (Esd 2: 43-54; Ne 7: 46-56). These 'given' lived on mount Ophel, near the Temple (Ne 3: 31; 11: 21). They formed the less important personnel of the sanctuary and were at the service of the Levites (Esd 8: 20). To some extent their names betray a foreign origin. Though the term does not appear in pre-exilic texts, there was a similar institution in existence, at least at the end of the monarchy: Ez 44: 7-9 reproaches the Israelites for introducing foreigners into the sanctuary and entrusting part of their duties to them. It is even likely that slaves of foreign origin were attached to Israelite sanctuaries from the beginning, as was the practice in all the temples of the ancient East, of Greece and of Rome. The editor of the book of Josue was already acquainted with

1. On the levy, cf. pp. 141-142.

Gibeonites who cut wood and carried water in the Temple (Jos 9: 27), saying that their fathers had been condemned to this task by Josue, for deceiving Israel (Jos 9: 23). It is such foreigners who are alluded to in Dt 29: 10. Esd 8: 20 ascribes the institution of the n'thînîm to David, but, in reaction against this employment of foreigners, Nb 3: 9; 8: 19 emphasizes that it is the Levites who were 'given' to the priests for the service of the sanctuary.

Under the monarchy, then, as in neighbouring countries, there were two classes of State slaves, the king's slaves and the Temple slaves, both of foreign origin, and usually prisoners of war or their descendants. After the Exile, with the disappearance of royal institutions, the 'slaves of Solomon' were merged with the 'given', and all were attached to the service of the Temple.

CHAPTER FOUR

THE ISRAELITE CONCEPT OF THE STATE

1. *Israel and the various Eastern notions of the State*

WHEN the Israelites conquered Canaan, the land was divided into a host of principalities. Jos 12: 9-24 records the defeat of thirty-one kings by Josue, and this list is not a complete inventory of the towns on the political map of Palestine. Two centuries earlier the Amarna letters reflect the same state of affairs and show that Syria too was divided into principalities. It was the form the Hyksos domination took in these regions, but it dates back still further: Egyptian decrees of banishment witness to it at the beginning of the second millennium B.C. These political units are confined to a fortified city with a small surrounding territory. Each was ruled by a king, who at the time of the Hyksos and in the Amarna period, was often of foreign birth, relying on an army drawn from his own people and reinforced by mercenaries. Succession to the throne was normally on the dynastic principle. The same idea of the State is found in the five Philistine principalities on the coast. It is true that these formed a federation (Jos 13: 3; Jg 3: 3; 1 S 5: 8), but this was true of the four Gibeonite towns also (Jos 9: 17), without counting the apparently *ad hoc* alliances between the Canaanite kings (Jos 10: 3f.; 11: 1-2).

In contrast with these pygmy states, there were vast empires: the Egyptian, which for centuries counted the petty kings of Palestine and Syria as its vassals, then the Assyrian, the Neo-Babylonian and the Persian Empires. These were highly organized states, uniting heterogeneous populations across vast territories won by conquest. National feeling was hardly developed at all, and the army which defended the territory and made the conquests was a professional army embodying mercenary formations. The authority was monarchical and the succession, in theory, hereditary.

At the end of the second millennium B.C. some national states made their appearance. They bore the names of peoples—Edom, Moab, Ammon and Aram. They were confined to the territory where the nation lived, and at first made no attempt to spread by conquest. The country was defended, not by a professional army, but by the nation in arms, by calling to arms all the menfolk in time of danger. The government was monarchical, though not necessarily hereditary. From the list of the first kings of Edom (Gn 36:31-39), it appears that the kings owed their power to the fact that they had been either chosen or accepted by the nation. If, later on, the dynastic principle was established, the change was no doubt due to a natural evolution or to the influence of the great neighbouring states.

According to one Biblical tradition, the Israelites asked for a king in order to be 'like the other nations' (1 S 8: 5). But they did not imitate the Canaanite principalities whom they had dislodged. Such a conception of the State never held sway in Israel.

Attempts were made, but they came to nothing: it was this type of royal rank, with hereditary succession, which Gideon refused (Jg 8: 22f.), and the short-lived kingdom of Abimelek at Shechem was based on non-Israelite elements (Jg 8: 31; 9: 1f.). It has recently been maintained that both Jerusalem (a Jebusite town conquered by David) and Samaria (a new town founded by Omri on land bought by him) had the status of city-states of the Canaanite type inside the kingdoms of Judah and Israel, but this conclusion seems to go beyond the texts on which its claims are based.

Nor were the original Israelites inclined to adopt their ideas on the State from the great Empires with which they had been in contact, particularly in Egypt. It was only at the end of David's reign and under Solomon that an attempt was made to realize the idea of empire. But its success was short-lived and all that remained were some features of administrative organization copied from Egypt.

The notion of the State in Israel is in fact closer to that of the Aramaean kingdoms of Syria and Transjordania. First Israel, then Israel and Judah, were, like them, national kingdoms; like them they bore the names of peoples, and like them they did not at once accept the dynastic principle. The parallel could no doubt be pursued further if we knew more about the early history and organization of these kingdoms. It is certainly noteworthy that these national states were formed about the same time as Israel, after a semi-nomadic existence. These states emerged as the result of the solidarity of the tribes which eventually settled down in a limited territory.

2. The Twelve Tribes of Israel

In the first stage of its settlement in Canaan, Israel consisted of a federation of twelve tribes. Parallels to this system are known, and precisely in those related peoples who had passed through the same stage of social evolution. According to Gn 22: 20-24, Nahor had twelve sons, who gave their names to the Aramaean tribes. Similarly the sons of Ishmael are 'twelve chiefs of as many tribes' (Gn 25: 12-16). Again, there were twelve tribes of Esau's descendants established in Transjordan (Gn 36: 10-14, to which v. 12 adds Amalek).

At Shechem the twelve Israelite tribes joined in a pact which sealed their religious unity and established a certain form of national unity between them (Jos 24). This organization has been compared to the amphictyonies in which Greek cities were grouped around a sanctuary: there they joined in common worship and their representatives took counsel together. The comparison is helpful, provided we do not press it too far and try to find all the features of the Greek amphictyonies in the Israelite federation. The twelve tribes were conscious of the bonds which united them, they shared the same name, and together they formed 'all Israel'.

They acknowledged one and the same God, Yahweh (Jos 24: 18, 21, 24), and celebrated his feasts at the same sanctuary, around the Ark, the symbol of Yahweh's presence in their midst. They shared a common statute and a common law (Jos 24:25) and they assembled to condemn violations of this customary or written law (Jos 24: 26), the 'infamies', the 'things which are not done in Israel' (Jg 19: 30; 20: 6, 10; cf. 2 S 13: 12).

The punishment of the outrage of Gibeah (Jg 19-20) shows us the tribes acting in concert to chastise a particularly odious crime. Apart from such an extreme case, perhaps they settled disputes and points of law by appealing to a judge whose authority was generally recognized: the list of 'lesser' judges (Jg 10: 1-5 and 12: 8-15) would be evidence of this institution.[1]

This may well be true, but the theory that there was a council of tribal representatives is far less probable. The narratives in the Book of Judges present the federation of tribes as a body without any organized government and lacking real political cohesion. The members formed one people and shared one worship, but they had no common head, and the oldest tradition never mentions any personality comparable to Moses or Josue. The editor of Judges has divided out the period between chiefs who are supposed to have reigned successively over all Israel, after liberating it from foreign oppression, but it has long been recognized that this is an artificial presentation. Their activity did sometimes involve a group of tribes (e.g. Gideon, and especially Deborah and Baraq), but this was quite unusual. Nothing is said about their actual functioning as rulers; only their military achievements are recorded and Gideon expressly refused a permanent authority (Jg 8: 22-23). The reign of Abimelek (Jg 9) was an isolated episode which affected only the Canaanite town of Shechem and a few Israelite clans.

However much these 'judges' differed from each other, they had one trait in common: they were chosen by God for a mission of salvation (Jg 3: 9, 15; 4: 7; 6: 14; 13: 5), and they were endowed with the spirit of Yahweh (Jg 3: 10; 6: 34; 11: 29; 13: 25; 14: 6, 19). The only authority manifest in Israel at that time was charismatic. This is an aspect which it is important to note, for it will reappear later.

1. See below, p. 151.

3. The institution of the monarchy

The related kingdoms of Ammon, Moab and Edom had been in existence for many decades when the Israelite federation was still politically shapeless. Suddenly it formed itself into a state, with Saul as the first king of Israel.

The Books of Samuel have preserved two parallel narratives of the institution of the monarchy, one of which is favourable to it (1 S 9: 1-10, 16; 11: 1-11, 15, continued in cc. 13 and 14, except for some additions). The other is opposed to it (1 S 8: 1-22; 10: 18-25, continued in cc. 12 and 15). According to the first account, the initiative came from God, who chose Saul as the liberator of his people (1 S 9: 16); according to the second, the people themselves demanded a king to be 'like the other nations' (1 S 8: 5, 20; cf. Dt 17: 14).

This development was hastened by the danger from Philistia, which threatened all Israel and made common action imperative. The first tradition is to this extent justified. In it Saul appears as one who continues the work of the Judges: like them he is a saviour appointed by God (1 S 9: 16; 10: 1); he receives the spirit of Yahweh (1 S 10: 6, 10; 11: 6); like them he effectively delivers his people (1 S 11: 1-11; cc. 13 and 14). But for the first time in Israel's history, the whole people respond to this choice by God: on the day after his victory over the Ammonites, Saul is acclaimed as king (1 S 10: 6). The 'charismatic leader', the *nagîd*[1] (1 S 9: 16; 10: 1), becomes the *melek*, the king (1 S 11: 15).

This is something quite new. The Israelite federation became a national state, and in the end took its pattern from the related kingdoms beyond the Jordan. This is where the imitation of other nations comes in, as the other tradition tells us. For this state had to have institutions. The 'law of the king' proclaimed by Samuel (1 S 8: 11-17) and written down (1 S 10: 25) is a warning against this imitation of foreign ways. The dynastic principle was no more readily accepted in Israel than in Edom (Gn 36: 31-39): no provision was made for the succession to Saul, and only Abner's personal authority made Ishbaal a puppet king (2 S 2: 8-9), while the men of Judah anointed David (2 S 2: 4). As in the national states, Saul summoned the militia to arms (1 S 11: 7; 15: 4; 17: 2; 28: 4), but against the Philistine commandos he sent troops of the same type, less numerous than the militia, but more experienced in battle (1 S 13: 2, 15; 14: 2); these he recruited specially (1 S 14: 52) with a corps of officers (1 S 18: 5, 13) whom he rewarded with fiefs (1 S 22: 7). It was the beginning of a professional army, a career open to foreign mercenaries (*e.g.* Doeg the Edomite, 1 S 21: 8; 22: 18). Ishbaal inherited his father's bodyguard (2 S 2: 12) and his two troop leaders from Gibeon, Baanah and Rekab (2 S 4: 2).

The institution of the monarchy had sprung from the tribal federation;

1. Cf. p. 70.

under Saul it was still in embryonic form. We do not know what authority Saul exercised apart from his military office. Except for his army commander, Abner (1 S 14: 50), none of his officers are known to us by name. There was no central government, and the tribes, or rather the clans, retained their administrative autonomy. A new and decisive stage was to open with the reign of David.

4. The dual monarchy

One tradition portrays David's kingdom as the continuation of Saul's, with the same charismatic aspect. God, who had rejected Saul, chose David as king over his people (1 S 16: 1). Hence David was anointed by Samuel (1 S 16: 12-13), as Saul had been; the spirit of Yahweh took hold of David (1 S 16: 13) as it had done of Saul. This tradition expresses the deep religious sense always attached to power in Israel; but it bears no direct relation to actual history. David's royal rank, both in its origins and in its developments, was very different from Saul's. David was a captain of mercenaries, at first in Saul's pay (1 S 18: 5), then on his own (1 S 22: 2), and then in the service of the Philistines, who made him prince of Siqlag (1 S 27: 6). After Saul's death he was anointed king, not by a prophet, but by the men of Judah (2 S 2: 4).

From the beginning Judah had had a history of its own. Together with Simeon, the Calebites and the Qenites, it had conquered its own territory, with no assistance from the House of Joseph (Jg 1: 3-19). In the days of the Judges, the Canaanite enclaves (Jerusalem, the Gibeonite towns, Gezer and Ayyalon, Jg 1: 21, 29, 35) formed a barrier between Judah and the northern tribes. This did not prevent religious and personal contacts (Jg 17: 7-8; 19: 1f.), but it did keep Judah apart from the communal life of the tribes: Judah is not even mentioned in the Hymn of Deborah (Jg 5), which praises the tribes taking part in the battle and blames those who did not come.

The rôle ascribed by Jg 20: 18 to Judah as leader of the coalition against Benjamin is an addition, based on Jg 1: 1-2. There was a *rapprochement* in the reign of Saul, who lived close by, in Benjamin, and had a certain authority over Judah (cf. especially 1 S 23: 12, 19f.; 27: 1). Yet Judah retained its separate identity and the division reappeared after Saul's death (2 S 2: 7 and 9). Indeed, to all appearances, David continued to be the vassal of the Philistines at the beginning of his reign in Hebron. Saul, to begin with, had relied on the general militia; David never did. He relied on a guard of mercenaries, even for the capture of Jerusalem (2 S 5: 6f.). Thus David's first kingship was very different from Saul's, and time did not alter the personal character of David's rule. After the murder of Ishbaal and in face of the Philistine menace, the men of Israel acknowledged David as their king, but they did not rally to the kingdom, already established, of Judah, nor was Judah absorbed by the more populous Israel. Just as the men of Judah had anointed David king over the House of Judah (2 S 2: 4), so the elders of Israel anointed him king over

Israel (2 S 5: 3). 2 S 5: 4-5 states clearly that David had reigned seven years and six months over Judah and thirty-three years 'over all Israel *and* over Judah'. When David named Solomon as his successor, he appointed him chief 'over Israel *and* over Judah' (1 K 1: 35). The kingdom of David and Solomon had, of course, a real unity, in the sense that the authority of the same sovereign was acknowledged everywhere, but it comprised two distinct elements. The list of Solomon's prefectures, 1 K 4: 7-19a, omits the territory of Judah, which had a separate administration; it is the 'land' of v. 19b.[1] The same distinction held good in military matters. When David ordered his census of the people for the general levy, two lists were compiled, one for Israel, the other for Judah (2 S 24: 1-9). At the siege of Rabbah, Israel *and* Judah were encamped (2 S 11: 11). The unity of the regime proceeded from the fact that the two states had one and the same sovereign: it was a United Kingdom like England and Scotland before the Act of Union, a Dual Monarchy like the old Austria-Hungary or, to take an example less remote in time and place, a double state like the kingdom of Hamath and La'ash, which is known to us from a Syrian inscription of the eighth century B.C.

Furthermore, the kingdom of David and Solomon was no longer merely a national kingdom. Though some authors have perhaps exaggerated the political influence of those Canaanite enclaves which were subjugated by David and Solomon, David's wars of aggression did bring into his kingdom non-Israelite populations, Philistines, Edomites, Ammonites, Moabites and Aramaeans (2 S 8: 1-14); sometimes their kings were left to rule as vassals (2 S 8: 2; 10: 19; 1 K 2: 39), at other times governors were set over them (2 S 8: 6, 14).

The notion of a national state gave way to that of an empire, which aspired to fill the place left vacant by the decline of Egyptian power. Its success was short-lived and its conquests were partly lost by David's successor (1 K 9: 10f.; 11: 14-25), but the idea of empire persisted, at least as an ideal, under Solomon (1 K 5: 1; 9: 19), who gave it practical expression by large commercial enterprises and by the external splendour of Israel's culture (1 K 9: 26-10: 29). This evolution involved an administrative development which was begun by David (2 S 20: 23-26), and completed by Solomon (1 K 4: 1-6 and 7-19); it was modelled, it seems, on the Egyptian administration.[2]

5. The kingdoms of Israel and Judah

This Dual Monarchy and this attempt at empire lasted only two generations. On Solomon's death, Israel and Judah parted company, and formed two national states, with their external provinces ever diminishing. But the notion of the State was rather different in the two kingdoms. In Israel the charismatic aspect of Saul's period was revived. The throne was promised

---

1. Cf. p. 135.   2. Cf. pp. 127ff.

to the first king, Jeroboam, by a prophet speaking in the name of Yahweh (1 K 11: 31, 37); later, Jeroboam was acknowledged by the people (1 K 12: 20). In the same way Jehu was named as king by Yahweh (1 K 19: 16), anointed by a disciple of Eliseus (2 K 9: 1f.), and acclaimed by the army (2 K 9: 13). God himself made and unmade the kings of Israel (1 K 14: 7f.; 16: 1f.; 21: 20f.; 2 K 9: 7f.; cf. Os 13: 11). But Osee also accuses the people of having made kings without God's sanction (Os 8: 4). The principle of hereditary succession was never recognized in Israel before Omri, and the dynastic principle was never taken for granted. Omri's dynasty lasted some forty years, Jehu's a century, thanks to the long reign of Jeroboam II, after which six kings, four of whom were assassinated, succeeded each other in twenty years; and then the kingdom was conquered by Assyria.

The kingdom of Judah presents a striking contrast. There the dynastic principle was admitted from the outset, and sanctioned by divine intervention: the prophecy of Nathan promised David a house and kingdom which would endure for ever (2 S 7: 8-16). God's choice, which in the days of the Judges, and at intervals in Israel, picked out an individual, here lights on a particular family; and once the choice was made, the succession followed human rules. There is no dispute round David's deathbed about the dynastic principle, but only as to which of David's sons is to succeed him, and it is David himself, not Yahweh, who names Solomon (1 K 1: 28-35). Later on, Judah, in contrast to Israel, accepts Roboam, Solomon's son, without dispute (1 K 12: 1-20). There were palace revolutions in plenty in Judah, but the Davidic line was always maintained, thanks to the loyalty of the 'people of the land', the nation (2 K 11: 13-20; 14: 21; 21: 24; 23: 30).

It is probable that if our information about the two kingdoms was fuller and more balanced, other institutional differences would come to light. One fact at any rate is very clear: Israel and Judah are sometimes allies, sometimes enemies, but they are always independent of each other, and other nations treat them as distinct entities. This political dualism, however, does not prevent the inhabitants feeling themselves to be one people; they are brethren (1 K 12: 24; cf. 2 Ch 28: 11), they have national traditions in common, and the Books of Kings, by their synchronized presentation of the history of Judah and Israel, claim to tell the story of one people. This people is united by its religion. Like a man of God before him, who came from Judah (1 K 13: 1f.) Amos the man of Judah preached at Bethel, in spite of the opposition of Amasias, who wanted to send him back to Judah (Am 7: 10-13). In the Temple of Jerusalem, worship was offered to 'Yahweh, the God of Israel'. Political conditions may frequently lead writers to contrast 'Israel', *i.e.* the northern kingdom with 'Judah'; but 'Israel' always retained its wider connotation and Is 8: 14 speaks of the 'two houses of Israel'. Thus, all through the political separation of the monarchy, there survived the religious idea of the federation of the Twelve Tribes, and the Prophets looked forward to its reunion in the future.

6. *The post-exilic community*

The fall of Jerusalem marked the end of Israel's political institutions. Henceforth Judaea was an integral part of the successive empires, Neo-Babylonian, Persian and Seleucid, which subjected it to the customary law of their provinces; even when the Hasmonaeans laid claim to the title of king, they were still vassals. Old customs were maintained, no doubt, at a municipal level, by the clans, *mishpahoth*, and their elders, *z'qenîm*, who represented the people before the authorities (Esd 5: 9; 6: 7), but there was no longer any idea of a State. Within the limits of what cultural and religious autonomy was left to them, the Jews formed a religious community, ruled by its own religious law under the government of their priests. It was a theo-cratic regime, and here again an ancient idea was reaffirmed and restated: Israel had God for king (Ex 15: 18; Nb 23:21; Jg 8:23; 1 S 8: 7; 12: 12; 1 K 22: 19; Is 6: 5). The idea was often expressed during and after the Exile, in the second part of Isaias (Is 41: 21; 43: 15; 44: 6) and in the Psalms about the reign of Yahweh (Ps 47; 93; 96-99). The kings who had governed Israel were only his viceroys (1 Ch 17: 14; 28: 5; 2 Ch 9: 8). The Chronicler, reviewing the history of his people, saw in the reign of David the realization of this kingdom of God on earth (1 Ch 11-29), and believed that the Jewish com-munity of the Return, that of Zorobabel and Nehemias, approximated to that ideal (Ne 12: 44-47).

7. *Was there an Israelite idea of the State?*

Clearly we cannot speak of *one* Israelite idea of the State. The federation of the Twelve Tribes, the kingship of Saul, that of David and Solomon, the kingdoms of Israel and Judah, the post-exilic community, all these are so many different regimes. We may even go further and say that there never was any Israelite idea of the State. Neither the federation of the Tribes nor the post-exilic community were states. Between the two, the monarchy, in its varying forms, held its ground for three centuries over the tribes of the North, for four and a half over Judah, but it is hard to say how far it pene-trated or modified the people's mentality. The post-exilic community returned to the pre-monarchical type of life with remarkable ease; this suggests some continuity of institutions at the level of clan and town. This municipal life is also the only aspect of public life considered by the legisla-tive texts. There is indeed the 'law of the king' (Dt 17: 14-20), and the 'rights of the king' in 1 S 8: 11-18 (cf. 10: 25), but these in no way resemble political charters. These texts accept the fact of kingship as something tolerated by Yahweh (1 S 8: 7-9) or as subordinate to his choice (Dt 17: 15); they warn against imitating aliens (1 S 8: 5; Dt 17: 14), and the evil which kingship entails (1 S 8: 11-18; Dt 17: 16-17). And that is all. To study royal institutions we must glean what occasional information we can from the historical books.

One current of opinion was hostile to the monarchy. It can be seen in one of the traditions about the institution of the kingdom (1 S 8: 1-22; 10: 18-25), in the omissions in Dt 17: 14-20, in the denunciations of Osee (Os 7: 3-7; 8: 4, 10; 10: 15; 13: 9-11), and Ezechiel (Ez 34: 1-10; 43: 7-9), who allots only a very obscure rôle to the 'prince' (he avoids the word 'king') in his programme of future restoration (Ez 45: 7f., 17, 22f.). The Deuteronomic editor of the Books of Kings condemns all the kings of Israel and nearly all those of Judah.

On the other hand there is a stream of thought which is favourable to it; it finds expression in the other tradition on the institution of the kingdom (1 S 9: 1-10: 16; 11: 1-11, 15) in all the passages glorifying David and his dynasty, from Nathan's prophecy onwards (2 S 7: 8-16), in the royal psalms (Ps 2; 18; 20; 21, etc.), and in all the texts on the royal Messiah, which proclaim that the future Saviour will be a descendant of David, a king after the image, idealized, of the great king of Israel (Is 7: 14; 9: 5-6; 11: 1-5; Jr 23: 5; Mi 5: 1; cf. the Messianic adaptation of the royal psalms).

But these two opposite convictions are inspired by the same conception of power, one which is fundamental to Israelite thought, the conception of theocracy. Israel is Yahweh's people and has no other master but him. That is why from the beginning to the end of its history Israel remained a religious community.

It was religion which federated the tribes when they settled in Canaan, as it was to gather the exiles on their return from Babylon. It was religion which preserved the unity of the nation under the monarchy, in spite of the division of the kingdoms. The human rulers of this people are chosen, accepted or tolerated by God, but they remain subordinate to him and they are judged by the degree of their fidelity to the indissoluble covenant between Yahweh and his people. In this view of things the State, which in practice means the monarchy, is merely an accessory element; in actual fact Israel lived without it for the greater part of its history. All this should warn us against the tendency of a certain modern school of thought to attach too much importance, in the study of Israel's religion, to what is called 'the ideology of kingship'.

CHAPTER FIVE

THE PERSON OF THE KING

THE fact remains that, for a period of several centuries, Israel lived under a monarchy, and this is precisely the period when its political organization is best known. Moreover, royal institutions had an undeniable influence on some of Israel's religious conceptions, though this influence may have been exaggerated by a recent school of exegesis. We must therefore devote some attention to them. Unfortunately our information is one-sided; it is mainly about Judah, from which most of our documents have come, and we have just seen that Israel held another view of the royal power. Moreover, it is incomplete, because the Biblical writers were not specially interested in studying institutions. We can of course make good this deficiency by examining the organization of the neighbouring countries, which is sometimes better known; this can be very helpful, but then we run the risk of attributing to Israel ideas or customs which were foreign to it.

1. *Accession to the throne*

We have seen that while the dynastic principle was never really accepted in the northern kingdom, it was always observed in Judah. Even in Judah, however, accession to the throne implies a divine choice: a man is 'king by the grace of God', not only because God made a covenant with the dynasty of David, but because his choice was exercised at each accession. If the kingdom descended to Solomon and not to his elder brother Adonias, it was 'because it came to him from Yahweh' (1 K 2: 15; cf. 1 Ch 28: 5), and, as we shall see, every enthronement meant a renewal of the Davidic covenant and an adoption of the new sovereign by Yahweh. This idea of divine choice is universal in the ancient East. It is affirmed in Mesopotamia, even when a king succeeds his father, as was the ordinary rule, and at all periods, from Gudea, who is 'the shepherd designed by Ningirsu in his heart', down to Nabonidus, whom 'Sin and Nergal chose to reign when he was yet in his mother's womb', and Cyrus, of whom a Babylonian document says, 'Marduk chose his name for the kingdom over the world.' With this we naturally compare Is 44: 28, 'It is I (Yahweh) who say to Cyrus: My shepherd', and Is 45: 1, 'Thus says Yahweh to Cyrus his anointed.' The idea is carried to extremes in Egypt, where every king is held to be a son of Ra, the sun-god. In the

Aramaean kingdoms of Syria, Zakir, king of Hamath and La'ash, says: 'Ba'al Shamaïn called me and stood by me, and Ba'al Shamaïn has made me king.' This Zakir was a usurper, but Bar-Rekub, king of Senjirli, was a legitimate heir, yet he said: 'My master Rekub-el has made me sit on the throne of my father.'

The dynastic principle does not necessarily involve primogeniture, but this was probably the rule among the Hittites, though not, apparently, in the Aramaean kingdoms of Syria. In Egypt and Assyria the father was usually, though not always, succeeded by his eldest son. The king appointed the heir-apparent and took him as a partner in the government during his lifetime. Similarly, at Ugarit the king appointed the heir from among his sons. In Israel too, primogeniture was a title to the succession, but appointment by the king was also required (2 Ch 21: 3), for the king was not bound to choose his eldest son. Though Adonias, the eldest surviving son of David, hoped to be king (1 K 2: 15 and 22), and was supported by a whole party (1 K 1: 5-9; 2: 22), a rival party supported Solomon (1 K 1: 10). It lay with David to choose his successor (1 K 1: 20, 27), and he chose the younger son, Solomon (1 K 1: 17, 30). Joachaz succeeded Josias, although he had an elder brother, who was later placed on the throne by the Pharaoh and given the name Joiaqim (2 K 23: 31 and 36). It is possible that this choice between the sons took place only if the first-born, the normal heir, was dead: with Solomon this would be Amnon, and with Joachaz it was the Yohanan mentioned in 1 Ch 3: 15, of whom nothing is said at the time of the succession. This seems to have been the custom also in Assyria. But the situation was complicated when a king had several wives: Roboam preferred Maakah, although she was not his first wife (compare David and Bathsheba) and he gave Abiyyah, Maakah's eldest son, precedence over his brothers, in the hope that he would be king (2 Ch 11: 21-22).

Solomon was anointed king during the lifetime of his father (1 K 1: 32-40), who did not die until some time later (1 K 2: 1-10). Similarly Yotham assumed power when his father Ozias became a leper (2 K 15: 5), but we are not told that he was at once anointed. These are the only two co-regencies expressly mentioned in the Bible, though there may have been others not mentioned. Some modern historians list a whole series of them: Josaphat, Ozias and Manasseh in Judah, and Jeroboam II in Israel, are all said to have reigned at the same time as their fathers. But these are only hypotheses whose main purpose is to harmonize the discordant data of Biblical chronology. In the two certain cases, Solomon and Yotham assumed power because their fathers were too old or too ill to rule; the term co-regency is therefore some-what inaccurate, and the situation is not quite the same as in Egypt or Assyria.

Women were excluded from the succession. In the kingdom of Israel, Joram succeeded his brother Ochozias because the latter died without male descendants (2 K 1: 17; cf. 3: 1). In Judah, Athaliah seized power on the death of her son and reigned for seven years, but her reign was regarded as unlawful and was terminated by a revolution (2 K 11).

2. The coronation rites

We possess two fairly detailed accounts of an enthronement, concerning Solomon (1 K 1: 32-48) and Joas (2 K 11: 12-20). Both situations are exceptional: Solomon's accession was the last event in a long intrigue and took place in his father's lifetime, while the accession of Joas brought to an end the usurpation of Athaliah. Though a century and a half passed between the two coronations, the two rites are so similar that they must represent the general custom, at least in Judah. There were two parts to the ceremony, the first of which was performed in the sanctuary, and the second in the royal palace. It included the following: investiture with the insignia (not mentioned for Solomon), anointing, acclamation, enthronement, homage of the high officials (not mentioned for Joas). We shall consider these points in order.

(a) *The setting: the sanctuary.* Solomon was consecrated at Gihon, the spring of Jerusalem. Is it because water played a part in the ceremonies, as in the rites of purification before the coronation of the Pharaoh? Some authors, interpreting Ps 110 as a coronation psalm, point to the allusion in v. 7: 'He drinks of the brook by the wayside', but it is a most flimsy theory. It is much more likely that Solomon was consecrated at Gihon because the sanctuary of the Ark was there. We are in fact told that when Sadoq came to Gihon he took the horn of oil 'in the tent' and anointed Solomon (1 K 1: 39): this, then, would be the tent which David had erected for the Ark (2 S 6: 17), and the 'tent of Yahweh' where Joab sought refuge (1 K 2: 28), and near it would be the altar at which Adonias (who was quite near by, at the Fuller's spring, 1 K 1: 9) took refuge on hearing that Solomon had been enthroned in the palace (1 K 1: 49-50). Joas was consecrated in the Temple, where, we presume, the consecration of the other kings of Judah after Solomon took place.

According to 2 K 11: 14, during the ceremony Joas remained 'standing near the pillar, as the custom was'. We may compare this with 2 K 23: 3, which shows us Josias 'standing near the pillar' during the reading of the law: the parallel passage 2 Ch 34: 31 merely says 'in his place'. Writing of Joas, 2 Ch 23: 13 adds the detail that this place was 'near the entrance'. So we may connect it with the 'king's dais' (in Greek) and the 'entrance for the king', which Achaz took out of the Temple to gratify the king of Assyria (2 K 16: 18). This dais is perhaps the one which Solomon erected in the middle of the court, according to 2 Ch 6: 13. This detail is illustrated by two stelae, one from Ras Shamra and one of Egyptian origin, which show the king (or a worshipper?) standing on a pedestal before an image of the God. We may then ask ourselves whether, in 2 K 11 : 14; 23 : 3 and 2 Ch 23 : 13, we should not translate 'on the dais' instead of 'near the pillar'. One fact is certain, that a special place was reserved for the king in the Temple, just as there was a place for the Pharaoh in the Egyptian temples; the new king stood in this place during the ceremonies of consecration.

(b) *The investiture with the insignia*. According to 2 K 11 : 12, the priest Yehoyada gave Joas the *nezer* and the *'edûth*. The meaning of *nezer* is certain: it is the diadem or crown, which is the royal emblem par excellence (2 S 1 : 10; Jr 13 : 18; Ez 21 : 30-31; Ps 89 : 40; 132 : 18). The word *'edûth* is more difficult: it means 'testimony' or 'solemn law', and is usually corrected to *s͑adôth*, 'bracelets'. And in fact, in 2 S 1 : 10, Saul's diadem and bracelets, which would have been royal insignia, are brought to David. But perhaps in the sacring rite we ought to keep *'edûth*. We find that Ps 89 : 40 gives 'diadem' as a parallel to the 'covenant', *b͑rîth*; now *b͑rîth* is sometimes synonymous with *'edûth*. Another synonym is *hôq*, 'decree'; Ps 2 : 6-7 speaks of the sacring of the king and the 'decree' of Yahweh. We may compare it with the 'protocol' mentioned by Egyptian enthronement rites, which was supposed to have been written by the hand of the god: *e.g.* Thutmoses III says: 'He has put my diadem on me and established my protocol', which would be a good parallel to 2 K 11 : 12. This protocol contained the Pharaoh's coronation names, the affirmation of his divine sonship and power; it was an act of legitimation. It may be that the new king of Judah was given a similar testimony affirming his adoption by God and promising him victory over his enemies, in the manner of Yahweh's 'decree' in Ps 2 : 7-9, or recalling the covenant between Yahweh and the house of David (2 S 7 : 8-16; Ps 89 : 20-38; 132 : 11-12, where the word *'edûth* occurs).

In Egypt it was the bestowal of the crowns and sceptres of Upper and Lower Egypt which made a man Pharaoh. In Assyria, the crown and sceptre were placed on cushions in front of the god; the priest crowned the king and handed him the sceptre. The Israelite accounts of enthronement do not mention a sceptre: it is not an exclusively royal emblem, there is no special name for it, and when it is carried by the king it seems to signify his executive power (Ps 2 : 9; 110 : 2) and his functions as judge (Ps 45 : 7).

(c) *The anointing*. The coronation or imposition of the diadem does not appear in Solomon's sacring, as it does in that of Joas, but the two accounts agree on the essential rite of anointing (1 K 1 : 39; 2 K 11 : 12). It is mentioned from the beginning of the monarchy, for Saul (1 S 9 : 16; 10 : 1), for David as king of Judah (2 S 2 : 4), then as king of Israel (2 S 5 : 3), in addition to the special tradition in 1 S 16 : 13. Apart from Solomon and Joas, it recurs in the story of Absalom's usurpation (2 S 19 : 11); it is recorded of Joachaz in the kingdom of Judah (2 K 23 : 30), and of Jehu in Israel (2 K 9 : 3, 6). But it is certain that all the kings of Judah were anointed, and it is probably true of all the kings of Israel. The prophet Samuel anointed Saul (1 S 10: 1) and David (according to the tradition of 1 S 16: 13). Jehu was anointed by a disciple of Eliseus. A priest anointed Solomon, according to 1 K 1: 39 (though v. 34 speaks of Sadoq and Nathan, a priest and a prophet) and Joas (2 K 11: 12). In the other instances the texts use a plural verb, but the rite was obviously performed by a single officiant, who was a religious personage. There can be no doubt that all the kings of Judah were consecrated in the Temple and anointed by a priest.

Anointing is a religious rite. It is accompanied by a coming of the Spirit: we would say that it confers a grace. Thus the spirit of God took hold of Saul after he was anointed (1 S 10: 10), and in the story of David the link between the two is even more direct according to 1 S 16: 13. The king is the Anointed of Yahweh (1 S 24: 7, 11; 26: 9, 11, 16, 23; 2 S 1: 14, 16 (Saul); 2 S 19: 22 (David); Lm 4: 20 (Sedecias); cf. 1 S 2: 10; 12: 3, 5; 2 S 22: 51; Ps 18: 51; 20: 7; 84: 10; 89: 39, 52; 132: 10). The king, a consecrated person, thus shares in the holiness of God; he is inviolable. David refuses to raise a finger against Saul because he is Yahweh's Anointed (1 S 24: 7, 11; 26: 9, 11, 23), and he executes the man who had dared to lift his hand against the king (2 S 1: 14, 16).

The anointing of a king is not, however, a rite peculiar to Israel. Yotham's fable about the kingship of Abimelek (Jg 9: 8, 15), shows that the rite existed in Canaan before the establishment of the Israelite monarchy, and the command to Elias to go and anoint Hazael as king of Aram (1 K 19: 15), may indicate that the rite was practised at Damascus, though this is not borne out either by the account of Hazael's accession (2 K 8: 9-15) or by the non-biblical documents. Concerning Canaan, extra-biblical documents do exist, though they are not all equally convincing. There is a text from Ras Shamra which may contain an allusion to the anointing of Baal as king, but the text is mutilated and its meaning uncertain. One of the Amarna letters tells us that the kings of Syria and Palestine were anointed as vassals of the Pharaoh, and an Egyptian balsam vase found in one of the royal tombs at Byblos may have served for such an investiture. These facts suggest an Egyptian practice rather than a native custom: we know from other sources that the high officials in Egypt were anointed on appointment to office, but the Pharaohs were not. The kings in Mesopotamia do not seem to have been anointed: the only text which might be quoted is of doubtful value: it is a mutilated passage of the Assyrian royal ritual, which may refer to anointing. Hittite kings, on the other hand, were anointed with 'the holy oil of kingship', and in their titles these sovereigns are styled, 'Tabarna, the Anointed, the Great King, etc.'

Was anointing, in Israel, a strictly royal rite? In 1 K 19: 15-16 God commands Elias to go and anoint Hazael, Jehu . . . and Eliseus. Hazael was to be king of Syria, Jehu would be anointed king of Israel by a disciple of Eliseus, but we hear nothing of the anointing of Eliseus or of any other prophet. Here the word was demanded by the context and is used metaphorically. In Is 61: 1, 'anointed' is used figuratively and signifies the prophet's consecration to Yahweh(cf.Jr. 1: 5).The same figurative use is found in Ps 105: 15=1 Ch 16: 22, where the Patriarchs are called 'anointed' and 'prophets'.

Many passages, however, say that priests were anointed, and according to Ex 40: 12-15, it was this anointing which conferred on them the priesthood in perpetuity, from generation to generation. These passages all belong to the Priestly tradition, and in them we can distinguish two parallel series of texts: in one, anointing is reserved to the high priest alone (Ex 29: 4-9; Lv 4: 3, 5, 16; 6: 13 (retaining the singular), 15; 8: 12; 16: 32), while in the other it is received by all priests (Ex 28: 41; 30: 30; 40: 12-15; Lv 7: 35-36; 10: 7; Nb 3: 3).

Everyone admits that all these texts were edited after the Exile. Before this the historical and prophetical books never mention the anointing of priests, not even of the high priest. It is therefore possible that, after the disappearance of the monarchy, the royal anointing was transferred to the high priest as head of the people, and later extended to all the priests. One should note, however, that, apart from these texts from the Pentateuch, there is no certain evidence for the anointing of priests before the Hellenistic period. Za 4: 14, it is true, speaks of the 'two sons of the oil', who are probably Josue and Zorobabel, the spiritual and temporal heads of the community; but even if we grant that this unusual expression refers to an anointing (which is a moot point), it is certain that Zorobabel was never anointed, and consequently we cannot conclude that the high priest Josue was ever anointed either. There remains the uncertain text of 1 Ch 29: 22, which mentions an anointing of Sadoq as priest, along with that of Solomon as king. This text only tells us how the practice of former times was then pictured (cf. the texts just quoted from the Pentateuch referring to Aaron), but it is no evidence of contemporary practice. On the contrary, the 'anointed prince' of Dn 9: 25 is probably the high priest Onias III, and the 'race of anointed priests' in 2 M 1: 10 is apparently that of the high priests. But the custom of anointing priests had ceased by the Roman era, and the Rabbis even thought that it had never been practised throughout the period of the Second Temple. Hence it is hard to say at what period the high priest or the priests in general were anointed, though it is clear that it was not under the monarchy.[1] In those days the king was the only Anointed One.

We have stressed somewhat this problem of anointing, because of its religious implications. Anointing, as we shall see, made the king a sacred person and empowered him to perform certain religious acts. Further, 'Anointed' and 'Messiah' are synonyms, being respectively the translation and the transliteration of the same Hebrew word, *mashiah*. The reigning king is therefore a Messiah, and we shall see that he is also a saviour.

These elements were to combine in the expectation of a future saviour who

1. Cf. pp. 399-400.

would be the Messiah King. But it was only in the last century before Christ, in the apocryphal Psalms of Solomon, that this combination became explicit and that the long-promised, long-expected saviour was called the Anointed, the Messiah.

(d) *The acclamation.* After the anointing, the new sovereign was acclaimed. The horn or the trumpet was sounded, the people clapped their hands and shouted: 'Long live the king!' (1 K 1: 34, 39; 2 K 11: 12, 14; cf. 2 K 9: 13). It is the same shout which the rebels must have raised at the banquet of Adonias (1 K 1: 25), and which greeted the appointment of Saul at Mispah (1 S 10: 24). This was the cry of Hushai when he pretended to go over to Absalom (2 S 16: 16).

This acclamation does not mean that the people chose the king, but that the people accepted the choice made by Yahweh and made effective by the anointing: the shout of 'Long live the king!' is not a wish, it is an acquiescence (cf. 'Jehu is king' after the anointing and the sounding of the horn in 2 K 9: 13). Men recognize the king's authority and submit to it. The same meaning must be given to similar expressions such as the greeting: 'May the king live for ever!' (1 K 1: 31), or the oaths by the life of the king (1 S 17: 55; 2 S 14: 19). This oath is sometimes coupled with one by the life of Yahweh (2 S 11: 11; 15: 21), and this double formula makes the king's authority parallel to that of God.

(e) *The enthronement.* After the acclamation all left the sanctuary and entered the palace, where the new king took his seat on the throne (1 K 1: 46, Solomon; 2 K 11: 19, Joas). This action marks the assumption of power, and 'to sit on the throne' becomes a synonym for 'to begin to reign' (1 K 16: 11; 2 K 13: 13). The same expressions recur in other Eastern cultures and in our modern languages. Thus the throne becomes the symbol of royal power (Gn 41: 40; Ps 45: 7), and is sometimes almost personified (2 S 14: 9). It is still called the throne of David, when speaking of his successors the kings of Judah (1 K 2: 24, 45; Is 9: 6; Jr 13: 13; 17: 25), to mark the permanence of the Davidic dynasty promised by Nathan's prophecy, 'Your throne shall be established for ever' (2 S 7: 16; cf. Ps 89: 5; 132: 11-12).

Solomon's throne of gold and ivory is described in 1 K 10: 18-20 as one of the wonders of the world; its back was surmounted by bulls' heads, two standing lions served as arm-rests and it was approached by six steps flanked by figures of lions. The thrones of gods or kings which archaeologists have unearthed provide analogies which illustrate this description, and there is no need to look for a cosmic symbolism, as some have done.

As Yahweh was held to be the true king of Israel,[1] the royal throne is called 'the throne of Yahweh' (1 Ch 29: 23), and more explicitly, 'the throne of the kingship of Yahweh over Israel' (1 Ch 28: 5). This throne of Yahweh had Justice and Right for its supports (Ps 89: 15; 97: 2). The king's throne, too,

1. Cf. p. 98.

was firmly established on justice (Pr 16: 12; 25: 5; 29: 14; cf. Ps 72: 1-2), or on right and justice (Is 9: 6).

(f) *The homage.* When the king had taken possession of his throne, the high officials came to do him homage (1 K 1: 47). This homage is mentioned only in the account of Solomon, but it must have taken place at every accession: the ministers made acts of obedience and the new sovereign confirmed them in their offices. Here the Assyrian royal ritual had a picturesque ceremony: the officials laid their insignia before the king, and then ranged themselves round in any order, without regard for precedence. The king then said: 'Let every man resume his office', and every one resumed his insignia and his place in the hierarchy.

3. *The coronation name*

At the coronation of the Pharaoh his full set of titles was proclaimed, comprising five names, of which the last two were the names of accession and of birth, each inscribed on a cartouche. In ancient Mesopotamia an old coronation text of Uruk says that the goddess Ishtar takes away the king's 'name of lowliness' and calls him by his 'name of lordship'. But the Assyrian royal ritual says nothing of a change of name, and one must not draw too sweeping a conclusion from expressions like those of Assurbanipal in his inscriptions: 'Assur and Sin have pronounced my name for power.' This is probably no more than a way of signifying predestination by God; we may compare a Babylonian text about Cyrus: 'Marduk has pronounced his name, Cyrus of Anshan, and has appointed his name for kingship over the world.' Consequently, it is not proved that the kings of Assyria took a new name at their coronation. Asarhaddon certainly received a new name when he became heir-apparent, but this name was hardly ever used in his reign. There remain three instances which are clearer: Tiglath-Pileser III took the name of Pulu when he became king of Babylon (cf. the Pul in the Bible, 2 K 15: 19; 1 Ch 5: 26), Salmanasar V reigned at Babylon under the name of Ululai, and Assurbanipal called himself Kandalanu at Babylon; perhaps they were conforming to a custom of Lower Mesopotamia. Several Hittite kings were known by two names, but as both names are used in official texts dating from their reigns, they cannot be birth and coronation names.

In Israel, the Messianic titles given to the child, probably the Emmanuel, whose birth is foretold in Is 9: 5, have been compared with the five names of the Egyptian protocol: there are in fact four double names, and perhaps the trace of a fifth. This is very probably a literary imitation of an Egyptian custom, but it does not justify the conclusion that the kings of Israel were given a similar set of titles at their accession.

On the other hand there are two certain instances of a change of name. When the Pharaoh made Elyaqim king, he gave him the name of Joiaqim (2 K 23: 34), and Mattanyah, placed on the throne by the king of Babylon, was named

Sedecias (2 K 24: 17). The two cases are similar in that each time a foreign suzerain intervenes, whereas Joiakin came to the throne between these two king without his suzerain intervening and with no mention of a change of name. The change might then be a mark of the bond of vassalage, except that one would expect the Pharaoh to give his vassal an Egyptian name (cf. Gn 41: 45), and the king of Babylon a Babylonian name (cf. Dn 1: 7), whereas the new names of these two kings are just as Hebrew and even Yahwist as those they had before. It is therefore possible that the change was an Israelite custom accepted by the foreign master.

If this is so, the kings of Judah—we find nothing similar in Israel—may have been given a coronation name or a reigning name, and this conclusion seems to be confirmed by other texts. Besides general expressions like 2 S 7: 9; 1 Ch 17: 8 (literally, 'I will make you a [great] name'), which have their equivalents in Egypt, certain facts are significant. To begin with the most cogent, the son and successor of Josias is called Joachaz in 2 K 23: 30, 31, 34, but Shallum in Jr 22: 11, and the list of Josias' sons in 1 Ch 3: 15 contains no Joachaz but does contain a Shallum. May this not be the birth name, and Joachaz the reigning name? We know that the successor of Amasias is some-times called Ozias and sometimes Azarias in the accounts of 2 K 14: 21—15: 34, but the prophets always call him Ozias (Is 1: 1; 6: 1; 7: 1; Os 1: 1; Am 1: 1; Za 14: 5), and so does 2 Ch 26, every time, in the account of his reign. Yet he is called Azarias in the genealogy of 1 Ch 3: 12. We may therefore conclude that Azarias was his birth name and Ozias his coronation name. According to 2 S 12: 24-25 the child of David and Bathsheba received the name of Solomon from his mother, but the prophet Nathan called him Yedidyah. It is curious that this latter name never appears again: could it have been his birth name, displaced by his reigning name? A still more hazardous conjecture is to consider David as the coronation name, in fact a royal title, of the first king of Israel, whose birth name was Elhanan: the same Elhanan who slew Goliath according to 2 S 21: 19, and the same as that Baalhanan, who, according to Gn 36: 38-39, reigned over Edom after a certain Saul.

If we have no more or no clearer examples, the reason may be that the reigning name, the only official one, almost always completely displaced the name given at birth, so that it was no longer even remembered. But in every instance we are still in the realm of hypothesis: the most one can say is that it is probable, though not certain, that the kings of Judah took a new name when they succeeded to the throne.

4. The enthronement psalms

The crowning of the king was accompanied by popular demonstrations. Besides the cry of 'Long live the king!' there was cheering, and playing on the flute and trumpet (1 K 1: 40; 2 K 11: 13-14). This music and cheering evidently provided an accompaniment to songs praising the new ruler, as in such demonstrations in the East to-day. Some of the 'royal' psalms may have been composed and sung in this most solemn of settings, as Ps 45 was composed for a royal wedding. The question concerns chiefly Ps 2 and 110, which seem to allude to the rites of enthronement.

In Ps 2, in reply to the princes of the earth who have conspired against Yahweh and his Anointed (v. 2), Yahweh declares that it is he who has established his king in Sion (v. 6). The king (or the cantor) then proclaims the decree, the *ḥôq*, of Yahweh: on this day of sacring he adopts him as his son and promises him dominion over all the land (vv. 7-9). Then the kings pay homage to him (v. 12). In this psalm, then, we find the anointing, the 'decree' (which is the equivalent of the 'testimony' delivered to Joas, 2 K 11: 12, and of the 'covenant' with the house of David, 2 S 7: 8-16[1]), and finally the homage. The supposed revolt of the vassal kings is understandable at the time of a change of reign, and has a parallel in the sham fight which was performed in Egypt at coronation feasts. The question of adoption will be considered later.[2]

In Ps 110, Yahweh seats the king on his right hand (v. 1), promises him the sceptre of power (v. 2), declares that he has begotten him (v. 3, according to the Greek, the text being corrupt and disputed), and declares him a priest after the order of Melchisedech (v. 4); the king slays his enemies, he is 'arbiter of the nations' (vv. 5-6). Here again we see the enthronement, the investiture, the promises and probably the adoption. The allusion to the priesthood of Melchisedech will be discussed later.[3]

These two psalms are therefore close akin and would be appropriate to a sacring feast. Against this it may be objected that the New Testament uses them as Messianic psalms, and that part of the Jewish tradition and all Christian tradition interpret them as such. Some writers point out that the psalmist could not promise universal empire to the human king of the little kingdom of Judah, and that he certainly could not address him as Yahweh's son. Yet there is nothing here which goes beyond the expressions of court etiquette, or the ideas the Israelites held about their king. On the first point, there are numerous parallels from other Eastern sources, but we need only recall the 'Psalm of David' (2 S 22 = Ps 18), in which the king sings of his victories over all his enemies in terms very like those of Ps 2 and 110, or the expressions of the royal wedding song in Ps 45, which also allude to the sacring, or the good wishes expressed at the accession of Solomon (1 K 1: 37 and 47). The title of 'son' is found in Nathan's prophecy (2 S 7: 14), where the primary reference is to the human king descended from David, as the next words (vv. 14b-15) show. Moreover, the terms of this prophecy are applied explicitly to Solomon by 1 Ch 17: 13; 22: 10; 28: 6. The two aspects

1. Cf. p. 103.   2. Cf. p. 111.   3. Cf. p. 114.

of universal dominion and divine adoption are combined in the commentary on this prophecy given in Ps 89: 20-38.

Other psalms, too, may have been sung on this occasion, even though they did not contain express references to the ceremonies of the day. Ps 72, for example, prays that the king may reign in justice and foretells that he will rule to the ends of the earth, and Ps 101 draws a portrait of the righteous prince.

It has been maintained that Ps 2, 72 and 110 were at first royal psalms, and were modified after the Exile in a Messianic sense; but it is very hard to say what the revisions were. It is more reasonable to suppose that these psalms, like Nathan's prophecy and other texts referring to royal Messianism, had a twofold meaning from the moment of their composition: every king of the Davidic line is a figure and a shadow of the ideal king of the future. In fact, none of these kings attained this ideal, but at the moment of enthronement, at each renewal of the Davidic covenant, the same hope was expressed, in the belief that one day it would be fulfilled. All these texts, then, are Messianic, for they contain a prophecy and a hope of salvation, which an individual chosen by God will bring to fulfilment.

5. The king as saviour

The king is *ipso facto* a saviour. It is a common idea among primitive peoples that the king embodies the good estate of his subjects: the country's prosperity depends on him, and he ensures the welfare of his people. The idea is common in Eastern countries, too. In Egypt, to cite only two examples, there is a hymn about Senusret III which reads: 'He has come to us, he has brought the people of Egypt to life, he has done away with their afflictions.' Another hymn describes the reign of Ramses IV in these words:

Those who had fled returned to their towns, those who had hidden showed themselves again;
those who had been hungry were fed, those who had been thirsty were given drink;
those who had been naked were clad, those who had been ragged were clothed in fine garments;
those who were in prison were set free, those who were in bonds were filled with joy . . .

In Mesopotamia, Assurbanipal says: 'From the moment that Assur, Sin, etc., placed me on the throne, Adad made his rain fall, Ea opened her springs, the corn grew five cubits high, the harvest of the land has been abundant.' Adad-shum-usur, a priest, wrote to the same king: 'Shamash and Adad . . . have destined for my lord the king . . . good government, days of justice, years of righteousness, abundant rains, powerful floods, good commerce . . . ; those who have been ill for many days are cured. The hungry are satisfied, the starved grow fat. . . . Women give birth, and in their joy tell their children: our lord the king has given you life.'

It is not surprising, then, to find similar developments of thought in Israel. So we read in Ps 72:

He will judge the lowly among the people with justice,
  he will prove himself a saviour to the children of the poor,
  and will crush their oppressors.

He will come down like gentle rain upon grass,
  like the showers which soften the earth.
In his days justice shall blossom forth,
  and widespread peace, until the moon be no more.

He will set free the poor who call for help,
  and the lowly, who stand helpless, alone;
he will show mercy to the weak and the poor,
  and will save the life of the poor.

Abundance of wheat on the earth,
  even on the tops of the hills!
Abundance like Lebanon's, when its fruit is awaking,
  and its flowering, like grass over the earth!

Just as in former times the Judges had been 'saviours' (Jg 3: 9, 15), so under the monarchy the king delivered the nation from its enemies (2 S 19: 10); he was a 'saviour' (2 K 13: 5), whom men called to their aid (2 K 6: 26).

6. Divine adoption

Some recent writers go further, and speak of the king's divine character, of a divine kingship, or of a divinization of the king, in Israel. Here too they appeal to Eastern parallels, but not all of them are equally convincing. It is clear enough that the Pharaoh was considered a god: he is called, without qualification, 'the god', or 'the good god': he is the son of Ra the creator god; during his life he is an incarnation of Horus and after his death he is assimilated to Osiris. This divine character is expressed in the royal titles, in religious literature, in the rites of coronation and in art, which represents the Pharaoh with divine attributes and more than human stature.

In Mesopotamia, it was from time to time acknowledged, in very early days, that the king had a divine character. Among the Babylonians and Assyrians, however, this is far less apparent. Despite the fiction of divine sonship and the fact that a certain supernatural power was ascribed to him, the king still remained a man among men. It was quite a different concept from that which the Egyptians had. Among the Hittites the king was deified after his death, but during his lifetime he was not recognized as a 'god'.

The limited evidence available from Palestine and Syria, apart from Israel, does not allow us to conclude that the kings were deified. In the Amarna letters, when the vassal kings address the Pharaoh as 'my Sun (god)' or 'my god', they are conforming to the Egyptian manner of expression, which need not necessarily be a true expression of their own thought. The Aramaean inscriptions seem to exclude the notion of the king's divinity by representing him as definitely subordinate to the god. The historical and ritual texts from Ras Shamra say nothing of any divinization of the king, and it is only by a forced interpretation that the mythological poems can be invoked as witnesses to it.

It is not true then, to say that the idea of a divine king was shared by all the peoples of the ancient Near East. And when we turn our attention to Israel, the arguments adduced are extremely flimsy. It is true that the anointed king stood in a special relationship to Yahweh.[1] David knew everything, 'like an angel of God' (2 S 14: 17, 20), but the very words of this flattery exclude the idea that he was a god (cf. 1 S 29: 9). The idea of any king-worship, whereby the king, on certain feasts, took the place of God, is based on mere conjectures. Thus, some writers appeal to Ps 45: 7, rendering it as 'Thy throne, O Elohim, endures for ever and ever.' Other possible interpretations have been suggested, such as 'divine throne', 'throne like that of God', but even if the text calls the king an Elohim, we must remember that the term 'Elohim' is applied not only to God but to beings of superhuman power or nature. Thus, for example, it is used of members of the court of heaven (Jb 1: 6; Ps 29: 1; 89: 7), of the shade of Samuel (1 S 28: 13), and even of exceptional men such as princes or judges (Ps 58: 2; 82: 1, 6). The Israelite idea is that while the king is not just a man like other men, he is not a god (cf. 2 K 5: 7 and Ez 28: 2, 9).

This leaves the affirmations of divine sonship in Ps 2: 7 and 110: 3 (Greek). The word of Yahweh in Ps 2: 7, 'Thou art my son, to-day I have begotten thee', is best understood as a formula of adoption. According to the Code of Hammurabi, when someone adopted a person, he said to him, 'You are my son', and if the latter wanted to break the bond thus created, he would say, 'You are not my father' or 'You are not my mother.' Such declarative formulas were used in Israel for engagements: 'To-day you shall be my son-in-law' (1 S 18: 21), for marriage: 'Henceforth you are her brother and she is your sister' (Tb 7: 11), and for divorce: 'She is no longer my wife' (Os 2: 4). In the same way, in Ps 2: 7, Yahweh declares that on this day of consecration, 'to-day', he acknowledges the king as his son; he adopts him. This brings us back to Nathan's prophecy: 'I shall be his father, and he shall be my son' (2 S 7: 14). It is no valid objection to say that the text speaks of the adoption

1. Cf. pp. 103-105.

of the entire Davidic dynasty, for this adoption, obviously, had to be made effective for each sovereign; thus the text is applied to Solomon by 1 Ch 22: 10 and 28: 6.

Granted that the king is adopted by Yahweh, this does not by any means imply that he is equal to him or deified. Ps 89: 27, commenting on Nathan's prophecy, makes the necessary distinction: 'He will call unto me, Thou art my father, my God, the Rock of my salvation.' Israel's religion, indeed, with its faith in Yahweh as a personal God, unique and transcendent, made any deification of the king impossible. Nor can it be said that this represents only the official religion, for if the popular religion or the royal ideology had accepted such a divine character of the king, we should find traces of it in the Prophets, who are anything but lenient towards unfaithful kings. They accuse the kings of many crimes, but never of claiming divinity. Israel never had, never could have had, any idea of a king who was a god.

7. The king and worship

The fact remains that the king, sanctified by his anointing and adopted by Yahweh, is a sacred person and seems thereby to be empowered to perform religious functions. One often hears of the royal priesthood in Israel. We recall that the kings of Egypt, Assyria and Phoenicia were priests. In the Bible, Melchisedech is both king of Salem and priest of El-Elyon (Gn 14: 18). And it is precisely Ps 110: 4, which we have interpreted as an enthronement psalm, which says: 'Thou art a priest for ever in the order of Melchisedech.'

In the historical books, the king appears several times as the leader in acts of worship. David sets up the first altar for Yahweh in Jerusalem (2 S 24: 25); it is David, too, who conceives the project of building him a temple (2 S 7: 2-3), and, according to 1 Ch 22-29, plans in detail how this is to be served. It is Solomon who actually builds the temple directly opposite his own palace, and who dedicates it (1 K 5-8). It is Jeroboam who founds the sanctuary in Bethel, recruits its clergy and arranges its calendar of feasts (1 K 12: 26-33); hence it is a 'royal sanctuary' (Am 7: 13). The chief priests are officials nominated and dismissed by the king (2 S 8: 17; 20: 25; 1 K 2: 26-27; 4: 2). Joas publishes ordinances concerning the Temple (2 K 12: 5-9), and Josias supervises their enforcement (2 K 22: 3-7). The same Josias takes the initiative in the reform of worship and directs it in person (2 K 23). The priest Uriyyah carries out the modifications introduced by Achaz in the sanctuary and its worship (2 K 16: 10-18).

But the kings go even further: the historical texts show them personally performing priestly acts. They offer sacrifices: e.g. Saul at Gilgal (1 S 13: 9-10), David at Jerusalem (2 S 6: 13, 17-18; 24: 25), Solomon at Gibeon (1 K 3: 4, 15), at Jerusalem for the dedication of the Temple (1 K 8: 5, 62-64), and then at the three great feasts of the year (1 K 9: 25). Some of these texts can, of course, be taken in a factitive sense, that the king 'had sacrifice offered', but not all are capable of this meaning. And other texts in fact exclude it: in 2 K 16: 12-15, Achaz goes up to the new altar he has had made, offers the first sacrifice, and then commands the priest to continue the liturgy there; in 1 K 12: 33 it is said that Jeroboam 'went up to the altar to offer sacrifice' (cf. 13: 1f.). Again, David and Solomon bless the people in the sanctuary (2 S 6: 18; 1 K 8: 14), which is a rite reserved to the priests by Nb 6: 22-27 and 1 Ch 23: 13. Solomon consecrates the middle of the court (1 K 8: 64). David wears the loincloth which is the vestment of officiating priests (2 S 6: 14). Neither the prophets nor the historical books before the exile make any protest against these intrusions by the king into liturgical worship. It is only after the end of the monarchy that they become a stumbling-block, and 2 Ch 26: 16-20 says that Ozias was struck with leprosy because he had dared to burn incense at the altar, thus usurping a privilege of the sons of Aaron (2 Ch 26: 18, cf. Nb 17: 5; 1 Ch 23: 13).

All this evidence calls for a carefully balanced solution. The part played by the king in the regulation and supervision of worship or the nomination of the clergy does not mean that he was himself a priest; it does not exceed the prerogatives which the head of State may have over the State religion. It is quite another thing when he performs actions which are properly sacerdotal. But we must note that the instances where the king's personal action is beyond question are all very special or exceptional: the transference of the Ark, the dedication of an altar or a sanctuary, the great annual festivals. Ordinarily, the conduct of worship was left to the priest (2 K 16: 15). Anointing did not confer on the king a priestly character, since, as we have seen,[1] priests were not anointed in the days of the monarchy; but it did make him a sacred person, with a special relationship to Yahweh, and in solemn circumstances he could act as the religious head of the people. But he was not a priest in the strict sense.

But, it may be objected, Ps 110 is a royal psalm, and it calls the king a 'priest'. It has recently been suggested that this verse (Ps 110: 4) was addressed, not to the king, but to the priest whom the newly enthroned king (vv. 1-3) was confirming in his functions, and that these words were originally addressed to Sadoq, the psalm being composed in David's reign. It is an interesting hypothesis, but without foundation. The text can be explained otherwise: it could mean that the king was a priest, but in the only way in which an Israelite king could be: that is, in the way we have described. He was a priest in the same way as Melchisedech, who, it was thought, had been king and priest in that same Jerusalem where the new king was being enthroned. It was the starting-point of the Messianic interpretation to be given to the verse in He 5: 6.

1. Cf. p. 105.

Chapter Six

THE ROYAL HOUSEHOLD

1. *The harem*

IN a society which tolerated polygamy, the possession of a large harem was a mark of wealth and power. It was also a luxury which few could afford, and it became the privilege of kings. Saul had at least one concubine (2 S 3:7), and elsewhere there is mention of his 'wives' (2 S 12:8). Even when David was reigning only in Hebron, he already had six wives (2 S 3: 2-5), and in Jerusalem he took more concubines and wives (2 S 5: 13; cf. 2 S 19: 6), including Bathsheba (2 S 11: 27). When he fled from Absalom he left ten concubines in Jerusalem (2 S 15: 16; 16: 21-22; 20: 3). According to 2 Ch 11: 21, Roboam had eighteen wives and sixty concubines. Abiyyah had fourteen wives according to 2 Ch 13: 21. According to 2 Ch 24: 3 Joas had at least two wives and so had Josias (cf. 2 K 23: 31, 34, 36). Ben-hadad called on Achab to surrender his wives (1 K 20: 3-7), and Nabuchodonosor deported Joaikin and his wives (2 K 24: 15). The same fate befell the wives of Joram (2 Ch 21: 14, 17) and of Sedecias (Jr 38: 23). Sennacherib, according to his Annals, accepted the women of Ezechias' harem as tribute. The 'king' in the Song of Songs has sixty queens and eighty concubines (Ct 6: 8). But all these are eclipsed by the fabulous harem of Solomon, who had, according to 1 K 11: 3, seven hundred wives and three hundred concubines. Whatever we may think of these last figures, Dt 17: 17 had good cause to warn the king against possessing too large a harem.

Things were probably much the same in the small states bordering on Israel, though we are poorly informed about them. In the Amarna period we learn, incidentally, that the king of Byblos had at least two wives, and the king of Alasia (Cyprus) speaks of his 'wives'. In the eighth and seventh centuries b.c., however, the Assyrian Annals attribute to the kings of Ascalon, Sidon and Ashdod only one wife each, who may have been the queen consort; this would still leave room for other wives and concubines.

We are better informed about the great empires. Among the Hittites there was only one queen consort, but the king had a harem of wives (free women) and of slave concubines also. Similarly, in Assyria, the king had other wives besides the queen, the 'Lady of the Palace'; often they were princesses from vassal countries. In Egypt the Pharaoh had only one 'great royal spouse'. Five persons, no doubt in succession, held this title in the very long reign of

Ramses II, but his one hundred and sixty-two children prove that he did not restrict himself to his official spouses. According to the Amarna letters, a Pharaoh's harem was the nearest approach to that attributed to Solomon: the princess from Mitanni whom Amenophis III married arrived with 317 young maidens, and the same Pharaoh ordered from the king of Gezer forty 'beautiful women' at forty shekels of silver each. The Pharaoh received thirty young girls as a present from the king of Mitanni, twenty-one from the king of Jerusalem and twenty or thirty from a Syrian prince.

Foreign women were often introduced into these harems to serve not only the king's pleasures but also his policy. Such marriages set the seal on alliances, maintained good relations and guaranteed the loyalty of subject countries. We saw that Amenophis III married a princess of Mitanni: he also married a sister of the king of Babylon. Thutmoses IV before him had married a daughter of the king of Mitanni, and after him Ramses II married a daughter of the Hittite king. Another Hittite king gave his daughter to Mattiwaza of Mitanni; Asarhaddon of Assyria gave his to a Scythian king. A daughter of the king of Amurru became queen at Ugarit, and such cases could be multiplied.

In the same way, David married Maakah, daughter of the Aramaean king of Geshur (2 S 3: 3). Solomon became the Pharaoh's son-in-law (1 K 3: 1), and if he took wives from among the Moabites, the Ammonites, the Edomites, the Sidonians and the Hittites (1 K 11: 1, cf. 14: 21), his motive was to strengthen the bonds with his allies and tributaries. The marriage of Achab with Jezabel, daughter of the king of Tyre (1 K 16: 31), was arranged by his father Omri, in order to strengthen his alliance with the Phoenicians.

From some passages it appears that the king's harem, at least in the early days of the monarchy, used to pass to his successor. In 2 S 12: 8, Nathan says that it was Yahweh himself who, by establishing David as king of Israel, had given him the wives of his master Saul. Absalom publicly approached the concubines whom David had left in Jerusalem: it was a way of asserting that he was now king (2 S 16: 21-22), for possession of the harem was a title to the throne. Ishbaal's anger against Abner, who had taken one of Saul's concubines (2 S 3: 7-8), is easy to explain if she had passed by inheritance to Ishbaal, for Abner's action would imply that he was disputing the power with him. Adonias desired to have Abishag, who had belonged to David's harem (although, according to 1 K 1: 4, he had not had carnal knowledge of her) and had entered Solomon's harem. But when Adonias persuaded Solomon's mother to present his request to the king, Solomon answered: 'Ask me to give him the kingdom, too!' (1 K 2: 13-22). No evidence has yet been found of any such custom among Israel's immediate neighbours, but we may note that it existed among the Persians: Herodotus (III, 68) records that the false Smerdis had usurped both Cambyses' throne and all his wives. Among the ancient Arabs, wives formed part of the inheritance, and the custom was not abolished at one stroke by the Koran's prohibition. In Israel, too, the voice of religion was raised in protest against this incestuous practice: Reuben lost his pre-eminence because he had taken his father's concubine (Gn 35: 22; 49: 3-4), and the laws of Lv 18: 8; Dt 23: 1; 27: 20 were meant for the king as well as the rest of the people; only he did not always observe them (cf. Ez 22: 10).

Among the ladies of the harem, one held the king's preference. This was evidently the privilege of Bathsheba under David, of Jezabel under Achab, of Athaliah under Joram, and it is explicitly stated of Maakah that Roboam 'loved her more than all his other wives and concubines' (2 Ch 11: 21). But the king's favour was not enough to give this wife official title and rank. It is remarkable that the Old Testament only once uses the word 'queen', the feminine of *melek*, 'King', in connection with Israel, and that is in a poetical passage and in the plural, to describe the 'queens' of the 'King' in the Song of Songs, as distinct from his concubines (Ct 6: 8). Elsewhere the singular is used of foreign queens: the queen of Sheba (1 K 10), the queen of Persia (Est *passim*, especially Est 2: 17: the king preferred Esther before all the other women—cf. 2 Ch 11: 21—'and chose her as queen'—nothing similar in 2 Ch 11).

2. The Great Lady

On the other hand, at the court of Judah, official rank was accorded to the *g'bîrah*. In ordinary speech the word means 'mistress' as opposed to servant, and corresponds to *'adôn*, 'lord', the feminine of which is not used in Hebrew (2 K 5: 3; Is 24: 2; Ps 123: 2; Pr 30: 23). In 1 K 11: 19 it is applied to the Pharaoh's wife and consort, but it is never used of the wife of a king of Judah; under Asa, the *g'bîrah* is his grandmother Maakah (1 K 15: 13; 2 Ch 15: 16). The *g'bîrah* carried into captivity in Jr 29: 2 is the king's mother, according to the parallel in 2 K 24: 15. The sons of the *g'bîrah* mentioned in 2 K 10: 13 along with the sons of the king must be distinct from them: they are the sons of the queen-mother (and therefore the king's brothers). In Jr 13: 18 the king and the *g'bîrah* are Joiakin and his mother. Etymology and usage suggest that the title should be rendered as Great Lady.

This title implied a certain dignity and special powers. Bathsheba was certainly *g'bîrah* under Solomon; he receives her with great honour and seats her on his right hand (1 K 2: 19). The power of the Great Lady did not proceed merely from the influence of a mother over her son, as with Bathsheba; it was much more extensive, and for abusing it, Maakah was deprived by Asa of her dignity of Great Lady (1 K 15: 13). This authority of the queen-mother explains how Athaliah could so easily seize power on the death of Ochozias (2 K 11: 1f.); the queen-mother had an official position in the kingdom, and hence the Books of Kings always mention the name of the king's

mother in the introduction to each reign in Judah—except in the cases of
Joram and Achaz, where no woman is named, and of Asa, where his grandmother's name takes the place of his mother's. It is possible that the Great
Lady was accorded her rank on the accession of her son, which would
explain the career of Hamital, wife of Josias, who was queen-mother under
Joachaz, was set aside under Joiaqim and Joiakin, and returned under
Sedecias, the brother of Joachaz (2 K 23: 31, 36; 24: 8, 18). It is also possible
that the mother became *gᵉbîrah* as soon as her son was designated heir to the
throne, as is suggested by 2 Ch 11: 21-22. The story of Bathsheba does not
enable us to decide this point, since Solomon's sacring took place immediately
after his nomination; but it does at least prove that before this nomination
Solomon's mother had not the dignity which she subsequently enjoyed (cf.
1 K 1: 15-16, 31 and 2: 13-19). Bathsheba was the first Great Lady in Israel.
On the other hand it seems that the Great Lady could keep her position after
her son's death: Maakah, wife of Roboam, was still *gᵉbîrah* under her grandson Asa, after the short reign of her son Abiyyam (1 K 15: 13). From the
same passage we see that the *gᵉbîrah* could be dismissed by the king: Maakah
had favoured the cult of Asherah.

Hittite parallels may help to elucidate this rather complicated question. The
tavannana was the lawful queen, the mother of the heir-apparent, and played
an important part in policy and religion. If she survived the king she retained
the same position during the reign of her son (or sons, if two brothers
succeeded to the throne); and only on her death did the dignity pass to her
daughter-in-law, the wife of the reigning king. Like Maakah, she could be
dismissed for a serious offence against the king or the state; but, as in Judah,
this seems to have been exceptional. The queen-mother must have held a
similar position in Ugarit, where several official letters are addressed to the
king's mother, also called the '*adath*, which is the feminine of '*adôn*, and therefore the equivalent of *gᵉbîrah*. The Akkadian texts of Ras Shamra indicate
that this queen-mother intervened in political affairs, and they also mention
a Great Lady of Amurru. For Assyria the evidence is less clear, but we should
remember the part played by the queens Sammuramat and Naqi'a during
the reigns of their husbands and then of their sons. This tradition is preserved
in the Greek legends of Semiramis and Nitokris. One may also point to the
influence of Adad-guppi', the mother of Nabonidus.

There is no direct evidence of the existence of a Great Lady in the northern
kingdom. In the introductions to the reigns of Israel, the name of the king's
mother is never given. 2 K 10: 13 mentions a *gᵉbîrah* who can only be Jezabel,
but the word is put in the mouth of the princes of Judah. The institution,
moreover, presupposes a dynastic stability which was not usually found in the
kingdom of Israel. But we must draw attention to a rare term, which is perhaps the Israelitic equivalent of the *gᵉbîrah* of Judah. In Ps 45: 10, the *shegal* is
mentioned as standing on the right hand of the king; she is not classed with

the other women of the harem, for she is the queen consort. Now Ps 45 has been interpreted as a wedding-hymn composed for a king of Israel. It is also very tempting to restore the word *shegal* at the end of Jg 5: 30 in the Hymn of Deborah, in place of the impossible *shalal*, 'booty'. The word is parallel to Sisera, and would denote the queen or queen-mother, cf. v. 28. Once again, the Hymn of Deborah is a composition of northern Israel. The only other examples of the term in the Old Testament, Ne 2: 6 (the queen of Persia) and Dn 5: 2, 3, 23 (the Aramaic plural form: the wives of Balthazar) do not prove that the word was an official term in Judah before the Exile.

3. *The royal children*

Our only information on the position of the king's daughters comes from the story of Tamar, the daughter of David. From this we may conclude that the princesses lived in the palace until their marriage, under the care of women (2 S 13: 7). They wore a distinctive dress (2 S 13: 18-19), probably a long-sleeved robe like that given by Jacob to his favourite son Joseph (Gn 37: 3, 23, 32). Their father would give them in marriage to his senior officers (1 K 4: 11, 15) or to friendly kings (2 K 8: 18).

The king's sons were brought up in the palace by nurses (2 K 11: 2), then entrusted to tutors chosen from the leading men of the city (2 K 10: 1, 6f.; cf. 1 Ch 27: 32). We are told that Achab had seventy sons. The figure is no doubt symbolic of a large family (cf. Jg 8: 30; 9: 2, 5), but this parallel shows that we must take 'sons' in the literal sense and not interpret it as descendants in general or as more distant relatives. We know besides that Achab had a harem (1 K 20: 2, 5, 7), which may have been a large one. In the same way, in the story of Absalom and Amnon, the 'king's sons' are certainly the sons of David (2 S 13: 23-38). Again, 2 K 10: 13 speaks of the sons of the king and the sons of the Great Lady; there is no good reason to interpret these terms as honorific titles instead of taking them in the strict sense. When they had grown up and, no doubt, married young, the king's sons led an independent life and were provided for by their father (2 Ch 21: 3; cf. Ez 46: 16). Amnon resided outside the palace (2 S 13: 5), and Absalom had his own house (2 S 13: 20; 14: 24) herds and lands (2 S 13: 23; 14: 30). But even when they were adults these sons were still subject to the authority of their father the king (2 S 13: 27).

Apart from the heir-apparent, who had special prerogatives (2 Ch 11: 22), the king's sons could perform certain duties at the court (2 S 8: 18; 1 Ch 18: 17). The expression *ben hammelek*, 'son of the king', is, however, used several times in contexts which seem to imply that it does not mean a son in the proper sense. In 1 K 22: 26-27 = 2 Ch 18: 25-26, the 'king's son' Yoash is named after the governor of the city, and both are ordered to put the prophet Micheas in prison. In Jr 36: 26, the 'king's son' Yerahmeel, and two other men are commanded to seize Baruch and Jeremias. In Jr 38: 6, Jeremias is thrown into the cistern of the 'king's son' Malkiyyahu. In 2 Ch 28: 7 the 'king's son' Maaseyahu is killed along with two of the king's officers. None of these men appear elsewhere as a member of the royal family. It seems therefore that in these four instances the title 'king's son' denotes an office. This conclusion is perhaps confirmed by two discoveries in Palestine, one of a seal, the other of a stamp from a signet-ring: both have a proper name, followed by 'king's son' in the place where other seals mention their owner's office. These officials were not of very high rank; Yoash is named after the governor of the city and in three instances out of four their intervention is connected with prisoners. Probably, therefore, the *ben hammelek* was a police officer. The explanation may be that this officer was perhaps chosen originally from among the king's sons.

A parallel from Egypt may be noted: 'royal son of Kush' is the title of the viceroy of Ethiopia, who was never a descendant of the Pharaoh, except perhaps for the first holder of that title, who would have been a grandson of the founder of the Eighteenth Dynasty.

4. *The king's attendants*

The royal family was surrounded by a court of officials and household servants (1 K 10: 4-5). All, whatever their office, were called the king's 'servants', from the soldiers of the guard (1 K 1: 33; 2 S 11: 9, 13; 20: 6), to the highest officials (1 K 11: 26; 2 K 19: 5; 22: 12; 2 Ch 34: 20; and for foreign courts cf. 2 K 5: 6; 25: 8; 2 Ch 32: 9).

The question has been raised whether the expression 'king's servant', *'ebed hammelek*, when used in the singular, may not sometimes denote a special office. For example the *'ebed hammelek* Asayah is named together with the secretary Shaphan (2 K 22: 12 = 2 Ch 34: 20). Further, we possess a number of seals bearing a proper name followed by *'ebed hammelek* or by *'ebed* with the name of a king. Seals of the same type, but of Phoenician, Ammonite, Edomite and perhaps Philistine origin, have also been discovered. Now it is true that the title stands in the place where an office is usually mentioned, but this does not prove that it denotes a particular office. As a matter of fact the title is given to Nebuzaradan (2 K 25: 8) who at the same time is called the commander of Nabuchodonosor's guard. Finally, the number of seals which have survived would be surprisingly large, if all their wearers had occupied the same office. We should rather conclude that it was a general title, borne by several officials who used their seals to stamp official documents. The corresponding Assyrian expression also covered different functions.

At the time of the capture of Jerusalem in 587 B.C., the Chaldaeans took prisoner five men 'who saw the king's face' (2 K 25: 19; in the parallel of

Jr 52: 25 there are seven). This is sometimes translated as 'counsellors', and in fact in Est 1: 14, the same words denote the seven members of the royal council of Persia. In itself, however, the expression has a general sense: it means those who are admitted to the king's presence (cf. 2 S 14: 24, 28, 32), just as the expression 'to go to see the face of Yahweh', means 'to go to the Temple' (Dt 31: 11; Ps 42: 3). The term then includes the king's personal servants, and also his friends and courtiers, all who 'stand before the king' (1 S 16: 21f.; Jr 52: 12; cf. the angels in Mt 18: 10). The expression is found in Assyrian with the same vague meaning. The king would naturally seek advice from his courtiers (1 K 12: 6; cf. the heavenly court in 1 K 22: 19f.; Jb 1: 6f.; 2: 1f.). The formal title of 'counsellor', *yô'es* was given to Ahitophel under David (2 S 15: 12; cf. 15: 31 and its sequel) and to David's uncle in 1 Ch 27: 32-33. The title is found under Amasias also (2 Ch 25: 16).

1 S 8: 15 mentions, along with the king's servants, the *sarîsîm*. They are named among the men of rank in Jr 34: 19, and among the men of war, the women and the children in Jr 41: 16. A *sarîs* is sent by Achab to the prophet Micheas ben Yimlah (1 K 22: 9 = 2 Ch 18: 8); another is charged with restoring her goods to the Shunamite (2 K 8: 6). Two or three *sarîsîm* join in throwing Jezabel down from the window (2 K 9: 32). The *sarîsîm* of Joiakin are sent into captivity (2 K 24: 12, 15; Jr 29: 2). The *sarîs* Nathan-Melek had a room in the Temple (2 K 23: 11). At the capture of Jerusalem a *sarîs* was in command of the men of war (2 K 25: 19; Jr 52: 25). It is usually translated by 'eunuch', and it certainly has this sense in other passages (Is 56: 3-5; Si 30: 20, and perhaps in 2 K 20: 18 = Is 39: 7, probably in Est 1 and 2, *passim*, and Dn 1, *passim*). But it is more than doubtful whether this sense holds good in the texts quoted earlier, where the *sarîsîm* figure simply as officials or courtiers. Outside Israel, the Bible uses this word to denote the captain of the guard, the chief cupbearer and the chief baker of the Pharaoh (Gn 37: 36; 39: 1; 40: 2); it mentions the chief *sarîsîm* of Sennacherib (2 K 18: 17 omitted in the parallel of Is 36: 2), and of Nabuchodonosor (Jr 39: 3, 13), both of whom took part in military expeditions.

The word itself is borrowed from Assyrian: it is transcribed *sha-reshi*, 'he at the head', simply a dignitary, a courtier, who goes before the king, one of his confidential advisers. For certain tasks, such as the supervision of the harem or the royal children, eunuchs were chosen, and the word acquired this meaning, as several cuneiform inscriptions show. This evolution in meaning also explains all the Biblical uses. The word passed into Egyptian at a late date, in the form *srs*, to signify Persian officials.

The king maintained male and female singers to entertain himself and the court. David, who was called to play the harp before Saul, is rather an exceptional figure anyway (1 S 16: 14-23; 18: 10; 19: 9), but Barzillai says he is too old to accept David's invitation to come and listen to the male and female singers at the palace (2 S 19: 36). The memory of Solomon's musicians is preserved in Qo 2: 8. Sennacherib mentions in his Annals the singers, male and female, of Ezechias, who were given to him in tribute.

These singers, men and women, used to enliven banquets. It was a signal mark of favour to be admitted to the royal table 'as one of the king's sons' (2 S 9: 7, 13; 19: 29, 34; cf. Lk 22: 30). Solomon's table was renowned for its lavish service and the high quality of its menu (1 K 10: 5), though the abundant victuals which reached it (1 K 5: 2-3, 7) supplied not only the king's own table but all the inmates of the palace and the king's pensioners, like the descendants of Barzillai (1 K 2: 7), and (later) the hundreds of prophets who 'ate at Jezabel's table' (1 K 18: 19, cf. Daniel and his companions, Dn 1: 5-15, and the table of Nehemias, Ne 5: 17-18). The great monarchies of the East had officials in charge of the king's table, cupbearers, bakers and carvers, just as the French monarchy had its *officiers de bouche*. The Old Testament speaks of the Pharaoh's chief cupbearer and chief baker (Gn 40: 1f.) and Sennacherib's chief cupbearer (2 K 18: 17f.; Is 36: 2f. where the context shows that such titles could be honorary and associated with other duties, as is abundantly confirmed by Assyrian documents). Nehemias, on the other hand, who was cupbearer to the king of Persia, did serve at the king's table (Ne 1: 11; 2: 1). The small courts of Israel and Judah may have had similar offices, but they are not mentioned in the Bible; in 1 K 10: 5=2 Ch 9: 4, the word usually translated 'cupbearers' really means a 'drinking service'.

The king, who had military duties and often went to war himself, had a squire. At first, he was called the king's 'armour-bearer': this was David's title when he was attached to Saul (1 S 16: 21), and another of Saul's squires took part in the battle of Gilboa (1 S 31: 4-6). Abimelek, king of Shechem, had his squire (Jg 9: 54), and the senior officers of course had theirs (1 S 14: 6f.; 2 S 23: 37). When Solomon began to use chariots, the squire was called the *shalîsh*, literally the 'third man'. The Hittite, Israelite and Assyrian chariots were in fact mounted by three men, the driver, the fighting man and the *shalîsh*, who carried the buckler and the weapons. (He was called in Assyrian the *shalshu*.) In Ex 14: 7; 15: 4, the word is extended to the Egyptian army, whose chariots carried only two men. Every Israelite charioteer had his *shalîsh*, but the king's squire was an important personage, his orderly officer or aide-de-camp; he was the man 'on whose arm the king leaned' (2 K 7: 2, 17, 19; cf. 2 K 5: 18). We hear of Jehu's squire (2 K 9: 25), and Peqahyah's, that Peqah who assassinated his master and reigned in his stead (2 K 15: 25). The word is twice employed in the plural, and in both texts the king's guards are mentioned too (1 K 9: 22; 2 K 10: 25). The name and the office disappeared when there were no more chariots, *i.e.*, at the fall of Samaria in the northern kingdom, and after Sennacherib's invasion in the kingdom of Judah.

Under David, Hushai is called the king's 'friend' (2 S 15: 37, also in v. 32, according to the Greek; 16: 16). The name has been taken as the name of an office by 1 Ch 27: 33, which includes Hushai among David's principal officials, and in fact the list of Solomon's officials also includes a 'friend' (1 K 4: 5). This word re'eh is generally explained as a different form of re'a, 'companion', which is the word used in 1 Ch. 27: 33. But the two words may be unconnected, and re'eh may be a word borrowed from abroad. In the Amarna letters the king of Jerusalem proclaims himself the ruḫi of the Pharaoh. Now there is an Egyptian title rḫ nsw.t, the man 'known by the king', a title of nobility given to men whom the Pharaoh wished to honour. The Hebrew word may be a transcription of this, via the Canaanite language. If so, 2 S 16: 16 is making a play on the words: Hushai is the re'eh, the man 'known by' David, and Absalom asks him why he has not departed with his re'a his 'friend'. The title carried with it no special function and it is not found after Solomon. Possibly it was replaced by a translation of this Egyptian expression; this would explain the 'known' or familiar men of Achab's court, the m'yudda'îm (2 K 10: 11). The equivalent mûdû is by then found at Ugarit.

5. The royal guard

David had a corps of foreign mercenaries, the Kerethites and the Pelethites, recruited in Philistia and the neighbouring regions. They were under a separate command from the army raised in Israel (2 S 8: 18 = 1 Ch 18: 17; 2 S 20: 23). The part played by these mercenary troops in war (cf. 2 S 20: 7) will be examined in connection with military institutions, but they also formed the king's bodyguard. They accompanied David on his flight from Absalom (2 S 15: 18), and formed the escort to Solomon on the day of his sacring (1 K 1: 38, 44). They are those 'servants of My Lord' (2 S 20: 6; 1 K 1: 33), who lodged at the palace gate (2 S 11: 9, 13). They are never again mentioned after Solomon's accession, but other foreign mercenaries, the Carites, were in the service of the Palace at the time of the revolt against Athaliah (2 K 11: 4, 19).

On this occasion the Carites are mentioned along with the raṣîm, the 'runners'. The latter furnished the escort platoon which ran before the king's chariot. Absalom, and later Adonias, in their attempts to seize the throne, provided themselves with a chariot-team and fifty runners (2 S 15: 1; 1 K 1: 5), for this was part of royal ceremonial. The runners appear in the reign of Saul (1 S 22: 17), where the context implies that they were recruited from the Israelites. We learn from 1 K 14: 27-28 = 2 Ch 12: 10-11, that their guardroom stood at the entrance to the Palace, and that they kept there the bronze bucklers worn when they accompanied the king to the Temple. There were six hundred of these; they had replaced the golden bucklers which Solomon made and which he had stored in the Gallery of the Forest of Lebanon (1 K 10: 16-17). This suggests that this gallery was the guardroom of Solomon's Palace. These runners kept watch by roster over the Palace and the Temple and they took a leading part in the deposition of Athaliah and the enthronement of Joas (2 K 11). The kings of Israel, too, had their guard: Jehu's accompanied him to Samaria and took part in the extirpation of the worship of Baal (2 K 10: 25).

6. The royal estate

All the kings of the ancient East were large landowners. The lands they owned were administered directly, or rented, or granted as fiefs in return for rents or personal services. This is especially true of Egypt, where the greater part of the land belonged to the king or the temples, and the statements of Gn 47: 20-26 are amply confirmed by the documents of the country. It is also true, though not to the same extent, of Mesopotamia, where the Code of Hammurabi, the Nuzu documents and those of the Kassite period all stress the importance of fiefs, and the texts of all periods mention royal possessions. It is also true of the little kingdoms of Syria, as is proved by the recently discovered archives of Alalakh and Ugarit.

It was equally true of Israel. Samuel warned the Israelites that the king they wanted would make his subjects till and harvest his fields, and would take their vineyards and olivegroves to give them to his servants (1 S 8: 12, 14). This happened as early as Saul's day. Before he became king he had only a small family property (1 S 9: 1f.; 11: 5), but afterwards he was able to distribute fields and vineyards to his officers (1 S 22: 7), and at his death he left a vast amount of property (2 S 9: 9-10). There was no clear distinction between the king's personal possession and the crown's, and everything passed to his successor, even if he were not of the family of the late king. David inherited Saul's harem and also his 'house' (2 S 12: 8). It was only as a favour that he 'restored' to Meribbaal the lands of his grandfather (2 S 9: 7) and he reserved his rights over them: he controlled their administration (2 S 9: 9-10), withdrew them from Meribbaal (2 S 16: 4), and then divided them between Meribbaal and Siba (2 S 19: 30). This power of the king over the estate of his predecessor certainly remained in force in the northern kingdom, where usurpations were frequent. In Judah, where the dynastic succession was uninterrupted, the transmission of the royal estate presented no problem.

This estate could be formed and increased in many ways. The king would acquire lands, as David bought the threshing-floor of Araunah (2 S 24: 24), and Omri the hill of Samaria (1 K 16: 24). Achab tried to buy Naboth's vineyard or to obtain it by exchange (1 K 21: 2). The rest of the story of Naboth could mean that the goods of men condemned to death were forfeit to the king (1 K 21: 15). It is also possible that the king took possession of property left vacant by their owners leaving the country: this would explain the story of the Shunamite (2 K 8: 1-6, especially vv. 3 and 6). It is clear too that an unjust king had no scruples about confiscating his subjects' goods: this had been foretold by 1 S 8: 14, and would itself be sufficient explanation of the story of Naboth. The king could also receive presents. Gezer, the wedding gift of the Pharaoh's daughter (1 K 9: 16), remained crown property, which is why its territory is omitted in the administrative organization of the revenues (1 K 4: 8-19, where one would expect mention of it in v. 9). The Arabs sent flocks to Josaphat (2 Ch 17: 11). The income which Solomon derived from his commercial enterprises certainly favoured the extension and exploitation of the royal estate. In Qo 2: 4-7 Solomon is represented as saying: 'I have planted vineyards for myself, laid out gardens and orchards, and placed in them every kind of fruit tree. I have dug out pools to water what I have planted, bought servants and maid-servants. I have owned men and flocks, cattle and sheep in abundance.' According to 2 Ch 26: 10 (which is confirmed by archaeological observations), Ozias had built towers in the desert and dug cisterns; he had many cattle, many labourers and vine-dressers. 2 Ch 32: 28-29 says that Ezechias had granaries for his grain, wine and oil, grazing grounds for his herds, many flocks and cattle. The king's estate is again mentioned in 2 Ch 31: 3; 35: 7. It is very significant that Ezechiel, in his plan for the future, reserves the prince's portion and makes regulations about it (Ez 45: 7; 46: 16-18; 48: 21). He was still dominated by the age-old tradition of the royal estate.

We are not very well informed about the administration of this estate. The Chronicler gives a list of the overseers of David's property (1 Ch 27: 25-31; cf. 28: 1): there are overseers for the grain crops and the vineyards, for the wine and the oil, for the herds and the flocks, the camels and the she-asses. This list is not invented, as is proved by the non-Israelite proper names in it, but we can verify neither the details nor the date.

The general administration of the estate was in the hands of a special official. He is apparently the man who is 'over the king's house', 'asher 'al habbayth, the master of the palace. This is the title conferred on Joseph by the Pharaoh (Gn 41: 40; cf. 45: 8), and Joseph's duties were in fact concerned with the royal estate (47: 20-26) and its revenues (41: 48-49, 55-56; 42: 6f.). Achab set out during the drought with Obadyahu, his master of the palace, to find forage for his horses, mules and livestock (1 K 18: 5). But the functions of the master of the palace far exceeded those of a royal steward, as is shown by the rest of the story of Joseph and other texts on the subject. He was also major-domo and he ended by becoming the king's first minister.[1] There is perhaps another title to indicate the estate manager. Siba, who is the steward of Saul's property, is called his na'ar, or the na'ar of his house (2 S 9: 9; 19: 18). Boaz too had a na'ar who supervised his harvesters (Rt 2: 5f.). Three seal-impressions have also been found, dating from the end of the monarchy, with the

1. Cf. pp. 129-130.

name of Eliakim, *na'ar* of the king. As the title does not appear in the texts which mention the highest officials of the realm, it may perhaps have been reserved for the steward of the estate.

This information may perhaps be completed by reference to some archaeological discoveries. Some seventy inscribed potsherds have been unearthed in the ruins of the royal palace at Samaria: they are delivery notes for wine or oil, with the name of the receiver and the deliverer, and often an indication of the place of origin. They are administrative receipts dating from the reign of Jeroboam II. It is very likely that they concern the administration of the royal estates near the capital: similar documents have been found in Egypt. It is much less likely that the Judaean jars which are stamped on the handles with *lammelek*, 'to the king', are connected with the management of the estate: obviously they could have been used for the delivery of revenue, but it is simpler and less hazardous to explain the stamp on them as a hall-mark of the royal workshop.[1]

1. Cf. pp. 77-78.

CHAPTER SEVEN

THE PRINCIPAL OFFICIALS OF THE KING

THE king was assisted in the administration of the kingdom by a number of high-ranking officials who lived close by and formed his government; they were his ministers. They are called the king's 'servants', but in relation to the people they are 'chiefs', *śarîm*[1] (1 K 4: 1); they are referred to by their office, or by the title 'set over' such and such a charge. As with other Eastern courts, their functions are sometimes difficult to define, and the Bible does not give a complete picture of this central administration.

1. *The ministers of David and Solomon*

We possess two lists of David's senior officials and one of Solomon's. They are certainly derived from documents preserved in archives, but they have been re-edited and their text has suffered to some extent.

The first list (2 S 8: 16-18 = 1 Ch 18: 14-17) is given after Nathan's prophecy and the summary of David's victories, and before the long story about the succession to the throne. Consequently, it represents the final and definitive arrangement after the foundation of the kingdom. The military command was shared between Joab, commander of the army, and Benayahu, commander of the guard. Yehoshaphat was herald, Serayah (or Shawsha in Ch) was secretary. Sadoq and Ebyathar were the priests, but at the end of the list is added: 'the sons of David were priests'. The order as we have it seems haphazard: commander of the army, heralds, priests, commander of the guard and finally the sons of David. Joab and Benayahu, Sadoq and Ebyathar, all figure in the same offices in the history of the reign. Neither Yehoshaphat the herald nor the sons of David play any part in it.

The mention of the latter is strange: their names, which one would think essential in a document of this kind, are not given, and their status as 'priests' is enigmatic. The most we can presume is that they assisted or did duty for their father in those sacerdotal functions which were occasionally performed by the king.[2] The parallel in 1 Ch 18: 17 has: 'and the sons of David held the first rank next to the king', which is proof of a Levite's scruple, but it does not clarify matters. The text about the two legitimate priests is doubtful. The Hebrew reading is 'Sadoq son of Ahitub and Ahimelek son of Ebyathar'; this must be corrected at least to 'and Ebyathar son of Ahimelek', according

1. Cf. p. 69.   2. Cf. p. 114.

to the Syriac (1 S 22: 20 and 2 S 20: 25). Perhaps we should even restore 'Sadoq and Ebyathar son of Ahimelek son of Ahitub', according to 2 S 22: 20; this would make Sadoq a newcomer, without Israelite ancestry. These questions will be dealt with in connection with the history of the priesthood.[1] Here it is enough to note that the religious leaders are included among the royal officials.

The second Davidic list (2 S 20: 23-26), which has no parallel in Chronicles, is given at the very end of David's reign. The same names are here arranged in a more logical order: commander of the army, commander of the guard, herald, secretary (here called Sheya or Shewa), and the priests. But before the herald it adds Adoram, the officer in charge of forced labour; and at the very end, instead of the sons of David who were 'priests', it gives Ira the Yairite, 'priest of David'. This repetition of a list of high officials is easily explained after the return of Joab to the post from which he had been dismissed (2 S 19: 14; 20: 22), and after the suppression of the revolt of Sheba (2 S 20: 1-22); but it is not so easy to account for its new features. It is doubtful whether Adoram, who was still in office after Solomon's death (1 K 12: 18), could already have been in charge of forced labour under David, for this post does not seem to have been instituted until the reign of Solomon (1 K 5: 27; 9: 15). The mention of a 'priest of David' along with Sadoq and Ebyathar is puzzling. According to one reading of the Greek, this Ira the Yairite might be a doublet of Ira the Yattirite, who is one of David's warriors, according to 2 S 23: 38. It is not impossible that this list presents a true account of the state of administration at the end of David's reign; it is also possible that the passage is a subsequent compilation.

The list for Solomon's reign (1 K 4: 1-6) raises some difficult problems of literary and textual criticism, to which no satisfactory solution has yet been found. Examination of external witnesses and the weight of internal evidence would suggest suppressing v. 4 on Benayahu, Sadoq and Ebyathar, and adding to v. 6 the mention of Eliab, son of Joab, as army commander. It would then read as follows (with the proper names often uncertain): the priest Azaryahu, son of Sadoq; the secretaries Elihoreph or Elihaph and Ahiyyah, who are sons of Shisha, evidently David's secretary; Yehoshaphat the herald; the chief prefect Azaryahu or Adoniyahu, son of Nathan; the king's friend, Zabud or Zakkur, another son of Nathan (to whom a gloss has added the title of 'priest'); the master of the palace, Ahishar or Ahhiyah (or 'his brother'?), with no mention of his father's name; the army commander, Eliab, son of Joab; the chief over the levy, Adoniram or Adoram, son of Abda.

The continuity with the Davidic administration is evident. Solomon employs the same herald as his father, the son of one of his priests, both the sons of his secretary, the son of his army commander and at least two sons of

---

[1] Cf. pp. 372-374.

the prophet Nathan, who had been an adviser of David and had favoured the accession of Solomon. On the whole, it represents a new generation coming to power; this proves that the list does not date from the beginning of Solomon's reign. This is confirmed by the appearance of new posts: there is a chief prefect, a fact which presumes the existence of the organization described in 1 K 4: 7-19, and an officer in charge of forced labour, the introduction of which is recorded in 1 K 5: 27 (with the reservation noted above about the second Davidic list).

It is noteworthy, too, that some of these high officials, or their fathers, have non-Israelite names, names which have puzzled the copyists or the translators: Adoram has a Phoenician name, like his father Abda. The names of Shisha or Shawsa (1 Ch 18: 16) and his son Elihoreph or Elihaph may be Egyptian or Hurrite. In fact it was to be expected that the young Israelite kingdom should recruit some of its officials from the neighbouring countries, which had an administrative tradition. Even for its organization it had to copy models abroad. Study of some offices suggests the influence of Egyptian institutions, but it does not enable us to decide whether this influence was direct, or whether it came indirectly to Israel from the Canaanite states which Israel displaced. Direct influence seems the more likely, for the kingdom of David and Solomon was far bigger than any of the little city-states of Canaan.

The king's 'friend' is rather an honorary title, probably Egyptian in origin[1]; he is perhaps an intruder in this list of officials. The rôles of army commander and commander of the guard will be studied under military institutions[2]. The officer in charge of the prefects, and the officer in charge of forced labour will be discussed in connection with the services they directed[3]; in any case they do not appear after Solomon. There remain three ministers whose functions continued until the end of the monarchy and who are again mentioned together in an important crisis, Sennacherib's invasion in 701 (cf. 2 K 18: 18): they are the master of the palace, the secretary and the herald. These three deserve to be studied on their own.

2. The master of the palace

In Solomon's list, Ahishar is *'asher 'al habbayth*, the master of the palace. The same title is given to Arsa, who had a house at Tirsah under Elah, king of Israel (1 K 16: 9); to Obadyahu, who was minister under Achab (1 K 18: 3); to Yotham, when he succeeded his sick father, the king Ozias (2 K 15: 5); and to Shebna, who was master of the palace under Ezechias (Is 22: 15), and later succeeded by Elyaqim (Is 22: 19-20); it was this Elyaqim who held the discussion with Sennacherib's envoy under the walls of Jerusalem (2 K 18: 18= Is 36: 3). Outside the Bible, the title appears in the inscription of a tomb in Siloam (the name is incomplete: could it be the tomb of Shebna? cf. Is 22:

1. Cf. pp. 122-123.   2. Cf. pp. 220-221.   3. Cf. pp. 134 and 142.

16), and on a seal-impression in the name of Godolias, doubtless the man whom Nabuchodonosor installed as governor of Judah after the capture of Jerusalem (2 K 25: 22; Jr 40: 7). He would formerly have been master of the palace under Sedecias, the last king of Judah. It has recently been suggested that the post was hereditary, and that Godolias was a descendant of Elyaqim, who was master of the palace under Ezechias; but there is no sufficient evidence for this suggestion in the texts. In the vocabulary of Chronicles, the equivalent is perhaps the n'gîd habbayth, the chief of the palace, a title given by Achaz to a certain Azriqam (2 Ch 28: 7).

The exact semantic equivalent in Assyrian and Babylonian is *sha pân êkalli* and in Egyptian *mr pr*. They were high officials, but their authority seems to have been restricted to the administration of the royal palace: they were the king's stewards or majordomos. In Israel the powers of the master of the palace were far more extensive and the similarity between his functions and those of the Egyptian vizier is even more important than the verbal resemblances. This vizier used to report every morning to the Pharaoh and receive his instructions. He saw to the opening of the 'gates of the royal house', that is, of the various offices of the palace, and then the official day began. All the affairs of the land passed through his hands, all important documents received his seal, all the officials were under his orders. He really governed in the Pharaoh's name and acted for him in his absence. This is obviously the dignity which Joseph exercised, according to Genesis. He had no one above him except the Pharaoh, and he was appointed over the whole land of Egypt; he held the royal seal (Gn 41: 40-44), and to describe his dignity the Bible says that the Pharaoh 'put him in charge of his house'; he made him, in fact, his master of the palace (Gn 41: 40; 45: 8).

The master of the palace had similar functions at the court of Judah. Announcing the promotion of Elyaqim, Is 22: 22 says:

> I lay the key of the house of David
>   upon his shoulder;
> If he opens, none will shut;
> If he shuts, none will open.

The Egyptian vizier's instructions are described in a very similar fashion. Every morning 'the vizier will send someone to open the gates of the king's house, to admit those who have to enter, and to send out those who have to go out'. One is reminded of our Lord's words to Peter, the Vizier of the Kingdom of Heaven (Mt 16: 19). Like the Egyptian vizier, the master of the palace was the highest official in the state: his name comes first in the list of 2 K 18: 18; he alone appears with the king in 1 K 18: 3; and Yotham bears this title when he acts as regent of the kingdom (2 K 15: 5), as the vizier did in the absence of the Pharaoh.

It seems, however, that the master of the palace only gradually came to be the first minister, and perhaps in the early days of the monarchy he was only the steward of the palace and of the royal estate.[1] This would account for his title and for the fact that he is not named among David's senior officials, and does not head the list of Solomon's civil servants. Under David and Solomon the secretary and the king's herald were the immediate representatives of the king: there was no place for a vizier.

In Is 22: 15 Shebna, the master of the palace, is called the *soken*. This word is found in the form *zukinu* in two Canaanite glosses of the Amarna letters, to denote the Pharaoh's commissary. In Akkadian, *shaknu* denotes first the prefect of Assur (*shakîn mâti*), then the governors of the conquered countries; and the term was adopted by the Pharaohs in their Akkadian correspondence. At Ras Shamra, however, the *skn* (in alphabetical script) or the *shakîn mâti* (in Akkadian) was an official at Ugarit, apparently the highest in the land; this corresponds to the position held in Judah by Shebna, *soken* and master of the palace.

3. The royal secretary

We have seen that the list of David's high officials included a secretary, whose two sons held the same office under Solomon. An edict of Joas, king of Judah, entrusted to the royal secretary the duty of collecting the contributions given for the repair of the Temple (2 K 12: 11; cf. 2 Ch 24: 11), and it was while performing this duty a century later that Shaphan the secretary learned of the discovery of the Book of the Law (2 K 22: 3, 8-10, 12; 2 Ch 34: 15, 18, 20). Shebna the secretary was one of the three ministers who held the discussion with Sennacherib's envoy (2 K 18: 18, 37; 19: 2; Is 36: 3, 11, 22). We know the names of the last secretaries under the monarchy: we have just said that Shaphan held the post in 622; he was succeeded by Elishama in 604 (Jr 36: 12, 20), and in 588 the secretary was Yehonathan (Jr 37: 15, 20).

This official, an indispensable link in the chain of power from the time of David, was both the king's private secretary and secretary of state. He was responsible for all correspondence, internal and external, and for the Temple collections (2 K 12: 11); he played a considerable part in public affairs. He ranked below the master of the palace (Shebna, who held the latter post, Is 22: 15, was demoted to that of secretary, Is 36: 3, etc.), but he comes immediately after the master of the palace in 2 K 18: 18f.; Is 36: 3f., and the fate of the kingdom hung on the mission they performed together. Shaphan the secretary brought to the king the Book of the Law discovered in the Temple, read it to him and went to consult Huldah the prophetess for him; this was the beginning of the religious reformation (2 K 23). The senior officials held a conference in the house of Elishama the secretary, and there prophecies of Jeremias were read to them (Jr 36: 11-20). The 'secretary's room' where they met (Jr 36: 12, 20, 21) was evidently his office, the state

1. Cf. pp. 125-126.

chancery. During the siege of Jerusalem the home of Yehonathan, the secretary, became a public prison (Jr 37: 15).

In Egypt, under the New Empire, the title 'royal scribe' occurs frequently, both on its own and in combination with other functions. There were innumerable clerks, but above them certain royal scribes had functions of the highest importance and were involved in all affairs of state. The 'scribe of the royal documents' was one of the four holders of the seal during the XIIIth Dynasty; the 'royal scribe', together with the vizier and the herald, conducted the enquiry into the pillage of the tombs in the time of Ramses IX. The same official transcribed the great edict of Horemheb at the dictation of the Pharaoh himself. There can hardly be any doubt that the Israelite post was a copy, on a reduced scale, of that which existed at the Egyptian court.

4. The royal herald

During the reigns of David and Solomon, Yehoshaphat was *mazkîr* and the post continued until the end of the monarchy, since we know of Yoah, the *mazkîr* of Ezechias, 2 K 18: 18, 37; Is 36: 3, 11, 22; and of another Yoah, *mazkîr* to Josias, according to 2 Ch 34: 8. He was not the king's annalist or archivist, as it is often translated. From the meaning of the root, and its causative (Hiphil) form, the *mazkîr* is the man who calls, names, reminds, reports. The exact equivalent is found in the Egyptian scheme of titles: the *whm.w* is 'he who repeats, calls, announces', *i.e.*, the Pharaoh's herald. He was in charge of the palace ceremonies and introduced people to audiences, but his duties far surpassed those of a modern Lord Chamberlain. He reported to the king on what concerned the people and the country, but also passed on to the people the commands of their sovereign. He was the Pharaoh's official spokesman. When the Pharaoh went abroad, he accompanied him, watched over his person, and prepared quarters for each stage of the journey.

In Israel too the herald was a very high official. The mission which received Sennacherib's envoy, himself a high ranking official, consisted only of the master of the palace, the secretary and the king's herald (2 K 18: 18). It is remarkable that in the very serious matter of the violation of the royal tombs under Ramses IX, the three corresponding Egyptian officials, the vizier, the royal scribe and the herald, are named in the same order as alone presiding over the enquiry. This parallelism confirms the connections we have noted, and underlines the Egyptian influence in the organization of the kingdom of Judah.

CHAPTER EIGHT

THE ADMINISTRATION OF THE KINGDOM

1. *The kingdom of David*

WE know nothing about the administration of the kingdom under David apart from the fact already noted,[1] that Israel and Judah remained distinct entities. It is true that 1 Ch 26: 29-32 names some Levites engaged in secular affairs under David, as civil servants or judges, and attributes to this king the establishment of a police force, also composed of Levites, who supervised all the affairs of Yahweh and the king on both sides of the Jordan; but what these statements mean, or from what period they date, cannot be decided.

It is also true that 1 Ch 27: 16-22 names the chiefs who commanded the tribes under David, but this list is obviously artificial. It follows the order of the sons of Jacob as given in 1 Ch 2: 1-2, it retains Simeon and Levi (not to mention Reuben) which under David were no longer autonomous tribes; it then divides Joseph into three (Ephraim and the two halves of Manasseh) and omits the last two names on the list, Gad and Aser, so as not to exceed the number of twelve. It is still probable, however, that in the strictly Israelite territory David retained the tribal organization as he found it established, and as we find it described, with only slight variations, in Gn 49 and Dt 33. Beyond these frontiers the subject lands were laid under tribute and administered by governors (2 S 8: 6, 14), or else left under their vassal kings (2 S 8: 2; 10: 19).

2. *The administration under Solomon*

In contrast to this, a most important document has survived from the reign of Solomon. It is a list of twelve prefects, *niṣṣabîm*, with the description of the lands they governed (1 K 4: 7-19). Five of them are named only by their patronymic, 'son of X', and it has been suggested that the redactor had before him an old document from the archives, the edge of which was damaged: this would account for the absence of certain personal names. On the other hand, the administrative lists of Ugarit show that this designation by patronymic alone was the rule for certain families, which served the king from father to son. The twelve prefectures are given in the following order:

1. Cf. pp. 95-96.

I. The hill-country of Ephraim, probably including part of the territory of Manasseh.

II. The former country of the Danites, augmented by the districts annexed from the Canaanites and Philistines.

III. The plain of Sharon, from Philistia in the south to the next district on the north.

IV. The prefecture of Dor, continuing from the plain of Sharon and bounded on the east by the ridge of Carmel.

V. The former Canaanite territories in the plain of Esdraelon and the region of Beisan.

VI. On the other side of the Jordan, with Ramoth-Gilead as its capital, what was formerly Eastern Manasseh, and what remained of David's Aramaean conquests.

VII. In Transjordan, the prefecture of Mahanaim, lying to the south of the last-named territory.

VIII. The territory of Nephthali, to the north of the Lake of Tiberias.

IX. The territory of Aser, lying between Nephthali and the Phoenician possessions along the coast.

X. The territory of Issachar, to the south of the Aser and Nephthali prefectures.

XI. The territory of Benjamin.

XII. The territory of Gad (following the Greek text, instead of Gilead) on the other side of the Jordan.

This list dates from the second half of Solomon's reign, as two of the prefects are the king's sons-in-law. The order followed is not always geographical, but follows a logical arrangement: the house of Joseph (I), to which are attached the former Canaanite territories (II, III, IV, V), then the conquests in Transjordan (VI, VII), the Northern tribes (VIII, IX, X), and finally Benjamin (XI) and Gad, facing it on the other side of the Jordan (XII). According to 1 K 4: 7; 5: 7-9, each of the twelve districts supplied on a monthly rota the provisions needed by the Palace (by which is meant the whole staff in the king's service) and the forage for the horses and draught animals. The whole system was under the central control of an officer who held authority over the prefects, Azaryahu son of Nathan, who was a member of Solomon's ministerial cabinet (1 K 4: 5). Mesopotamian documents provide evidence of a vaguely similar organization in the Neo-Babylonian period, and Herodotus (I, 192) states that under Cyrus the victualling of the court and the army was allotted to the provinces according to the month of the year, four months being imposed on Babylonia because of its exceptional wealth.

The avowed object of the Israelite system was to ensure the raising of the revenue. The rôle of the prefects was of course wider than that: they were the governors of their districts, which represented the administrative divisions of the kingdom. But one must remember that in Eastern monarchies, both ancient and modern, the essential task of the administrators, apart from the maintenance of order, is the collection of the taxes and tithes. It will be noticed that six of the prefectures are described by the names of tribes. Evidently Solomon did not try to destroy the administrative units which existed before him; in fact he preserved them when he could, but he had to integrate the Canaanite enclaves conquered by David into the old tribal territories, or group them with each other. He also had to ensure a measure of equality between the districts, since they had to take turns in providing the needs of the State for a month at a time. In point of fact we do not know how the system worked in practice, and it is doubtful whether the small district of Benjamin, for example, was obliged to provide as much as the whole of Ephraim.

It is still more surprising that Judah does not figure in this list. Some exegetes, in fact, have been so surprised that they have modified the text in order to bring Judah in. None the less, Judah is implicitly mentioned: it is 'the land' which, according to 1 K 4: 19b, had a governor of its own (in the same way, in Assyrian, *matu*, 'the land', means the central province of the empire). But this mention comes after the end of the list of the twelve prefectures; Judah, then, was not incorporated in this system. It would be rash to conclude that it was exempted from all taxation, but one must at least admit that it had an administration of its own. Perhaps the reason why the organization of Judah is not described is that Solomon did not modify it, because he had no new territories to integrate in this region. But this difference of treatment emphasizes the dualist nature of Solomon's monarchy.[1]

We do not know how Solomon administered his external possessions. The allusions to the tribute of the vassal kingdoms (1 K 5: 1), and to what was paid in by the 'pashas of the land' (1 K 10: 15b), occur in glosses added to the text, and in any case give us no details. As far as he could, Solomon must have preserved the organizations created by his father, in the regions which he succeeded in retaining (1 K 2: 10-14; 11: 14-25).

3. *The districts of Judah*

We have just said that nothing is known about the organization of Judah under Solomon, but we are perhaps better informed on the situation after the schism. In Jos 15: 21-62 (excepting vv. 45-47, which are later insertions) there is a list of the towns of Judah, forming eleven groups introduced by geographical titles.

A list of the towns of Benjamin (Jos 18: 21-28) makes a twelfth group; this list has been separated from the previous list to furnish names of towns in the territory of Benjamin, whose boundaries, like those of the other tribes, are described in accordance with a premonarchical document. It is less certain

1. Cf. p. 96.

that we should include in this list the groups of towns of Simeon (Jos 19: 2-8), and of Dan (Jos 19: 41-46), which have been inserted here accidentally, and are of composite origin. We thus obtain a picture of twelve districts, covering the whole kingdom of Judah. The administrative centres are not indicated; from the towns mentioned we have chosen whichever seems to be the most important, or which gives the best indication of the geographical position of the district.

In the Negeb:
    I. Beersheba (Jos 15: 21-32).

In the Plain:
    II. Azeqah (Jos 15: 33-36).
    III. Lakish (Jos 15: 37-41).
    IV. Mareshah (Jos 15: 42-44).

In the Hill-country:
    V. Debir (Jos 15: 48-51).
    VI. Hebron (Jos 15: 52-54).
    VII. Maon (Jos 15: 55-57).
    VIII. Beth-Sur (Jos 15: 58-59a).
    IX. Bethlehem (Jos 15: 59b Greek; missing in Hebrew).
    X. Qiryath-Yearim (Jos 15: 60).
    XI. Gibeon (to be taken from Jos 18: 25-28).

In the desert:
    XII. Engaddi (Jos 15: 61-62).

This table reveals an organization similar to that of Solomon's twelve prefectures, and no doubt designed, like the former, to ensure the collection of the taxes. In this connection we may recall the governors and the collecting centres established by Josaphat (2 Ch 17: 2, 12). An organization of this kind may have existed even under David and Solomon, but if so, we have no knowledge of it, and according to 1 K 4: 19b, the 'Land', i.e. Judah, was administered by a single governor (the word is different from that used for Solomon's prefects, and the same as that in 2 Ch 17: 2). In any case, the organization we have reconstructed from the lists in Josue is certainly later than the schism, since it includes a part of Israel's two most southerly prefectures under Solomon. But it is impossible to decide how late we should date the list. One authoritative opinion has it that these lists represent the state of the kingdom under Josias, but good arguments have recently been brought forward in favour of an earlier date, viz. the reign of Josaphat, in the ninth century. It is hard to decide, because the document was revised either before, or when, it was inserted into the book of Josue. It is enough for our purpose that it gives us the scheme of an administrative division of the kingdom of Judah.

4. *The districts of the kingdom of Israel*

For the kingdom of Israel we have nothing like this. One is tempted to apply the same method to the lists of towns given by the book of Josue for the northern tribes, but these lists are a medley of points vaguely marking the tribal frontiers and filled with names of towns borrowed from other Biblical lists. We can only presume that the northern kingdom preserved the system of Solomon's prefectures in so far as it retained control over their territory. There is casual mention in 1 K 20: 14-20 of the chiefs of districts, here called *m'dînôth*, the word used in the Book of Esther for the satrapies of the Persian empire.

The ostraka from Samaria, which have already been quoted in connection with the royal estate,[1] provide some details about the central region of the kingdom. Certain geographical names appear as those of districts, each comprising several villages: Abiezer, Heleq, Shechem, Shemida, Noah, Hoglah, Soreq. Except for the last, these districts are given as the clans of Manasseh in Jos 17: 2-3, along with several other names which probably correspond to administrative divisions. This is certainly true of Tirsah, the ancient capital, for the excavations at Tell el-Farah have proved that it retained its importance until the eighth century B.C. Naturally these ostraka do not provide a complete picture, for it is sheer chance that has preserved them, and it seems that they all refer to the management of the royal estate. All these districts were dependent on Samaria, where these ostraka were found: Samaria was both the capital of the kingdom and the administrative centre of a province. It has been suggested, with less probability, that they cover all the territory left to Joachaz of Israel after the incursions of the Aramaeans and the men of Judah.

5. *Local administration*

Mesopotamian documents, especially for the time of Hammurabi, provide ample information about their internal administration of the provinces, and about the numerous duties of their governors and the staff which assisted them; but very little of the kind survives about Israel.

We learn incidentally that the two capitals, Jerusalem and Samaria, each had a governor. He bore the title of *śar ha'îr*, 'chief of the town', or (once) *'asher 'al ha'îr*, 'he who is over the town'. The 'town' suffices to describe the capital, as in 2 K 11: 20; Is 66: 6; Ez 7: 23. It is Amon, governor of Samaria, who is ordered by Achab to put the prophet Michaeas ben Yimlah in prison (1 K 22: 26). An unnamed governor of Samaria appears, together with the master of the palace and the Elders, in the time of Jehu (2 K 10: 5). Under Josias there was at Jerusalem a 'gate of Joshua, governor of the town' (2 K 23: 8), but one of his successors was by then in charge, called Maaseyahu,

1. Cf. p. 126.

according to 2 Ch 34: 8, where he is mentioned with the royal secretary and
the herald. He was evidently an important person, nominated by the king.
Much earlier, in the abortive attempt at monarchy at Shechem, a governor of
the town is mentioned (Jg 9: 30); he had been appointed by Abimelek
(Jg 9: 28). We have no proof that there was a similar post in towns other than
the capitals. There may perhaps be an indication to the contrary: in 2 K 10:
5, the governor of Samaria, with the master of the palace and the Elders,
replies to a message addressed to them by Jehu; but when Jezabel plots the
death of Naboth she writes only to the Elders and notables of Yizreel, and no
governor of the town appears in the story, though as an official appointed by
the king he would have had a major part to play in it (1 K 21: 8-11). In
Assyria and Babylonia we know there was a head of the town (*rab âli*), and
that there were mayors (*ḥazânu*) in the small towns; there is also evidence for
these in the kingdoms of Mari on the Euphrates. But at Ugarit the burgo-
master (*ḥazanu* or *ḥazan âli*) seems to have been the governor of the capital,
where he had authority over all the inhabitants except those who had been
ennobled by the king. This is certainly the nearest parallel with the *śar ha'îr*
of the Bible.

Outside the two capitals, local affairs were, it seems, left in the hands of the
Elders, the *z'qenîm*.¹ They formed a sort of municipal council. They are the
men who take action under the laws of Dt 19; 21: 1-9, 18-21; 22: 13-21; 25:
5-10. At the end of Saul's reign, David sent messages and gifts to the Elders
of the different towns of Judah (1 S 30: 26-31). Jezabel wrote to the Elders of
Yizreel (1 K 21: 8) and Jehu addressed himself to the Elders of Samaria
and to the royal officials (2 K 10: 1, 5). The Elders of Judah and Jerusalem
were convened by Josias to hear the reading of the Law (2 K 23: 1). In
Mesopotamia, from the archives of Mari in the eighteenth century B.C.
down to the royal correspondence of the Sargon dynasty in the eighth, the
Elders appear as the people's representatives and the defenders of their interests, but without any administrative functions. In the Hittite empire, however, municipal affairs seem to have been left to the council of the Elders,
which also settled local disputes in co-operation with the commander of the
garrison. The Phoenician towns also had their assemblies of Elders, attested,
for Byblos and Tyre, by non-Biblical documents, and cf. Ez 27: 9. In Israel
the Elders had a similar rôle; under the monarchy they continued to regulate
the life of the clans, thereafter identified with the towns and villages.² They
survived the collapse of the royal institutions; we meet them again during
the Exile (Ez 8: 1; 14: 1; 20: 1, 3), and after the Return (Esd 10: 8, 14).

1. Cf. p. 69.   2. Cf. p. 13.

CHAPTER NINE

FINANCE AND PUBLIC WORKS

1. *Royal revenues and State revenues*

LITTLE is known about the fiscal system of Israel or the resources at the disposal of the State. First of all, it must be admitted that there was no distinction between the king's revenues and those of the kingdom. A sovereign's wealth was the expression of his own power and of that of the kingdom he ruled (cf. 1 K 10: 23; 2 Ch 17: 5; 26: 8). The king bore all the expenses (the upkeep of the administration and the army, national defence and public works), but he also enjoyed absolute control of the entire revenue. Similarly, there was only a theoretical distinction between the national and religious treasuries (cf. 1 K 14: 26). The king might deposit in the sanctuary booty taken from the enemy (cf. Jos 6: 19) and his personal gifts (2 S 8: 11; 1 K 7: 51; 15: 15; 2 K 12: 19); his officials too were in charge of the offerings made by the people (2 K 12: 10f.; 22: 3-4); but to meet urgent demands he would draw on both the Temple and Palace treasuries (1 K 15: 18; 2 K 12: 19; 16: 8; 18: 15; cf. even Jg 9: 4).

The king had at his disposal the produce of the royal estate,[1] the profits of his commercial and industrial enterprises,[2] the import or transit taxes paid by the caravan merchants (1 K 10: 15), and the tribute of the vassal states. This last source was an abundant one under David (2 S 8: 2, 6) and under Solomon (according to 1 K 5: 1), but shrank as the external possessions were lost. Mesha king of Moab, before he shook off the yoke of Israel, paid a tribute in kind for which 2 K 3: 4 gives some fantastic figures: 100,000 lambs and the wool of 100,000 rams. According to 2 Ch 17: 11, the Philistines paid tribute to Josaphat, and the Arabs brought him in tribute or gifts 7,700 rams and 7,700 goats. The Ammonites paid tribute to Ozias, according to 2 Ch 26: 8.

2. *'Voluntary' or exceptional contributions*

In addition there were the presents brought by foreign embassies. All the kings of the earth, it was said, wished to be received by Solomon, and each brought his gift (1 K 10: 24-25), but none surpassed the queen of Saba in

1. Cf. pp. 124-125.　　　　　　　2. Cf. p. 78.

lavishness (1 K 10: 2, 10). Before this the king of Hamath had sent gold, silver and bronze to David (2 S 8: 10), and Merodak-Baladan sent a present to Ezechias (2 K 20: 12=Is 39: 1). But these transactions were scarcely profitable, since the king of Israel had to return these courtesies with an equally lavish gesture (1 K 10: 13). The custom was in fact general among the kings of the East.

The sovereign made a clearer profit from the presents which had to be offered by all who presented themselves at court. When David was admitted to Saul's presence he brought only a modest offering (1 S 16: 20), but when Naaman was sent by his master to the king of Israel, his present was a princely one (2 K 5: 5). On the occasion of the king's coronation, custom obliged men to make presents to the king when they swore him fidelity (1 S 10: 27). Such more or less voluntary contributions are also mentioned in Ugaritic documents.

In grave circumstances the king would decree an exceptional tax. Menahem, for example, levied a thousand talents of silver on all the men of rank in Israel, at the rate of fifty shekels a head, in order to buy the favour of Tiglath-Pileser III (2 K 15: 19-20). Joiaqim raised the hundred talents of silver and ten talents of gold demanded by the Pharaoh by taxing the people of Judah, according to their wealth (2 K 23: 33-35).

3. Tithes

Some exegetes have argued that, apart from these occasional contributions, the Israelites were not subject to regular taxation, but this is contradicted by several facts. Solomon's prefectures[1] presuppose a system of revenues in kind which did not derive solely from the royal estates, and when 2 Ch 17: 5 says that all Judah brought its tribute to Josaphat, this is best understood as an annual tax, like the tribute of the vassal states. Though Gn 47: 13-26 describes the land system of Egypt as something strange, owing its origin to Joseph, what surprises the redactor is not that revenues are paid to the Pharaoh but that all the lands, except those of the temples, belong to him and that all the Egyptians are serfs of the crown, in contrast with the system of private property prevailing in Israel.

In particular, 1 S 8: 15, 17 predicts that the king will levy the tithe on the fields, the vineyards and the herds. This is what went on in the neighbouring kingdoms, as is clearly proved by the Ugarit texts. The Bible states that the king may leave this revenue to his officers; this custom is attested by Ugaritic documents also, and there is perhaps an allusion to this practice in Am 5: 11, where the prophet rebukes the men of rank for crushing the poor man by extorting tribute from his corn.

The king seems to have had a right over the first mowing of the meadows

1. Cf. pp. 133-135.

(Am 7: 1), similar, perhaps, to the right of pasturage exercised by the sovereign of Ugarit. Both there and in Israel an individual or his family could be exempted, by the king's favour, from tithes and forced labour (1 S 17: 25).

It is on the model of this institution of the monarchical period that Ezechiel, over and above the estate he reserves for the prince of Israel, fixes the revenue which all the people of the land will owe him, in wheat, barley, oil and live-stock (Ez 45: 13-16); in return for this, and in accordance with the ideals of theocracy envisaged by Ezechiel, the prince will be responsible for all the public sacrifices and oblations (Ez 45: 17).

A final stage was reached when the theocracy was actually set up after the return from the Exile; the people solemnly undertook to pay into the Temple a third of a shekel annually, the first fruits of the earth and the flocks, a tithe on the soil and certain offerings of wood (Ne 10: 33-40). Trustworthy men were charged with collecting, storing and distributing these revenues (Ne 12: 44-47; 13: 10-13). These measures can no doubt be interpreted as the fulfilment of the Priestly laws about the tithe due to the sanctuary and its ministers, but whatever be the date of these regulations, it can scarcely be doubted that this religious legislation is the parallel to, or the memory of, a similar civil institution.

4. *Forced labour*

Forced labour was universal in the ancient East. There is evidence of it in Lower Mesopotamia from the earliest times down to the Neo-Babylonian period. The Assyrian laws condemn certain criminals to a period of forced labour for the king. The Israelites preserved a harrowing memory of the tasks imposed on their ancestors in Egypt (Ex 1: 11-14; 5: 4-19; cf. Dt 26: 6), though their lot had been no worse than that of all the Pharaoh's subjects. Forced labour is also mentioned in the documents of Syria and Palestine before the Israelite settlement.

In Israel it was not organized till after the institution of the monarchy; it was one of the disadvantages foretold by 1 S 8: 12, 16-17. David imposed it on the Ammonites (2 S 12: 31), unless this means that they were reduced to utter slavery.[1] A defeated enemy, if he survived, became liable to this levy (Is 31:8; Lm 1:1). At the end of his reign, David is said to have had a minister set over the levy (2 S 20: 24), but this statement is not certain.[2] In any case it is under Solomon that the institution appears in its full development. The great works undertaken by the king, the building of the Temple and the Palace, the fortification of Jerusalem and the garrison towns (1 K 9: 15-19), required a considerable labour force. Solomon of course had state slaves at his disposal, whom he used on the Red Sea fleet and in his factory at Esyon-Geber,[3] and they probably worked also on the great buildings of his reign. The text of 1 K 9: 20-22 implies that all the men employed on them were

1. Cf. p. 89.   2. Cf. p. 128.   3. Cf. p. 89.

descendants of those Canaanites who had escaped extermination and that the Israelites furnished only soldiers and officers for the king. This information, however, does not come from an early document; the text is in the style of Deuteronomy and reflects an opinion from the end of the monarchical period. The same opinion recurs in Chronicles (2 Ch 2: 16-17; 8: 7-9), where it is explicitly stated that only resident aliens had been employed on these buildings.

But the earlier texts are equally explicit in stating that Israelites were involved. It was in 'all Israel' (1 K 5: 27) that Solomon raised the men for the levy, *mas*, and he had 30,000 workmen, of whom 10,000 went in their turn to the Lebanon to cart the wood cut by the king of Tyre's woodcutters (1 K 5: 20, 23, 27-28). Further, it is said, he had 70,000 porters and 80,000 quarrymen employed at Jerusalem with Hiram's masons and carpenters (1 K 5: 29-32). The 'levy of the house of Joseph' over which Jeroboam was placed (1 K 11: 28) was made up of Israelites. It was in fact this burden laid on the Israelites which incited Jeroboam to revolt (1 K 11: 26f.), and after Solomon's death it is given as the main cause of the political schism (1 K 12: 4-16).

The levy was staffed by supervisors and officers (1 K 5: 30; 9: 23; 11: 28), under the orders of the chief of the levy, Adoram, son of Abda, apparently a Phoenician, who was one of Solomon's ministers (1 K 4: 6; 5: 28).[1] It was this Adoram, whom Roboam, through stupidity or for provocation, sent to subdue the rebels of Israel, and who was stoned to death by them (1 K 12: 18).

Later history contains no mention of any other chief of the levy, and it would appear that this ceased to be a regular institution after Solomon's reign. Yet from time to time the kings of Israel and Judah must have resorted to it for the building programmes attributed to them; there is explicit evidence for this in the reign of Asa, who called up every single man in Judah to fortify Geba and Mispah (1 K 15: 22). But popular sentiment regarded this forced labour as an exaction, and Jeremias denounces Joiaqim for building his palace with no respect for justice, making men work without pay (Jr 22: 13). This explains the reluctance of the redactors of the Books of Kings and Chronicles to admit that Solomon had used free Israelites in the levy. Under Nehemias the walls of Jerusalem were rebuilt by teams of volunteers; the writer merely observes that the leading men from Teqoa refused to take part in it (Ne 3: 5).

1. Cf. p. 128.

Chapter Ten

LAW AND JUSTICE

1. *Legislative codes*

THE Law, *Tôrah*, means in the first place a teaching, a doctrine, a decision given for a particular case. Collectively, the word means the whole body of rules governing men's relations with God and with each other. Finally the word comes to mean the first five books of the Bible, the Pentateuch, containing God's instructions to his people, the prescriptions which his people had to observe in their moral, social and religious life. All the legislative codes of the Old Testament are found in the Pentateuch.

(a) *The Decalogue* contains the 'Ten Words' of Yahweh, the essential precepts of morality and religion. It is set out twice (Ex 20: 2-17 and Dt 5: 6-21) with some significant variants, but the two texts stem from a shorter primitive form which may justifiably be assigned to the Mosaic Age.

(b) *The Code of the Covenant* (Ex 20: 22-23: 33) is a composite collection, in which one can easily distinguish a central portion (Ex 21: 1-22: 16), where 'sentences' or 'judgments', *mishpaṭim*, of civil and criminal law are grouped together: it is a law for a community of shepherds and peasants. The present context (cf. Ex 24: 3-8) connects it, like the Decalogue which precedes it, with the Sinaitic Covenant, but the directions about slaves, cattle, fields, vineyards and houses can only apply to an already settled population. This code has obvious connections with the curses of Dt 27: 15-26, the 'law' (Dt 27: 26) which was to be proclaimed on Mount Ebal (or Garizim?) after the entry into Canaan (Dt 27: 11-14). This command of Moses was carried out by Josue, according to Jos 8: 30-35, the opening words of which recall in turn the law of the altar with which the Code of the Covenant begins (Ex 20: 24-25). But this passage in Jos 8 does not fit in with its present context nearly so well as with the assembly at Shechem, where Joshua gave the people a law (*mishpaṭ*) written in a 'book of the law' (Jos 24: 25-26). We cannot be certain that the Code of the Covenant, in the form in which it has come down to us, is the actual law promulgated by Josue at Shechem, but we can say that internal evidence and the witness of tradition agree in dating this Code from the early days of the settlement in Canaan, before the organization of the State. It is the law of the tribal federation.

(c) *Deuteronomy*, in its legislative part (Dt 12-26), forms another code which brings together, in ill-defined order, some short collections of laws which may have originated in different ways. Some of them repeat the directions of the Code of the Covenant, others, *e.g.* the laws on the one sanctuary and on the slaves, modify them, and many others are added. This code seems designed to replace the old code by taking account of a whole social and religious evolution; it also reveals a change of spirit by its appeals to the heart and by the tone of exhortation in which its prescriptions are often couched. Fundamentally, it is certainly the 'law' discovered in the Temple in the time of Josias (2 K 22:8f.). It contains ancient elements which seem to stem, at least in part, from the Northern kingdom, but it is difficult to say how long before the reign of Josias they were collected and completed. One plausible hypothesis is that they were brought to Judah after the fall of Samaria and put together under Ezechias.

(d) *The Law of Holiness* (Lv 17-26) is also a compilation, containing a number of doublets. But it constitutes a unity which, like Deuteronomy, begins with rules about sacrifices and ends with blessings and curses. It differs from it by its strong preoccupation with rites and the priesthood, and its constant reminders of the holiness of Yahweh and his people. It may represent the customs in vogue at the end of the monarchy, originating in a different *milieu* from that of Deuteronomy, and codified during the Exile. It may well have received some additions before or after its inclusion in the Pentateuch.

(e) *The Priestly Code*. The rest of Leviticus is composed of other collections: laws about sacrifices (Lv 1-7); the ritual for the installation of priests (Lv 8-10); the law of purity (Lv 11-16), to which must be added the legislative texts scattered throughout Ex and Nb and associated with events of the desert period. The sum total of these enactments and the narratives in which they are set, together with the Law of Holiness, form what critics call the Priestly Code. It contains some rules which are very ancient and others which are much more recent, and it received its final form only in the Jewish community after its return from Exile.

This brief survey is enough to make clear how inorganic was the legislation of Israel, how it varied with the background and time, and how much more closely connected it was with religious than with civil life. These are points to which we shall have to return, but before embarking on them we must compare this body of law with those of the other peoples in the ancient East.

2. *Eastern law in ancient times*

It is a remarkable fact that Egypt, where there was so much writing and so much litigation, has left us no body of laws (the Edict of Horemheb is only an administrative document); nor is there any record of any Egyptian king's having been a law-giver, apart from some traditions collected at a very late date by Diodorus of Sicily (I 94), which we cannot check. It was a foreign conqueror, Darius, who issued the only codification recorded by an Egyptian text. Egypt seems to have felt no need for a written law because it had a living law, the Pharaoh, son of Ra, a god upon earth, whose word laid down the law. The language has no word to denote law as such. The nearest term is *ma'at*, which covers the concepts of truth and justice and is an attribute, itself divine, of the Pharaoh. The judges gave their decisions according to the principles of this 'truth which is justice' and by applying the unwritten customs or the directive of the sovereign.

Babylonia, on the other hand, has bequeathed several collections of laws ascribed to the initiative of a king or placed under his name, and they are very ancient. The Code of Ur-Nammu or Ur is to be dated about 2050 B.C., that of Lipit-Ishtar of Isin, about 1850; the law of the city of Eshnunna was promulgated by an unknown king long before Hammurabi and perhaps before Lipit-Ishtar; lastly, the Code of Hammurabi of Babylon, issued about 1700, was the first to be discovered and is the most complete. These are not, strictly speaking, 'codes' in our modern sense, *i.e.* bodies of law to which the judge is obliged to refer in giving judgment. It is noteworthy that in Mesopotamian texts we never come across expressions like 'by application of the law' or 'in virtue of such and such a law'. There is not even any word meaning 'law' in general. The king governs and the judges decide according to 'justice' (*mesharu*) or 'the truth' (*kittu*), following the accepted custom in similar cases. The practice was therefore not very different from that in Egypt, but in Mesopotamia this legal tradition or jurisprudence was, in certain circumstances, collected and put into writing, rather for the benefit of the people, it seems, than for that of the judges. These 'codes', however, were not binding texts, as is evident from the number of divergent solutions given to the same cases by contemporary juridical acts.

The Collection of Assyrian Laws, compiled about 1100 but making use of older material, has long been recognized as a book of law, a manual of jurisprudence, but it covers only certain fields, and does not attempt to set forth the general law of the State. It is perhaps the work of a private jurist, but even if it was compiled for the use of the judges by an official authority, it would still be a reference-book rather than an authoritative code.

The Hittite laws are preserved in copies probably dating from the thirteenth century B.C., but they were compiled, apparently, about 1500. They frequently contrast 'what must be done' now with 'what was done formerly', the change being usually a reduction of the penalty. They are based, then, on an older customary law. They do not constitute a code; they form an even looser collection than that of the Assyrian laws. They refer mostly to very particular cases, the presumption being that ordinary cases will be settled by simple and generally accepted rules.

No similar collection is forthcoming from Syria or Palestine, where juridical texts are extremely rare, apart from the two lots recently discovered

in northern Syria, at Ras Shamra and Alalakh. Their principal characteristic
is the special place assigned to the king, acting as representative of public
authority: judgment is represented as his personal act, without reference to a
law of the State. Their usages and formularies have certain peculiar features,
but on the whole they have little which is not found in some other province
of the ancient East, whether in Asia Minor, Babylonia or more distant Elam.

This fundamental unity of Eastern law is of greater importance than the
variations to be found between regions and epochs. It is the expression of a
common civilization, in which the application of the same juridical principles
has produced a similar customary law.

3. *The sources of Israelite law*

The civil legislation of the Old Testament belongs to the same ancient
world, though it certainly has an originality which will be emphasized
later. The very close connections and even the occasional identity of expression which we find between Israelite law and the Code of Hammurabi, the
Assyrian Collection or the Hittite laws, is not to be explained by direct
borrowing but by the influence of a single widespread customary law.

The legislative codes of the Old Testament are collections of particular
rules, like the Eastern 'codes', and they are even less unified than the latter.
They are also more heterogeneous; ethical, religious or ritual prescriptions
are found side by side with articles of civil or criminal law. The laws fall into
two groups according to their style. There are laws in casuistical form, in
which the conjunction 'if' or 'supposing that' introduces a typical case,
followed by the solution. 'If you take a man's cloak as security, you must
return it to him at nightfall' (Ex 22: 25). 'Supposing that a bull gores a
man ... that bull shall be stoned' (Ex 21: 28, etc.). Other laws are in an
apodictic form and lay down commands or prohibitions in the second person
future. 'You shall not allow a witch to live' (Ex 22: 17). 'You shall not boil a
kid in its mother's milk' (Ex 23: 19; Dt 14: 21, etc.). The casuistic form is
used chiefly for secular law, the apodictic form chiefly for laws covering
worship. But we must observe that the distinction of styles and their use is
less rigid than is usually thought.

What was the origin of these forms? A theory at present in favour holds
that 'casuistic' law is a wholesale borrowing from the Canaanite legislation
which the Israelites encountered when they settled in the land, and that the
'apodictic' law represents the strictly Israelite tradition. It is mere guesswork
to speculate about the formulation of Canaanite law so long as we possess
none of the legislative texts which embodied it, and the juridical texts of
Alalakh and Ras Shamra suggest that it hardly differed at all from other
Oriental laws. The fact remains that the Mesopotamian codes are compiled
in casuistic form, and part of the Israelitic law closely resembles them in style.

Like these codes, the legislative collections of Israel bring together customary decisions.

The apodictic form is not found in these codes. But the originality of Israel in this respect is less striking if we compare it with the treaties imposed by the Hittite kings on their vassals. The treaties very frequently contain clauses introduced by 'if', and also imperative clauses, as for example: 'You shall keep the land which I have given you and shall not covet any territory of the land of Hatti.' The form is like that of the Decalogue: 'You shall not covet your neighbour's house, etc.' (Ex 20: 17). We also have the remains, though badly damaged, of three Assyrian treaties of vassalage, and an important part of a treaty in Aramaic, found at Sfiré near Aleppo; and a treaty of vassalage imposed by Asarhaddon on certain princes of Media has recently been discovered. The essential points of the Hittite treaties are also found in these Assyrian ones; the texts date from the first millennium and may be compared with the legislation of the Old Testament. The structure of Old Testament legislation, however, is much closer to that of the Hittite documents, which date from the second half of the second millennium. In addition, Ras Shamra has yielded fragments of treaties which were imposed on the king of Ugarit by a Hittite sovereign.

4. *Characteristics of Israelite law*

These resemblances are not accidental. The Covenant between Yahweh and his people had to be sealed by a treaty, and between God and men this could only be a treaty of vassalage. The ancient legal codes of Israel do in fact read like the clauses of such a treaty. The Decalogue is the deed of the Sinaitic covenant, inscribed on large stones entrusted by God to Moses (Ex 24: 12), which are the tables of the law (*'edûth*: Ex 31: 18), or the tables of the covenant (*b'rîth*: Dt 9: 9). The Code of the Covenant, as we have seen, may be connected with the pact at Shechem, where Josue concluded a covenant between Yahweh and the people, and gave the people a statute and a law (Jos 24: 25-26). The Code of Deuteronomy is also the expression of a pact: it is set forth as the sum total of the conditions accompanying the gift of the Holy Land (Dt 12: 1; cf. 11: 31-32), and after the curses and blessings it culminates in these words: 'These are the words of the covenant which Yahweh commanded Moses to make with the children of Israel, in the land of Moab, in addition to the covenant he had made with them at Horeb' (Dt 28: 69); the Deuteronomic law is thus connected with the Decalogue, by-passing the Code of the Covenant, which it professes to replace. Under Josias, this Deuteronomic law was accepted by the king and the people as a covenant with Yahweh (2 K 23: 2-3). The fiction of a treaty is still maintained in the Law of Holiness, which ends by recalling the covenant (Lv 26: 42-45), and concludes: 'These are the customs, rules and laws which Yahweh established between himself and the Israelites' (Lv 26: 46).

If this is granted, other points of resemblance appear between the legal codes of the Old Testament and Oriental treaties. The latter begin with a historical introduction, sometimes fairly long, recalling the events leading up to the treaty. Similarly, the two promulgations of the Decalogue are introduced by a very short summary of previous facts (Ex 20: 1; Dt 5: 4-5). This is more developed in the narrative of the pact at Shechem (Jos 24: 2-13), to which we assigned the Code of the Covenant; in the first chapters of Deuteronomy it becomes a record of the entire history of the people. Oriental treaties end with formulas of cursing and blessing, as sanctions for the keeping or breaking of the engagements undertaken. So too the Law of Holiness and the Code of Deuteronomy conclude with blessings and curses (Lv 26: 3-41; Dt 28). The Code of the Covenant has no similar conclusion in its present context, but this context is not the original one, and if we were right in associating this Code with the pact at Shechem, it too involved curses and blessings (cf. Jos 8: 34; Dt 11: 26-29; 27: 12-13): the curses would then be those recorded in Dt 27: 15-26, which, as we have already noted, were closely connected with the Code of the Covenant.

Oriental treaties were inscribed on tablets, or engraved on a stele, and placed in a sanctuary in the presence of the gods. The Decalogue was engraved on two tablets and deposited in the sacred tent, in the Ark 'of the Covenant' or 'of the Law'. The pact at Shechem was written in a book, according to Jos 24: 26, on stones according to Jos 8: 35; Dt 27: 2-4, and the record of this pact was preserved in the sanctuary of Yahweh (Jos 24: 26-27). Again, the 'book of the law', Deuteronomy, was discovered in the Temple at Jerusalem (2 K 22: 8).

Finally, several Hittite treaties order the text to be read periodically before the vassal king and his people. So too Dt 31: 10-13 prescribes a public reading of the law every seven years. It is very likely that such readings actually took place, perhaps even more often, *e.g.* in connection with an annual ceremony for renewing the Covenant, similar to that recorded by the Dead Sea scrolls among the Qumran sect. The historical books have recorded only readings which took place in certain exceptional circumstances, at the reform of Josaphat (2 Ch 17: 9), after the discovery of the Deuteronomy (2 K 23: 2), and after the promulgation of the law by Esdras (Ne 8: 4-18).

But since these pacts governed the relations of Israel's dependence on Yahweh, not on a human suzerain, the Israelite law, for all its resemblances in form and content, differs radically from the clauses of the Oriental 'treaties' and the articles of their 'codes'. It is a religious law. It established the principles of the Covenant with Yahweh: its aim was to ensure that this Covenant remained in force. It is perfectly true that the Hittite and Assyrian treaties invoke their gods as guarantors, and that in the prologue and epilogue of their codes Lipit-Ishtar purports to be the interpreter of Enlil, and Hammurabi to be 'the king of justice to whom Shamash has entrusted the law'; but God was not merely a guarantor of the Covenant, he was a party to it, and no Oriental code can be compared with the Israelite law, which is ascribed in its entirety to God as its author. If it contains, and often mingles, ethical and ritual prescriptions, this is because it covers the whole field of the divine Covenant, and because this Covenant governed the relations of men with one another as well as their relations with God.

The law was the charter of the covenant with God; hence it contained the obligations undertaken by the people, but it was also a body of teaching directed to them. From this notion another characteristic of Israelite legislation proceeds. Unlike all other Eastern laws, its prescriptions are often supported by a justifying motive. This may be a simple explanation based on common sense: if a man has violated an already betrothed girl in the town, both are put to death, 'the girl because she did not call for help, the man because he has abused his neighbour's wife' (Dt 22: 24). Alternatively, the motive may be moral: in judicial actions, gifts must not be accepted 'because gifts blind the eyes of the clear-sighted' (Ex 23: 8). Often it is a religious motive, as in the Decalogue itself: idolatry is forbidden, 'for I, Yahweh your God, am a jealous God' (Ex 20: 5): this is often found in the Law of Holiness, where the prescriptions are punctuated with the refrain, 'I am Yahweh, your God.' Finally, it may be an appeal to history, especially the remembrance of the deliverance from Egypt (Ex 23: 9; Lv 19: 36; Dt 5: 15; 24: 18, etc.). The examples quoted show that these motives are attached to apodictical and casuisitical laws alike and are found in different collections. They are proportionately more numerous in Deuteronomy and the Law of Holiness, but they are found as early as the Decalogue and the Code of the Covenant, and they are certainly a primitive feature of the law in Israel.

This connection between the law and religion explains one last characteristic of Israelite legislation. Because it is designed to safeguard the Covenant, it enjoins severe penalties for all crimes against God, idolatry and blasphemy, and for crimes which tarnish the holiness of the chosen people, e.g., bestiality, sodomy and incest. But it is further distinguished from other Eastern codes (even the Hittite, which is the most lenient) by the humaneness of its sentences. Bodily mutilation is exacted only in one very special case (Dt 25: 11-12) which the Assyrian law punishes in the same way. Flogging is limited to forty strokes, 'lest the bruises be dangerous and your brother be degraded' (Dt 25: 3). Certain dispositions in the Code of the Covenant, more developed in Deuteronomy, protect the stranger, the poor, the oppressed, the widow and the orphan, even the personal enemy (Ex 22: 20-26; 23: 4-9; Dt 23: 16, 20; 24 passim). Exemptions from military service are very generous (Dt 20: 5-9). The law of retaliation, however, the lex talionis, is expressed in all its crudeness: 'life for life, eye for eye, tooth for tooth, hand for hand, foot for foot, burning for burning, bruise for bruise, wound for wound' (Ex 21: 23-25; cf. Lv 24: 19-20; Dt 19: 21). But this formula seems to have lost its force, merely asserting the principle of proportionate compensation. In the oldest text, that of Exodus, it is in fact followed immediately by a law which orders the liberation of a slave in compensation for the loss of an eye or a tooth (Ex 21: 26-27), and it is preceded by a law which, for a wound inflicted in a fight, orders only the payment of compensation and medical expenses (Ex 21: 18-19). Only in one case is strict retaliation exacted: the guilty murderer must die and cannot buy his freedom. This rigour is justified by a religious reason: the blood which has been shed has profaned the land in which Yahweh dwells (Nb 35: 31-34). Thus again we meet the religious sanctions mentioned in the beginning of this paragraph.[1] The Israelites could repeat with pride these words of Deuteronomy: 'What great nation is there whose laws and customs are so just as all this Law?' (Dt 4: 8).

5. The king's legislative and judicial powers

The 'codes' which have come down to us from Mesopotamia are all attributed to a king. As we have seen, they were rather collections of customary law than laws of the State, decreed by the sovereign, but they were at least promulgated by royal authority. In Israel, granted the religious nature of the law and its connection with the Covenant, nothing of the sort was possible, and in fact the historical books never allude to any legislative power of the king. The nearest example is the order said to have been given by David, to share the booty between the combatants and those who had been left to guard the baggage, which became 'a rule and a custom' for Israel (1 S 30: 24-25). But David was not then king: as commander, he decided a particular case and his decision became a custom. During the siege of Jerusalem, Sedecias ordered that all slaves should be freed; but this was after he had consulted the people—he did not act on his own authority (Jr 34: 8). The king had of course an extensive administrative authority; he organized his kingdom, appointed his officials and made decrees, but he did not enact law. It is remarkable that the two 'laws of the king' (1 S 8: 11-18; Dt 17: 14-20) make no allusion to any power of the king to lay down laws. On the contrary, the first warns the people against his arbitrary acts, and the second orders him to have a copy of the divine law and obey it to the last detail. It is also noteworthy that apart from this passage the king is nowhere mentioned in the Deuteronomic Code. When Josaphat reformed the administration of justice, he told his judges to apply the law of Yahweh (2 Ch 19: 5-7), and his envoys were to take with them, and to explain everywhere, not a law of the king, but 'the law of Yahweh' (2 Ch 17: 9). The king was not even in the full sense the promulgator of this law, as if it became the law of the State by his authority. That is not the meaning to be ascribed to the reading of Deuteronomy by Josias in the Temple (2 K 23: 1-2). Josias was the

1. Cf. also p. 12.

human intermediary in the covenant between God and his people; he published its clauses and watched over its observance. He performed the same function as Moses on Sinai (Ex 24: 7-8), as Josue at Shechem (Jos 24: 25-26), and Esdras in days still to come at Jerusalem (Ne 8). But the king could add nothing to the authority of a law to which he himself was subject (Dt 17: 19; 1 K 8: 58; 2 K 23: 3). There was no such thing as State law in Israel, and it was only under the foreign rule of Artaxerxes that 'the law of God brought by Esdras' was imposed as 'the law of the king' (Esd 7: 26).

On the other hand, the king was a judge, and held judicial power. This is an essential function of the chief: every sheikh wields it in his tribe and Moses exercised it in the desert (Ex 18: 16). Josue, Moses' successor at the head of the people, 'was filled with the spirit of wisdom' and everyone obeyed him (Dt 34: 9; cf. Nb 27: 18-23). He acted as a judge in condemning Akan (Jos 7: 19-25). This was, of course, an exceptional case, but it was natural that the man who determined the law of the people (Jos 24: 25) should also see to its enforcement. Between the death of Josue and the institution of the monarchy came the period of the 'Judges'. This title has been wrongly extended to the heroes who saved some part of the people from oppression, but it seems to belong properly to the 'lesser' Judges, whose names are given in Jg 10: 1-5; 12: 8-15, along with whom we should count at least Jephthah (cf. Jg 12: 7), who combined this rôle with that of a great 'saviour' Judge. It seems that these Judges were a permanent institution of the tribal federation: instead of a political head, it had a judge to whom all could appeal. Samuel performed the same function when he judged Israel at his home-town, Ramah, and also at Bethel, Gilgal and Mispah (1 S 7: 16-17); he claimed that no one could accuse him of denying any man justice or taking bribes (1 S 12: 3-5). In his old age he appointed his two sons as judges at Beersheba, but they 'accepted gifts and bent justice to their own ends' (1 S 8: 1-3).

It was then that the Israelites begged Samuel to give them a king, 'that he may be our judge' (1 S 8: 5). There is no reason to suspect this passage, which represents the king as heir to an office which already had a long history in Israel. The same passage says that the people asked for a judge-king 'to be like other nations'. Among the texts lately discovered at Ras Shamra and Alalakh there are, in fact, judgments given by the king and contracts guaranteed by his seal. On a wider scale, the preambles of Mesopotamian codes, the poems of Ras Shamra, and Aramaean and Phoenician inscriptions all demand as the first quality of a king the virtue of justice. In Israel, too, men prayed that the king might be given justice (Ps 72: 1-2), the foundation of his throne (Pr 16: 12; 25: 5; 29: 14; cf. Is 9: 6).[1] The list of David's senior officials (2 S 8: 15) is introduced with these words: 'David reigned over all Israel, doing right and justice to all his people', which seems to reserve the administration of justice to the sovereign. In the same way, the list of Solomon's

1. Cf. p. 107.

senior officials (1 K 4: 1–6) is immediately preceded by the story of the famous judgment which proved to all that there was in the king 'a divine wisdom for doing justice' (1 K 3: 28) *i.e.* both to settle quarrels and to assist every man to obtain his rights. This was the wisdom for which Solomon had prayed, to 'judge the people' (1 K 3: 9). Thus 'to judge' was almost a synonym for 'to govern' (cf. again 2 K 15: 5), and 'governors' could be called 'judges' (Ps 2: 10; 148: 11). It is the king who is called the 'judge of Israel' in Mi 4: 14, following what is still the likeliest interpretation.

When Absalom exclaimed: 'Ah! who will make me judge in this land?' If everyone who had a lawsuit and a judgment were to come to me, I would do them justice' (2 S 15: 4), he was coveting the crown itself. The whole story shows that there was at Jerusalem a king's court, to which every man in Israel could appeal. So too, Solomon's palace contained a 'porch of judgment' where the king administered justice (1 K 7: 7). The real or fictitious cases recorded in the historical books show that appeal was made to the king even in cases which we should leave to lower courts: the theft of a sheep (2 S 12: 6), a family blood feud (2 S 14: 4-11), the substitution of a child (1 K 3: 16-28), the recovery of a house and land (2 K 8: 3). The woman of Teqoa is supposed to be appealing from a judgment given by her clan (2 S 14: 4-11), and the king here appears as the judge in the final court of appeal, which he certainly was, but the other examples presume that recourse could also be made to him in the first instance.

6. Judges and courts of law

In practice the majority of cases went to judges other than the king, and increasingly so as institutions developed. It was said that Moses himself was unequal to this task and, on the advice of his father-in-law, Jethro the Midianite, he appointed chiefs to administer justice, reserving to himself only the most difficult cases (Ex 18: 13-26; cf. Dt 1: 9-17).

We are by no means so well informed on the courts of Israel as on those of Mesopotamia, the composition and procedure of which are described in many cuneiform documents. They reveal some interesting parallels with what the Old Testament tells us about the administration of justice. Like ancient Babylonia, Israel had three different jurisdictions, though it is hard to define what was the precise competence of each: the communal jurisdiction of the Elders, the jurisdiction of the king and that of the priests.

In every town disputes and trials were settled by the Elders, that is, the heads of families in the clan, the leading citizens of the place.[1] They sat at the gate of the town, where all the community's affairs were discussed (cf. Gn 23: 10, 18; Jb 29: 7; Pr 24: 7; 31: 23). These are the courts to which the prophets refer when they demand respect for justice 'at the gate' (Am 5: 10, 12, 15; Za 8: 16). The Deuteronomic law describes 'the Elders at the gate of the

1. Cf. pp. 68 and 138.

town' (Dt 21: 19; 22: 15), or 'the Elders of the town' (Dt 19: 12; 21: 3, 8;
25: 7f.) as judges in certain causes. An actual example of the working of these
courts is provided by Rt 4: 1-12. Boaz sits at the gate of the town, stops the
kinsman who has the right of redemption over Naomi's field and chooses ten
Elders. They take their places beside him. The case is stated and discussed
between the parties, the man renounces his right and Boaz calls the Elders and
all the people to witness it. When the judgment involves a penalty, the
Elders impose it (Dt 22: 18-19). When it is the death penalty, it is immediately
carried out by the witnesses present (Dt 21: 18-21). The practice is illustrated
by the story of Naboth. The Elders and the leading citizens summon Naboth
to appear before them, and two false witnesses accuse him of cursing God
and the king, a crime which incurs the death penalty (cf. Ex 22: 27; Lv 24:
14). Then 'they took him out of the city, they stoned him and he died' (1 K 21:
11-13). The members of these popular courts are addressed in the exhorta-
tions of Ex 23: 1-3, 6-8; cf. Lv 19: 15, 35: they must not bear false witness
nor follow the majority in defiance of justice, nor accept gifts; they must
acquit the innocent and condemn the guilty. In the Mesopotamian courts
the Elders had a definite rôle; and among the Hittites they administered
justice under the presidency of a royal official.

But there were also professional judges in Israel, instituted by an authority
which can only have been the king's. They could claim as their prototypes the
competent laymen appointed by Moses to dispense justice (Ex 18: 13-26).
Among the collections of laws, the Deuteronomic Code is the only one
which refers to them. It commands that judges and registrars, or scribes, be
appointed in every town, and that they are to give just judgments (Dt 16: 18-
20). According to Dt 19: 16-18, the false witnesses in a religious trial must
appear before the priests and the judges then in office, and they are to conduct
the enquiry. According to Dt 25: 2, when a judge finds a man guilty, the
flogging is to take place in his presence. Dt 17: 8-13 orders the Elders or the
local judge to refer cases they cannot decide to a higher court. They must go
to 'the place chosen by Yahweh', that is, to Jerusalem, and submit the case to
the priests and the officiating judge (v. 9) or to the priest (singular) and the
judge (v. 12). Their judgment is without appeal. There was then at Jerusalem
a final court of appeal, both religious and secular. The text hesitates between
one priest and several, but is definite in denoting one secular judge. In this
legal context, it is not the king who can be called 'judge', as in Mi 4: 14, but
an official appointed by the king.

The directions of Dt 16: 18-20 and 17: 8-13 should be compared with
Josaphat's reform as described in 2 Ch 19: 4-11. This king appointed 'in
every town, in each walled town', judges who were to show themselves
incorruptible. At Jerusalem he established a court of priests, Levites, and the
heads of Israelite families, who were to act as a court of first instance for the
inhabitants of Jerusalem (according to the Greek) and as a court of appeal for

cases referred to them from other towns. This court was presided over by Amaryahu, the high priest, for all matters touching Yahweh, and by Zebed-yahu, chief of the house of Judah, for all the king's matters; the Levites served as notaries. The literary expression of this text may have been influenced by Deuteronomy and may reflect certain special interests of the time of the Chronicler, but there is no reason to suspect its basic accuracy. It will then be admitted that under Josaphat, at the beginning of Judah's monarchy, there was a judicial reform which established a royal jurisdiction alongside the communal jurisdiction and which relieved the king of his office of supreme judge. The texts from Deuteronomy which we have just analysed probably refer to the same institution.

With these measures of Josaphat's we may compare the Edict of Pharaoh Horemheb in the fourteenth century B.C. It concerns a reorganization of the courts of justice: the inhabitants of every town are to be judged by the priests of the temples, the priests of the gods and the magistrates appointed by the sovereign. These are men of discernment who are forbidden to respect persons or to accept bribes. The parallel is striking. But whereas the god-king of Egypt had simply 'taken counsel of his heart' in order to dictate to the scribe these 'excellent dispositions', and his judges had to apply 'the words of the Palace and the laws of the Throne-room', Josaphat's measures form part of his religious reform (2 Ch 19: 4; cf. 17: 7-9), and his magistrates 'judge not in the name of men but in the name of Yahweh' (2 Ch 19: 6). In the administration of justice as in everything else, the difference between the royal ideology of Israel and that of Egypt is conspicuous.

In Josaphat's ordinance (2 Ch 19: 8, 11) and in Dt 17: 9, 12; 19: 17, priests are mentioned along with judges. There is no ground for disputing the existence of this priestly jurisdiction; it is found in Mesopotamia, and also in Egypt, as we have just seen from the Edict of Horemheb. It was almost inevitable in Israel, where there was no distinction between civil and religious law, and where all legislation emanated from God. Moses brought the people's disputes 'before God' (Ex 18: 19). The fact that Samuel exercised his judicial functions in three sanctuaries, Bethel, Gilgal and Mispah (1 S 7: 16) and that his sons were judges at Beersheba, another place of worship (1 S 8: 2) is not an irrelevant detail. In certain cases the Code of the Covenant prescribes a procedure 'before God' (Ex 21: 6; 22: 6-8); the law of Dt 21: 1-9 on murder by a person unknown prescribes a ritual act. All this presupposes that the priest took a certain part in judicial affairs. The problem is to know exactly what their competence was. The priests gave *tôrôth*, 'decisions' in the name of God, and according to Dt 33: 10 (reading, probably, the plural) it was their exclusive privilege. According to Lv 13-14, it is the priest who decides whether a man, a garment or a house are infected with 'leprosy' or are clear of it. In Ag 2: 11f., the priests are asked for a *tôrah* on the conditions in which cleanness and uncleanness are passed on. In Za 7: 3 they are asked whether the fast in commemoration of the ruin of the Temple is still of obligation. It would seem, then, that the priests' rôle was only to distinguish between the sacred and the profane, clean and unclean, and this is certainly the function assigned to them in Lv 10: 10 and Ez 44: 23. But Lv 10: 11 extends their competence to 'any law whatever', and Ez 44: 24 adds 'they shall be judges in quarrels; they shall judge according to my law', while Dt 21: 5 says 'that it is their office to pronounce on all disputes and all assaults'. But in the absence of any concrete examples no certain conclusion can be drawn. It seems that the priests were the authentic interpreters of the law, that they judged all strictly religious matters, the 'affairs of Yahweh' (2 Ch 19: 11), and intervened in civil cases at least when these involved some religious law or religious procedure. Their competence was perhaps extended with time. When we read in 1 Ch 23: 4, cf. 26: 29, of 6,000 Levites who were clerks and judges under David, it is evidently the idealized projection into the past of a later situation, probably after the Exile. In New Testament times the Sanhedrin included priests, laymen and scribes; it was presided over by the high priest and it acted as the supreme court of justice.

According to 2 Ch 19: 11, the tribunal instituted by Josaphat at Jerusalem employed Levites as *shôṭ'rîm*. The root *shṭr* means, in Akkadian and several other Semitic languages, 'to write', but the *shôṭ'rîm* were not mere scribes, for they are distinguished from them in 2 Ch 34: 13. They seem to have been clerks of the court, and more generally, clerks attached to the judges (cf. Dt 16: 18; 1 Ch 23: 4; 26: 29). 'Clerk' would also be a good translation of the other uses of the word, which denotes the officials in charge of forced labour (Ex 5: 6f.; perhaps 2 Ch 34: 13), and also the administrative officers of the army (Dt 20: 5f.). To complete this review of the judicial authorities, we may remember that there was a person at the king's court called 'the king's son', who seems to have been a police officer.[1]

7. *Procedure*

The legislative codes tell us little about judicial procedure, but the process of a trial can be reconstructed by piecing together the allusions in other books of the Bible and by making use of passages which represent God's disputes with men as a formal trial, especially in Job and the second part of Isaias.

Justice was administered in public, at the gate of the town (Dt 21: 19; Am 5: 10), in a holy place or a sanctuary (Ex 21: 6; 22: 7; Jg 4: 5; 1 S 7: 16; Jr 26: 10). The king gave his judgments in the porch of judgment (1 K 7: 7), which was open to all. As a general rule the action, *rîb*, was brought by a private person who appeared as plaintiff (Dt 25: 7, 8; Jb 9: 19; 13: 18; 23: 4; Pr 25: 8; Jr 49: 19; cf. Mt 5: 25). In certain religious cases, such as idolatry (Dt 17:

1. Cf. pp. 119-120.

2-5) or blasphemy against God and the king (1 K 21: 10f.), the tribunal took cognisance of the case after a denunciation.

During the arguments the judge was seated (Is 16: 5; Dn 7: 9-10; 13: 50; cf. Jb 29: 7), but he stood up to pronounce sentence (Is 3: 13; Ps 76: 10). The parties remained standing (Is 50: 8, literally, 'let us stand up together'; cf. 41: 1) and 'to stand before the judge' (Dt 19: 17) means 'to appear in court'. The accuser was the 'adversary', the *satan*; he stood on the right of the accused (Ps 109: 6; Za 3: 1). The defender also stood on the right (Ps 109: 31; cf. 16: 8; 142: 5), but he was rather a witness for the defence than an advocate, for which there is no word in Hebrew. Nor was there any public prosecutor: each party pressed or defended his own case.

In the majority of cases the accusation was presented orally, but Jb 21: 35b-36 indicates that it could be done in writing (cf. Is 65: 6; Dn 7: 10). The accused was heard (Dt 17: 4; Jb 13: 22; Is 41: 21; cf. Jn 7: 51), but Jb 31: 35a does not prove that he did or could present a written defence. The examination of the case then began (Dt 13: 15; 17: 4; 19: 18).

Both parties called witnesses. There were witnesses for the prosecution, like the accusers of 1 K 21: 10, 13, like the hills and the mountains on which Yahweh calls in the action he brings against his people (Mi 6: 1), and witnesses for the defence (Pr 14: 25; Is 43: 9, 10, 12; Jr 26: 17). Otherwise the rôles were not very clearly defined. The accuser gave evidence (1 K 21: 10, 13; Mi 1: 2), and in actions heard by the Elders the latter could be witnesses as well as judges; Is 5: 3 and Mi 6: 1 can be understood in either sense. For a death sentence the law required at least two witnesses for the prosecution (Nb 35: 30; Dt 17: 6; cf. 1 K 21: 10; Dn 13: 34; Mt 26: 59-60; He 10: 28), and possibly for every case, according to Dt 19: 15; cf. Is 8: 2. These witnesses accepted responsibility for the sentence, which is why they had to throw the first stones if the condemned party were stoned (Dt 17: 7; cf. 13: 10; Jn 8: 7). But their evidence had to be verified by the judges, and false witnesses were condemned to the punishment which would have befallen the accused (Dt 19: 18-19; cf. Dn 13: 62). This prospect does not seem to have prevented miscarriages of justice (Ps 27: 12; 35: 11; Pr 6: 19; 12: 17; etc., and cf. the trials of Naboth in 1 K 21: 10f., of Susanna in Dn 13: 28f., of our Lord in Mt 26: 59f., and of Stephen in Ac 6: 11f.). According to the historian Josephus, women and slaves could not give evidence; if the rule is ancient, Israel's practice differed from that of Mesopotamia.

Proofs of fact were produced before the judges: the herdsman accused of losing a beast had to produce the remains of the animal if it had been mangled by a wild beast (Ex 22: 12; cf. Gn 31: 39; Am 3: 12). The wife accused by her husband of having lost her virginity before her marriage presented the bed-linen of the wedding-night, showing the signs of her virginity (Dt 22: 13-17). Tamar, accused before Judah, made him acknowledge the signet, the cord and the staff she had received from him (Gn 38: 25).

When everything had been thoroughly examined, the court 'declared guilty' or 'declared just, innocent', that is, gave its verdict of condemnation or acquittal (Ex 22: 8; Dt 25: 1; 1 K 8: 32; Pr 17: 15). The rôle of the judge, however, was not so much to impose a sentence as to settle a dispute while respecting justice. He was more a defender of right than a punisher of crime. He was a just arbitrator (Jb 9: 33).

8. The judgment of God

When no decision could be reached after the examination, or if the accused could not produce witnesses for the defence, they had recourse to an oath. In the Code of the Covenant, several cases are grouped together (Ex 22: 6-10): if an object entrusted to someone disappears and the thief is not found, the trustee goes to Elohim to attest that he has not taken another man's goods; if a dispute arises over a lost object, the matter is brought before Elohim, and he decides who is responsible; if a beast entrusted to someone's care dies or is wounded or is stolen unseen, an oath by Yahweh decides whether the keeper is at fault or not. The last case clearly presumes a judicial oath, so the two former cases must be interpreted in the same way, giving 'Elohim' its regular sense of 'God', not of 'judges', as some ancient versions and several modern expositors take it, or of 'domestic idols' (teraphîm) as has lately been suggested. It may be associated with another method of religious test, where the oath is perhaps understood. When a murder has been committed in the country by some person unknown, the Elders of the nearest town kill a heifer near a stream and wash their hands over the animal, saying: 'Our hands have not shed this blood and our eyes have seen nothing.' They are then covered against blood-vengeance (Dt 21: 1-8).

The judicial oath by the gods or the king was also practised in Babylonia, in Assyria, at Nuzu and in the Jewish colony of Elephantine, especially when property rights were in question; as in the cases quoted from the Code of the Covenant, an oath terminated the action. A man might refuse the oath, but that was to own himself guilty: he feared that if he perjured himself he would be stricken by the curse accompanying the oath. It is to such a refusal that Qo 9: 2 alludes, speaking of 'him who swears an oath' and 'him who fears to swear an oath'. It was therefore an imprecatory oath, as in Nb 5: 21.

The oath itself is therefore an ordeal, a judgment of God (cf. 1 K 8: 31). In Nb 5: 11-31 it is only one action of a fuller ritual. The husband who suspects his wife of misconduct presents her to the priest. The priest sprinkles some of the dust of the sanctuary over a vessel of water, proffers the oath to the woman, dissolves the writing containing the words of the oath into the water, and then makes the woman drink the mixture. If she is guilty this water becomes for her a 'water of bitterness and cursing' which makes her barren for ever, a fearful example to all. It will be observed there is here no question of bringing an action, and that the priest is not acting as a judge but as the minister of a rite. We may connect it with the last part of the story of the golden calf in Ex 32: 20: the idol is ground to a fine powder which the Israelites are made to swallow in water; the conclusion is doubtless to be found in v. 35: 'And Yahweh chastised the people.' The story of the massacre by the Levites (vv. 25f.) would come from another tradition.

This ordeal of bitter waters has no analogy in the ancient East. On the other hand, Israel knew nothing of the judicial ordeal by throwing the accused into a river. It was practised in Babylonia, in Assyria, in Elam, east of the Tigris at Nuzu, and on the banks of the Euphrates at Mari and Carchemish. If it is not found in Palestine, this may simply be because, apart from the Jordan, the country has no river in which anyone could possibly be drowned.

Another form of the judgment of God is the drawing of lots. 'The lot puts an end to quarrels and decides between the mighty' (Pr 18: 18). It serves to pick out one guilty man from a group, as with Akan (Jos 7: 14-15), and Jonathan (1 S 14: 38-42). In the latter case it is stated that the sacred lots were used, the *urim* and the *thummim,* which only a priest could handle. The high priest's breastplate, which contained the lots, is called for that reason the 'breastplate of judgment' (Ex 28: 15). Aaron bears on his breast the 'judgment of the children of Israel' (Ex 28: 30). But again we should note that the procedure here is extra-judicial, and the priest is acting only as the minister of the divine oracle.

9. Penalties

The death penalty is laid down for the following crimes:

Intentional homicide (Ex 21: 12; Lv 24: 17; Nb 35: 16-21) for which monetary compensation is never accepted (Nb 35: 31; Dt 19: 11-12); the abduction of a man in order to make him a slave (Ex 21: 16; Dt 24: 7).

Grave sins against God: idolatry (Ex 22: 19; Lv 20: 1-5; Dt 13: 2-19; 17: 2-7; cf. Nb 25: 1-5); blasphemy (Lv 24: 15-16); profanation of the sabbath (Ex 31: 14-15; cf. Nb 15: 32-36); sorcery (Ex 22: 17; Lv 20: 27; cf. 1 S 28: 3, 9); prostitution by a priest's daughter (Lv 21: 9).

Grave sins against parents (Ex 21: 15, 17; Lv 20: 8; Dt 21: 18-21); abuses of sexual relations: adultery (Lv 20: 10; Dt 22: 22); different forms of incest (Lv 20: 11, 12, 14, 17); sodomy (Lv 20: 13); bestiality (Lv 20: 15-16).

Thus Israelite law, unlike other Eastern laws, limits capital punishment to offences against the purity of worship, against the sanctity of life and the sources of life, and this religious motive is usually expressed in the laws. It is a consequence of the peculiar character of Israel's legislation.[1]

1. Cf. p. 149.

As to the execution of the penalty, the murderer was handed over to the avenger of blood, who employed whatever means he chose. Stoning is ordered for idolaters (Dt 13: 10-11; 17: 5-7), for blasphemers (Lv 24: 14, 23), for a woman who concealed the fact that she was not a virgin at the time of her marriage (Dt 22: 21), for the guilty fiancée and her accomplice (Dt 22: 24), for the rebellious son (Dt 21: 21) and the man who profaned the sabbath (Nb 15: 35-36). A man who disobeyed an order of extermination and one who was guilty of lese-majesty were also stoned, according to Jos 7: 25 and 1 K 21: 10. It was the normal method of execution and it must also be presumed when the text does not state it precisely (cf. Jn 8: 5 for the woman taken in adultery). The condemned person was taken out of the town (1 K 21: 10, 13; cf Lv 24: 14; Nb 15: 36). The witnesses for the prosecution cast the first stones and the people continued till death ensued. The collective character of communal justice was thus expressed to the end.

The penalty could be increased by exposure of the bodies of the condemned. They were 'hung on the gibbet', but had to be taken down before night (Dt 21: 22-23; cf. Jos 8: 29; 10: 27). This was not the punishment of hanging, for the condemned had already been executed (cf. in particular Jos 10: 26; 2 S 4: 12). It was a mark of infamy and an example. We should probably interpret the texts of Nb 25: 4 and 2 S 21: 9 in this way and understand that the corpses of the guilty were impaled.

Death by crucifixion was a punishment unknown in the Old Testament. It is attested among the Persians (impalement or crucifixion), sporadically among the Greeks, frequently among the Romans. The first mention of it in Palestine occurs in Flavius Josephus, writing of the persecution under Antiochus Epiphanes.

Death by burning is prescribed in the law for two cases only: prostitution by a priest's daughter (Lv 21: 9) and the incest of a man who weds both mother and daughter (Lv 20: 14). The same mode of death is ordered in the Code of Hammurabi for similar cases. According to Gn 38: 24, the same punishment was inflicted in ancient times on an adulterous wife.

The punishment of flogging seems to be applied by Dt 22: 18 to the man who has slandered his wife, and by Dt 21: 18 to a disobedient son, according to the parallels in 1 K 12: 11, 14 and Pr 19: 18, where the same verb is employed. According to Dt 25: 1-3, the judge could impose up to forty strokes of the whip (or rod?) on the guilty man, who was stretched on the ground before him (cf. Jr 20: 2). By a legalistic scruple, later Jewish custom restricted the number to 'forty save one' (cf. 2 Co 11: 24).

Bodily mutilation as a consequence of the *lex talionis* is fairly common in the Code of Hammurabi and the Assyrian laws, but it is found in Israelite law only in the special case of Dt 25: 11-12, where it is a symbolic retaliation.[1]

Strictly speaking, there are no pecuniary penalties, in the sense of fines

1. Cf. p. 149.

payable to the State or the community. The money paid to the priests in satisfaction for a crime or sin (2 K 12: 17) is not in the nature of a fine and arises from religious institutions. On the other hand, a wrong done to an individual in his goods or rights is equitably redressed, and this compensation has a penal aspect, as it is generally larger than the damage caused. A man who has slandered his wife pays her father a hundred pieces of silver, which is much more than he had paid in order to marry her (Dt 22: 19). A seducer pays damages to his victim's father (Ex 22: 16). A man who has let his beasts graze in the field or vineyard of another reimburses him on the basis of his best harvest (Ex 22: 4). One who is responsible for a fire which has spread to his neighbour's land and destroyed his crop compensates him for what the fire has destroyed (Ex 22: 5). A man who has caused the death of an animal by leaving a pit open pays the price of it to the owner (Ex 21: 34). A man who has stolen a beast and slaughtered it must pay compensation, fivefold for cattle, fourfold for sheep or goats (Ex 21: 37; cf. 2 S 12: 6; Lk 19: 8). The 'sevenfold' claimed in Pr 6: 31 and 2 S 12: 6, in the Greek, is not to be taken literally and simply means perfect restitution.

Imprisonment by judicial order does not appear till after the Exile, in Esd 7: 26, as an application of a foreign legislation. But there were prisons, in which accused persons were kept pending a decision (Lv 24: 12; Nb 15: 34), and suspects were shut up by police action, often arbitrarily (1 K 22: 27; Jr 37: 15-18). Putting a man in the pillory or the stocks was a further punishment (2 Ch 16: 10; Jr 20: 2; 29: 26). Bodily restraint of one sentenced to make restitution or of a defaulting debtor (Mt 5: 25-26; 18: 30; Lk 12: 58-59) is something borrowed from Hellenistic law. Under ancient legislation, thieves who could not make restitution were sold as slaves (Ex 22: 2) and an insolvent debtor would sell himself or his dependents into slavery to discharge his debt (Lv 25: 39f.; Dt 15: 2f.).[1]

10. Private vengeance and Cities of Refuge

The very ancient custom of blood-vengeance, carried out by the *go'el*,[2] never disappeared and was recognized by law. But the same law tried to limit the abuses which could easily arise from this exercise of private justice. It did so by distinguishing between voluntary and involuntary homicide, and by establishing places of refuge where an involuntary killer could find safety.

The principle is laid down in the Code of the Covenant: the man who has killed without premeditation may take refuge in a place which God will appoint, but the wilful murderer must be dragged from the altar itself to be put to death (Ex 21: 13-14). The 'place' thus denoted is evidently a sanctuary, where there is an altar, apparently any lawful sanctuary of Yahweh, but first

1. Cf. pp. 82-83.   2. Cf. pp. 11 and 21-22.

and foremost the central sanctuary of the tribal federation, that of the Ark. There Adonias took refuge (1 K 1: 50-53), and Joab after him. But Joab, who had murdered Abner and Amasa, was not protected by the law of asylum and was put to death in the sanctuary itself, which he refused to leave (1 K 2: 28-31). There is no other actual example of this recourse to a sanctuary as a place of refuge, though certain expressions in the Psalms seem to refer to it. Thus the Temple is a shelter against enemies and anyone dwells there in safety (Ps 27: 2-5); there one is covered by the wings of Yahweh (Ps 61: 4-5), but the wicked are not allowed in (Ps 5: 5).

A more stable institution is that of the Cities of Refuge. Unfortunately the texts describing them are hard to interpret. In the order of the books of the Bible they are as follows:

Nb 35: 9-34: the Israelites are ordered by God to have cities where an involuntary killer can take refuge from blood-vengeance. There are to be three cities of refuge in Transjordan and three west of the Jordan, but they are not indicated by name. Asylum is granted only to the involuntary killer: the wilful murderer may not be received and must die at the hands of the avenger of blood. The community decides the question of guilt, rejects the murderer and watches over the involuntary killer, who must not leave the city of refuge till the death of the high priest.

Dt 4: 41-43, unconnected with its context: Moses chooses three cities of refuge across the Jordan: Beser, Ramoth of Gilead, Golan.

Dt 19: 1-13: after the conquest, the land must be divided into three regions and three cities chosen, which are not named (vv. 8-9, an obvious addition, orders that if the land should become greater still, three other cities shall be added). They are to welcome the involuntary killer, but the murderer is to be rearrested by the Elders of his city and handed over to the avenger of blood.

Jos 20: 1-9: at Yahweh's command and in pursuance of the instructions given to Moses, Josue chooses the cities of refuge where an involuntary killer will be protected from blood-vengeance. It is the Elders of these cities who admit the fugitive after inquiry. He remains there till he has been judged by the community, till the death of the high priest. The list of these towns is given in vv. 7-8: Qedesh of Galilee in the hill-country of Nephthali, Shechem in the hill-country of Ephraim, Hebron in the hill-country of Judah; on the other side of the Jordan, Beser on the plateau, Ramoth in Gilead, Golan in Bashan.

These passages show us the development of the institution in apparent conformity with the course of events recorded in the Pentateuch. The command of Nb 35, associated with the period on the steppes of Moab, fixes the rules but states neither the number nor the names of the cities: the land is not yet conquered. In Dt 4, Moses chooses three cities in the territory already occupied by the Israelites on the far side of the Jordan. Dt 19 provides for three cities in the land of Canaan, which has still to be conquered, but does not name them; the additional verses, 8 and 9, provide for three other unnamed cities in order to complete the traditional number of six, without seeing that the three missing cities are those of Dt 4. Finally, when the conquest is complete, Jos 20 recalls the rules proclaimed earlier and at last gives the names of the six cities with their geographical positions.

The picture is changed, however, if we examine and compare the vocabulary and context of the various texts. The latest of all is obviously Nb 35: the rôle accorded to the religious community, the 'edah, and the mention of the high priest, whose death is the occasion for a general amnesty, show that it was edited after the Exile. This late date and the absence of precise details about the towns show that it was never actually in force. Dt 19 and Jos 20: 4 and 9a, on the contrary, which allot a rôle to the Elders of the murderer's town or of the city of refuge, and which also preserve the primitive idea of blood-vengeance, are ancient. But Jos 20: 6 and 9b, at least, are later retouchings, which mention the community and the high priest in order to bring the text into line with Nb 35, and even so they do not avoid all incoherence. On the other hand, Dt 19 was never a real law, for the towns are not named, which would be necessary for the law to be applicable. But this passage prescribes three cities and three territories in Canaan, which are given, with their names, in Jos 20: 7. If no city in Transjordan is provided for by Dt 19, that is because the land was no longer in Israelite hands. The addition in vv. 8-9, however, shows that the tradition of six cities of refuge was still remembered. Dt 19 thus appears as a project of reform which was never carried out: this reform presumes that the institution described in Jos 20: 7-9a is known, and maintains its principles, but adapts it to new circumstances and secularizes it by taking away from certain towns a privilege which they owed, as we are about to explain, to the existence of a sanctuary, now condemned by the law on centralization of worship. The oldest element in all this documentation is therefore Jos 20: 7-9a, which guarantees the existence of cities of refuge, with the motives and rules for their institution (cf. Jos 20: 4 and Dt 19: 11-12). The list of cities of refuge in Transjordan in Dt 4 come in its turn from Jos 20: 8.

All the towns mentioned in Jos 20 are mentioned elsewhere as Levitical towns. The list is not invented: Beser and Golan do not appear apart from these two contexts, but Beser is mentioned as an Israelite town by the stele of Mesha, and the name of Golan is still preserved in the Bashan region. Further, among the six towns named, Qedesh was captured by Tiglath-Pileser in 734 B.C. and Beser was conquered by Mesha about 850. Ramoth of Gilead, before being finally severed from Israel, was a town over which Israel and the Aramaeans disputed in the first half of the ninth century. Golan and its region were lost soon after the death of Solomon. It is difficult to trace the list back beyond Solomon to the tribal federation, or even to the reign of David, for the towns are chosen and determined by their geographical situation, not by their attachment to a tribe; the mention of Reuben, Gad and Manasseh in connection with the three towns in Transjordan simply gives a second geographical designation and must be considered as secondary. The institution is therefore independent of tribal organization, and does not antedate the reign of Solomon. One may wonder whether it remained long in force and how it developed, but there are no sufficient grounds for asserting that it was a late invention to which nothing corresponded in reality.

Qedesh, the 'holy town', Shechem, hallowed by the memory of Abraham and Jacob, by the tomb of Joseph and the covenant under Josue, and Hebron, which possessed the tomb of the Patriarchs, had each its famous sanctuary. Very probably the three cities across the Jordan were also holy places. Thus the institution of the Cities of Refuge is linked with the right of asylum recognized at the sanctuaries. But it appears on the other hand as the secularizing of an originally religious custom (cf. Ex 21: 13-14). The prerogatives of the sanctuaries and their ministers were in the end transferred to the Cities and their councils of Elders.

Chapter Eleven

ECONOMIC LIFE

1. *Landed property*

IN Egypt all the land belonged to the Pharaoh or the temples, and the Israelites were astonished at this land system which was so different from their own (Gn 47: 20-26). In Mesopotamia, though, the king and the sanctuaries owned large estates, but the oldest texts show that communities, families and individuals already had certain lands, which the king could acquire only by purchase from the owners. With these and other lands of his estates, the king used to found fiefs. A fief is a grant of immovable property, made to an individual in return for the obligation to render personal services. This feudal system was very widespread in the Near East. The Code of Hammurabi and the Hittite Code devote several articles to it and it is frequently alluded to in the Nuzu and Ugarit documents. These texts span the second millennium B.C. At first the fief appears as an inalienable charge, to which personal services are attached. Gradually it took on the character of heritable property, of which a man might freely dispose, and the feudal services attached to it became attached to the property, not to any person or persons.

This development of the fief was already far advanced when Israel first appeared as a people. It was even later that this people became a centralized state, and apparently they never experienced a feudal regime. Those rare texts where some have tried to see an allusion to fiefs are capable of another interpretation. For example, 1 S 8: 14 predicts that the king will seize fields and vineyards and give them to his officers; according to 1 S 22: 7, this was already happening in Saul's time, but these lands were given as gifts rather than fiefs, for there is no mention of any service attached to them. When Saul promises to exempt the family of the man who slays the Philistine champion (1 S 17: 25), the reference is to exemption from taxes or forced labour rather than enfranchisement from the service of a fief. Only once is there an unmistakable reference to feudal services: David received the town of Siqlag from the Philistine prince of Gath on condition that he ensured the policing of the desert and followed his suzerain to war (1 S 27: 6, 10; 28: 1); it was a military fief, but we are on Philistine territory.

Nevertheless, the feudal idea was found in Israel, though transferred on to the theological plane. As Yahweh is the only true king of Israel (Jg 8: 23;

I S 12: 12), so he is the sole lord of the soil.[1] The Holy Land is the 'domain of Yahweh' (Jos 22: 19), the 'land of Yahweh' (Os 9: 3; cf. Ps. 85: 2; Jr 16: 18; Ez 36: 5). It is the land he had promised to the Fathers (Gn 12: 7; 13: 15; 15: 18; 26: 4; Ex 32: 13; Dt 1: 35-36), the land he has conquered and given to his people (Nb 32: 4; Jos 23: 3, 10; 24: 11-13; Ps 44: 4). This property-right which God retains over all lands was invoked as the basis of the law of Jubilee (Lv 25: 23).[2] It is also in virtue of God's supreme dominion that religious law limits the rights of the human occupants: hence the duty of leaving gleanings of corn and vines for the poor (Lv 19: 9-10; 23: 22; Dt 24: 19-21; cf. Rt 2); the right of every passer-by to satisfy his hunger when passing through a field or a vineyard (Dt 23: 25-26); the annual tithe due to Yahweh (Lv 27: 30-32), to be eaten in Yahweh's presence (Dt 14: 22-27), given to the Levites (Nb 18: 21-32); the tithe every third year for the poor (Dt 14: 28-29; 26: 12-15), and the law about fallow ground in the sabbatical year (Ex 23: 10-11; Lv 25: 2-7;).[3]

In the second millennium B.C., at Nuzu and in Assyria, the fiefs were distributed by drawing lots; in the same way, the Promised Land, at Yahweh's command, was shared by lot between the tribes, according to Jos 13: 6; 15: 1; 16: 1; 17: 1; 18: 6—19: 49, *passim*: Jg 1: 3. This 'sharing out' by lot of the 'plots' in which the tribes were in fact already settled, or which they had still to conquer, is the expression of God's sovereign dominion over the land; in actual fact the tribes acquired their territories by the hazards of a conquest which is schematized in Jos 6-12, and represented in Jg 1 as still incomplete. But probably the drawing of lots among the Tribes for the Holy Land is only an imaginative extension to the whole people of what in fact took place at the level of the clan and the family. In the nomadic system, pastures and watering places are the common property of the tribe.[4] When the tribe becomes settled, the same system may be applied to the arable land. This idea of common property still survives in modern times, and it is interesting to find it attested in ancient Mesopotamia, from the Kassite period onwards; it is particularly noticeable among the Aramaean tribes on the Tigris banks, whose social structure was like that of the earliest Israelites. These communal lands are often mentioned in the *kudurrus*, land-survey documents which were used to authenticate the purchase of a tribal property by the king and its transfer to an individual or a temple.

The use of these common lands, however, is divided among the members of the group, each member of which cultivates a part for his own benefit. There has been a similar system in modern Palestine, traces of which still remain. Outside the village and its immediate surroundings, which were private property (*mulk*), the rest was Government land (*miri*) and allotted to the village as common land (*mesha'*). This was divided into plots which were distributed in rotation, generally every year, or drawn for by lot among the

1. Cf. p. 98.   2. Cf. pp. 175-177.   3. Cf. p. 173.   4. Cf. p. 9.

heads of families. Except for its temporary nature, this is the same division by lot between clans and families as that prescribed by Nb 26: 55-56; 33: 54; 36: 2; cf. 27: 7; this too is what Ezechiel foretold for the future Israel (Ez 45: 1; 47: 22). The same word *gôral*, originally 'a pebble', means both the 'lot' which was drawn and the 'plot' assigned by the lot. According to Is 34: 17, Yahweh himself 'drew by lot the portion of each one', and 'divided the land to them by line'; in Mi 2: 5, the monopolizers will be despoiled and 'will have none to cast the line for them on a plot in the assembly of Yahweh'; according to Ps 16: 5-6, the faithful man has Yahweh for his plot, the line marks out for him a choice portion. The use of such figures would have no meaning unless there existed an actual custom similar to the modern practice, and perhaps a partition of this kind is alluded to in Jr 37: 12.

2. *Family property and large estates*

This communal property, the temporary use of which was divided among a number of families, is far less in evidence than family property, which, it seems, was the normal system in Israel. In our texts the word *gôral*, 'lot' and 'plot', alternates with *ḥeleq*, 'portion' and *nahalah*, 'heritage'. This ancestral estate often contained the family tomb (Jos 24: 30, 32; 1 S 25: 1; 1 K 2: 34; cf. Gn 23). It was defined by boundaries which it was strictly forbidden by law to remove (Dt 19: 14; 27: 17; cf. Jb 24: 2; Pr 22: 28; 23: 10; Os 5: 10). The peasant was deeply attached to the piece of ground he had inherited from his fathers: Naboth refused to surrender his vineyard at Yizreel to Achab, and the king could not legally force him to do so (1 K 21). The social ideal was that every man should live 'under his vine and under his fig-tree' (1 K 5: 5; Mi 4: 4; Za 3: 10).

Public feeling and custom took care that this patrimony was not alienated, or that at least it should not pass out of the family. It is probable that when land was inherited it was not shared like the other property but passed to the eldest son or remained undivided.[1] If a man dies without male heirs, the land is bequeathed to his daughters (Nb 27: 7-8), but they must marry within their tribe, so that their portion may not be transferred to another tribe (Nb 36: 6-9). If the owner dies childless, the inheritance reverts to his brothers, his uncles or his nearest kinsman (Nb 27: 9-11). If the Law of Levirate binds a man to marry his widowed and childless sister-in-law, the object is no doubt to raise up descendants to the deceased, but it is also to prevent the alienation of the family property.[2]

Sometimes, however, an Israelite was obliged by poverty to sell his patrimony. One of the duties of the *go'el*[3] was to buy the land which his near relation had to abandon. Hence Jeremias buys the field of his cousin Hanameel (Jr 32: 6-9), and Boaz, in place of the nearest *go'el*, buys the land of

1. Cf. p. 53.   2. Cf. p. 38.   3. Cf. pp. 11 and 21-22.

Elimelek, which Naomi, his widow, was offering for sale (Rt 4: 9). Note that in these cases there is no question of the repurchase of a property already sold, but of a prior right to purchase a property offered for sale, and that the land is not restored to the impoverished kinsman, but becomes the property of the *go'el*. These are the only concrete cases recorded in the Bible and it is in their light that the law of Lv 25: 25 must be interpreted: if an Israelite falls into distress and has to sell his land, his nearest *go'el* comes 'to his house' (generally omitted by translators) and buys what he has to sell. The aim of this institution is to keep for kinsfolk the property which the head of a family cannot keep for himself and his direct descendants; it thus links up with the laws on the marriage of heiresses and inheritance in the collateral line. But in Lv 25 this ancient arrangement is recalled in a different context: the object of the Law of Jubilee is in fact to restore property to the individual or family which used to possess it, not merely to retain it in the clan; compared with the institution of the *go'el*, it is something new and, as we shall see, Utopian.

But the *go'el* did not always exercise his right of pre-emption and the economic development of the first centuries of the monarchy[1] hastened the break-up of family properties in favour of rich landlords. Is 5: 8 curses 'those who add house to house and join field to field, until there is no room left for anyone else'; Mi 2: 2 condemns those 'who covet fields and seize them, houses and they take them'. These *latifundia* (large estates) were worked by slaves (2 S 9: 10), or by paid workmen.[2] The system of rent-holding or *métayage*, land tenure in which the farmer pays a part (usually half) of the produce as rent to the owner, who furnishes stock and seed, was apparently never practised in Israel in early days, though it was known in Mesopotamia, and was later provided for in the Rabbinic period. Am 5: 11 blames the rich for taking tribute from the corn of the poor, which could be an allusion to a *métayage*, but it may refer to the tithe, the collection and profits of which were left by the king to his officers (cf. 1 S 8: 15). The first mention of the renting of lands is found in the parable in Mt 21: 33-41, and the earliest documents are the contracts of *métayage* discovered in the caves of Murabba'at, datad A.D. 133.

Finally, it will be recalled that the king owned large estates.[3] The royal estate was managed by stewards (1 Ch 27: 25-31), and worked by the labour of State slaves and the levy of free men (1 S 8: 12).

3. *Conveyances and similar formalities*

The sale of a property was recorded by a contract. This might be simply an oral contract, made in the presence of witnesses in a public place, at the town gate: thus Boaz acquires the property of Naomi and the right to marry her daughter-in-law (Rt 4: 9-11). Abraham's purchase of the field of Ephron is

---

1. Cf. pp. 72-73.   2. Cf. p. 76.   3. Cf. pp. 124-125.

also represented as an oral transaction, made in the sight of all who passed through the gate of the town (Gn 23: 17-18). But its terms are as precise as a legal deed and comparable to the contracts on cuneiform tablets: a description of the land acquired, the names of the contracting parties and the witnesses. Mention of the gate of the town recalls the clause in certain contracts at Nuzu, drawn up 'after proclamation at the gate'. The transaction at Hebron may well have been concluded by the drawing up of such a contract.

The use of written contracts, which had long existed in Canaan and all the Near East, was certainly widespread in Israel. Two cuneiform tablets found at Gezer contain contracts of sale made under Assyrian rule in the seventh century B.C. and drawn up in Assyrian. It is mere chance that the Bible speaks only once of a written contract, but it does so in great detail (Jr 32: 6-14). Jeremias buys the field offered for sale by his cousin Hanameel. The contract is drawn up, sealed and signed by the witnesses; the money is weighed out. The deed is made out in duplicate; one document is sealed, the other 'open'. All is done 'according to the prescribed rules' and the two copies are given to Baruch to be preserved in an earthen vase. This has been compared with the duplicate documents of Mesopotamia: the tablet of the contract was wrapped in a sheath of clay on which the same text was reproduced. But in Jeremias' time this custom no longer survived in Mesopotamia, and moreover his deed of purchase, drawn up in Hebrew, would be written on papyrus or, less probably, on parchment. This is the earliest evidence of a type of document of which there are many examples in Egypt, from the Hellenistic period onwards; some, dating from the beginning of the second century of our era, have lately been discovered in Palestine. On the same sheet of papyrus two copies of the contract were written, separated by a blank space. The first copy was rolled up and sealed, the other rolled up but not sealed: this is the 'open' copy of which Jeremias speaks. It could be consulted at will but was liable to be falsified; if a dispute arose the sealed copy was opened. Baruch was to put the contract in an earthen vessel: the custom of preserving family archives in this way is attested by many archaeological finds.

The Old Testament tells us little about the value of land. Abraham buys the field and cave of Macpelah for 400 shekels (Gn 23: 15). Jacob pays a hundred qeṣitah (value unknown) for the land of Shechem (Gn 33: 19; Jos 24: 32). David buys the threshing-floor and oxen of Araunah for fifty shekels (2 S 24: 24). Omri pays two talents of silver (6,000 shekels) for the hill of Samaria (1 K 16: 24); Jeremias' field costs him seventeen shekels (Jr 32: 9). These statements give us a certain order of values but nothing exact, since we know neither the area of the lands nor the exact weight of the shekel, nor the purchasing power of silver at the different periods. According to Lv 27: 16 the value of a field is calculated at fifty shekels for every ḥomer of barley produced.

In early days the transfer of property was ratified by a symbolic action. According to Rt 4: 7, it was once the custom in Israel to validate all transactions in this way: one of the parties removed his sandal and gave it to the other. This action, performed before witnesses, signified the abandonment of a right. Naomi's first *go'el* in this way renounces his right of pre-emption in favour of Boaz (Rt 4: 8); the brother-in-law who declines the moral obligation of the levirate has his shoe removed (Dt 25: 9-10); he is dispossessed of the right he had over his brother's widow.[1] The shoe seems to have served as a probative instrument in transfers of land: in Ps 60: 10= 108: 10, the phrase 'over Edom I cast my sandal' implies taking possession. At Nuzu, the seller lifted his foot off the ground he was selling, and placed the buyer's foot on it. Here, too, a pair of shoes (and a garment) appears as a fictitious payment to convalidate certain irregular transactions. This may explain, in Am 2: 6; 8: 6, the poor man who is sold, or bought, for a pair of sandals: he has been unjustly dispossessed, while the exaction has been given a cloak of legality. The same meaning would then be found in the Greek of 1 S 12: 3, confirmed by Si 46: 19; Samuel has not taken a pair of sandals from any man, that is, he has not twisted the law to make an illicit profit.

4. *Deposit and hiring*

Deposit is a free contract by which a man places an object in the safe keeping of another, who does not make use of it and gives it back on demand. The Code of the Covenant (Ex 22: 6-12) provides for the deposit of money, movable objects and animals. If the thing deposited disappears or is damaged through no fault of the depositary, he may exonerate himself by taking an oath; otherwise he owes compensation. The law of Lv 5: 21-26 adds that if he makes a false declaration he must restore the deposit and one fifth. The Babylonian law of Eshnunna and the Code of Hammurabi contain similar provisions, and the latter requires the deposit to be made before witnesses and registered by a contract. A late example of this procedure occurs in the Book of Tobias (Tb 1: 14; 4: 1, 20; 5: 3; 9: 5). The elder Tobias deposited ten talents of silver with Gabael in sealed bags. The deposit was confirmed in writing, signed by the depositor and the depositary, each of whom kept half of the document. On presentation of the document the representative of Tobias was given back the deposit.

A deposit involves no charge on either of the parties. This is not true of hiring, but this form of contract—apart from the hiring of services from wage-earners[2]—was scarcely known among the Israelites. There is only the text of Ex 22: 14, which, if interpreted in the light of the Hittite law, may refer to the hiring of a beast. We have already said that Am 5: 11 contains only an uncertain allusion to the hiring of lands. The hiring of money and

1. Cf. p. 37.   2. Cf. p. 76.

foodstuffs, on the other hand, was developed in the form of loans at interest, in spite of legal prohibitions.

5. Loans

When an Israelite fell on hard times and was reduced to borrowing, he should have found help among his clan or tribe. Lending to the poor is a good deed (Ps 37: 21; 112: 5; Si 29: 1-2; cf. Mt 5: 42). But many refused because the borrowers did not honour their obligations and did not discharge them, even when they were able to (Si 29: 3-7; cf. 8: 12).

All this concerns loans without interest, the only kind of loan allowed by the Code of the Covenant (Ex 22: 24), which contemplates only loans between Israelites. This provision is developed by the law of Dt 23: 20; one may not take interest on money, food or anything whatever lent to one's brother, and the same precept is found in Lv 25: 35-38; but one may lend at interest to a foreigner (Dt 23: 21; cf. 15: 6). Lending at interest was in fact practised by all Israel's neighbours.

Interest is called in Hebrew *neshek*, literally, 'a bite', and *tarbîth*, literally, 'increase'. The former word is found alone in the laws of Ex and Dt and in Ps 15: 5. In later texts it is always used along with the second, and it is hard to distinguish between them. Possibly *neshek* at first referred to any kind of loan (cf. Dt 23: 20) and was later restricted to loans of money, *tarbîth* then applying to loans in kind (cf. Lv 25: 37, where we have, as an exception, the cognate form *marbîth*). In that case the Aramaic of Elephantine, in the fifth century B.C., would give us the final stage in the development: here *marbîth* is the only word used for interest, even in money. Possibly, too, the vocabulary reflects an evolution in the system of lending: either the borrower signs a receipt for sixty shekels and only receives forty (*neshek*, a bite) or else he signs a receipt for forty shekels and undertakes to pay sixty on maturity (*tarbîth*, increase). Alternatively, *tarbîth* may be an increase provided for in case of non-execution, or finally an increment to take account of the depreciation of the provisions borrowed in winter and restored after the harvest, when prices stand lower. Information is so scarce that we can only guess.

Economic development and example from abroad led to frequent violation of these laws. The just man does not lend at interest, says Ps 15: 5, but the wicked does so (Pr 28: 8; cf. Ez 18: 8, 13, 17). It is one of the sins for which Jerusalem is condemned (Ez 22: 12). Things were no better after the Exile, and in Ne 5: 1-13 we find the people burdened with debts. Lending at interest, at rates which strike us as usury, was practised by the Jews at Elephantine. From Rabbinic sources it appears that the Jerusalem Temple itself lent at interest, and the parable in Mt 25: 27; Lk 19: 23 presumes that the custom was common and accepted. The Greek papyri of Egypt, however, show that the Jews did not take to these strictly banking operations till a late period.

The annual rate of interest in the ancient Near East was very high: in Babylonia and Assyria it was generally a quarter or a fifth for money loans, a third for loans in kind, and often much more. In Upper Mesopotamia and in Elam, the interest on money was higher—up to one-third or a half, but the interest on loans of corn was the same as in Babylonia. In Egypt the rate dropped in the Ptolemaic period and seems to have been twelve per cent per annum at Elephantine; this was also the maximum permitted rate at Rome at the beginning of our era. We do not know what the practice was in Israel. The Massoretic text of Ne 5: 11 was interpreted by the Vulgate, in the light of Roman usage, as meaning an interest of one per cent a month, but this text is corrupt.

6. Securities

To guard against his debtor's defaulting, the creditor could demand a security. In Gn 38: 17-18, Judah gives Tamar his signet, cord and staff as pledge, 'erabôn (whence, through Greek and Latin, comes the English 'an earnest'), of her fee. According to 1 S 17: 18, when David was sent to his brothers he had to bring back to his father a pledge, 'arubbah, as proof that he had fulfilled his errand. In credit operations the pledge is a surety, an object in the possession of the debtor which he hands over to the creditor as guarantee for his debt.

A movable pledge is called ḥăbol, ḥăbolah, or 'ăbôt, 'abtît, and the cognate verbs mean 'to engage'. In spite of attempts to distinguish between their meanings, these words seem to be synonymous (cf. the identical prescriptions of Ex 22: 25-26, ḥbl, and Dt 24: 12-13, 'bt). These pledges were sureties accepted when the loan was granted: they remained the property of the debtor and there is nothing to show that the creditor had the right to realize them in order to recoup himself: the pledge must be returned (Ez 18: 12, 16; 35: 15). According to Dt 24: 10-11, the creditor may not enter the debtor's house to take his pledge for himself; it must be handed to him outside, no doubt in order to avoid all appearance of seizure. It was forbidden to accept as sureties objects which are means of livelihood, such as the mill or the millstone (Dt 24: 6). The pledge was often a garment, a substitute for the person, but the Code of the Covenant says that the poor man's garment must be given back to him at dusk, because it is all he has to cover himself with at night (Ex 22: 25-26; the law is repeated in Dt 24: 12-13; cf. Jb 22: 6; 24: 9 (corr.); Am 2: 8). This garment, which the creditor was forbidden to keep except in the daytime, was not a real pledge, proportionate in value to the credit, but a symbolic instrument, a probative pledge, which seems to have been generally true of movable pledges in Israel. But the orphan's ass and the widow's ox (in Jb 24: 3) are real sureties, which can even be used to profit.

Only once is there any question of immovable pledges: according to Ne

5: 3 the Jews pledged their fields, vineyards and houses in order to get corn. It is more than a mortgage, for the creditors were already installed in these properties (v. 5) and Nehemias demanded restitution (v. 11). It is at least a profit-bearing surety, the revenue from which goes to pay off the debt; it is perhaps an alienation pure and simple, since the property 'belongs to others' (v. 5), a fact which contradicts the notion of a pledge.

It is possible that movable pledges, especially garments, were only probative instruments of a weightier guarantee, the pledge of a man's own person. According to Dt 24: 10, the man who lends against security (*mashsha'ah*) must not go into the debtor's house to seize the pledge ('*abôt*) which, according to vv. 12-13, is a garment. Now in Dt 15: 2 the *mashsheh* is a person who works for the creditor, and this is also the sense which must be given to *mashsha'* in Ne 10: 32, referring to the sabbatical year, like Dt 15. The context again allows us to understand it as a personal pledge in Ne 5: 7, 10, 11 (corr.), where the same word is used. The debt contracted on this guarantee is called *mashsha'ah* (Dt 24: 10; Pr 22: 26).

The person who stood as security was handed over to the creditor only when the debt matured and in case of non-payment. He passed into the service of the creditor, who employed him to recover the interest and, if necessary, the principal. This is clear from the story in 2 K 4: 1-7: the lender against security, the *nôshe'*, comes to take the widow's two sons to make them his slaves, but they are still with her, and thanks to the miracle of Eliseus she redeems her pledge (*n'shî*) and keeps her children. The same passage shows us that the pledge was someone dependent on the debtor and not the debtor himself. In Ne 5:2 (corr.) and 5, the Jews pledge their sons and daughters, who are handed over into slavery (cf. Is 50:1: Yahweh has not sold his children, the Israelites, to lenders on pledge). Such men easily made themselves odious through the exercise of their rights. The Code of the Covenant rebukes the practice (Ex 22: 24) and Nehemias was bitterly angry at it (Ne 5: 6f.; cf. 1 S 22: 2; Ps 109: 11).

If he had no personal pledge the defaulting debtor had to enter the service of his creditor, or sell himself to a third party so as to repay his debt (Dt 15: 12; Lv 25: 39, 47). Insolvency was the main cause of Israelites being reduced to slavery.[1]

7. *Sureties and bail*

The seizure of the pledged person or the actual debtor could be prevented by entering bail or surety. In Biblical law the surety is the person who, when the debt matures, 'intervenes' (the root '*rb*), in favour of the insolvent debtor and assumes responsibility for the payment of the debt, either by obtaining it from the debtor or by substituting himself for him. The collections of laws do not mention it, but there are many allusions to it in the Sapiential books,

1. Cf. p. 83.

and the texts in Pr 11: 15; 17: 18; 20: 16=26: 13, which belong to the 'Salomonic' collections, show that the practice was not of late date in Israel. There is very early evidence of it in Mesopotamia.

The surety intervened by the symbolic gesture of 'striking the hands', that is, shaking hands (Pr 6: 1; 11: 15; 17: 18; 22: 26; Jb 17: 3). In Mesopotamia he 'struck the forehead' of the debtor, but the resemblance between the actions is probably only outward. The surety had to try to free himself by importuning the debtor till he paid up (Pr 6: 3-5); otherwise he himself became liable to seizure (Pr 20: 16=27: 13; 22: 27). The Book of Proverbs warns rash men against thus going surety for their friends or for strangers. Sirach is less unfavourable to the practice: a good man goes surety for his neighbour, but his beneficiary is not always grateful, and going surety has brought many to their ruin; in any case, one must not go surety beyond one's means (Si 29: 14-20; cf. 8: 13).

8. The sabbatical year

Alienation of family property and the development of lending at interest led to the growth of pauperism and the enslavement of defaulting debtors or their dependants. This destroyed that social equality which had existed at the time of the tribal federation and which still remained as an ideal. Religious legislation attempted to remedy these evils by two institutions, the sabbatical year and the jubilee year.

The Code of the Covenant provided that an Israelite slave should not be kept more than six years: he was set at liberty in the seventh year, unless he preferred to stay with his master (Ex 21: 2-6).[1] This passage apparently means that the six years are counted from the time a man enters into service. According to the Code of the Covenant again, the fields, vineyards and olive groves are to lie fallow every seventh year and their produce is to be left for the poor (Ex 23: 10-11). The text does not say whether this reckoning varies with each field and owner, or whether the law orders a general measure, applicable at a fixed date. The latter solution is favoured by the following verse, which refers to the sabbath day and is formulated in the same way (Ex 23: 12).

There is no such uncertainty in the law of Deuteronomy (Dt 15: 1-18). The 'remission' (sh'miṭṭah) occurs every seventh year, and then all persons who have been enslaved for non-payment of a debt are set free (vv. 1-6). Verses 12-28, which repeat the law of Ex 21: 2-6 in this new context, are an invitation to interpret that law in the same manner: the slaves are insolvent debtors who have 'sold' themselves or have been 'sold', and setting them free involves writing off the debt. Vv. 7-11, however, prove that this remission is general and happens at fixed dates: no one may refuse a loan to his poorer brother, thinking: 'Soon it will be the seventh year, the year of remission.'

1. Cf. p. 87.

The general and periodic nature of this institution is confirmed by Dt 31: 10-11, which orders the reading of the Law 'every seven years, the time fixed for the year of remission'.

The law of Ex 23: 10-11 about land, not found in Deuteronomy, is repeated by Lv 25: 2-7: every seventh year the land is to have its sabbatical rest, according to a cycle which is reckoned to begin, by a sabbath year, from the people's entry into the Promised Land. God pledges his blessing for the sixth year, the produce of which will enable them to live through the year of fallow and the next year too, till the harvest (Lv 25: 18-22).

From all these provisions it appears that the sabbatical year was marked by a rest for the land and the setting free of Israelite slaves, signifying the abandonment of debts. The cycle of seven years is obviously inspired by the week of seven days, ending in the sabbath rest, whence the use of the same word 'sabbath' to denote both this year of rest and the whole period (Lv 25: 8; 26: 34, 35, 43). The seven-year periods recur in other Biblical contexts (Gn 41: 25-36; Dn 9: 24-27), and in Oriental literature. But no exact parallel has been found for the remission in the sabbatical year; a Ptolemaic papyrus remitting a debt contracted seven years earlier does not necessarily imply either the same practice or Jewish influence.

In the Bible itself there is scarcely any evidence for the institution apart from the legislative texts. It is very unlikely that the 'sign' given by Isaias (2 K 19: 29 = Is 37: 30) refers to the sabbatical (or jubilee) year, in spite of the analogies of the text with Lv 25: 21-22. The freeing of the slaves under Sedecias is an exceptional measure, in connection with which Jeremias quotes Dt 15: 12-13, but complains that the law is not observed. According to the tradition of Lv 26: 35-36, 43; cf. 2 Ch 36: 21, the Holy Land was never able to 'enjoy its sabbaths' till the Jews were deported. After the Exile, Nehemias made them promise to give up in the seventh year the produce of the soil and persons held as sureties, which obviously refers to the prescriptions of the sabbatical year (Ne 10:32). Though Ne 5: 1-13 makes no allusion to it, this does not mean that the law was then unknown, nor even that it was known but not observed, for the social crisis demanded an immediate solution (cf. v. 11) without waiting for the sabbatical cycle.

It is not, however, till the Hellenistic period that we find clear proof that the law was applied, at least in leaving land fallow: in 163-162 B.C. the Jews lacked provisions, 'for it was a sabbatical year granted to the land' (1 M 6: 49, 53). Other historical data are provided by the historian Josephus; these, if they were more reliable, would allow us to trace this observance down to the beginning of the reign of Herod the Great. For the reign of Herod we have another piece of evidence that the law existed and was a source of embarrassment to lenders. During this period Hillel invented a way of circumventing the law by the *prosbol*: a clause was inserted in the contract by which the debtor renounced the advantage he would have gained from the sabbatical

year. An acknowledgment of a debt containing such a clause has been discovered at Murabba'at. The land, too, was given rest: it is significant that
contracts of *métayage* found in the same place are concluded up to the next
sabbatical year (*sh'miṭṭah*). They are dated in February, A.D. 133, which would
mark the beginning, more or less, of a sabbatical period, the time when
contracts of land tenure would be renewed.

The sabbatical year is therefore an ancient institution, but it is hard to say
how faithfully the Israelites observed it. Positive evidence is rare and late, and
comes from periods of national and religious fervour.

9. *The Jubilee Year*

In Lv 25 prescriptions about the sabbatical year are combined with those on
the jubilee year (Lv 25: 8-17, 23-55, several parts of which apply equally to
both). This text raises some difficult problems. The jubilee (*yôbel*) is so called
because its opening was announced by the sound of the trumpet (*yôbel*). It
recurred every fifty years, at the end of seven weeks of years. It was a general
emancipation (*d'rôr*) of all the inhabitants of the land. The fields lay fallow:
every man re-entered his ancestral property, *i.e.* the fields and houses which
had been alienated returned to their original owners, except for the town
houses, which could only be re-purchased in the year after their sale. Consequently, transactions in land had to be made by calculating the number of
years before the next jubilee: one did not buy the ground but so many harvests. Finally, defaulting debtors and Israelite slaves were set free, so the purchase price of these slaves was reckoned from the number of years still to
elapse before the next jubilee. Religious grounds are given for these measures:
the land cannot be sold absolutely, for it belongs to God; Israelites cannot be
cast into perpetual slavery, for they are the servants of God, who brought
them out of Egypt.

The practical application of this law seems to encounter insuperable
obstacles. Unless we arbitrarily suppose, against the evidence of vv. 8-10, that
this fiftieth year was really the forty-ninth, the last of the sabbatical years, the
lands must have been left fallow for two consecutive years. The law presumes
that the transfer of property, loans at interest and enslavement for debt are
current practice, and such was indeed the case in the period of the monarchy.
But in such a developed society it is hard to suppose that there was a general
return of lands and real property to their original owners or their heirs.
Secondly, the directions on the redemption or liberation of the slaves would
be ineffective in themselves[1] and are in contradiction to the law of the
sabbatical year, which provides for their liberation every seventh year.

There is no evidence that the law was ever in fact applied. Two legislative
passages refer to it (Lv 27: 16-25 and Nb 36: 4) but they belong to the final

1. Cf. p. 88.

revision of the Pentateuch and clearly depend on Lv 25. No historical text mentions it, even when it seems to be required by the context. On the subject of the liberation of the Hebrew slaves, Jr 34: 14 quotes Dt 15, but not Lv 25. Nehemias makes the people promise to observe the sabbatical year, but says nothing about the jubilee year (Ne 10: 32). In the prophetical books, Ez 46: 17 apparently refers to it: if the prince makes a gift from his domain to one of his servants, the gift reverts to the prince 'in the year of emancipation' (d*rôr), as in Lv 25: 10. But Ezechiel's directions are for a future time, and moreover this particular text is generally considered to be an addition. Another even less probable allusion may be found in Is 61: 1-2, where the prophet proclaims a year of grace and emancipation (d*rôr) for the captives; but this text is post-Exilic.

The Law of Jubilee thus appears to set out an ideal of justice and social equality which was never realized. It is difficult to say when it was thought out. It forms part of the Code of Holiness (Lv 17-26), which is the oldest section of Leviticus and may have been compiled by the priests at Jerusalem at the end of the monarchy: but the Law of Jubilee is an addition to the Code of Holiness. It is set forth as a development of the sabbatical law, and is still unknown in the time of Jeremias. It might have been written during the Exile, in which case Ez 46: 17 would reflect the same preoccupations, if this passage is the work of Ezechiel. Or it might have been written after the Exile, even after Nehemias, for he does not refer to it.

Some arguments, on the other hand, would favour a much earlier date. The inalienable nature of the patrimony, which this law safeguards, is an ancient idea. The seven sabbatical years, followed by the jubilee of the fiftieth year, have their parallel in the seven sabbaths between the presentation of the first sheaf and the Feast of Weeks, celebrated on the fiftieth day, Pentecost (Lv 23: 15-16). Now the cycles of fifty days are the basis of an agricultural calendar which may have been used in Canaan and which still survives to some extent among the peasants of Palestine.[1] But we must note that nowhere outside the Bible is the fiftieth year marked by a redistribution of the land or a remission of debts and of persons taken as sureties; nor is there any evidence whatever of such a general liberation, at any time whatever. Some have appealed to the evidence of cuneiform tablets which mention that the tablets (of contracts) have been broken, but this action merely signifies the repudiation or annulment of an agreement, or its invalidation for a legal flaw, or the fulfilment of the obligation. A connection has been suggested with the Akkadian word a(n)duraru or duraru, meaning exemption, emancipation or declaration of a state of freedom, which is obviously related to the Hebrew d*rôr: but this term never denotes a general and periodical remission of obligations.

Taking all these elements into account, one may advance the hypothesis

1. Cf. p. 180.

that the Law of Jubilee was a late and ineffective attempt to make the sabbatical law more stringent by extending it to landed property, and at the same time to make it easier to observe, by spacing out the years of remission. It was inspired by ancient ideas, and made use of the framework of an archaic calendar, which had not lost all its value in rural practice and in the religious sphere. But it was a Utopian law and it remained a dead letter.

Chapter Twelve

DIVISIONS OF TIME

1. *Ancient Eastern calendars*

WE read in Gn 1: 14 that God created the sun and the moon 'to divide the day from the night and to serve as signs, for feasts and for the days and the years', and time is in practice reckoned by the courses of these two bodies. The day is measured by the apparent revolution of the sun round the earth, the month by the moon's revolution round the earth, the year by the earth's revolution round the sun. The day, the easiest unit to observe, which regulates all life, public and private, has necessarily been taken as the basic unit by all systems, but the lunar month does not equal an integral number of days, and twelve lunar months amount to 354 days, 8 hours and a fraction, whereas a year based on the sun has 365 days, 5 hours and a fraction. The lunar year is therefore nearly eleven days shorter than the solar year. In a primitive society these differences are of little importance and only need to be corrected from time to time by empirical readjustments. But very early in the East, the development of civil and religious institutions, the taxes periodically due to the State, religious festivals, contracts between individuals, all made it necessary to fix past and future dates, in short, to establish an official calendar. These systems varied in different times and places, and the ancient history of the calendar is very complicated.

The Egyptians adopted at first a lunar calendar, adjusted to ensure that the heliacal rising of Sirius (Sothis)—whose feast had to fall in the last month of the year—should mark the year's end. In order to keep this agreement between the lunar and solar years a lunar month was added from time to time. This calendar regulated the seasonal religious feasts throughout the whole of Egyptian history. At the beginning of the third millennium B.C., to avoid these arbitrary readjustments and to meet the needs of civil life, a solar year was decreed, with twelve months of thirty days each, *plus* five supernumerary days, making 365 days, starting from the heliacal rising of Sirius. It was the nearest possible number of days to the natural year, but the latter dropped a day behind the civil year every four years. The Egyptians took a long time to deal with this, and the civil year gradually drew apart from the natural year: the first day of the first month could not fall on the heliacal rising of Sirius for another 1460 years (Sothiac period). After a century or two of the 'New' civil calendar, the discrepancy between the civil and natural year had become too flagrant; but since they did not dare to touch the civil year, they duplicated it by a new lunar calendar, in which a supplementary month was intercalated, according to a simple rule founded on a twenty-five-year cycle. The right solution would have been to add a day to every fourth civil year, but this was not proposed till 237 B.C., by the decree of Canopus, which remained a dead letter. It was only applied by the reform of Julius Caesar instituting a leap year, the system which is still with us.

Mesopotamia was faithful to a lunar calendar from very early days: the year comprised twelve months of 29 or 30 days without fixed order, the next month beginning on the evening when the new crescent moon was sighted. The names of the months varied at first in different regions, but from the time of Hammurabi the calendar of Nippur gradually won favour. The Nuzu calendar, however, in the middle of the second millennium, has a high proportion of Hurrite names, and Assyria had several calendars concurrently down to Tiglath-Pileser I, who had the Babylonian calendar adopted. In this, the year began in the spring, on the first day of Nisanu, and ended on the last day of Addaru. The discrepancy of eleven days between this lunar year and the solar year was corrected every two or three years by the addition of a thirteenth month, called second Ululu (the sixth month), or second Addaru (the twelfth month). Public authority decided the years in which intercalation was to be made. Thus Hammurabi wrote to one of his officials: 'This year has an intercalary month. The coming month must then be called second Ululu.' This was still the practice in the Persian period. Babylonian astronomers were well aware that the two years coincided at the end of nineteen years if seven lunar months had been intercalated, but it was only at the beginning of the fourth century B.C. that rules for intercalation within this cycle were fixed.

The Moslem calendar, which follows a non-rectified lunar year, in which the months do not remain constant with the seasons, is not primitive. It is a rather practical innovation of Islam. The pre-Islamic Arabs followed a lunar year, adapted to the natural year by intercalary months, and the names of their months were partly connected with agricultural operations.

We still know little about the ancient calendar of Syria and Palestine. They were subject to various influences under the stress of invasions and foreign rule. When the Egyptians were masters they introduced their own reckoning, at least for official documents: an inscription of the thirteenth century B.C. found at Tell ed-Duweir (Lakish) mentions deliveries of wheat in the second and fourth months of the flooding (of the Nile), one of the three seasons of the Egyptian year. In Northern Syria the Hurrite names of months appear side by side with Semitic names, and the nomenclature is in every case different from that of Mesopotamia. Inscriptions reveal a certain number of Phoenician month-names, but do not enable us to determine their order. The general impression is one of great confusion, but it is probable that a rectified lunar calendar was followed everywhere, for this is the only one based on the observance of the months which preserves a year related to the rhythm of agricultural operations. There is no proof that a real solar calendar was used, apart from the superficial and temporary influence of the Egyptian system.

There has recently been an attempt to prove the existence of an entirely different system in ancient Mesopotamia. The theory is that the Assyrian merchants who traded in Cappadocia at the beginning of the second millennium B.C. divided the year into seven periods of fifty days, each fifty comprising seven weeks, *plus* a day of festival. As seven fifties make only 350 days, and since the needs of both agriculture and commerce required agreement with the natural year, a period of sixteen days (the *shapattum*) was added at the end of this year. This calendar, it is claimed, was used in Cappadocia concurrently with that of the rectified lunar year. The system could be extended to longer periods, and they reckoned by periods of seven years and fifty years (the *dârum*). About the same time in Babylonia, there is evidence of a reckoning by seven-year periods. But this hypothesis rests on weak arguments; the key argument is the word *ḥamushtum*, translated by 'a fifty' of days, but the word means far more probably a period of five days or a fifth of a month. Besides, the use of this reckoning in Assyria and Babylonia must have been restricted to the first centuries of the second millennium B.C. However, we have traces of a similar system in the institution of the Jubilee[1] and the festal calendar of Israel.[2] The calendar of the Qumran sectaries enumerates agricultural feasts which were celebrated approximately every fifty days. A partial application of this quinquagesimal system is found also in the calendar of Nestorian Christians and, through this Christian adaptation, in the calendar of Palestinian peasants, who reckon seven fifties of days, going from one feast to another.

2. *The Israelite calendar. The day*

The same complexity is found in Israel, which stood at the crossroads of several civilizations and was subjected to varied influences in the course of its history. But no one can deny that the complexity has been increased by the contradictory hypotheses of modern scholars, and it seems that a simpler and more coherent solution can be found than those which have recently been proposed.

As everywhere, the basic unit is the solar day. The Egyptians reckoned it from one morning to the next and divided it into twelve hours of day time and twelve of night; the hours varied in length with the latitude and the season. In Mesopotamia the day was reckoned from one evening to the next; it was divided into twelve *bêru* of two hours each, and each *bêru* had thirty units of four minutes each. The night and the day were divided into six

1. Cf. pp. 175 177.   2. Cf. p. 493.

watches, each lasting for two *bêru*, or four hours. Thus there was, as in Egypt, a difference between the seasonal hour and the real hour, but they were able to fix tables of concordance for the different months.

In Israel, the day was for a long time reckoned from morning to morning. When they wanted to indicate the whole length of a day of twenty-four hours, they said 'day and night' or some such phrase, putting the day first: scores of references could be quoted (Dt 28: 66-67; 1 S 30: 12; Is 28: 19; Jr 33: 20, etc.). This suggests that they reckoned the day starting from the morning, and it was in fact in the morning, with the creation of light, that the world began; the distinction of day and night, and time too, began on a morning (Gn 1: 3-5, cf. 14, 16, 18). The opposite conclusion has been drawn from the refrain which punctuates the story of Creation: 'There was an evening and there was a morning, the first, second, etc., day'; this phrase, however, coming after the description of each creative work (which clearly happens during the period of light), indicates rather the vacant time till the morning, the end of a day and the beginning of the next work.

In the latest books of the Old Testament the expression 'day and night' is reversed: Judith praises God 'night and day' (Jdt 11: 17); Esther asks for a fast of three days 'night and day' (Est 4: 16); Daniel speaks of 2,300 'evenings and mornings' (Dn 8: 14). The same form is found in texts which are not so late but certainly post-Exilic: Ps 55: 18, 'at evening, at morning and at noon'; Is 27: 3, 'night and day', Is 34: 10, 'neither night nor day'. This order is found in only two pre-exilic passages, 1 K 8: 29 and Jr 14: 17, but the parallel of 2 Ch 6: 20 in the former case and the readings of the ancient versions in both cases suggest that the Massoretic text should be corrected. On the contrary, where we find the order 'day and night' in late passages, it is explained by the importance, in the context, of the day as opposed to the night (Za 14: 7; Qo 8: 16), or by the survival of a formula rooted in the spoken language.

The same conclusions clearly emerge from certain biblical stories. Thus in the story of the daughters of Lot: 'The next day the elder said to the younger, Last night I slept with my father; let us make him drink wine again to-night' (Gn 19: 34). In the story of the Levite of Ephraim: he stays three days with his father-in-law and stops the night there. The fourth day, he wakes and wants to depart. He is detained and again stops the night. The fifth day, the father-in-law says to him: 'Behold, the day is far advanced towards evening. Spend the night here again. . . . To-morrow, early in the morning, you will depart. . . .' (Jg 19: 4-9). Saul's henchmen arrive at night to take David by surprise, and Mikal says to him: 'If you do not escape to-night, to-morrow you are a dead man' (1 S 19: 11). In the house of the witch of Endor, Samuel appears to Saul during the night and says to him: 'To-morrow, you and your sons will be with me' (1 S 28: 19). Other passages could be quoted, but they are less decisive (Jg 21: 2-4; 1 S 5: 2-4).

Nehemias, on the other hand, to prevent the merchants breaking the sabbath, orders the gates of Jerusalem to be shut at nightfall, before the sabbath, and not to be opened till after the sabbath (Ne 13: 19). Here the day seems to begin at sunset.

The same duality is found in the liturgical texts, but it is more difficult to argue from them since their dates are uncertain. According to Lv 7: 15 and 22: 30, the meat of sacrifices must be eaten the same day, not leaving anything to be eaten to the morning of the next day. Had the day begun in the evening the wording would have ordered the meat to be eaten before the evening. The Passover is celebrated on the fourteenth day of the first month, after sunset; the feast of the Unleavened Bread, which lasts seven days, begins on the fifteenth day (Lv 23: 5-6: cf. Nb 28: 16) and this fifteenth day is the day after the Passover (Nb 33: 3; cf. Jos 5: 10). All this presumes that the day began in the morning. But the other reckoning appears clearly in the date of the day of Atonement, 'the evening of the ninth day of the month, from this evening to the next evening' (Lv 23: 32), and in Ex 12: 18, in which Unleavened Bread must be eaten from the evening of the fourteenth day to the evening of the twenty-first. These two passages belong to the final redaction of the Pentateuch. This method of reckoning is used in New Testament times and under later Judaism for the sabbath, the religious feasts and civil life.

The change of reckoning must therefore have taken place between the end of the monarchy and the age of Nehemias. One could date it more precisely if it were certain that in Ez 33: 21-22 the evening and the morning of v. 22 both applied to the fifth day of v. 21. This would bring us to the beginning of the Exile; unfortunately the text is not explicit.

The day was divided without precision according to natural phenomena: the morning and the evening (Ex 18: 13, etc.), mid-day (Gn 43: 16, 25; 1 K 18: 29, etc.), dawn (Gn 19: 15; Jos 6: 15; 1 S 30: 17), the setting of the sun (Gn 15: 12, 17), the breeze which blows before sunrise (Ct 2: 17; 4: 6), the evening breeze (Gn 3: 8), the hottest time of the day (Gn 18: 1; 1 S 11: 11; 2 S 4: 5). Sometimes reference was made to the ritual: the time of the evening sacrifice is an indication of time in 1 K 18: 29; Esd 9: 4, 5; Dn 9: 21. Certain religious actions had to be performed 'between the two evenings' (Ex 12: 6; 16: 12; 29: 39, 41; 30: 8; Nb 9: 3, 5, 11; 28: 4, 8). This expression denotes the time between the sun's disappearance and nightfall, that is to say, twilight, which in the East is very short. So the Samaritans continued to interpret it: the Pharisees explained it as the time preceding sunset.

The night was divided into three watches: the first watch (perhaps Lm 2: 19), the midnight watch (Jg 7: 19), and the last or morning watch (Ex 14: 24; 1 S 11: 11). This was on the whole the Mesopotamian practice, but by New Testament times the Egyptian and Roman custom of four night watches had been adopted (Mt 14: 25; Mk 13: 35).

We know of no terms for the smaller divisions of time. The word *sha'ah*, which later meant 'hour', is only employed in the Aramaic of Daniel, in the vague sense of a moment or instant (Dn 4: 16; cf. 3: 6, 15; 4: 30; 5: 5). But the Israelites had ways of telling the hours of the day. In Mesopotamia and Egypt water-clocks and gnomons were used from the second millennium B.C. and an Egyptian sundial of the thirteenth century has been found at Gezer. The 'degrees of Achaz' on which the sun receded six degrees at the prayer of Isaias (2 K 20: 9–11 = Is 38: 8) are not a gnomon, but a stairway built by Achaz, perhaps in connection with the 'high chamber' mentioned in a gloss in 2 K 23: 12. The miracle in question is not that of a 'clock' going forwards or backwards, but of the sudden movement of a shadow on a stairway.

3. *The month*

As the Egyptians reckoned the day from morning to morning, so they reckoned the lunar month to start from the morning when the last quarter of the preceding moon disappeared. The Babylonians, who reckoned the day from one evening to the next, made the month begin from the appearance of the crescent new moon at sunset. As long as the Israelites counted the day from morning to morning, they probably followed the Egyptian custom to fix the beginning of the month, but this cannot be stated for certain. If it could, the detailed story in 1 S 20: 18–35 would be more easily understood, and the transfer of the beginning of the feast of the Unleavened Bread from the fifteenth day (Lv 23: 6) to the fourteenth (Ex 12: 8), and its being joined with the Passover, could be explained by a change of reckoning; the Babylonian method of reckoning the day had replaced the Egyptian one.

What is certain in any case is that the Israelites followed a lunar month. Like the Canaanites, they called the month *yerah*, which also means the moon: the month is a lunation. But very soon, too (cf. Ex 23: 15; 34: 18; 1 S 6: 1; 10: 27; 1 K 4: 7) and more often thereafter, they called the month *hodesh*, which means primarily the new moon. In 1 K 6: 38 and 8: 2 the word *yerah*, with the Canaanite name of the month, is glossed by the word *hodesh* with the number of the month.[1]

As a lunation takes 29 days, 12 hours and a fraction, the lunar months had 29 and 30 days alternatively. At first they were given Canaanite names, which were connected with the seasons; Abib, the month of the ears of corn (Ex 13: 4; 23: 15; 34: 18; Dt 16: 1); Ziv, the month of flowers (1 K 6: 1, 37); Etanim, the month in which only the permanent water-courses still flow (1 K 8: 2); Bul, the month of the great rains (1 K 6: 38). The last three names are found with others in Phoenician inscriptions: Abib has not yet been attested there, but has been deciphered in the proto-Sinaitic inscriptions, though the reading is uncertain.

This Canaanite nomenclature was long preserved, since it was still used in Deuteronomy, which fixes the feast of the Passover in the month of Abib (Dt 16: 1), and it is only by chance that the names do not appear in the historical books after Solomon. It was an official calendar, and it seems that in daily life other names were used. A limestone tablet has been discovered at Gezer, which has an inscription attributed to the tenth century B.C. The text was certainly drawn up by an Israelite. It is a calendar, giving the following table:

Two months: *'sp*   = Ingathering
Two months: *zr'*   = Seedtime
Two months: *lqsh*   = Late seedtime
One month: *'ṣd psht* = Flax gathering
One month: *qṣr s'rm* = Barley harvest
One month: *qṣr wkl*   = Harvest (of wheat) and accounting(?)
Two months: *zmr*   = Pruning
One month: *qṣ*   = Summer fruits

This is not a memorandum of tasks to be carried out in the different months of the year, but a concordance table between twelve lunations (the months of the official year, listed here without their proper names) and the periods of the agricultural year, which the peasants called after the tasks they performed in them. The Old Testament uses several of these terms to mark dates. In the oldest liturgical calendars, Ex 23: 16 orders the feast of the Harvest, *qaṣîr*, to be observed, and that of the Ingathering, *'asîph*; Ex 34: 22 prescribes the feast of Weeks at the wheat harvest and the feast of Ingathering. Ruth and her mother-in-law arrive at Bethlehem 'at the beginning of the barley harvest' (Rt 1: 22). Reuben goes out 'at the time of the wheat harvest' (Gn 30: 14). Samson comes to visit his wife 'at the time of the wheat harvest' (Jg 15: 1). In 1 S 12: 17, 'the wheat harvest' is an indication of the season, like 'the barley harvest' in 2 S 21: 9-10. Amos sees the locusts swarming 'at the time when the late growth, *leqesh*, begins to shoot' (Am 7: 1). Much later, the Rule of the Qumran sect, naming the four seasons borrowed from the Greeks, gave them names drawn from agriculture, *qaṣîr*, harvest; *qayṣ*, summer fruits; *zera'*, seedtime; *deshe'*, tender shoots. The first three were already in the Gezer calendar, but here they are matched with the Greek seasons and the order is that of a year beginning in the spring. There seems to be evidence that this same Qumran community had a more complete agricultural calendar, comparable to the 'fifties' of the modern Palestinian peasants.[1]

In the official calendar the Canaanite names of the months were at some time replaced by the ordinal numerals: they were then counted from the first to the twelfth month. As an argument for the antiquity of such a system, one might quote the Egyptian practice of numbering the months of the three annual seasons from one to four, or Mesopotamian passages such as these: 'From the beginning of the year to the fifth month, and from the sixth month to the end of the year' (in the Code of Hammurabi), or 'I have taken

1. Cf. p. 180.

the omens . . . for the sixth month' (in the archives of Mari) or 'In the sixth month I shall send' (in the Amarna letters). But the Egyptian division of the year into three seasons never penetrated into Israel, and the Akkadian expressions just quoted are exceptional and do not form part of genuine dating formulae.

There is in fact no evidence of this system in the historical books before the account of the capture of Jerusalem by Nabuchodonosor (2 K 25=Jr 52). The other passages (Jos 4: 19 and 1 K 12: 32f.) are from the hand of the redactor, and in 1 K 6: 38 and 8: 2 the numeral of the month is a gloss, explaining the Canaanite name. In the Book of Jeremias, the practice appears under Joiaqim (Jr 36: 9, 22), under Sedecias (Jr 28: 1, 17; 39: 1, 2; cf. 1: 3), and after the fall of Jerusalem (Jr 41: 1). The change was made, then, after the reign of Josias, and this is confirmed by Deuteronomy, which still uses the old name of the month Abib (Dt 16: 1). As we shall see, the change coincided with the adoption of the Babylonian year, beginning in the spring.

But the Babylonian month-names were not accepted at first, probably because of their association with heathen worship, and the ordinal numbers were substituted for them. Two cuneiform tablets of the seventh century B.C., found at Gezer, are dated with the Babylonian name of the month, but they are written in Assyrian and under Assyrian rule. Reference to the months by the ordinal numbers remains the regular practice in Ezechiel and, after the Exile, in Aggaeus. In the Book of Zacharias, the eleventh month is explained as being the month of Shebat (Za 1: 7), the ninth as being the month of Kisleu (Za 7: 1), but these are later glosses. The Babylonian names are used in the Aramaic document of Esd 6: 15 and in the memoirs of Nehemias (Ne 1: 1; 2: 1; 6: 15), which is not surprising, since the Persians had adopted the Babylonian calendar[1]. But the redactor of Esdras and Nehemias and Chronicles never uses any but the ordinal numbers. The Book of Esther always refers to the months by an ordinal, followed, with one exception, by the Babylonian name. In the Books of Maccabees, the ordinal number is sometimes given alone (1 M 9: 3, 54; 10: 21; 13: 51) and sometimes followed by the Babylonian name (1 M 4: 52; 16: 14; 2 M 15: 36), but the Babylonian name in its Greek form is generally given alone. These variations show that the Babylonian names were only introduced long after the Exile and did not become current till very late. Apocryphal works like the Book of Jubilees and the Qumran literature show what obstinate resistance there was in some religious circles. In spite of it, however, the Babylonian month-names were in the end accepted by orthodox Judaism. We give here their order in the year, beginning in the spring, with their approximate equivalents in our calendar:

I. Nisân	March–April
II. Iyyar	April–May
III. Siwân	May–June

[1] And also, at the same period, and for the same reason, in the papyri of Elephantine.

IV.	Tammuz	June–July
V.	Ab	July–August
VI.	Elul	August–September
VII.	Tishri	September–October
VIII.	Marheshwân	October–November
IX.	Kisleu	November–December
X.	Tebeth	December–January
XI.	Shebat	January–February
XII.	Adar	February–March

From the Hellenistic period onwards the Macedonian names of months were introduced into official usage. A man of letters like the historian Josephus uses this system, but it never became familiar to the Jews. In the Greek Old Testament we encounter only the months of Xanthicus and Dioscurus (?) in the foreign documents of 2 M 11: 21, 30, 33, 38, and the month of Dystros in Tb 2: 12.

4. The week

In the Egyptian civil calendar the month of thirty days was divided into three decades. Some think they can find traces of a similar reckoning in the Old Testament. The mourning for Moses and that for Aaron each lasted thirty days (Nb 20: 29; Dt 34: 8), and it may be compared with the mourning of the captive woman which lasted a month (Dt 21: 13; cf. also Est 4: 11; Dn 8: 13). Ten days is a unit of time in Gn 24: 55; 1 S 25: 38. The tenth day of the month appears as the date of a feast or an event (Ex 12: 3; Lv 16: 29 (parallels: 23: 27; 25: 9; Nb 29: 7): Jos 4: 19; 2 K 25: 1 (parallels Jr 52: 4; Ez 24: 1); Ez 20: 1; 40: 1); the twentieth day is mentioned less frequently (Nb 10: 11; 11: 19). At Tell el-Farah in the south, and at Tell ed-Duweir bone tablets have been found, pierced with three parallel lines of ten holes each. These are perhaps 'calendars' for counting the days of the month: they date from the beginning of the monarchy.

All this does not amount to proof. Since the lunar months had alternately twenty-nine and thirty days, one can speak in round terms of thirty days as a month, and if the little 'calendars' found in excavations had to serve for all the months, they would have needed thirty holes. The fact that a feast was celebrated or that an event took place on the tenth of the month proves nothing about the month's division in time. The context of Gn 24: 55 and of 1 S 25: 38 show that this 'decade' is only a rough reckoning, 'ten days or so'.

The only unit less than the month for which there is good evidence is the period of seven days (shabū'a), the week. The origins of this institution, so familiar to us, are very obscure. In a lunar calendar the month would naturally be divided according to the moon's phases. The most obvious division is that marking the full moon in the middle of the month, and in fact the fifteenth day was of special importance in the Assyro-Babylonian calendar: it was the *shapattu*. Now there are certain passages in the Old Testament (2 K 4: 23; Is 1: 13; 66: 23; Os 2: 13; Am 8: 5) in which the *shabbath* is coupled with the new moon as a festal day. Ps 81: 4, in an identical context, employs the very rare word *kese'* ('full moon') so that *shabbath* may possibly have the same sense in the preceding passages as *shapattu* has in Akkadian. It must be remembered that the two great Israelite feasts, the Passover and Tents, were celebrated on the fourteenth-fifteenth days of the first and seventh months respectively, that is, at the full moon; the later feast of Purim was also fixed at the full moon, in the twelfth month.

The division of the month into four according to the moon's quarters is much less evident in the texts. It is true that in the Babylonian Poem of Creation the moon is assigned the function of marking the periods of the month by its phases, and that the Babylonian calendar, at least from the seventh century B.C., picks out as 'unlucky days' the 7th, 14th (19th), 21st and 28th days, which correspond with the lunar phases; but the Assyro-Babylonian calendar, at least till the eleventh century B.C., noted several other unlucky days. If a division into weeks is indicated by the later calendar—which is far from proved—the cycle was interrupted at the end of each month, which comprised twenty-nine or thirty days, and started again at each new moon. In Egypt there seems to have been a division of the months into seven, eight, eight and seven days, with lunar names, but it is obvious that the number of days is not constant, a fact which contradicts the very idea of the week.

Some novel explanations of the week have recently been proposed. According to one author, the seven days of the week are derived from the seven winds which blew from the seven directions, according to the most ancient Babylonian cosmology. Another says that the *ḥamushtu* of the Cappadocian texts being interpreted as a fifth of the month,[1] a 'week' of six days in the old Assyrian calendar was supplemented by the Israelites with a seventh day, reserved for rest. A discussion of these hypotheses would be to little purpose: it will be more useful to recall the sacred and symbolic value of the number seven and the seven-day periods which recur in the Babylonian poem of Gilgamesh and the poems of Ras Shamra. One of the passages in the Gilgamesh poems has an exact parallel in the story of the Flood (Gn 8: 10-12) and seven-day periods are often found in the Old Testament: for marriage celebrations (Gn 29: 27; Jg 14: 12), for mourning (Gn 50: 10), for the condolences of Job's friends (Jb 2: 13); for banquets (Est 1: 5), for a long march (Gn 31: 23; 2 K 3: 9, etc.). These expressions have no formal connection with the calendar, but their frequency makes it probable that from an early date the period of seven days was a calendar-unit.

If such a reckoning is uniformly applied, it is independent of the lunar months, since these are not exactly divisible into weeks. It is possible that the

1. Cf. p. 180.

idea of the week arose from rough observation of the moon's phases, but it became the element of a cycle of its own, overriding those of the months and the years. This in itself distinguishes the Israelite week from the Egyptian and the Babylonian 'weeks'. There are more important differences: the week is marked by the repose of the seventh day, the sabbath, which is an ancient religious institution, peculiar to Israel. We shall deal with it at greater length in connection with religious institutions[1] and would here note only one consequence; the reckoning by weeks—not merely the indication of seven-day periods, as in the passages just quoted—is only found in liturgical texts, except for the late passages in Dn 10: 2 and 9: 24-27 (where they are weeks of years).

The calendar of one religious group in Judaism is entirely governed by the week. It is found most clearly in the apocryphal Book of Jubilees: fifty-two weeks make a year and 364 days, divided into quarters of thirteen weeks that is, of ninety-one days; seven years make a week of years (as in Daniel), seven weeks of years form a jubilee. This same calendar is found in a part of the Apocrypha ascribed to Henoch, and in the Qumran literature. The purpose of this reckoning is to make the same feasts fall every year on the same days of the week. The liturgical days are the first, fourth and sixth days of the week; the sabbath is the day of rest. The originators of this calendar do not seem to have been concerned over the divergence between this year of 364 days and the real year of $365\frac{1}{4}$ days. But this discrepancy must have appeared very soon, and this calendar cannot have been followed for long, unless there were periodical adjustments not mentioned in any text. The recent attempt to connect this with an ancient priestly calendar, whose influence may be found in the redaction of the Pentateuch, is still no more than a hypothesis. We shall now see, moreover, that the Pentateuch gives evidence of another reckoning.

5. The year

The 364-day year of this calendar of Jubilees is a solar year, only less accurately reckoned than the Egyptian year of 365 days. The latter was evidently known to the Israelites and appears in two passages of Genesis. According to Gn 5: 23, the patriarch Henoch lived 365 years. If we remember that according to later tradition Henoch was favoured with revelations on astronomy and the calculation of time, we realize that 365 represents a perfect number, that of the days in a solar year. The chronology of the Flood is even more convincing: the disaster begins on the seventeenth day of the second month (Gn 7: 11) and ends on the twenty-seventh day of the second month of the next year (Gn 8: 14). Hence it lasted twelve months and eleven days, the exact period required to equate the year of twelve lunar months, 354 days, with the solar year of 365 days. The redactor wanted to say that the Flood lasted exactly one solar year. In the same context, compari-

1. Cf. pp. 475-483.

son of Gn 7: 11, 24 with Gn 8: 3-4 indicates that five months make a total of 150 days, that is, five Egyptian months of thirty days. This passage is of late redaction; it appears as a scholar's note to show the correspondence between the solar year and the rectified lunar year, or lunisolar year, which regulated daily life and the liturgy. But in this lunisolar year the feasts did not fall each year on the same days of the week. The calendar of the Jubilees, mentioned above, must have been a reform aimed at tying the feasts to fixed days of the week.

Apart from these scholarly calculations and abortive attempts, there is no proof that a truly solar year ever prevailed in Israel. The intentional chronology of Gn 7: 11; 8: 15 itself emphasizes that the description of the months by the ordinal numbers belonged to a lunar reckoning. We noted earlier that the ordinal system had done away with the use of Canaanite names. These names, being drawn from seasonal events, can only fit a year which is at least approximately adjusted to the natural year; this might be either a solar year or a lunisolar year with an intercalary month. This latter solution is indicated by the Canaanite word for a month (*yerah*, meaning the moon) and by Mesopotamian analogy. There is no reason to doubt that it was the same in ancient Israel, where the same word stood for the month and the moon, and the beginning of the month was marked by the new moon.

The intercalary month, however, is never mentioned in the Old Testament, except at the very end, for a non-Israelite calendar: the Macedonian month of Dioscorus (2 M 11: 21) is perhaps an intercalary month. The sacred writers invariably speak of only twelve months (1 K 4: 7; 1 Ch 27: 1-15; cf. Jr 52: 31; Ez 32: 1; Dn 4: 26) and we saw that the Gezer calendar too reckoned twelve months. But in 1 K 4: 7 one would have expected the intercalary month to be mentioned: Solomon's twelve districts had each to supply the king and his household for a month of the year; and in 1 Ch 27 each of David's stewards was on duty for a month. What happened when the year had thirteen months? The uncertainty arises from our lack of information: these passages only tell what happened in ordinary years.

In any case, the intercalation of a supplementary month was, for a long time, made in an empirical manner. Even at the end of the first century of our era, the Rabbi Gamaliel II was writing to the communities of the Diaspora: 'The lambs are still too weak and the chickens too small: the grain is not ripe. Therefore it has seemed good to us and our colleagues to add thirty days to this year.' In the end, the Babylonian cycle of nineteen years was adopted, with intercalations at fixed dates. The duplicated month was Adar, the last month of the year; there is no proof that a second Elul month was sometimes intercalated, as in Babylonia.

The year was divided into two seasons, the winter, *horeph*, and summer, *qays*, corresponding roughly to the cold and hot seasons, to seedtime and harvest (Gn 8: 22; cf. Ps 74: 17; Is 18: 6; Za 14: 8). Kings and the rich had their summer and winter houses (Am 3: 15; Jr 36: 22). This simple division corresponds to the climate of Palestine, where the hot, dry season and the cold, wet season succeed each other fairly quickly, leaving no distinct sensation of spring and autumn, as in more temperate countries. The Egyptians had three seasons, governed by the rise of the Nile and its effects: Flooding, Seedtime and Harvest. The Greeks at first had three seasons and later four, by the addition of autumn. They were defined by the spring and autumn equinoxes and the summer and winter solstices. This division was introduced among the Jews in the Hellenistic period. We have noted earlier that it appeared in the Qumran documents, with agricultural names. Later, the seasons were called after those months which included the equinoxes and solstices.

6. *The beginning of the year*

The two oldest liturgical calendars (Ex 23: 14-17 and 34: 18-23) list three great annual feasts: Unleavened Bread, Harvest and Ingathering. As the Unleavened Bread was celebrated in the month of Abib, later called Nisan, one might see in this order the indication of a year beginning in the spring, if a date were not defined for Ingathering. According to Ex 23: 16, it falls *b'ṣe'th hashshannah*, at the 'going out' of the year, which most probably means the beginning of the year, as the same word elsewhere means the rising of the sun (Jg 5: 31; Is 13: 10) or of the stars (Ne 4: 15). According to Ex 34: 22, the feast of the Ingathering marks the *t'qûphath hashshannah*, etymologically the 'revolution' of the year, but strictly the end of this revolution (cf. 1 S 1: 20; Ps 19: 7, and the use of the corresponding verb in Jb 1: 5), and therefore the end of the year. We must not introduce into these ancient texts the notion of solstice and equinox which later Judaism gave to *t'qûphah*. How the feast was fixed, whether at the beginning or at the end of the year, is a problem which will claim attention under religious institutions[1]: here it is enough to show that the two calendars presuppose a year beginning in autumn.

The list of agricultural tasks in the Gezer tablet also begins in autumn: it is not the natural order, which would begin with the sowing, but the text shows that it agrees with a civil year beginning in autumn.[2]

In 2 S 11: 1 = 1 Ch 20: 1 and in 1 K 20: 22, 26, we find the expression *t'shûbath hashshannah*, literally the 'return' of the year; in the first text and its parallel it is explained as 'the time when kings take the field', and in the other two it is used to date a military expedition. According to repeated indications in the Assyrian annals, this was usually in the spring. This 'return' of the year would be the time when the year was half over, and beginning to return from winter to summer, when the days began to equal the nights, our spring equinox. This again presumes an autumnal year. The expression continued to be attached to this time of the year after the change of the calendar,

and in 2 Ch 36: 10 it again refers to the spring: from other sources we are able
to date the event referred to, the capture of Jerusalem, in March 597.

The story of Josias' reform (2 K 22-23) tells of the discovery of the Book
of the Law, how it was read before the king, then before the whole people
assembled in Jerusalem, how measures of reform were applied in the capital,
in Judah and the former kingdom of Israel, and finally of the celebration of
the Passover. All these events took place in the eighteenth year of the king:
this would be impossible if the year began in the spring, just before the
Passover, and postulates a year beginning in autumn.

Finally we may recall that Mesopotamia too originally had an autumnal
year: the seventh month of the Babylonian spring year kept its name of
Teshrîtu, that is 'beginning'.

But there are other Old Testament texts which presume a different
reckoning. When the scroll of the prophecies of Jeremias was read to Joiaqim,
the king was in his winter house, warming himself at a brazier, because 'it
was the ninth month' (Jr 36: 22), evidently the ninth month of a year beginning in spring, that is, November-December.

According to 2 K 25: 8 = Jr 52: 12, the Temple was destroyed by Nabuchodonosor in the fifth month. Josephus and Jewish tradition say that it was at
the same time of the year that the second Temple was burnt by the Romans,
and we know that this event took place in August. The tradition is ancient:
according to Zacharias, at a time when the spring calendar was certainly in
use (cf. the dates of Aggaeus in connection with the years of Darius), the
destruction of the Temple was commemorated by a fast in the fifth month
(Za 7: 3 and 5). This is confirmed by Jr 40-41, which records the events
immediately after the capture of Jerusalem: wine, fruit and oil were gathered
in (Jr 40: 10), and after the murder of Godolias, in the seventh month of the
same year, wheat, barley, oil and honey were already stored (Jr 41: 8); all
this is inexplicable except in a spring year.

Some of the liturgical texts are quite explicit. The law of the Passover begins thus in Ex 12: 2: 'This month comes to you as the head of the months;
it is for you the first month of the year.' This insistence is intentional,
emphasizing something new. According to Ex 23: 15 and also Dt 16: 1, the
Passover must be celebrated in the month of Abib in the autumnal year.
Between these texts and the redaction of Ex 12, the date of the feast was not
altered, but the calendar was changed: a spring year was being followed.
(The same remarks apply to the religious calendars of Lv 23, Nb 28-29 and
Ez 45: 18-25.)

All the Old Testament passages in which the months are denoted by
ordinal numbers are easily explained if the year begins in the spring. We
have already shown that this new nomenclature was introduced after the
death of Josias[1]; if we compare the story of Josias' reform (2 K 22-23) with

1. Cf. p. 185.

that of the capture of Jerusalem (2 K 25), we observe that the spring year had also been introduced by this date. Possibly, too, this was the time when they began to reckon the day from evening to evening,[1] and the months from the appearance of the new moon at sunset.[2] All this points to the adoption of the Babylonian calendar and is explained by the historical circumstance that under Joiaqim, son of Josias, the kingdom of Judah became a vassal state of Nabuchodonosor.

These conclusions hold good for the kingdom of Judah, about which we are better informed. It may be presumed that the autumnal calendar was also followed in the kingdom of Israel so long as it remained independent, but that the Babylonian calendar was imposed, at least for official use, in the Assyrian provinces constituted after the conquests of Tiglath-Pileser III in 733 B.C., and then for the rest of the territory after the fall of Samaria. The cuneiform contracts at Gezer, dated in the Assyrian manner, are evidence of this. An earlier date has been suggested for the adoption of the spring calendar in Israel, in order to throw light on the way in which the Books of Kings synchronize the reigns in Israel with those in Judah; but this synchronization raises difficult problems in itself, which the addition of another unknown element is not likely to solve.

The spring year was naturally retained when the Babylonian month-names replaced the ordinal numbers. Only one passage raises a difficulty. According to Ne 1: 1 and 2: 1, the month of Kisleu and the following month of Nisan fell in the same twentieth year of Artaxerxes, which would imply an autumnal year. But it is unlikely that Nehemias, living at the Persian court, where the Babylonian calendar was followed and the Babylonian month-names were used, did not also follow the official reckoning of the year. On the other hand, the Hebrew text of Ne 1: 1 has only 'the twentieth year', without the name of the reigning king, which is strange. The text must be corrupt, and the likeliest explanation is that originally it did not contain, or it accidentally lost, the mention of the year, which was later supplied mechanically from Ne 2: 1; it was really the nineteenth year of Artaxerxes. It has also been suggested that an autumnal year is found in one of the Elephantine papyri, but the date is apparently incorrect.

The Seleucids introduced an autumnal year at Antioch and in the Macedonian colonies, but in Babylonia they conformed to the spring calendar, which the Jews had already adopted. The first Book of Maccabees dates the events of general history by the Syro-Macedonian reckoning, but keeps the Babylonian reckoning for facts directly concerning the Jewish community. The few dates in the second Book are given according to the same calendar, except for the foreign documents of 2 M 11.

These variations in the course of the Old Testament history puzzled the Rabbis, who did not distinguish between the relative ages of the texts. They

---

1. Cf. pp. 181-182.   2. Cf. p. 183.

reckoned four beginnings to the year: in Nisan, the New Year for kings and for festivals; in Elul, the New Year for the tithe on cattle; in Tishri, the New Year for years, the sabbatical year and the Jubilee year; in Shebat, the New Year for the tithe on trees.

7. The eras

An era is the starting-point of a chronology which in theory continues for ever, such as the Christian era, the Moslem era, etc. Jewish chronologers have calculated an era of Creation, based on Biblical data, which is still followed by Judaism: the year 5718 of Creation began on September 26th, 1957. But the Old Testament knew nothing of the kind. It has been suggested that Nb 13: 22, according to which Hebron was founded seven years before Tanis, and Ex 12: 40, which gives the sojourn in Egypt as 430 years, refer to an 'era of Tanis', going back to the establishment of the Hyksos in Egypt. It is a mere hypothesis, and this chronology is in any case foreign to Israel. Figures like the 300 years of Jg 11: 26 and the 480 years of 1 K 6: 1 are based on calculations of the redactors of the Bible. To fix a date, reference was made to a roughly contemporary event which had made an impression: the prophecy of Amos is dated 'two years before the earthquake' (Am 1: 1). The oracle of Is 20: 1f. is in 'the year that the chief cupbearer came to Ashdod . . . and took it.' Ezechiel reckons the years from the deportation of Joiakin (Ez 1: 2; 8: 1; 20: 1; 24: 1; 26: 1, etc.) and 2 K 25: 27 (=Jr 52: 31) does the same.

This way of reckoning simply carries on the official reckoning of the kingdoms of Israel and Judah, in which events were dated by the years of the reign of each king. This system lasted till the end of the kingdom of Israel (2 K 17: 6), and of the kingdom of Judah (2 K 25: 1-2), and it went back at least to Solomon (1 K 6: 1, 37, 38). Something of the same sort may even be found in the time of the tribal federation, if we suppose that the 'lesser' Judges of Jg 10: 1-5; 12: 8-15 represent a permanent institution[1]: men would have reckoned time by the years of their office, the precise duration of which is noted in the texts.

It has been suggested that in the lists of Solomon's officials (1 K 4: 3) there is an official of the priestly caste 'over the year'; he would be an eponymous magistrate, one whose name served to describe the year: the list of these eponyms would provide a chronology. Israel would then have the equivalent of the eponyms of Assyria (*līmu*) and of Southern Arabia (*kabîr*). But this interpretation of a word which both the text and the versions represent as a proper name (Elihoreph or Elihaph) is a very fragile theory.

If dates were computed by the year of the reigning king, and if, as seems likely, this year coincided with the civil year, all that remains is to decide how the beginning of the reign was reckoned. The months between the enthronement and the next New Year might be counted as a complete year, the first year of the reign: this is the system of antedating, in which the year of a

1. Cf. pp. 93 and 151.

king's death and his successor's enthronement is counted twice. Alternatively the months before the New Year could go uncounted, the first year of the reign being reckoned from the New Year following the accession. This is the system of postdating.

The reigns of Assyria and Babylon were postdated. This system, it seems, was followed in Judah at the end of the monarchy: Jr 26: 1 gives as a date the 'beginning of the reign', re'shîth mamleketh, of Joiaqim, which is the exact equivalent of the Akkadian rêsh sharruti, meaning the incomplete year of the accession. On the other hand we cannot take into account Jr 27: 1 and 28: 1, where the same expression is found in passages which are corrupt or glossed. The re'shîth malkûth of Sedecias in Jr 49: 34 could be interpreted in the same way and would give a precise date: recently published Babylonian documents have shown us that there was exactly a month between the accession of Sedecias and the next New Year. We have no reliable information on earlier times. Various conjectures have been made, some of which result in a regular criss-cross of antedating and postdating between Israel and Judah. The object of these hypotheses is to support the synchronization given by the Book of Kings, but, as we have already remarked, this raises a special problem of chronology, which is perhaps insoluble. Simply on the basis of the evolution of the calendar, as we have traced it in the preceding pages, one would be inclined to suppose that postdating, a Babylonian custom, began with the adoption of the Babylonian calendar under Joiaqim, and that in earlier reigns the custom was to antedate, as it was in Egypt.

It was only under the Seleucids that a genuine era was inaugurated, the era of the 'kingdom of the Greeks', as it is called in 1 M 1: 10. Its beginning was fixed by Seleucus I in the year in which he conquered Babylon. The difference between the autumnal year observed at Antioch and the spring year observed in Babylon makes this era begin in the autumn of 312 B.C. in the Syro-Macedonian reckoning, but in the spring of 311 B.C. in the Babylonian. The dates in the Books of Maccabees are divided between these two reckonings in the manner already stated with reference to the beginning of the year.[1] When the autonomy of the Jewish nation was recognized in 142 B.C., acts and contracts began to be dated 'in the first year, under Simon the high priest, eminent general and leader of the Jews' (1 M 13: 41-42). This was not the foundation of a new era, but a return to the custom followed under the independent monarchy. All the same, the era of the Greeks continued in use (1 M 14: 1; 15: 10), and even serves to date the death of Simon (1 M 16: 14). The Jews resumed an independent but short-lived reckoning during their two revolts against the Romans in A.D. 66-70 and 132-135.

The special era of the free cities of Syria and Palestine at the end of the Hellenistic and Roman periods, and the more general eras of Pompey and of Arabia, are of no interest for the Old Testament.

1. Cf. p. 192.

CHAPTER THIRTEEN

WEIGHTS AND MEASURES

1. Israelite 'metrology'

METROLOGY is by definition an exact science. It presumes that units of length, volume and weight can be mathematically determined and rigorously classified. In practice, it requires the sanction of an authority to impose a system and to ensure that the measures used by everyone are in conformity with the statutory standards. This is the law in modern states and was, in varying degrees, the practice in the great empires of antiquity, but it is doubtful whether any such regulations existed in Israel. Some have claimed that 2 S 8: 1 contains a mention of a 'standard cubit' captured by David from the Philistines, but the text is corrupt and may conceal a geographical name. We hear of swindlers who gave short measure and overcharged (Am 8: 5), of weights which were 'heavy' or 'light' (Dt 25: 13), of a short bushel and of faked weights (Mi 6: 10-11; cf. Pr 20: 10). By contrast, Lv 19: 35-36 prescribes just weights, a just measure, a just ephah (cf. Ez 45: 10). But all these texts refer to commonly accepted estimates, not to official standards. The Rabbinical tradition that samples of the standard cubit were kept in the Temple is unverifiable and is perhaps based only on 1 Ch 23: 29, where the Levites are placed in charge of the loaves of oblation, the flour of wheat, the wafers and all sorts of measures. From the context, this simply means they were to see that the offerings were of the required quantity (cf., e.g. Ex 29: 40) and that God was not defrauded (cf. Ml 3: 8-10). We must not turn them into inspectors of weights and measures. We may appreciate these texts better if we see what happens to-day in Jerusalem, even after the metric system has been imposed, and all are required to use the authorized measures; certain shopkeepers in the bazaars weigh their wares with a small stone or a horse-shoe, peasants measure out milk or oil in jam-pots, Bedouin measure the rope they buy with outstretched arms. Like the Arabs of to-day, the Israelites of old were satisfied with a measure which conformed to custom. We shall see that in certain cases this measure was guaranteed by a mark or inscription on the receptacle or the measuring instrument, but this was not as accurate as our modern systems, nor, it seems, as those of ancient Mesopotamia or Egypt. It is useful to compare the data of the Bible with these ancient Eastern systems and (by way of filling the gaps) with the Graeco-Roman metrology. But it must be remembered that our estimate of their

units is often uncertain and that there is no guarantee that the Israelite
measures were exactly equivalent to those used in these foreign countries. In
our own day, measures with the same name have had, and sometimes still
have, appreciably different values in Syria, in Egypt and in Palestine, and even
in different regions of Palestine itself. Moreover, values changed with the
passage of time, both in Israel and in the adjacent countries. Finally, when we
are confined, as here, to the Old Testament, the data gleaned from the texts
and excavations is very inadequate.

These factors should incline us to a degree of prudence which has not
always been observed by authors of specialized works on biblical metrology.
One may, with a certain degree of probability, arrange the measures of each
category in their order, but it is futile and misleading to give their modern
equivalents to four or five places of decimals, when we can be sure neither of
the ancient standard nor of its relation to our system. Approximations are all
that can be given. Biblical 'metrology' will probably never become an
exact science.

2. Linear measures

According to the universal practice of antiquity, the commonest measures
of length were named from the limbs of the human body, and in Israel, from
the arm and the hand which the craftsman employed for his art.

The cubit, *'ammah*, is the distance between the point of the elbow and the
tip of the middle finger. The span, *zereth*, is measured from the tip of the
thumb to the tip of the little finger, the hand being extended and the fingers
apart: the Vulgate, by translating this as *palmus*, has caused confusion with the
following term. The palm or handbreadth, *ṭephaḥ* or *ṭophaḥ*, is in fact the
breadth of the hand at the base of the fingers. The finger or thumb, *'eṣba'*,
which is frequently mentioned in ancient metrologies and in the Talmud,
is found only once in the Old Testament as a unit of measurement
(Jr 52: 21).

The rod, *qaneh*, employed in Ezechiel's description of the Temple, is an
instrument for measuring rather than a unit of measurement (cf. Ez 40: 3).
This rod of Ezechiel was of six 'great' cubits, like the measure of the same
name in Mesopotamia. The flaxen cord of Ez 40: 3 and the measuring cord
of Am 7: 17; Za 1: 16; 2: 5, are also measuring instruments, and we do not
know whether they were standardized, like the Mesopotamian cord.

Finally, Jg 3: 16 says that Ehud had a sword one *gomed* in length. The word
is a *hapaxlegomenon* in the Bible, and neither the conjectures of ancient
versions ('span' or 'palm') nor those of modern scholars ('short cubit')
throw any light on the size of this measure.

The Old Testament nowhere indicates the relation of these units to one
another, but they obviously had the same proportional relations as the limbs
of the human body from which they took their names. Probably, too, these

relations were adjusted in the same way as in Mesopotamia and Egypt, which have an identical subdivision of the common cubit:

Cubit	1			
Span	2	1		
Palm	6	3	1	
Finger	24	12	4	1

According to Herodotus, Mesopotamia had, in addition, a 'royal cubit' which measures 27 fingers. In Egypt, too, there was a royal cubit of 7 palms or 28 fingers. A greater and a smaller cubit seem to have existed in Israel also, though not at one and the same time. Repeating the dimensions of Solomon's Temple as they are given in the books of Kings, 2 Ch 3 : 3 states clearly that they are 'cubits of the old measure'. The rod of the heavenly measurer in Ez 40-42 (cf. Ap 21 : 15-16) measured six cubits 'of a cubit and a palm' (Ez 40 : 5; cf. 43 : 13). Probably Ezechiel adopted the ancient measure for the description of the future Temple and gave its equivalent in the measure of his time: the old cubit would then have 6 palms of 24 fingers, but these were bigger. On the other hand we must not forget the Egyptian royal cubit, divided into 7 palms or 28 fingers.

The length of a cubit according to our modern systems of measurement can be found by comparing the neighbouring systems; but these are not all the same. The graduated rules engraved on two statues of Gudea, prince of Lagash about 2000 B.C., show a cubit of 19½ inches (0·495 metres), which is probably the greater cubit of the time. According to graduated rules found in Egypt, the royal cubit measured 20⅔ inches (0·525 or 0·53 metres). Excavations in Palestine have so far not yielded any similar standards, and we have only one positive piece of information to use: the inscription engraved in the tunnel of Ezechias says that it is 1,200 cubits long, and it is in fact 583 yards long (533·10 metres); this would make the cubit 17·490 inches (0·44425 metres) long. Such precision, however, is absurd, for 1,200 is evidently a round number, like the 100 cubits in the same line of the inscription indicating how far underground the tunnel is, and secondly, there is the inevitable margin of error in the measurement of its winding course. Next, one would have to decide whether this cubit of Ezechias' time was still the old cubit mentioned in 2 Ch 3 : 3, or the longer cubit of Ez 40 : 5, or the shorter cubit implied by the same text. There is consequently something rather arbitrary in the estimates given in books, and they vary from about 17·716 inches (0·45 metres) for the common cubit to about 20·472 inches (0·52 metres) for the cubit of Ezechiel.

These calculations are in any case rather pointless because there was no official standard. In practice, the architects, masons and craftsmen measured with their own arms, their extended hands, their palms and their fingers.

Arab metrology mentions a 'black cubit': it was one measured by a tall negro in the service of the Caliph.

Travelling distances are indicated only by empirical methods in the Hebrew books of the Old Testament. The step or pace (*peśa'*) is mentioned only in 1 S 20: 3, and then as a metaphor: 'there is but one step between me and death'. The reckoning by days of marching is equally vague: one day (Nb 11: 31), three days (Gn 30: 36; Ex 3: 18; Jon 3: 3), seven days (Gn 31: 23). In Gn 35: 16=48: 7; 2 K 5: 19, the distance is indicated by the expression *kibrath ha'areṣ*, 'an extent of country': it is anything but an exact measurement, and simply means 'some distance'.

Two Hellenistic measures appear in the books of Maccabees. Bethsur is about five *schoinoi* from Jerusalem (2 M 11: 5). The *schoinos* is an ancient Egyptian measure, which in the Ptolemaic period was equal to approximately $3\frac{3}{4}$ miles or 6 kilometres: Bethsur is in fact 18 miles (29 kilometres) from Jerusalem. The *stadion* is mentioned several times, all grouped, as it happens, in the same chapter (2 M 12: 9, 10, 16, 17, 29). The *stadion* is a Greek unit which was in use in Palestine during the Hellenistic, and later, during the Roman, period. The Alexandrian *stadion*, which the author of 2 M must have had in mind, for it was almost certainly the one employed by the Jews in Palestine, measured just over 202 yards (a little less than 185 metres). The distance of 600 *stadia* (2 M 12: 29) between Jerusalem and Scythopolis (Beth Shan) corresponds exactly to this measure: the two places are just over 68 miles (110 kilometres) apart. The 248 *stadia* of 2 M 12: 9, however, if calculated at the same length, are definitely too short for the distance between Jerusalem and the port of Jamnia. The 750 *stadia* of 2 M 12: 17 cannot be estimated because the terminal points are unknown.

There are no terms in Hebrew for measures of area, and these are indicated by giving the lengths of the sides of a rectangle or square, the diameter and the circumference of a circular space (1 K 6: 2f.; 7: 23; 2 Ch 4: 1, 2; Ez 40: 47, 49; 41: 2, 4, etc.).

Agricultural measurements were empirical. The acre (*ṣemed*), literally a 'yoke' or 'harnessing', is the area which a team of oxen can work in a day: it is mentioned as a measurement in Is 5: 10 and in the corrupted text of 1 S 14: 14. The area of a piece of ground was also calculated by the amount of grain needed to sow it. This method was also used throughout the ancient East and is attested in Palestine in the Talmudic period, but in the Bible it occurs only in 1 K 18: 32, a passage which is difficult to interpret. Elias digs a ditch round the altar, with a content of two *s°ah* of seed. Whatever the size of the *s°ah* may have been, and however densely we suppose it to be sowed, whether we apply the measure to the surface area of the ditch itself or extend it to the space it enclosed, the estimate is still highly exaggerated.

It is not likely that Lv 27: 16 means that a field is to be valued at fifty shekels per *homer* of barley needed to sow it, for that would mean a vast area could be bought for a ridiculously small price. The text must refer to the grain to be harvested, and is an estimate of the value of the field, not of its area.

3. *Measures of capacity*

The names used are generally those of the receptacles which contained provisions and which were used to measure them, as in many metrologies, included those of our own country, like the tun, the hogshead, the bushel and so on. When these words are used to translate Hebrew terms, it is only to indicate a measure of roughly the same size, not to give an exact equivalent. To avoid all confusion, we shall here use only transcriptions of Hebrew words.

The *homer* is, by derivation, an 'ass-load'. It is a large measure for cereals (Lv 27: 16; Ez 45: 13; Os 3: 2). In Nb 11: 32, the *homer* is used, by way of exception, as a measure for the quails which fell in the desert: they covered the ground to a depth of 2 cubits for a day's march around the camp, and each man gathered ten *homer*; the figures are deliberately fantastic, to show the people's gluttony and to justify their chastisement. The text of Is 5: 10 is meant to produce astonishment, but for the opposite reason: a *homer* of seed will produce only an *'ephah* of crop: it is a curse.

Similarly, the *kor* is a large measure for flour (1 K 5: 2), for wheat and barley (1 K 5: 25; 2 Ch 2: 9; 27: 5; Esd 7: 22). The mention of *kor* for oil in 1 K 5: 25 is a mistake for *bath* (cf. the Greek word and the parallel in 1 Ch 2: 9), but the confused and overloaded text of Ez 45: 13 makes *kor* a measure for liquids and the equal of the *homer*.

The *letek* is mentioned only in Os 3: 2 as a measure for barley, smaller than the *homer*. The versions interpret it as half a *homer*.

The *'ephah* in the vision of Za 5: 6-10, denotes a large receptacle, closed with a lid and large enough to hold a woman. It is often the name for a measuring instrument: there must be a just, a perfect *'ephah* (Lv 19: 36; Dt 25: 15); the *'ephah* must not be made too small (Am 8: 5; Mi 6: 10); there must not be two kinds of *'ephah*, large and small (Dt 25: 14; Pr 20: 10). Usually the word means the measure itself: an *'ephah* (Jg 6: 19; Rt 2: 17; 1 S 1: 24, etc.), one-sixth of an *'ephah* (Ez 45: 13; 46: 14), one-tenth of an *'ephah* (Lv 5: 11; 6: 13; Nb 5: 15; 28: 5; cf. Ex 16: 36). The articles measured are flour, meal, barley or roasted corn, but never liquids. It is the commonest unit of measure for solids.

For liquids the equivalent is the *bath*. The measure must be just (Ez 45: 10). It is used for water (1 K 7: 26, 38; 2 Ch 4: 5), wine (2 Ch 2: 9; Is 5: 10) and oil (2 Ch 2: 9; Ez 45: 14; 1 K 5: 25, corrected).

The *shalish*, found only in Is 40: 12 and Ps 80: 6, is an instrument for measuring one-third of an indeterminate unit.

The *se'ah* is a measure for flour and cereals in ancient historical texts (Gn 18: 6; 1 S 25: 18; 1 K 18: 32; 2 K 7: 1, 16, 18).

The *hîn* is a measure for liquids. Apart from Ez 4: 11, where one-sixth of a *hîn* represents the minimum a man needs to drink in a day, the *hîn* is only mentioned in rituals, for offerings of wine and oil: the whole *hîn* (Ex 30: 24; Ez 45: 24; 46: 5, 7, 11), the half-*hîn* (Nb 15: 9, 10; 28: 14), one-third of a *hîn* (Nb 15: 6, 7; Ez 46: 14), one-quarter *hîn* (Ex 29: 40; Lv 23: 13; Nb 15: 4, 5; 28: 5, 7, 14).

The *'omer*, a word meaning 'sheaf', is used only in the story of the manna (Ex 16 *passim*): every man gathers an *'omer* a day. The gloss of Ex 16: 36 reckons it as one-tenth of an *'ephah*.

The *'iśśarôn* (one-tenth) is a measure of meal in the liturgical texts (Ex 29: 40; Lv 14: 10, 21, etc.).

The *qab* appears only in 2 K 6: 25: during the siege of Samaria a quarter of a *qab* of wild onions is sold for five shekels of silver.

The *log* is a small unit for liquids, mentioned only in the ritual for the purification of lepers (Lv 14 *passim*).

If we try to arrange these terms in order of size, the gloss of Ex 16: 36 indicates that the *'omer* is one-tenth of an *'ephah*, and probably the 'tenth' (*iśśarôn*) is also one-tenth of an *'ephah*. According to Ez 45: 11, the *'ephah* and the *bath* are of the same capacity and are equal to one-tenth of a *homer*. This gives the following series:

homer	I	
'ephah = *bath*	10	I
'omer = *'iśśaron*	100	10	I

This is all that can be deduced from the Hebrew text alone. But Mesopotamian metrology enables us to establish another series: in the Neo-Babylonian period the proportions between the three units of measure are: 1 *gur* = 30 *sûtu* = 180 *qa*. The resemblance of the names justifies our drawing up the following table for the exilic and post-exilic period:

gur = *kor*	I	
sûtu = *s^eah*	30	I
qa = *qab*	180	6	I

These proportions are confirmed by the documents of the Jewish period and the Talmud.

These two series, one of which is founded on the decimal system and the other on the sexagesimal, are apparently independent. Their interrelation is only a hypothesis, founded on the Greek version of Ex 16: 36 and Is 5: 10, which renders an *'ephah* by τρία μέτρα; now μέτρον is the ordinary translation of *s^eah*, which would then be one-third of an *'ephah*. On the other hand, though the text of Ez 45: 14 is obscure, we can deduce that the *homer* and the *kor* are equivalent, and so we can draw up the following table:

ḥomer = *kor*	I				
'ephah = *bath*	10	I			
s''ah	30	3	I		
'omer = *'iśśarôn*	100	10	–	I	
qab	180	18	6	–	I

The position of the *hîn* and the *log* can only be deduced from sources which are even later: the comparison made by Josephus with the Graeco-Roman metrology, the interpretations of St Jerome and Talmudic data. From them we conclude that 1 *qab*= 4 *log* and 1 *bath*= 6 *hîn*. Leaving aside the *lethek* and the *shalîsh*, which are too seldom mentioned to concern us, the complete table would be as follows:

ḥomer = *kor*	I					
'ephah = *bath*	10	I				
s''ah	30	3	I			
hîn	60	6	2	I		
'omer = *'śśarôn*	100	10	–	–	I	
qab	180	18	6	3	–	I
log	720	72	24	12	–	4	I

This table, we must insist, is hypothetical, and in any case is valid only for a very late date. It depends on identifications which are sometimes uncertain and always late, the oldest being those of Ezechiel. And even of these last, no one can say whether they record measurements which had fallen into disuse, or foretell a reform which was perhaps never put into effect in biblical times.

It must be admitted that we have no means of drawing up a table, however limited in its accuracy, for proportions in use before the Exile. The only useful term of comparison would be the Assyrian system, which preceded the Neo-Babylonian used above. The Assyrian nomenclature was as follows: 1 *imêru* = 10 *sûtu*= 100 *qa*. As it is generally agreed that the *qa* did not change its value in Mesopotamia, the *imêru* is almost half the Babylonian *sûtu*. The Hebrew *ḥomer* has the same name as the *imêru*, which also means 'an ass-load'. This makes it doubtful, in spite of Ez 45: 14, whether the *ḥomer* was the equivalent of the *kor*, which corresponded to the *gur*. The position of the *s''ah*= *sûtu* is equally puzzling: according to the Assyrian system, it should be $\frac{1}{10}$ of an *imêru*= *ḥomer*, and therefore equal to the *'ephah*= *bath*, as it was later defined in Ez 45: 11. All the same, it would be surprising if the *s''ah* of the monarchical period had the same value as the *'ephah*= *bath*, also mentioned in ancient texts, though we do not know their relative values.

These gaps in our knowledge make it impossible to give, for the Old Testament period, a table of equivalents with our modern systems. The most one could attempt would be to determine the value of a particular unit at a particular period. We can compare the Hebrew measures *ḥomer*, *kor* and *s''ah* with the Mesopotamian measures of the same names, which are better known. In the Neo-Babylonian period, according to recent calculations, the *kor* was equal to 53 gallons and $\frac{1}{10}$ pint (241·20 litres), and the *s'ah* to 14·15 pints (8·04 litres): the basic unit, the *qa* was 2·35 pints or 1·34 litres. In the Assyrian system the *imêru=homer* would be 29 gallons 3 pints (134 litres), the *sûtu* (=*s'ah? 'ephah?*) 2 gallons 7½ pints (13·4 litres). Unfortunately, the estimate of the *qa* is uncertain and other authors value it as 1·42 pints (0·81 litres); an inscribed vase recently found at Persepolis would point to a *qa* of 1·62 pints (0·92 litres), or a little more. Egypt had a measure called *'pt= 'ephah* for solid and *hnw= hîn* for liquids; but their values are even more doubtful. Different authors reckon the *hnw* between 4⅔ and 8⅘ pints (2·5 and 5 litres), and the number of *hnw* in the *'pt* is not certain—perhaps 40; even taking the lowest estimate for the *hnw*, this would demand a higher capacity for the *'ephah* than anything yet proposed.

One might think that a start could be made from the apparently precise data of the Bible: the sea of bronze in Solomon's Temple had a diameter of 10 cubits, a depth of 5 cubits and it contained 2,000 *bath* (1 K 7: 23, 26). But we do not know exactly either the value of the cubit or the form of the receptacle, and the parallel passage in 2 Ch 4: 5 gives a capacity of 3,000 *bath*, with the same measurements in cubits. The facts about the bronze basins (1 K 7: 38) are even less adequate.

Archaeology alone might provide us with more reliable information. At Tell ed-Duweir (Lakish) the upper part of a jar has been found on which has been engraved *bt mlk* (royal *bath*): the same inscription can perhaps be restored on a handle from Tell en-Nasbeh, and a fragment inscribed *bt* comes from Tell Beit-Mirsim (Debir?). Having been engraved before baking, these inscriptions are evidently meant to indicate a recognized official capacity. Unfortunately the largest fragment, that from Tell ed-Duweir, does not allow of our calculating the capacity of these jars with any accuracy. Other vases had only the stamp *lmlk*. It has been possible to reconstruct entirely only one example, also from Tell ed-Duweir, whose capacity is nearly 10 gallons (45·33 litres). But at Tell en-Nasbeh there is an almost complete jar, stamped *lmlk*, which contains only 40·7 litres. If this stamp certified that these jars conformed to an official measure, and if, as used to be thought, the jars stamped *bt* or *bt lmlk* had the same capacity, we could then arrive at the approximate size of the *bath*. But the fragments marked *bt* certainly belong to receptacles smaller than the jars marked *lmlk*. It has therefore been suggested that the latter were of double capacity and represented two *bath*; the size of the *bath* would then be about 4 gallons 7 pints (22 or 23 litres). Such a string of hypotheses hardly leads to a certain conclusion.

The inscriptions *bt lmlk* are of the eighth century B.C. and some of the stamps *lmlk* are rather later. A final piece of evidence comes from the Roman period. In a cave at Qumran an unbroken jar was discovered on which is written in charcoal: '2 *s'ah* 7 *log*'. Its capacity is about 61 pints or 35 litres, which would make the *log* just about one pint (0·64 litres) and the *s*"*ah* about 27 pints (15·30 litres). This could agree with the 10-gallon (45-litre) estimate of the *lmlk* jars, which contained 1 *bath* = 3 *s*"*ah*. Unfortunately, this inscription, being traced in charcoal and not inscribed before baking, may not be an indication of capacity at all, but simply the amount of provisions put in the jar, without filling it. This makes it useless for fixing a metrology. Moreover, it would only hold good for the Roman period. Here we need only say that the tables which have been drawn up for this period, after comparison with Graeco-Roman metrology and after consulting the Talmud, vary as much as 100%, and are then, quite wrongly, applied to the Israelite period. If such tables must be given, the probabilities, at least, should be respected: a *homer*, being originally an ass-load, may have been as much as 5 bushels, 6 gallons (209 litres), the lowest figure proposed, but certainly not the 12 bushels, 3 gallons (450 litres) suggested by an alternative reckoning.

4. *Measures of weight*

While foodstuffs were measured by volume, precious materials and metals were weighed. Small things were weighed on a beam-balance with two scales. The weights, usually of hard stone, were called *'eben*, which means both 'stone' and 'weight'; they were kept in a purse (Dt 25: 13; Mi 6: 11; Pr 16: 11).

'To weigh' is *shaqal* and the *sheqel* or shekel was consequently the basic unit of weight. This unit is common to all ancient Semitic metrologies. The original text of 2 S 14: 26 speaks of 200 shekels 'at the king's weight', and a series of post-exilic texts mentions the 'shekel of the sanctuary' (Ex 30: 13, 24; 38: 24-26; Lv 5: 15; 27: 3, 25; Nb 3: 47, 50; 7 *passim*; 18: 16). In all these references it is the weight which conforms to the official standard, or else a unit of the same name but heavier; some of the Ugaritic texts reckon in 'heavy' shekels and in Mesopotamia there was a series of 'royal' weights, double the ordinary weights. In a story from the patriarchal period, before the institution of the State, there is a reference to shekels which were 'current among the merchants' (Gn 23: 16). But it sometimes happened that traders had large and small 'stones' (Dt 25: 13), two kinds of weights (Pr 20: 23), according to whether they were buying or selling.

The multiples of the shekel are the mina and the talent. The mina (*maneh*) appears only rarely and is apparently late (1 K 10: 17, perhaps radactional; Ez 45: 12; Esd 2: 69; Ne 7: 70, 71; cf. Dn 5: 25). The mina is often mentioned in Mesopotamian texts, but we may note that at Ugarit it is attested only in Akkadian texts of foreign origin, or by Ugaritic translations of them; in practice, however, weights of 50 shekels were used, the equivalent of one mina. The talent (*kikkar*) takes its name from the fact that it is a weight of circular shape (root: *krr*). It is a unit for gross reckoning, often used in the historical books but seldom in the Pentateuch (Ex 25: 39; 37: 24; 38: 24-29).

Several fractions of the shekel are mentioned: a half-shekel (Ex 30: 13), one-third of a shekel (Ne 10: 33), a quarter-shekel (1 S 9: 8). But there are also special names for the small units of weight. The *beqa'*, literally a 'fraction', is mentioned only in Gn 24: 22 and Ex 38: 26, and is a half-shekel. The *gerah* (probably 'grain') is the smallest unit of weight (Ex 30: 13; Lv 27: 25; Nb 3: 47; 18: 16; Ez 45: 12). The *payim*, familiar to archaeologists, is mentioned in 1 S 13: 21, a text which was for a long time incomprehensible; it represents two-thirds of a shekel (cf. Za 13: 8). Another term occurring only once in the Bible, but known in Akkadian, is quoted in Dn 5: 25, 28 (Aramaic), along with the mina and the shekel: it is the *p'res*, with the plural or dual *parsin* ('part'), representing half a mina or, more probably, half a shekel.

Finally we must mention the *q'sitah*, an otherwise unknown unit of weight, used by Jacob when paying for the field of Shechem (Gn 33: 19; cf. Jos 24: 32, and repeated in Jb 42: 11 by a deliberate archaism).

The basic elements of these units are found among Israel's neighbours. In Mesopotamia they are arranged on a sexagesimal basis: the shekel contains 180 'grains' and is also divided into multiple fractions, from two-thirds to a twenty-fourth of a shekel. The mina is 60 shekels and the talent is 60 minas = 3,600 shekels. At Ugarit the talent is only 3,000 shekels; the value of the mina is not given by the texts where it is mentioned, but it appears from the series of weights that it was only 50 shekels, and so there were 60 minas in the talent.

For Israel, the following values are given by the texts: according to Ex 38: 25-26, the talent is worth 3,000 shekels and the *beqa'* is a half-shekel. From Lv 27: 25; Nb 3: 47; 18: 16; Ez 45: 12, the shekel contains 20 *gerah*, and the first three texts make clear that this is the shekel of the sanctuary. Evaluation of the mina is more difficult: the Hebrew of Ez 45: 12 reads: 'the mina shall be for you 20 shekels and 25 shekels and 15 shekels', which gives a total of 60 shekels, like the Babylonian mina. The manner of counting is odd, but is perhaps explained by the existence of weights of 15, 20 and 25 shekels, the last representing half a mina of 50 shekels, as at Ugarit. Ezechiel seems to try to revalue the mina, as Ez 40: 5 would revalue the cubit and Ez 45: 11 would perhaps revalue the *'ephah* and the *bath*. Reckoning the shekel as 20 *gerah* Ez 45: 12, followed by the later texts, would then be part of the scheme of reform. The best plan is therefore to draw up two tables. One depends on Ex 38: 25-26, and runs as follows:

talent	. . . .	1			
mina	. . . .	60	1		
shekel	. . . .	3,000	50	1	
beqa'	. . . .	6,000	100	2	1

These values seem to be confirmed by the penalties of 100 shekels (Dt 22: 19) and 50 shekels (Dt 22: 29) and the tax of 50 shekels imposed on the wealthy by Menahem (2 K 15: 20). We must remember that the name of the mina is very rare and that here we have its equivalent in shekels. The system is of a respectable antiquity, and, as we have seen, obtained at Ugarit.

From the data given by Ezechiel, we can produce another table:

talent	1			
mina	60	1		
shekel	3,600	60	1	
gerah	72,000	1,200	20	1

This value for the mina seems to be found in an ancient text: according to Ex 21: 32, a fine of 30 shekels is imposed in a case where the Code of Hammurabi imposes half a mina.

To transpose these weights into our modern systems is very difficult. In the system most commonly used in Mesopotamia, the shekel weighed 0·30 ounces (8·4 grams), but there was a series derived from the 'royal' talent in which all the units weighed double. At Ugarit a collection of weights postulates a light shekel of 0·34 ounces (9·5 grams), and the texts speak of a 'heavy' shekel, perhaps its double, which would give a weight of 0·67 ounces (18·7 grams).

For Israel, excavations in Palestine have yielded numerous weights, some of which bear a numerical mark or the name of a unit of weight, or both together. Though their archaeological context is rarely beyond dispute, these inscribed weights can generally be dated, by epigraphic criteria, towards the end of the monarchy. But there are notable differences of weight between specimens belonging to the same type and apparently to the same period, and found in the same site (*e.g.* at Tell ed-Duweir, which has produced a large collection). Only the small units are represented by inscribed weights, and none bears the name 'shekel'; it is replaced by a symbol, followed by a number. Since it was the commonest unit, the word 'shekel' must also be supplied in many reckonings in the Bible.

The longest series of inscribed weights bears the symbol and the numbers 1, 2, 4 or 8. At least twenty-five examples are known, a dozen of them for eight units. The mark is that of the shekel, and they weigh about 0·41 ounces (11·5 grams). A small bronze weight, found at Gezer, is marked *lmlk* with a figure 2; this would be a 'royal' weight. It actually weighs 0·79 ounces (22·28 grams), which would give a shekel of 0·39 ounces (11·14 grams), but the metal may have lost some of its weight through oxidization.

Half a dozen weights connected with this series are inscribed *pym*; the word can be recognized, as we said, in 1 S 13: 21, and stands for two-thirds of a shekel. Judging by what they weigh, a shekel is about 0·42 ounces (12 grams).

The weights inscribed *bq'* evidently represent half-shekels (cf. Ex 38: 26). The six known specimens weigh roughly 0·21 ounces (6 grams) and suggest a shekel of at least 0·42 ounces or 12 grams.

Besides these, we possess a dozen weights inscribed *nṣp*. This seems to mean the 'half' of a unit, but the unit is not the Israelite shekel, for judging by what they weigh the *nṣp* averages 0·35 ounces (10 grams). It belongs, therefore, to another system, also represented by a small weight, marked ¼ *nṣp*, weighing 0·09 ounces (2·54 grams), and perhaps by certain uninscribed weights, some of which weight 0·18 ounces (5 grams) and others 0·72 ounces (20 grams). Clearly, they represent ½ and 2 *nṣp* respectively. The name is never found in the Old Testament as that of a weight, but it is found in the Ugaritic texts together with the shekel, and is perhaps represented by a weight of 0·34 ounces (9·5 grams) in the weight system: in the Ugaritic system, the *nṣp* would be a 'light' shekel, 'half' of the 'heavy' shekel. Perhaps the *nṣp* weights found in Palestine were lost there by 'Canaanite' traders.[1]

Uncertainty about the exact value of the shekel and the theoretical nature of Ezechiel's classification prevent us suggesting more than approximate values for the mina and the talent. The ancient mina must have weighed between 1·213 and 1·323 pounds (550 and 600 grams), the talent between 75 and 80 pounds (34 and 36 kilograms). In Ezechiel's system the mina would have weighed about 1·54 pounds (700 grams). It is useless to be too precise in what has always been a fluctuating metrology.

5. *The coinage*

Study of weights leads us naturally to that of the coinage. The earliest form of trade was bartering merchandise, and payment was made, at first, in goods which could be measured or counted—so many measures of barley or oil, so many head of cattle, etc. For the sake of convenience, metal was soon adopted as the means of payment; sometimes it was wrought, sometimes in ingots, the quality and weight of which determined the value in exchange. Metal was used in large quantities for the payment of tribute (2 K 15: 19; 18: 14, etc.), in small amounts for individual transactions with foreign countries (Gn 42: 25, 35; 43: 12f.; 1 S 13: 21; 1 K 10: 29), and always, it seems, for the purchase of land (Gn 23: 14f.; 2 S 24: 24; 1 K 16: 24; 21: 2; Jr 32: 9). Solomon paid Hiram in kind (1 K 5: 25) and Mesha used to pay a tribute of sheep and wool (2 K 3: 4). The two methods of payment might be combined: Osee acquired his wife for 15 shekels of silver, a *homer* of barley and a *lethek* of barley (Os 3: 2).

The metals of exchange were copper, gold and, chiefly, silver. The word *keseph*, silver, thus came to mean both the metal itself and the medium of payment, like *kaspu* in Akkadian, *argent* in French and 'silver' in Scottish

1. Cf. pp. 77-78.

usage. At a very early date in the Eastern Mediterranean, at Mycenae, in Cyprus, in Egypt, in Mesopotamia and in Syria, the metal was melted into ingots of different shapes, or into discs, bars, brooches and rings, sometimes bearing signs certifying their weight and purity, but this was not yet coinage. Payments were always made by weight. The weight of the silver or gold is often mentioned on Egyptian monuments and is described in one of the Ras Shamra poems. This remained the only method of payment among the Israelites until the Exile; the q'sîṭah of Gn 33: 19 is not 'coinage of the patriarchal period', but a weight of unknown value. The verb shaqal means both 'to weigh' and 'to pay', and the shekel became the basic unit in the Jewish monetary system after first being the basic unit of the Israelite weight-system. To pay for the cave of Macpelah Abraham 'weighs' 400 shekels to Ephron (Gn 23: 16); Jeremias 'weighs' 17 shekels to his cousin for the field at Anathoth (Jr 32: 9, etc.). Merchants are called 'weighers of silver' in So 1: 11. The State acted in exactly the same way. To finance the repairing of the Temple, King Joas placed at the entrance to the sanctuary a chest, prototype of our church alms-boxes, in which the faithful deposited silver of every shape. When they saw the chest contained a large amount of silver, the royal secretary came and the silver found in the Temple of Yahweh was melted down and calculated. Then they sent the silver, after checking it, to the master-builders, who paid it out (2 K 12: 10-13). This should be compared with what Herodotus relates about Darius: 'The gold and silver of the tribute are kept by the king in this fashion: he has them melted down and poured into earthenware jars. When the vessel is full, the clay covering is taken off and, when the king needs money, he has so much metal broken into pieces as is required for each occasion' (Hist. III, 96).

But between Joas and Darius came the invention of coinage. A coin is a piece of metal stamped with a mark which guarantees its denomination and weight. In theory, then, it can be accepted at sight, without weighing or checking. It was invented in Asia Minor in the seventh century B.C., and the custom spread through the Near East, largely through the influence of the Persians. The earliest coins were made of electrum, a natural alloy of gold and silver, which was collected in the sands of river-beds, especially in the Pactolus. Croesus invented a bimetallic system of gold and silver staters. These 'croesids' were replaced under Darius by 'darics' of gold and shekels of silver. The daric had no rival as a gold coin, but the use of the Median shekel was not widespread and it did not compete with the Greek silver coins.

Naturally, then, the first references to coinage in the Bible appear in the post-exilic books. Gold darics are mentioned in Esd 8: 27 and, by an anachronism, in 1 Ch 29: 7, which refers to the time of David. The reckonings of Esd 2: 69 and Ne 7: 69-71 are made in gold drachmas. The silver drachma was the Greek coin most highly valued, especially the Athenian drachma, the 'owl' of the fifth century B.C. But the gold drachmas were struck only rarely, and were never in wide circulation. It seems certain, then, that the 'drachmas' of Esd and Ne are darics, the confusion being due to the redactor, or to a copyist's fault. We cannot tell whether the silver shekels of Ne 5: 15; 10: 33 refer to a weight or a coin; but they are certainly not Median shekels, for these were never current in Palestine.

The oldest coins discovered in Palestine are Greek Macedonian coins: an electrum coin dated *circa* 500 B.C. comes from the latest excavations at Balata (Shechem), and a silver four-drachma piece struck at Aegaea about 480 has been found in a tomb at Athlith. It is obvious that these coins from remote lands were not current in Palestine, and circulated only for their value as ingots, estimated by their weight.

But Judaea, like other provinces of the Persian Empire, eventually struck its own coinage. The first Jewish coin seems to have been a small silver piece of the fifth century B.C., originating from Hebron and similar to those, of uncertain series, from Arabia and Philistia in the same period. It bears the inscription *bq'* in old Hebrew script, and weighs 0·14 ounces (3·88 grams), which is approximately the weight of the Attic drachma. It has been ascribed to the time when Nehemias was governor of Judaea, but this is only a hypothesis, and it is not even certain that the coin is Jewish: the type is not characteristic, and the Phoenician alphabet was then in use far beyond the boundaries of Judaea. More authentic are two silver pieces with the legend *yhd*, that is, *Y'hud*, the official name of the Persian province of Judah in the Aramaic Esd 5: 1, 8; 7: 14 (cf. Dn 2: 25; 5: 13; 6: 14). A silver coin found at Bethsur also carries the stamp *Y'hûd* and the proper name 'Ezechias'. This is probably the priest Ezechias who, according to Josephus, became in old age the friend of Ptolemy I around 315 B.C.; but it is scarcely probable that the Ptolemies would have authorized silver coinage to be struck locally. The coin must date from the time when Ezechias administered the province of Judaea, immediately after the conquest of Alexander or at the very end of the Persian rule. The other two coins inscribed *Y'hûd* are earlier.

Palestine, and indeed, the entire Near East, then came under the monetary systems of the Seleucids or the Ptolemies. This followed the Phoenician standard, the silver drachma of 0·13 ounces (3·6 grams) and the tetradrachma, or shekel, of approximately 0·51 ounces (14·4 grams). It was only when Simon Maccabaeus was recognized by Antiochus VII Sidetes as priest and ethnarch of the Jews that he received the right to strike a coinage (1 M 15: 6). As in similar concessions made by the Seleucids, this only extended to a bronze coinage for local use. This event took place in 138 B.C. But Simon did not use his privilege, and it must have been revoked by the same Antiochus, who very soon turned against him (1 M 15: 27), and Simon died shortly after, in 134. In any case, no bronze coins of his age have reached us: the silver and bronze coins which were for a long time attributed to him date in fact from the First Revolt, in A.D. 66-70. Jewish coinage began only with Simon's successor, John Hyrcanus, and then only when he considered himself independent, after the conquest of Samaria, around 110 B.C. It was an inferior bronze coinage, which continued under his successors, the Hasmoneans; among silver coins, Tyrian money, which was valued for its alloy, circulated almost to the exclusion of all others. The history of this coinage and its successors under Herod and the Procurators does not concern us here. The Jews began to strike bronze and silver coins again during their two revolts against the Romans, in A.D. 66-70 and 132-135. Their coins have an inscription in Hebrew and are dated from the years of the 'deliverance of Sion' or the 'deliverance of Israel'. But this has taken us far beyond the Old Testament era.

III

MILITARY INSTITUTIONS

CHAPTER ONE

THE ARMIES OF ISRAEL

WE have a fair knowledge of the military organization of the Egyptians, the Assyro-Babylonians and the Hittites. Reliefs, paintings and drawings portray their soldiers, their battles, their camps and their strongholds; inscriptions describe their campaigns; and copies of peace treaties record the titles, functions and careers of particular individuals in the army.

Our information about the military organization of Israel is by no means so complete. Not a single relief or drawing of a military kind has survived; perhaps there never were any. Even the fortifications and weapons brought to light by excavations belong, for the most part, to the Canaanites, whom the Israelites conquered and displaced. There are, of course, numerous texts, and the historical books of the Bible are full of wars. But these narratives are not contemporary records of the events. There are, it is true, some very old traditions in the books of Josue and Judges; but it was nearly six hundred years later, just before the Exile, when the military history of this period received its final literary form in the books as we possess them to-day. The books of Samuel and Kings, on the other hand, do contain passages committed to writing very soon after the events took place, but the vivid and life-like character of these passages does not compensate for their lack of precision about military details. Quite the most detailed information on the military organization under the monarchy is to be found in Chronicles; but these two books were written in an age when there was neither independence nor an army to defend it. Lastly, the Exodus itself and the wanderings in the deserts were described, centuries later, as the movements of a well-disciplined army. Such are the sources of our information, and yet they can be used to good purpose, provided they are carefully tested and dated by literary and historical criticism. The military institutions of a people change more rapidly than any other form of its social organization, for they are subject to many kinds of influence. The army is affected by every change in the type of government, by the varying requirements of policy, by the enemy it may have to face, and, of course, by progress in the development of armaments. The period between the Conquest under Josue and Nabuchodonosor's siege of Jerusalem is longer than that which separates the Hundred Years' War from the second World War, and though the organization of the army and field tactics evolved more slowly in ancient times, those six centuries saw extensive changes in both.

It is obvious, therefore, that the military institutions of Israel must be studied in the order in which they developed. Secondly, the general character of the sources must be taken into account: the texts are religious texts, and as a rule they are not concerned with merely military matters such as the constitution of the army or the technique of war. Moreover, even the texts treating directly of war need careful interpretation, and this is particularly true of the older texts, for war was regarded as a sacral undertaking with a ritual of its own. Indeed, this notion of a holy war persisted to the very end of Old Testament times; but the concept underwent many transformations until it emerged as a kind of holy ideal. The religious character of these military institutions will be treated at the end of this part of the book; we must first concern ourselves with their non-sacred aspects.

1. *A people under arms*

Among nomads[1] there is no distinction between the army and the people: every able-bodied man can join in a raid and must be prepared to defend the tribe's property and rights against an enemy, under his sheikh or another commander. As a rule, each tribe acts on its own, but from time to time several tribes will unite for a common enterprise. There are customs of war and rules for fighting, but there is no stable military organization. This was probably true of Israel also, as long as it was leading a semi-nomadic life, but it is not easy to perceive the true situation which underlies the stories of Exodus and Numbers. Ex 12: 37; 13: 18 and 14: 19-20 picture a people in arms marching out of Egypt; Nb 1: 3, 20, 22, etc.; 2: 1-31 and 10: 11-28 show them marching through the desert in formation; but these pictures are idealizations composed in a later age when the entire people was called to arms in times of national danger. In Josue, too, the Conquest is presented as the achievement of a unified Israelite army, though certain passages, with the parallels in Jg 1, give a more realistic picture of what actually happened. These latter texts show tribes or groups of tribes, such as Judah and Simeon and the house of Joseph, conquering their part of the Holy Land independently of each other; and the very ancient notes preserved in Nb 32: 1, 16, 39-42, which record the settlement of Reuben, Gad and Manasseh (Eastern half), are of a similar character. There was never any question of an organized army.

We are somewhat better informed on the period of the Judges. Each tribe is securing its hold on its own territory and defending this land against the counter-attacks of the Canaanites who formerly held it; neighbouring peoples wage war against them, and nomads make raids. Sometimes the tribes, who

1. Cf. p. 9.

were bound together by the pact of Shechem (Jos 24) join together for military enterprises. Gideon, for example, summons to arms not only his own tribe, Manasseh, but Aser, Zebulon and Nephthali as well (Jg 6: 35); in the end he calls upon Ephraim too (Jg 7: 24) where men were complaining because they had not been called to arms at the beginning (Jg 8: 1). The prose narrative in Jg 4: 6f. tells how Baraq mobilized Zabulon and Nephthali against the Canaanites, but the Song of Deborah (Jg 5: 14f.) includes in its list contingents from Ephraim, Benjamin, Makir and Issachar as well, and takes to task Reuben, Gilead, Dan and Aser for remaining neutral. Similarly, to avenge the outrage committed at Gibeah, all Israel, except the men of Yabesh in Gilead (Jg 21: 8f.) takes up arms (Jg 20).

In the same way Saul called 'all Israel' to arms against the Ammonites (1 S 11: 1-11), and the subsequent victory ensured him the throne. By this, political unity was at last achieved, and the people had a king 'who would lead it forth and fight its battles' (1 S 8: 20). Saul called upon the entire people for the holy war against the Amalekites (1 S 15: 4) and assembled 'all Israel' against the Philistines (1 S 17: 2, 11); this is the reason why David's three brothers went to the war (1 S 17: 13), leaving in Bethlehem only their aged father and David, who was too young to bear arms. According to 1 S 23: 8, the king even called out 'the entire people' to pursue David when he took refuge in Qeilah. For the battle of Gilboa, where he would meet defeat and death at the hands of the Philistines, Saul had gathered 'all Israel' (1 S 28: 4). Certainly things had changed considerably since the period of the Judges, but it was a smooth evolution. The 'Judges' were 'saviours' marked out by God to set his people free, and Saul himself was a leader of the charismatic type, moved by the spirit of Yahweh (1 S 10: 10 and especially 11: 6), smashing the Ammonites in a way which recalls the military successes which marked out the greater Judges.

There were various ways for the leader, Judge or King, to call the people to arms. Sometimes a trumpet was sounded (Jg 3: 27, Ehud; 6: 34, Gideon; 1 S 13: 3, Saul), or messengers were sent around the tribes (Jg 6: 35; 7: 24). Sometimes the message was underlined by a symbolic action, as when Saul cut to pieces a yoke of oxen and sent their quarters to every part of the territory of Israel with the threat: 'Whoever does not follow Saul to battle will have his own oxen treated in the same way' (1 S 11: 7). When the men of Gibeah so maltreated a Levite's concubine that she died, the Levite cut her body into twelve pieces and sent one to each tribe in order to rouse the entire people against the men of that town (Jg 19: 29-30). During the period of the Judges, the response to these appeals depended on each group, which made its own decision. The Song of Deborah twice insists on this freedom to fight or not to fight (Jg 5: 2 and 9), and expresses nothing stronger than reproach or regret about the tribes which chose to stand aside (Jg 5: 15-17). Meroz alone, a town in Nephthali which did not follow its tribe, is cursed (Jg 5: 23), for Nephthali was the first of all the tribes to take up arms. Threats might be uttered against those who refused to do their duty (Jg 21: 5; 1 S 11: 7), but we do not know what sanctions were in fact applied. According to the tradition recorded in Jg 21: 6-12, the expedition against the men of Yabesh was not a punitive expedition because of their abstention; its sole purpose was to find wives for the rest of the tribe of Benjamin without breaking the oath which the other combatants had taken.

In spite of this mass call-up, the number of fighting men was small. Exaggerated numbers have crept into the older narratives; they tell us that 400,000 men marched against Benjamin (Jg 20: 17), that 300,000 Israelites and 30,000 men of Judah answered the call of Saul (1 S 11: 8), that 200,000 infantrymen followed him when he marched on the Amalekites (1 S 15: 4). Other texts are more sober: Jg 4: 10 reckons the joint forces at Zabulon and Nephthali at not more than 10,000, and Jg 5: 8 gives 40,000 as the greatest number which could be mustered from all the tribes; this latter figure, 40,000, is also the size of the entire army of Israel facing Jericho (Jos 4: 13). But these figures, too, are symbolic.

The men assembled in battle dress ḥalûṣîm (literally, 'unclothed', 'stripped', i.e. in short cloaks). They provided their own arms, of a very simple kind. The usual weapons were swords and slings (the tribe of Benjamin had some expert slingers, Jg 20: 16). In Deborah's day there was 'not a shield or spear among the forty thousand men of Israel' (Jg 5: 8). The Philistines disarmed the Israelites at the beginning of Saul's reign, and at the battle of Mikmas only Saul and Jonathan had a sword and a lance (1 S 13: 19-22). Saul's spear became the symbol of his royal rank (1 S 22: 6; 26: 7, 16, 22; 2 S 1: 6; cf. 1 S 18: 11; 19: 9), but his shield is mentioned only in David's elegy (2 S 1: 21). Jonathan, on the other hand is shown as an archer (1 S 18: 4; 20: 20f.; 2 S 1: 22). The bronze helmet and the breast-plate which Saul wanted David to wear produce a splendid literary effect, but they are probably an anachronism (1 S 17: 38f.).

The units of the army were based on those of society. The unit was the clan (mishpaḥah), which in theory provided a contingent of 1,000 men, though in fact the number was far smaller; compare 1 S 1: 10 ('eleph) with verse 21 (mishpaḥah), and the use of 'a thousand men' for 'a clan' in Jg 6: 15; 1 S 23: 23. When the people take up arms, they are referred to as the 'thousands of Israel' (Nb 31: 5; Jos 22: 21, 30; Jg 5: 8). These units were commanded by a 'leader of a thousand', śar 'eleph (1 S 17: 18; 18: 13). They could be divided into small units of 100 men (1 S 22: 7; cf. Jg 7: 16) and 50 (1 S 8: 12). The term ḥamushîm, which (apart from Ex 13: 18 and Nb 32: 17, corrected by the ancient versions) occurs only in Jos 1: 14; 4: 12 and Jg 7: 11, is sometimes explained by the fact that the army was divided into groups of fifty. More probably, however, the word refers to soldiers drawn up in 'five' corps on the march and in camp. Arabic dictionaries give, as one meaning of the

Arabic *hamîsh* ('five'), the formation of an army with a vanguard, main body, two flanks and a rearguard. This brings to mind the arrangement of the camp in the desert, where, according to Nb 2: 2-31, four divisions (*d'galîm*) surrounded the Tabernacle, which was guarded by the Levites—five units in all; it recalls the *hamushîm* in the Midianite camp (Jg 7: 11) and the marching order described in Nb 10: 11-28: first the divisions of Judah and Reuben, then the Tabernacle with its Levites, lastly the divisions of Ephraim and Dan. (Compare also the *hamushîm* of Ex 13: 18; Jos 1: 14; 4: 12.)

These ill-armed and poorly trained troops were terrified at the fortified cities of Canaan (Nb 13: 28; Dt 1: 28), at iron-clad chariots (Jos 17: 16-18; Jg 1: 19; 4: 13; 1 S 13: 5; 2 S 1: 6) and at the heavily armed Philistine warriors (1 S 17: 4-7). Yet, in the very first stages of the conquest, the Israelites took advantage of the fact that the Canaanite forces were scattered, and that the withdrawal of Egypt had left a void. They infiltrated where victory was theirs, but stopped short at the edge of the plains, where fortified cities and chariots barred their way (Jos 17: 12, 16; Jg 1: 19, 27-35). Whenever the capture of a town is related in any detail, it is always prepared by espionage, and victory itself is secured either by treachery or by guile (cf. Jericho in Jos 6, Ai—which was already in ruins—in Jos 8; Bethel in Jg 1: 23-25). The Canaanite enclaves which survived were only gradually absorbed.

Pitched battles were fatal for the Israelites (1 S 4: 1-11; 31: 1-7). To compensate for their inferior armament and for their lack of military formation they would attack with a small group of picked men (cf., even during their days in the desert, Ex 17: 9; Nb 31: 3-4). The men of Dan who set off to conquer land were a mere 600 (Jg 18: 11); Saul picked 3,000 men out of all Israel to wage war on the Philistines (1 S 13: 2) and he gained his first victory with a force of only 600 (1 S 13: 15; 14: 2). By the skilful use of daring attacks, bold tricks and ambushes, these small groups of troops, under the firm control of good leaders, succeeded in worsting enemy forces which were superior in numbers or in weapons. Jonathan and his armour-bearer went forward unaccompanied to attack the Philistine post at Mikmas and threw the place into panic; then 600 of Saul's men fell upon the enemy, the 'Hebrew' auxiliaries deserted from the Philistine side, the Israelites from the hill country of Ephraim joined in the chase, and the Philistine defeat was turned into a rout (1 S 14: 1-23). Gideon's action against the Midianites is even more typical; of the 32,000 men who answered his call, he sent home all who had no heart to fight, and only 10,000 remained; of these, he chose 300, and divided them into three columns. Reconnaissance showed him that the morale of the enemy was low, and he made careful preparations for a night operation. His troops covered their torches with jars until the signal for attack, when the trumpet-sounds and the war-cries were calculated to throw the enemy camp into confusion by creating the impression of a vast force. The trick succeeded; the Midianites lost their heads and took to flight (Jg 6:

33-7: 22). There follows the exploitation of victory; other Israelite contingents took part in the pursuit (as in 1 S 14: 22), the Ephraimites cut off the enemy's retreat (Jg 7: 23-25), and Gideon's tiny force harassed the survivors right to the edge of the desert (Jg 8: 4-12). Though the story combines a series of distinct episodes, it gives a fair idea of warfare in the period of the Judges.

From time to time, two enemy forces would agree to settle the issue by single combat. There is evidence of this custom as early as the 18th century B.C.; an Egyptian story about a certain Sinuhet says it was practised among the Canaanite semi-nomads. The Philistine's challenge to the Israelites in 1 S 17: 8-10 is quite clearly a proposal that the fate of the two peoples should be settled by a single combat. The individual feats of arms attributed to David's heroes (2 S 21: 15-21) can be explained in the same way. The champions, it seems, were called *'îsh habbenaym*, 'the man-between-two' or 'the man for combat between two' (1 S 17: 4, 23). The term is never found again except in the Qumran work entitled 'The Order of the War' and there its meaning is not the same; in the Qumran scroll it means light infantry.

During the war between Saul's partisans and those of David, Abner proposed to Joab that they should decide the issue by a fight between twelve picked men from each side, but no decision was reached, because all twenty-four were killed and a general fight ensued (2 S 2: 14f.). These customs used to obtain among Arab tribes, and persisted until modern times. At the most critical moment in the conquest of Algeria, when the Duke of Aumale had been sent by his father Louis-Philippe to take over command of the army, the Emir Abd-el-Kader suggested to the Duke that they should end the war either by a single combat between the two of them before both armies, or by engaging an equal number of soldiers picked from either side.

This study of military institutions before the time of David has not taken into account their religious aspect, which will be discussed later.[1] But it must not be forgotten, even now, that the warriors of Israel were upheld by their firm belief that Yahweh fought with them and that he could grant them victory whatever the odds against them (1 S 14: 6; 17: 47).

2. *The professional army*

The enemies of Israel, the Canaanites and the Philistines, had standing armies, including both infantry and charioteers; the soldiers were professional soldiers, some native-born, some foreigners. Such a military organization was incompatible with the spirit and the traditions of the federation of the Twelve Tribes. There were exceptions, of course, but these can be explained. Abimelek recruited mercenaries (Jg 9: 4), but he was only half-Israelite by birth and was scheming to set up a kingdom on the model of the Canaanites.

1. Cf. pp. 258-267.

Jephthah, too, collected a band of armed supporters, but this was outside the territory of Israel (Jg 11: 3). Nevertheless, the setbacks encountered in the war against the Philistines proved to the Israelites that wholesale conscription of the nation would not provide a force capable of effective opposition to a professional army; the latter might be the smaller force, but it would be well trained and ready for action at a moment's notice. The creation of a similar army was the work of the first kings of Israel.

(a) *The corps of mercenaries*. Saul began the recruiting of mercenaries: whenever he saw a brave and fearless man, he took him into his service (1 S 14: 52). He preferred, presumably, men from his own tribe, Benjamin (cf. 1 S 22: 7), but he took men from other Israelite tribes also, like David, from Judah (1 S 16: 18f.; 18: 2), and even foreigners, like the Edomite Doeg (1 S 21: 8; 22: 18). They were never very numerous, for they had to be paid (cf. Jg 9: 4), and Saul's kingdom was poor. After breaking with Saul, David recruited mercenaries for himself: he had 400 men at first (1 S 22: 2), and later 600 (1 S 25: 13), with whom he went over into the service of the Philistines (1 S 27: 2). These partisans stayed with him when he became king of Judah and of Israel, and their numbers increased as the victories of David widened his field for recruiting and provided the necessary income to pay them. They came from everywhere: among the Thirty heroes of David (2 S 23: 24-39), whom we shall discuss later,[1] the majority came from Judah and the neighbouring regions, but there was also an Ephraimite, a man from Manasseh, a man from Gad and several foreigners, including an Aramaean from Sobah, an Ammonite, and Uriah the Hittite, the husband of Bathsheba (cf. 2 S 11: 3f.). After conquering the Philistines, David recruited among them and their vassals a corps of K'rethi and P'lethi (2 S 8: 18; 15: 18; 20: 7, 23; 1 K 1: 38, 44). There was also a contingent of 600 men from Gath in Philistia (2 S 15: 18f.). By this policy David was copying an institution of the Canaanite and Philistine principalities. It has recently been suggested that the special term for these mercenaries may have been preserved in the expressions y'lîdê ha'anaq (Nb 13: 22, 28; Jos 15: 14) and y'lîdê haraphah (2 S 21: 16, 18). The word yalîd would not mean 'descendant', but 'dependent, serf', and would be applied to professional soldiers because they gave up their freedom to enter a military corps, such as the corps of Anaq or of Raphah (the meaning of these words remaining open to investigation).[2] The other uses of the word yalîd, in the expression y'lîdê bayth would be a confirmation of this hypothesis: it refers to slaves who have a particular status in the family, and Gn 14: 14 shows they were used for military purposes. The hypothesis is not without interest, but for lack of a sufficient number of clearer texts it cannot be classed as certain.

These mercenaries did not enjoy the rank of free men. They were directly under the king. They were Saul's 'men' (1 S 23: 25-26) or David's 'men'

1. Cf. p. 220.　　　　2. Cf. p. 242.

(1 S 23 *passim*; 24: 3f.; 27: 3, 8, etc.), the servants ('*abadîm*) of Saul (1 S 18: 5, 30; 22: 17) or David (1 S 25: 40; 2 S 2: 17; 3: 22; 11: 9, 11, 13; 18: 7, 9; 20: 6; 1 K 1: 33). The king acknowledged their services by exempting them from taxes or forced labour (1 S 17: 25), by granting them lands, or a claim on tithes (1 S 8: 14-15). When the king died, his mercenaries passed to his heir: thus the 'servants' of Saul became the servants of Ishbaal (2 S 2: 12; 4: 2). They were stationed near the king at Jerusalem under David (2 S 11: 9, 13; 15: 14; 20: 7; 1 K 1: 33).

They formed the royal bodyguard.[1] We cannot say anything precise about its organization, for it seems to have been rather flexible. Apart from the general term "'*abadîm*", and indications of racial origin, the soldiers who composed this bodyguard are referred to by different names, but we do not know the precise relation which these names bear to each other. Saul's (and later David's) personal bodyguard is called, collectively, the *mishma'ath*, meaning, literally, 'those who obey, who answer the call' (1 S 22: 14; 2 S 23: 23). David was its leader under Saul, and Benayahu commanded it under David; but Benayahu was also the leader of *K'rethi* and the *P'lethi* (2 S 8: 18; 20: 23; cf. 1 K 1: 38, 44). The latter seem to constitute the entire bodyguard at the time: they are put alongside the army of the people in 2 S 8: 16; 20: 23, like the '*abadîm* in 2 S 11: 11. On the other hand, the 'champions' (*gibbôrîm*) are mentioned in 2 S 20: 7 alongside the *K'rethi* and the *P'lethi*. But the *gibbôrîm* seem to be the same as the *K'rethi* and the *P'lethi* (2 S 16: 6 compared with 2 S 15: 18, and 1 K 1: 8, 10 compared with 1 K 1: 38, 44), and the *gibbôrîm* alone are mentioned alongside the people's army in 2 S 10: 7.

Among these 'champions' two groups were outstanding for their bravery; the Three, whose leader was Ishbaal (2 S 23: 8-12), and the Thirty, commanded by Abishai (2 S 23: 18 and 24-39). Since the majority of them came from Southern Judah, it is probable that they were the bravest of David's companions in the early days, and that they were formed into a special company of picked men when he was living at Siqlag. (An Egyptian text mentions a 'troop of thirty' among the immediate attendants of Ramses III.)

These soldiers, or a group of them, are sometimes called *n''arîm*, literally, 'youngsters', but in the military sense of 'cadets'. When David fled for his life, they accompanied him (1 S 21: 3, 5; 25: 5f.) and no one knows precisely what distinguished them from the rest of David's 'men' (1 S 25: 13, 20). Saul too had his cadets (1 S 26: 22). The 'cadets' of David and Ishbaal, Saul's son, faced each other at Gibeon (2 S 2: 14), and they are called the '*abadîm* of David and Ishbaal in the same passage (2 S 2: 12-13). The 'cadets' of 2 S 16: 2 seem to be the same as the soldiers of the guard who accompanied David on his flight, as the mercenaries of 15: 18, and the *gibbôrîm* of 16: 6; cf. also 2 S 4: 12. Later, we meet the 'cadets' of the district commissioners, who were distinct from the national army (1 K 20: 14-19). Although they sometimes acted

1. Cf. p. 123.

as squires or armour-bearers (1 S 20: 21f., 35 f.; 2 S 18: 15), they were not, apparently, young recruits in contrast to veterans, for when the term is to be taken in a strictly military sense, it means simply professional soldiers (cf. also Ne 4: 10). The word had a military sense in Canaanite, and passed into the Egyptian language, where na'aruna means an army corps, possibly recruited from Canaan.

Lastly, Saul had raṣîm, 'runners' (1 S 22: 17); Doeg the Edomite was probably their commander (21: 8, corrected). They are called 'abadim and, in this context, figure as men who carry out the king's orders for revenge (like the n'̔arîm in 2 S 4: 12). They were a personal bodyguard, an escort platoon,[1] like the fifty runners who went before Absalom and Adonias when they were affecting a royal retinue (2 S 15: 1; 1 K 1: 5). They are mentioned, perhaps for the same reason, along with the squires (shalishîm) in the story of Jehu (2 K 10: 25). They were responsible, together with the Carite mercenaries, for guarding the palace in Jerusalem, which had a room for the 'runners' and a gate called the 'Runners' Gate' (1 K 14: 27-28; 2 K 11: 4, 6, 11, 19). They must therefore have been numerous enough to be divided into companies, or centuries.

Saul used his household troops against the Philistines (1 S 18: 27, 30; cf. 23: 27) and in the pursuit of David (1 S 23: 25f.), but the professional army did not really show its capabilities until the reign of David. He used his mercenaries for the capture of Jerusalem (2 S 5: 6) and to defeat the Philistines (2 S 5: 21; 21: 15) and daring feats of his champions became the subject of a story (2 S 21: 15-22; 23: 8-23). These professional troops formed a special command, and remained distinct from the contingents which Israel and Judah furnished in times of emergency. In the list of David's officials there are two soldiers: Joab is commander of the army, and Benayahu is commander of the Kerethites and Pelethites, that is, of the household troops (2 S 8: 16, 18; 20: 23). The detailed account of the Ammonite War throws light on the relationship between the two forces: both the household troops and all Israel are sent into action (2 S 11: 1), but during the investment of Rabbah of the Ammonites, Israel and Judah camp in huts while the guards sleep in the open country (11: 11); attacks are launched by the guards (11: 14-17; 12: 26) and the contingents of Israel and Judah are held in reserve until the final assault (12: 29). The same tactics are used in the Aramaean wars of Achab: the 'cadets' of the district commissioners, professional soldiers, are sent off first to launch the offensive, and then Israel (i.e. the national army) comes up in support and gives chase to the enemy (1 K 20: 15-20).

This last text reminds us that the professional army continued in existence long after the reign of David. We have already referred to the 'runners' of Roboam (1 K 14: 27-28) and of Jehu (2 K 10: 25), and to the 'runners' and the Carites under Athaliah (2 K 11: 4). The forts built by Roboam were

1. Cf. p. 123-124.

undoubtedly manned by professional soldiers (2 Ch 11: 11-12). Again, 2 Ch 25: 6f. states that Amasias, king of Judah, recruited mercenaries in Israel, and the Annals of Sennacherib mention the auxiliaries of Ezechias who deserted during the siege of 701 B.C. This is the last unquestionable reference to these mercenary troops.

(b) *The chariotry.* When the Israelites were still consolidating their position in the Promised Land, they had to contend with the war-chariots of the Canaanites and of the Philistines (Jos 17: 16-18; Jg 1: 19; 4: 13; 1 S 13: 5; 2 S 1: 6), for, from about 1500 B.C., chariotry had become the essential, and sometimes the principal, arm in the military forces of the Near East. It was first introduced by the Indo-Europeans who helped to build the state of Mitanni in Northern Mesopotamia; they were men skilled in breeding horses, and in the art of making light but strong two-wheeled chariots. The new weapon was quickly copied by the Hittites, and was soon adopted throughout Mesopotamia, Egypt and Syria-Palestine. Every little Canaanite state had its chariots and its charioteers, and they were known by the Indo-European name of *maryannu.* The Philistines and the other 'Peoples of the Sea' who lived along the coast of Palestine soon had their charioteers, too, and the new Aramaean states which were just coming into being in Syria could not afford to be without chariots either.

To set up and to maintain a chariot corps was an expensive undertaking, and in the early days the Israelites were poor; hence they were unable to adopt this new and important weapon for some time. After his victory over the Aramaeans at Sobah, David had the captured chariot horses hamstrung (cf. Jos 11: 6-9; 2 S 10: 18); he kept only one hundred of them (2 S 8: 4). He may have acted in the same way when he annexed Canaanite cities, and in this way he may have built up a small chariot force for his own use; but if he did, the chariot force must have been very unimportant compared with his foot-soldiers, for it is never once mentioned in the accounts of his campaigns. On the other hand, we do find that both Absalom and Adonias, when each was plotting for the throne, drove out in a chariot, with runners going before them (2 S 15: 1; 1 K 1: 5).

Solomon's great military innovation was the establishment of a strong chariot force. This force quite overshadowed the mercenary foot-soldiers, who are never once mentioned in his reign. They were not disbanded, but they were relegated to a secondary position, so that the situation was exactly the reverse of what had obtained in David's reign. Since Solomon had not made any conquests himself, he must have raised this chariot force from the money in the exchequer. The text of 1 K 10: 28-29 is far from plain, but it seems that the king bought chariots in Egypt (where they made excellent ones) and horses in Cilicia (which had a reputation for stud-farms). As a result, he had 1,400 chariots and 12,000 horses, according to 1 K 10: 26. The number of chariots is quite feasible: at the battle of Qarqar, in 835 B.C.,

Achab, king of Israel, put into the field 2,000 chariots, and the king of Damascus, 1,200. The number of horses, however, seems too high: reliefs, paintings, and non-biblical texts inform us that each chariot had three horses attached, two in harness and one in reserve. The number 12,000 may have originated in a tradition which estimated that Solomon could put 4,000 chariots into the field (2 Ch 9: 25; cf. the gloss on 1 K 5: 6).

These troops were quartered in Jerusalem, where there was a 'Horses Gate' (2 K 11: 16) and in the 'Chariot towns' (1 K 10: 26). These 'Towns for chariots and horses' or garrison towns, are listed in 1 K 9: 15-19: Hazor, Megiddo, Gezer, Lower Beth-Horon, Baalath, Tamar. Fortified by conscripts of the national labour forces (1 K 9: 15), these places formed a defence network which straddled the main roads leading to the heart of the kingdom, and all lay close to level country where the chariots could manoeuvre. Of these towns, at least the first four were formerly royal cities of the Canaanites, which had once possessed their own chariot force: Solomon was continuing a tradition. Solomon's prefects organized the supplies of corn and fodder for this force (1 K 5: 8). Excavations at Megiddo have shown what these 'chariot towns' looked like: part of the town was given over to enormous stables with a separate stall for each horse. In the middle was an open courtyard with drinking troughs; the courtyard was used to exercise and to train the horses. The stables discovered at Megiddo could hold 450 horses.

In Egyptian chariots, there were two riders, one to hold the reins and one to fight; Hittite chariots had a driver, a combatant and an armour bearer, but in the Neo-Hittite states the number was reduced to two. In Assyria, at the time of the Israelite monarchy, the team had three men; this number was raised to four at some date between Tiglath-Pileser III and Assurbanipal, but afterwards they reverted to a three-man team. The 'third' was called, in Assyrian, *shalshu(rakbu)* or *tashlishu*. Israelite chariots also carried three men, the driver (called simply *rakkab* or 'charioteer' in 1 K 22: 34), the combatant and the 'third' (*shalîsh*: 1 K 9: 22; 2 K 10: 25). The king's armour-bearer or squire enjoyed a special rank and was rather like an aide-de-camp.[1]

When the kingdom was split after the death of Solomon, the principal chariot garrisons (Hazor, Megiddo, Gezer and probably Lower Beth-Horon) fell into the hands of the Israelites. Judah had very few chariot troops left, and we do not know whether Roboam posted any in the new towns he fortified. Nevertheless, the horses of Judah fought side by side with those of Israel in the war against Moab (2 K 3: 7), and Joram had chariots which were defeated by the Edomites (2 K 8: 21). The chariot force of Judah seems to have been increased in the eighth century, when Isaias says: 'Its land is full of horses, and of chariots too numerous to count' (Is 2: 7), and curses those who place their trust in horses and a large chariot force (Is 31: 1; cf. 30: 16; Mi 1: 13; 5: 9). These armaments came from Egypt, where Judah had once more

1. Cf. p. 122.

turned in quest of an ally (Is 31: 1-3), and Isaias seems to be condemning this recourse to armaments as something new. The country did not benefit thereby, for in 701 Sennacherib captured every town in Judah except Jerusalem without fighting a single battle in which chariots were engaged. It seems that chariot troops were never again raised after this time. The only witness is the text of 2 Ch 35: 24, more detailed and unquestionably more exact than the parallel in 2 K 23: 30: when Josias was wounded at Megiddo, they took him out of his chariot and carried him to Jerusalem in his 'second chariot'. It shows that the king had two chariots at his disposal, but it does not prove that there was a chariot corps.

The greater part of Solomon's chariotry fell to the kingdom of Israel, where Canaanite traditions still persisted; consequently, mounted troops retained a greater measure of importance. Under Elah, they were divided into two corps, one of which was commanded by Zimri (1 K 16: 9). According to the Annals of Shalmaneser III, 2,000 Israelite chariots took part in the battle of Qarqar, but the reverse suffered in the Aramaean wars weakened this branch of the army very considerably. There were still some chariots at Samaria (2 K 7: 13; 10: 2), though not very many (cf. 2 K 7: 6), and at the most critical moment in these struggles, Joachaz had only ten chariots left (2 K 13: 7). The losses were never made good: Sargon of Assyria, who boasted that he captured 300 chariots at Hamath, gained only 50 by his conquest of Samaria.

About 1000 B.C. mounted cavalry made its first timid appearance in the Near East, though it had long been used among certain Northern peoples and was to remain the principal fighting arm of the Scythians. Warriors on horseback are represented on the bas-reliefs of Tell Halaf at the beginning of the ninth century B.C., and some elements of cavalry were introduced into the Assyrian army about the same time; but troops in chariots still preponderated. The Egyptian army never had any cavalry except for mounted scouts. Nor did the Israelites; Sennacherib's envoy made the ironical proposal to Ezechias that he would give him 2,000 horses if he could find horsemen to ride them (2 K 18: 23). In the stories of the monarchical period, the term *parashîm*, often translated 'horsemen' or 'cavalry', means either chariot teams or the men who rode in chariots. Sometimes men did jump on horseback to flee more quickly (1 K 20: 20; Is 30: 16; Am 2: 15). Moreover, horsemen could be used as scouts or despatch riders, as in Egypt (2 K 9: 17f.; cf. Za 1: 8-11). The description of the war-horse given in Jb 39: 19-25 is inspired by foreign customs, and the horsemen referred to in Ez 23: 6, 12 (Assyrians), 38: 4 (the army of Gog), Esd 8: 22 and Ne 2: 9 (Persians) are all foreigners. These texts, moreover, date from after the fall of the monarchy. Much later, in the early Maccabean wars, the Jews could field only infantry against the powerful Greek cavalry and elephant mounts (1 M 1: 17; 6: 30f.; 8: 6; 2 M 11: 4; 13: 2, 15). The accounts of the defeat at Bethzacharia (1 M 6: 29-47) and of

Jonathan's victory over Apollonius (1 M 10: 73-83) are particularly significant. A corps of Jewish cavalry appears for the first time under Simon in 136/135 B.C., but it was still very small (1 M 16: 4, 7). Herod had 30,000 infantrymen in his army, but only 6,000 cavalry.

3. *The conscript army*

We have seen that, in all probability, the mercenary and mounted troops of the kingdom of Judah were not re-formed after the events of 701 B.C.: they were too costly to maintain. Instead, the territory secured its freedom, and later defended itself, with an army of conscripts. These are the only soldiers mentioned in the accounts of the capture of Jerusalem by Nabuchodonosor. We hear nothing of mercenaries or chariots, but only of 'men of war' ('*anshê* (*ham*)*milḥamah*, in 2 K 25: 4, 19; Jr 38: 4, or '*osê milḥamah*, 2 K 24: 16). It is true that officers and their men are spoken of (2 K 25: 23f.; Jr 40: 7f., and also in the ostraka from Lakish), but these soldiers, or 'men of war', are men of Judah who had been called to arms and who would return to their homes and the fields after the war (Jr 40: 10).

According to 2 K 25: 19 Nabuchodonosor took prisoner a high ranking official, a *saris*,[1] 'set over the men of war'; perhaps he was a commander-in-chief, or a civilian in charge of the administration of the army, *i.e.* a minister of national defence, for the supreme command was exercised by the king himself. Among the prisoners there was also a scribe (*sôpher*), 'charged to enlist the people of the country'. This text should be compared with 2 Ch 26: 11, where we are told that a register of the army of Ozias was made under the secretary Yeiel and a *shôṭer* or clerk[2] named Maaseyahu.

According to Dt 20: 5-9 there were several *shôṭrîm*, who were responsible for recruiting, obviously in different districts. The same text makes provision for a certain number of men who are to be exempted: those who own a new and as yet unoccupied house, or a vineyard which has not yielded its first harvest, and men who are engaged but have not yet married: according to Dt 24: 5, newly-weds had a deferment for one year. The dismissal of the faint-hearted (Dt 20: 8) is perhaps an addition inspired by Jg 7: 3. (The same rules were applied by Judas Maccabee when he raised the liberation army, 1 M 3: 56.) Mobilization affected everyone aged 20 or over (2 Ch 25: 5; cf. Nb 1: 3; 26: 2). Enrolment was by family groups, and therefore by localities (2 Ch 17: 14; 25: 5), and a distinction was drawn between the contingents from Judah and those from Benjamin (2 Ch 17: 14-17; 25: 5). The recruits did not bring their own arms, as in olden times; they were provided by the king (2 Ch 26: 14).

After enlistment, the men were put under the command of their officers (*śarîm*: Dt 20: 9). The latter were normally the heads of families or clans, the

1. Cf. p. 121.   2. Cf. p. 155.

rô'šê ha'abôth (2 Ch 26: 12). The structure of the army and its efficiency in the field, however, necessitated a corps of professional officers permanently in the service of the king; they were part of his *'abadîm* or *śarîm* (2 K 24: 12, 14; Jr 52: 10; cf. 2 Ch 26: 11). The king remained, as in the time of Saul and David, the supreme head of the army and took an active part in operations (1 K 22: 29; 2 K 3: 9; 14: 11; 23: 29; 25: 4-5), even though he might (again like David) have a general to command his troops (2 Ch 26: 11; perhaps 2 K 25: 19).

The units were composed of 1,000, 100, 50 and 10 men. This organization dated back to the desert period, according to Ex 18: 21 and Dt 1: 15. Perhaps Ishbaal, who came with ten men to assassinate Godolias just after the fall of Jerusalem, was a leader of a group of ten (Jr 41: 1, 2; cf. 15). Leaders of fifty men are mentioned in the story of Elias (2 K 1: 9, 11, 13). The commanders of one hundred and of a thousand men are listed in the statistics of 2 Ch 25: 5, and the same organization of the conscript army dated back to the period of David, according to 1 Ch 27: 1. The last statement, however, is not wholly arbitrary, for units of one hundred and of a thousand men were already in existence when the entire people used to take up arms (1 S 22: 7; 17: 18) and among the mercenary troops (2 K 11: 4).

Except for these names which indicate numbers, the words used for army units are of uncertain meaning. According to 2 Ch 26: 11, the army was divided into *g'dûd*. In other passages the word means a troop of armed men, often brigands (1 S 30: 8f.; 2 K 13: 20, etc.), or sometimes (and the meaning is closely allied), soldiers sent on a raid into enemy territory (2 K 5: 2; 6: 23; 24: 2), and thirdly (and this meaning is not very unlike the others), a troop of mercenaries (2 S 4: 2; 2 Ch 25: 9; cf. 13). The use of the word in 2 Ch 26: 11 to denote the formations of the conscript army is quite exceptional. If it is a legitimate use, then it may be noted that the proportion between officers and soldiers in 2 Ch 26: 12-13 would give each officer roughly 120 men to command: the *g'dûd* or 'company' would be roughly equivalent to a hundred men. The *degel* seems to have been a higher unit. This word does not mean a standard or ensign, as so many modern dictionaries and translations interpret it, but a division of the army. This is the right meaning in Nb 1: 52; 2: 2-34; 10: 14-25; it is also the sense given by the ancient versions, and it is used with this meaning in the papyri of Elephantine and in the Order of the War from Qumran. The only questionable point is the size of this unit. In the Qumran text, the *degel* comprises about 1,000 men, but in the Elephantine documents it must be smaller, for there were several *d'galîm* in the colony. On the other hand, according to Nb 2 and 10, the men of the twelve tribes formed only four *d'gallîm* and even if we do not accept the colossal figures which are cited in Nb 2, each *degel* must have included several thousand men. Another argument in support of this theory is the use of 'a thousand' for *mishpaḥah*.[1]

1. Cf. p. 216.

If *degel* means a 'division', there is little evidence left for the existence of standards or ensigns in the Israelite army. In one text only, Nb 2: 2, the word *'oth* ('sign, signal, miraculous sign') may mean the emblem or standard around which men of the same clan camped; there are good parallels to this custom among the Bedouin, but there is no certain evidence for the use of the word in the sense of military ensign except in the Dead Sea Scrolls, where it may be a translation of the Latin *signum*. The *nes*, often translated 'banner', is not really an ensign, but a pole or mast, which was raised on a hill to give the signal to take up arms or to rally together (Is 5: 26; 11: 10, 12; 13: 2; 18: 3; Jr 4: 6; 50: 2; 51: 12, 27; cf. Ex 17: 15); but apart from these references in the prophets, the word is never used in texts concerning the army or in accounts of battles. The same custom exists among the Arabs, and only a few years ago, when a surveyor named Schumacher was making topographical surveys in Galilee, he brought about the mobilization of a neighbouring tribe by fixing a sighting picket on the top of a hill. The main argument in favour of ensigns in the army of ancient Israel is that all the Eastern armies had ensigns at the time; but the ensigns of other nations were usually religious emblems, and this may have been the reason which dissuaded the Israelites from copying them. We may note, however, that at the beginning of the monarchic period, the Ark of the Covenant played a similar role; we shall return to this later.[1]

This national army was never called to arms except in time of war. But when the mercenaries had fallen in numbers, or perhaps even ceased to exist, probably a certain number of recruits were kept under arms in peace-time to ensure the security of the territory and to garrison the fortresses. Information however, is lacking, and anyone should be wary of using the text of 1 Ch 27: 1-15, which says that David divided the people into twelve classes of 24,000 men, each of which did service for the king for one month of the year. The figures quoted are too high, and the names of the commanders of these classes are the names of David's champions, who had quite a different function. The information certainly does not date back to the reign of David, but, if we suppress the figures and the names, it may have been true of a later epoch. On the other hand, the idea may have originated with the Chronicler himself, drawing his inspiration from Solomon's twelve prefectures, each of which supported the king, his household and his troops for a month of each year (1 K 5: 7-8).

One recent suggestion is that the conscript army was an innovation of Josias, and that the notes scattered throughout Chronicles, which have been used in the last few pages, should all be referred to this age. This conclusion is unfounded. It is perfectly true that the mercenary troops had lost their importance, that they may even have ceased to exist towards the end of the monarchy, and that the conscript army (alone, it appears) ensured the defence

1. Cf. p. 259.

of the country during these times. But this same conscript army was already in existence, years before, alongside the mercenary troops. During the Aramaean wars, a census was made of the entire 'people' as well as of the 'youngsters' or 'cadets' (1 K 2: 15, cf. 19). The people of Israel and the people of Judah were involved in the alliance between Josaphat and Achab (1 K 22: 4), and in that between Joram and the king of Judah (2 K 3: 7). Thus the tradition of a people under arms persisted, but the mass response to a call from a leader inspired by God had given place to mobilization organized by the royal administration. The first indication of this development can be seen as early as David's reign: his census (2 S 24: 1-9) had a military purpose and was equivalent to drawing up a register for conscription, but this step was condemned as an abandonment of the rules of a holy war, and a profanation (cf. verses 3 and 10). Putting names on a register was seen as a usurpation of a divine prerogative: Yahweh alone keeps the register of those who are to live or to die (Ex 32: 32-33); a census is a move fraught with danger, against which one must take religious precautions. The new texts from Mari throw light on passages from the Bible such as this: 'When you make a census of the Israelites, each one of them must pay Yahweh the ransom-price of his life, so that no plague may break out against them on the occasion of the census' (Ex 30: 12). David, by disregarding this right of God's, brought a plague down on the people (2 S 24: 10-15). War, however, was becoming a non-religious matter, and the system of conscription forced itself upon them in the end. There is no reason to doubt that military registrations took place under Asa (2 Ch 14: 7), Josaphat (2 Ch 17: 14-18), Amasias (2 Ch 25: 5), and Ozias (2 Ch 26: 11-13); certain details show that the Chronicler has made use of ancient sources. Yet no one will deny that he has introduced into his text figures which are improbably high.

CHAPTER TWO

FORTIFIED CITIES AND SIEGE WARFARE

THE ancient cities of Canaan, each of which was the centre of a tiny State, were encircled by ramparts and defended by towers and fortified gates. The Egyptian illustrations of campaigns under the Pharaohs of the New Empire give a picture of what they looked like, and excavations in Palestine allow us to study the plan of these defences and the techniques employed in their construction. It is understandable that these heavily fortified towns struck fear into the Israelite invaders (Nb 13 : 28), for their ramparts reached 'to the sky' (Dt 1 : 28); they were 'strongholds enclosed by high walls, protected by gates and bars' (Dt 3 : 5). After their conquest or occupation of these towns, the Israelites took care to rebuild the defences (though archaeological evidence of this begins only at the reign of Saul); they preserved intact the parts which remained, and repaired them if necessary. Where the destruction had been complete, they rebuilt the ramparts in new ways, and they applied these new methods in the towns they themselves founded. These latter fortifications, replanned or erected by the Israelites, are the only ones which interest us here.

1. Fortified towns

Every town ('ir) was normally encircled by a rampart, which distinguished it from an open village (ḥaṣer, cf. Lv 25 : 31). But a town which was defended by solid constructions was called a 'fortified town' ('ir mibṣar: cf. Jr 34 : 7 and many other texts).

The entire population of the neighbourhood would seek protection behind these defences in times of danger (Jr 4 : 5; 8 : 14). Lists of strongholds and isolated references to them occur in the Old Testament; but though these texts throw some light on the system of protecting the territory, the information is incomplete, and applies only to certain periods.

David's first objective after the capture of Jerusalem was to build a wall around it (2 S 5 : 9): we should take it to mean that he merely repaired the Jebusite ramparts. The Bible mentions no similar work outside the capital during his reign, but it is quite certain that he secured the defences of other places as well, and archaeologists attribute to him the building of the ramparts at Tell Beit-Mirsim and at Beth Shemesh. Solomon's chariot garrisons[1] were obviously quartered in fortified towns, and at Megiddo, archaeologists have found a gate and rampart contemporary with the stables.

One passage of Chronicles, which has no parallel in the books of Kings, gives a list of fifteen places fortified by Roboam (2 Ch 11: 6-10). There is no good reason for assigning this text to the age of Josias, as some authors have proposed. It is sound historical information, recording a fact which is relevant in the reign of Roboam: the campaign of the Pharaoh Sheshonq in Palestine (1 K 14: 25) had proved that the country needed to reinforce its defences. A line of fortified towns guarded the ridge road running from the south towards Jerusalem, and dominated the Eastern desert: Jerusalem, Bethlehem, Etham, Teqoa, Bethsur, Hebron, Ziph. From Ziph to the west, the southern front was protected by Adorayim, Lakish and Gath. Northwards from Gath, the principal passes into the hill-country of Judah were closed on the western side by: (1) Gath, Mareshah; (2) Azeqah, Soko, Adullam; (3) Soreah; (4) Ayyalon. These fortresses were not strung out along the frontiers of the kingdom, but built along routes where resistance was practicable, and at the most favourable strategic points; the list is probably incomplete, for it mentions only the new ones built by Roboam, without counting the towns which David and Solomon had fortified and which were still in existence.

The northern front still lay open, for the boundary between the new kingdoms of Israel and Judah was at first undecided. Basha of Israel attempted to fortify Ramah, about six miles north of Jerusalem, but Asa of Judah drove him out and brought his own frontier forward to Geba in Benjamin and to Mispah, which he equipped for defence (1 K 15: 17-22). He restored other strongholds in Judah, too, according to 1 K 15: 23 and 2 Ch 14: 5-6. They were still in commission under Josaphat, who posted troops in them (2 Ch 17: 2, 19; 19: 5). Ozias, in addition to his work at Jerusalem (2 Ch 26: 9), built forts in the desert and improved the methods of defence (2 Ch 26: 10 and 15); we shall return to these last texts further on.

Besides rebuilding its chariot force, Judah 'built many strongholds' (Os 8: 14), in the eighth century[2]; Sennacherib boasted that he had besieged and captured 46 fortified towns in Judah. The biblical account, too, states that Sennacherib attacked the fortresses in Judah and captured them (2 K 18: 13), mentioning Lakish and Libnah by name (2 K 18: 17 and 19: 8); it was only by a miracle that Jerusalem itself was saved. (A most interesting Assyrian bas-relief is extant which does in fact represent the capture of Lakish by Sennacherib.) We do not know to what extent the destruction caused by the Assyrians was ever made good. The defence work undertaken at Jerusalem by Ezechias (2 Ch 32: 5; cf. Is 22: 9-11) was continued by Manasseh (2 Ch 33: 14), and there is no reason to doubt this precise information of the Chronicler. We know for certain that shortly before the

---

1. Cf. p. 223.   2. Cf. p. 223.

final ruin of the kingdom of Judah, the people placed its trust in strongholds (Jr 5: 17) and that, during the siege of Jerusalem, two cities, Lakish and Azeqah, were still holding out against Nabuchodonosor (Jr 34: 7); these two places are also mentioned in an ostrakon found at Lakish and written at the very time.

After their victory the Chaldeans razed to the ground the fortifications of Jerusalem (2 K 25: 10) and of every town in Judah (Lm 2: 2, 5), and archaeological evidence confirms this. The walls of Jerusalem were not rebuilt until the time of Nehemias, and those of other towns, like Gezer and Bethsur, not until the Hellenistic period.

The Bible gives us very little information about the northern kingdom. Jeroboam I fortified Shechem and Penuel in Transjordan (1 K 12: 25). We have already mentioned the abortive enterprise of Basha at Ramah (1 K 15: 17f.). Under Achab, Jericho was rebuilt and fortified with a gate (1 K 16: 34). In his letter to the leading men of Samaria (2 K 10: 2) Jehu writes that they have on their side a 'strong place'. The Massoretic text is often corrected to the plural 'strong places', but there is no doubt that the singular should be retained; he is referring to Samaria alone. Samaria had powerful defences, as is proved by the long sieges it withstood (1 K 20: 1f.; 2 K 6: 24f.; 17: 5; 18: 9-10), and excavations have confirmed the fact. Outside the Bible, the stele of Mesha speaks of the towns of Ataroth and of Yahas as 'built' (*i.e.* fortified) in Moab by Omri and Achab. The penury of biblical information is due to the Judahite origin of the historical books, and should not mislead us: there is no doubt that the northern kingdom had a defence system just as elaborate as Judah's.

As long as the chariot force and the mercenaries existed, these professional soldiers provided the garrisons of strongholds, but we do not know how the staffing was organized. We know only that Josaphat stationed troops in the fortified towns of Judah and that there were at Jerusalem a garrison and an officers' corps to form the backbone of the conscript army (cf. 2 Ch 17: 2, 13b-19). The numbers quoted are fantastic, but, these apart, the information may stem from an ancient source. According to 2 Ch 33: 14, Manasseh posted officers in the fortified towns of Judah; but there is no mention of troops being sent with them. This, however, is after the destruction of the military power of Judah by Sennacherib, and it is possible that in these last days of the monarchy the garrisons of the strongholds were reduced to token forces; they would employ forced labour (following the very old and extreme example cited in 1 K 15: 22) to keep the defences in good repair, and in times of crisis, they would man them with defenders raised on the spot.

It has been argued from 1 Ch 27: 1-15 that the strongholds were held by contingents of conscripts who served by turns for one month of each year, but the meaning and value of this text are far from certain (cf. p. 227).

2. Ramparts

Archaeology contributes to a better understanding of the biblical evidence by revealing the lay-out and the construction of defences. We have mentioned that the Israelites refitted some of the old Canaanite fortifications: apart from these, two distinct types of Israelite ramparts can be distinguished, casemated ramparts, and ramparts with redans.

A casemated rampart is a wall along which stand blind rooms, which used to be filled with earth or rubble, or which served as stores. The purpose of these rooms is to widen the rampart, and thereby to strengthen it, while economizing in building by furnishing the store-rooms necessary for any garrison town. Splendid examples of this type have been brought to light at Tell Beit-Mirsim (the ancient Debir), and at Beth Shemesh, both dating from the reign of David or Solomon; similar ones have been discovered at Tell Qasileh, near Jaffa (going back to the first Israelite occupation, probably under Solomon), at Hazor and at Gezer (also from the time of Solomon). This type of fortification seems to have originated in Asia Minor: there is evidence of it at Boghazkoi and at Mersin in the 14th-13th century B.C., and, at a slightly later date, in the fortresses of Senjirli and Charchemish. In Palestine, it was generally replaced by the type with redans, but a magnificent specimen of casemated rampart is still to be seen at Samaria in the palace walls, which must have been built by Achab in the ninth century B.C. Another casemated rampart, also from this period, has recently been uncovered at Ramath Rachel, just south of Jerusalem.

In building their ramparts, Canaanite architects were anxious to follow as closely as possible the escarpment of the hill; consequently, they would often follow a curved line, or break the straight line of the walls; they thus obtained a series of redans. This procedure was adopted as a principle in certain Israelite fortifications, even when the configuration of the terrain did not demand it. The most obvious reason was to provide a series of salients which would give more effective defence against an enemy which had come close to the walls. But these salients were sometimes so unimpressive that they hardly increased the range of weapons at all; clearly, the main advantage of the process was to strengthen the rampart without increasing its thickness: several angles well knit together and firmly anchored in the soil offered more resistance to the rams or to the undermining techniques used by assailants. Megiddo is a very fine example, probably later than Solomon: the entire town was encircled by a rampart four yards wide, divided into stretches six yards long, which are placed, alternately, half a yard forward and half a yard back. The rampart of Tell en-Nasbeh = Mispah follows the same design, but it is less regular: it may be dated to the time of Asa, who fortified Mispah (1 K 15: 22). There is a similar plan at Tell ed-Duweir = Lakish. These walls with redans were reinforced here and there by towers: there are a dozen of them at Mispah. At Gezer, along a rampart of the tenth or ninth century, the exterior and interior redans do not correspond, but go in opposite directions, which gives a series of reinforcements, of wide towers, all along the rampart. These flanking constructions, salients or towers, were called 'angles' or 'corners' (*pinnah*, 2 Ch 26: 15; So 1: 16; 3: 6).

Ramparts of this kind could be protected by a glacis, which would put to good use the slope of the hill (as at Mispah), or by a forward wall built some distance below (as at Lakish). This forward wall is the *ḥel* spoken of in Is 26: 1; Lm 2: 8; Na 3: 8, in contrast to the *ḥômah* or rampart. The text of 2 S 20: 15-16 is eloquent, and needs no correcting: during the siege of Abel Beth-Maaka, they heaped up an embankment on the forward wall (*ḥel*) and began tunnelling to bring down the rampart (*ḥômah*).

We do not know the shape of the top of these walls. On the basis of a find at Megiddo, it has been suggested that they were surmounted by crenelated battlements—a view which could claim the support of some Assyrian representations; but the connection of the stonework found at Megiddo with the rampart is only a hypothesis. The word *shemesh* could mean 'crenel' in Is 54: 12; Ps 84: 12, but it can also mean (from its ordinary sense of 'sun'), round shields, rondaches, which were fixed on the top of the walls. They are shown on the top of the rampart in the Assyrian bas-relief of the capture of Lakish. We may compare with this Ez 27: 11: 'They hung their shields all around thy walls', and Ct 4: 4: 'Thy neck is like the tower of David . . . a thousand shields are hung around it.'

All the Israelite fortifications which have so far been uncovered by excavations were built in the first half of the monarchical period, between 1100 and 900 B.C., and it is difficult to lay down any characteristics for ramparts of the following period. In some towns, *e.g.* in the two capitals and in the garrison towns, as long as there were any, the Israelites kept the defences in good repair, but elsewhere they allowed them to deteriorate. Men were happy enough with the indifferent protection afforded by the half-ruined ramparts or by the line of houses built over their ruins; the houses would be squeezed against each other, with no windows on the outside. Only a few strong points were retained, such as the gates, or a tower or bastion. The majority of the '46 fortified towns' of Judah which Sennacherib captured in 701 must have been just as feebly defended, and archaeology does not justify (no more than history did) the confidence which the men of Judah placed in their 'countless strong places' during the eighth century (Os 8: 14; Jr 5: 17).

3. Fortified gates and citadels

The gate was fortified in a special way. In Canaanite towns, the gate with tenailles was a classical type: two or three pairs of pilasters protruding in the bay made narrows (tenailles) in the entry. The object was to strengthen the walls and to establish successive barriers. The Israelites kept this type of gate in service, with or without modification, at Beth Shemesh, Shechem, Megiddo and Tirsah, and themselves built a few similar ones at the beginning of the monarchical period. Very soon, however, their pilasters began to protrude far more than the Canaanite ones had done, and so formed small rooms at the entry where the guards could lodge. Solomon's gate at Megiddo is a very fine example; it had four pairs of pilasters, though this is exceptional; an identical plan, from the same period, was adopted at Hazor and Gezer also. (Note that Ezechiel foresees the same plan being used in the porches of the Temple, cf. Ez 40: 6-16). The gate of Esyon Geber, also from Solomon's reign, had three pairs of pilasters, and the first Israelite gate at Tell ed-Duweir perhaps had three as well. In the following period, the gate of Megiddo had only two pairs, like that at Tell en-Nasbeh and the oldest gate at Tell Beit-Mirsim. Sometimes, as at Tell en-Nasbeh, in the modified gate at the northern Tell el-Far'ah (= Tirsah), and later at Tell ed-Duweir, benches were fixed against the wall: this at once brings to mind the biblical texts about the Elders 'who sat at the gate' to give judgement in law suits or to settle municipal affairs.[1]

As a rule, the gate was flanked by towers, either at each side or jutting out in front, and sometimes there was yet another bastion before it with a preliminary entry, as at Megiddo. The axis of the gate generally ran at right angles to the rampart, but at Tell en-Nasbeh it runs parallel, and you entered through a wide detour in the line of fortifications.

Towards the end of the monarchy, another type of gate appears, a gate with indirect access: it had been foreshadowed in the Solomonian gate at Megiddo. A good example of this type of gate has been discovered at Tell ed-Duweir: a bastion covered the entry, and you had first to walk along the rampart until you entered a courtyard; from here a simple right turn took you through the ordinary gate which stood open in the town wall. Further development led to a zigzag gate, one example of which is the last gate of Tell Beit-Mirsim; it reappears in far later times in Eastern towns.

In addition to the defences provided by the fortified gates and by the towers on the rampart, the capital cities had a second surrounding wall and bastions which shut off the royal palace and its outbuildings; it was the acropolis of the town. The clearest example is in Samaria, where a casemated wall flanked by a massive tower surrounds the palace with its arsenals and stores. Jerusalem had the equivalent in the City of David, which was the former citadel of Sion (2 S 5: 7 and 9). Rabbah of the Ammonites had its acropolis, too, which David stormed after Joab had captured the lower city (2 S 12: 26-29). Other towns had at least a citadel built on the highest point, and the citizens would gather there for their last resistance. Excavations have uncovered some which date from the Israelite period, but unfortunately they

1. Cf. pp. 152-153.

are badly damaged. The oldest is at Tell el-Ful= Gibeah, Saul's capital; it was a rectangular building, with a casemated wall and towers at the corners. Others can be recognized at Tell Zakariyah= Azeqah, at Tell el-Hesy= Eglon(?), and at Tell Ta'annak= Tanak. The plan is always polygonal, with small towers and buttresses to reinforce the walls.

These fortifications inside a town are called by the name *migdal*. The term is usually translated 'tower', and in fact it does denote towers or bastions raised on or near the ramparts in Jr 31: 38; 2 Ch 14: 6; 26: 9, 15; 32: 5; Ne 3: 1, 11, 25—all late texts. In older texts, however, the word *migdal* is better rendered by 'citadel' or 'castle', in the sense of the Latin *castellum*. This explains the story about Abimelek at Tebes: the town had been captured, but 'inside the town there was a redoubtable *migdal* where all the men and women and the leading figures in the town had taken refuge, etc.' (Jg 9: 50f.). There is no doubt that we should interpret the more difficult story of the destruction of Shechem, which comes immediately before this (Jg 9: 45-49), in the light of this text: the town had been taken, but the inmates of the *migdal* of Shechem took refuge in the crypt of the temple of Baal-berith, where, in the end, they were burned alive; this *migdal* is the citadel of Shechem, with a fortified temple, and it has been cleared by excavations at Tell Balata, the site of ancient Shechem. It has been suggested, however, that Migdal-Shechem is a place-name, and that the place was distinct from Shechem. Similar 'castles' are mentioned at Penuel (Jg 8: 9 and 17) and at Yizreel (2 K 9: 17).

The sense 'castles' (Latin *castella*) would also give a good meaning for the *migdalîm* which Ozias and Yotham built in the desert (2 Ch 26: 10; 2 Ch 27: 4). One of these little forts, perhaps even earlier than Ozias' time, is recognizable at Qedeirat near Qadesh; its plan reminds us of the citadels at Tell Zachariyah and at Tell el-Ful. Another has recently been identified at Khirbet Ghazza, about 20 miles east of Beersheba. This provides an explanation of place-names composed with *migdal*: they would be little places grouped around a small citadel. (One might compare the French place-names compounded with Château, Châtel- or Castel-.) When the second element is a divine name, such as Migdal-El or Migdal-Gad, this 'castle' would be a fortified temple, like that of Baal-berith in Shechem.

Yotham built *migdalîm* and *bîraniyyôth* (2 Ch 27: 4). The two words seem to be almost synonymous, the latter being a more modern word (cf. 2 Ch 17: 12). For example, in later texts the singular *bîrah* takes the place of *migdal* when the reference is to a citadel inside a town: thus it is used of the citadel of Jerusalem under Nehemias (Ne 2: 8; 7: 2) and the same term is used abroad for the citadel or for the whole of the fortified town of Susa (Ne 1: 1; Dn 8: 2 and frequently in Est) and for the fortress of Ecbatane (Esd 6: 2 *bîrta'*, the Aramaic form).

In the palaces at Tirsah and Samaria, there was a more heavily fortified part called the *'armôn* (1 K 16: 18; 2 K 15: 25): it was the keep. In the plural, the word means the fortified dwellings in Jerusalem (Jr 17: 27; Lm 2: 7; Ps 48: 4, 14; 122: 7) or elsewhere (Am 1: 4, 12; 2: 2, 5, etc.).

4. Siege warfare

Ramparts and bastions gave towns effective protection against assailants whose only long-range weapons were bows and slings. The latter had to resort to stratagems or to resign themselves to the prospect of a siege.

Stratagem is the method which figures in the accounts of the conquest. Josue sent spies to reconnoitre the defences of Jericho; the spies made contact with Rahab, and agreed on a sign (Jos 2): this story is apparently all that remains of a tradition which explained the capture of Jericho by an act of treason on the part of Rahab, a tradition which was eclipsed by the other tradition about the miraculous collapse of its walls. The text about Bethel is clear: a traitor tells the spies of a passage-way, where the Israelites gain entry (Jg 1: 23-25). At other times they coaxed the defenders out of the town: at Ai, the Israelites pretend to run away, the whole town gives chase, and a contingent which Josue has concealed then enters the town and sets it on fire (Jos 8: 3-22). It was a classic trick, which was successfully employed on another occasion at Gibeah, in the war against the Benjamites (Jg 20: 29-41); the king of Israel suspected the Aramaeans of the same trick when they raised the siege of Samaria (2 K 7: 12). Lastly, a group of determined men could effect an entry by surprise: this, apparently, was how David conquered Jerusalem (2 S 5: 7-8): Joab climbed up the tunnel which led from the spring to the interior of the town.

A powerful enemy could dispense with such subterfuges: it could intimidate a town into opening its gates or accepting its conditions (cf. Dt 20: 10-11). The inhabitants of Yabesh Gilead would have been prepared to surrender to Nahash the Ammonite if only his demands had not been so cruel (1 S 11: 1f.). When Ben-hadad pitched his camp below the walls of Samaria, Achab accepted the very first demands he made (1 K 20: 1f.). Sennacherib's envoy tried to bring about the surrender of Jerusalem by describing the power of the Assyrians, the futility of resistance and the horrors of a siege (2 K 18: 17f.).

If the town could not be captured by stratagem or surprise, and if negotiations failed, then the assailants had to mount a regular siege. They pitched camp near the city (2 S 11: 1; 1 K 16: 15-16, etc.), blocked the roads, occupied the watering-places (cf. the late text of Jdt 7: 12, 17-18) and waited until hunger and thirst got the better of the inhabitants (2 K 6: 25f.; Jdt 7: 20f.). The assailants would harry the defenders posted on the walls (2 K 3: 25). The besieged might try to break the grip by making sorties (2 S 11: 17; 1 K 20: 15-21), or, if they thought they were beaten, might try to escape (2 K 3: 26; 25: 4).

If resistance was too stiff, or if the defenders showed signs of weakening, the besiegers might hasten a decision by mounting an assault. A mound would be thrown up against the wall to provide a ramp giving access to the town; sappers might try to break through the wall (the operation is described at the siege of Abel Beth-Maakah under David, 2 S 20 : 15-16). The technical term for this ramp or embankment is *solalah* (cf. once more 2 K 19 : 32, Sennacherib at Jerusalem; Jr 32 : 24 and 33 : 4, the Chaldeans at Jerusalem, and the texts of Ezechiel which will be cited later). Attempts would be made to set fire to the gates (Jg 9 : 52). When the assailants reached the foot of the rampart, they were exposed to the onslaught of the defenders, who would redouble their efforts at this critical moment: at Tebes, Abimelek was killed by a mill-stone thrown by a woman (Jg 9 : 53). But the defenders, as a rule, had only these chance weapons or ordinary arms. True, according to 2 Ch 26 : 15, Ozias 'built machines designed by engineers, at Jerusalem, to install them on the castles and corners to shoot arrows and big stones'. It has often been thought that this was a kind of artillery, of ballistic machines or catapults; and those who have refused to allow Ozias the honour of possessing machines the Assyrians themselves did not possess have simply denied the historical value of the text. In fact, this text refers to something quite different: these 'engines' were simply frames arranged as corbelling along the curtains of the walls and bastions, so that the archers and slingers could shoot at the foot of the wall without exposing themselves to the enemy missiles. It was the equivalent of the hoardings which were used in military architecture during the Middle Ages. And, in fact, these contrivances do surmount the walls of Lakish in the Assyrian bas-relief of the capture of the city. The Jews never used machines to attack or to defend towns before the Maccabean wars, and then they were copying the Greeks against whom they were fighting (1 M 6 : 20, 51-52; 11 : 20; 13 : 43f.).

The religious rules for siege warfare are given in Dt 20 : 10-20. When the town lies in foreign territory, it must first be offered peace terms: if it thereupon opens its gates, the population may be subjected to forced labour, but to nothing else; if it refuses, then it should be invested, its menfolk put to the sword, and everything else, people and property alike, could be taken as spoil of war.

Where the town is a Canaanite town inside the frontiers of the Promised Land, all its inhabitants were to be put to the sword without giving them the choice of surrender. During the siege of a town, fruit trees were to be left standing, but other trees might be felled and used for the siege-works. These commands were not always followed in early times (2 K 3 : 19, 25), and when Deuteronomy was promulgated under Josias, there was scarcely any occasion to apply them: there were no Canaanites left to exterminate, and the Israelites were no longer likely to besiege foreign towns: they had quite enough to do in defending their own against the Assyrians.

The Assyrians were past masters of siege by encirclement, and their monuments give a vivid picture of their methods of attack. The besieged city was encircled by a mound, ramps were constructed and machines brought up. These machines were mobile redoubts sheltering archers and men who manœuvred a ram, *i.e.* a long wooden beam with a metal-covered head for battering the wall. Those inside the city would throw flaming torches and stones down on these machines, or try to immobilize the rams by means of grappling hooks. The infantry moved up to the assault behind the machines, and were given covering fire by archers: these archers were in turn protected by movable mantelets held by servants. Once the rams had opened a breach in the walls, the assailants could enter there; alternatively, they would scale the walls with ladders. The bas-relief of the capture of Lakish shows these different methods of attack in action, and the Annals of Sennacherib state that the king captured the towns of Judah 'by using earthen ramps, rams taken up to the walls, infantry attack, mines, breaches and tunnels'. The biblical texts provide the corresponding Hebrew words. The collective *maṣôr* is used for siege operations as a whole. We have seen that *solalah* meant a ramp; this ramp could be covered with stones or wooden logs to enable machines to pass (cf. Jr 6: 6). The encircling mound or trench is called *dayeq*, the mantelet or great siege-shield is the *ṣinnah*, and the rams are called *karîm*. When Ezechiel is ordered by God to do a mime of the siege of Jerusalem, he takes a brick to represent the city, and then builds around it a trench, makes a ramp and sets up rams (Ez 4: 2). In another text the same prophet shows Nabuchodonosor drawing lots to march to Jerusalem 'to bring rams against its walls, to pile up a ramp, to dig a trench' (Ez 21: 27). In his prediction of the siege of Tyre (Ez 26: 8-9), there are two obscure terms in addition to these others: 'he will direct against thy walls the blows of his *q'bol*' (clearly a type of ram), 'and will dismantle thy castles with his *ḥarabôth*', where the ordinary meaning (sword) is out of place: *ḥarabôth*, in this context, must mean either rams with pointed heads or sappers' picks (cf. Ex 20: 25, where it means 'chisel').

5. *The water supply*

It was not sufficient for the besieged to lie behind the shelter of a solid rampart; they had to live there, and the water supply was a problem which had to be tackled. It was solved, too, for Samaria held out for over two years against the Assyrians in 723-721, and Jerusalem withstood Nabuchodonosor for a year and a half in 587. Famine eventually raged inside Jerusalem (2 K 25: 3), as it did at Samaria during a siege by the Aramaeans (2 K 6: 25); but in neither instance are we told they were short of water. If such precautions had not been taken, however, disaster was inevitable: in the story of Judith, the army of Holofernes had occupied the springs outside the city, and the inhabitants of Bethulia were fainting from thirst after thirty-four days (Jdt 7: 20-22), though there is no question of a famine.

The Canaanites had already faced the problem and had resolved it in different ways. Here we shall discuss only the hydraulic installations built, or re-used, by the Israelites. Since the towns were built on hills and never had a spring within their walls, there were only three possible solutions, all of which were used: (*a*) a tunnel from inside the town, running under the ramparts to a water-supply outside the town; alternatively, a canal running from a water-supply outside the town which would bring water into the town; (*b*) deep wells dug inside the city down to the underground water level; (*c*) reservoirs and cisterns to collect rain water.

(*a*) *Water Tunnels.* There is archaeological evidence for these at Jerusalem and at Megiddo from the Canaanite period onwards, at Gibeon during the Israelite period, at Etham and at Yibleam at a date which cannot be fixed for certain. At Jerusalem, there is a tunnel, and a well cut through the rock, down to the spring of Gihon. It has been rediscovered by archaeologists and 2 S 5: 8 probably refers to this. The text would then mean that Joab climbed up it into the city; the word *ṣinnôr*, which is used here, can mean this type of canal and, in common usage, the name was extended to similar installations. At Megiddo, a very rudimentary Canaanite shaft was replaced by a most elaborate installation, which was modified several times during the period of the Israelite monarchy: a large rectangular well with flights of steps led into a sloping shaft, then into a horizontal tunnel which continued as far as the the water pool; when the water-supply was normal, the water flowed to the end of the horizontal tunnel, which lay within the ramparts. The shaft which has recently been uncovered at Gibeon followed a sloping line to the spring; it was dug out like a tunnel, except for the central part, which was a deep trench covered by flag-stones. The installations at Etham and at Yibleam have so far not been explored; that at Etham may be connected with the fortification of the town by Roboam (2 Ch 11: 6).

At Jerusalem, the configuration of the terrain eventually made a much more practical system possible. When the old Canaanite shaft had been abandoned, the Israelites had dug out a canal along the side of the Kedron Valley, running from the spring of Gihon; this canal, however, lay outside the rampart and would have served the enemy rather than the city during a siege. Faced with the threat of an Assyrian attack, Ezechias had a tunnel dug under the hill of Ophel; it brought the water from the spring at Gihon to a pool in the Tyropoeon valley, inside the ramparts. It was a masterly piece of work, which still survives as a water supply; an inscription was carved in the rock to mark the event, and the story is told with pride in 2 K 20: 20; 2 Ch 32: 30; Si 48: 17.

(*b*) Elsewhere, attempts were made to reach water-level by digging deep wells inside the town. At Beth Shemesh a well ten feet in diameter went down 67 feet; it was dug out by the Canaanites, and remained in use until the end of the Israelite period. On the crest of Tell ed-Duweir, a well protected by a salient part of the rampart reached water level at a depth of 120 feet; it was probably Canaanite to begin with, but it remained in use until the capture of the town by Nabuchodonosor. At Gezer, a series of steps over 40 yards long led down to a cave where a spring flowed, still within the ramparts; the work seems to date from the very early part of the second millennium B.C and may have been in use at the beginning of the Israelite period. At Gibeon, a large circular well has recently been discovered: it was reached by a flight of steps leading into a sloping shaft which ended in a cave where water dripped from the rock: this well at Gibeon seems to have been in use at the same time as the sloping tunnel mentioned above. We do not know how the Israelite engineers found these deep-water supplies without a considerable amount of digging. Perhaps the spring at Gezer originally flowed into the open on the side of the hill. At Gibeon, perhaps the first idea was to install a system like that at Megiddo, but when they came up against the dripping water, they stopped the project; the flow was too small, so they then dug a shaft going straight to the source.

(c) Finally, *reservoirs and cisterns* could be provided inside the city. Progress in the art of making waterproof coatings allowed the Israelites to build more cisterns as the number of dwelling-houses or public buildings increased. The excavations at Tell en-Nasbeh and Samaria have shown that they were particularly numerous from the ninth century B.C. onwards. During a siege, these two towns would have had no other water supply at all.

At Lakish, they decided to dig a large ditch in the form of a cube 20 yards square and deep; it was to drain off all the water from a particular quarter, and more especially from the plastered esplanades near the governor's residence; this ambitious project was never finished. It dates from the last days of the monarchy; perhaps it was only begun after the first attack of Nabuchodonosor in 597, when they started to rebuild the fortifications.

CHAPTER THREE

ARMAMENTS

VERY little is known about the equipment of Israelite soldiers. The biblical texts do not describe their weapons; indeed, the very words used for military equipment are far from precise, and their meaning is often uncertain. Archaeology might be expected to help, but only a few weapons have been found in the course of excavations. Illustrations from Egyptian and Mesopotamian monuments are certainly helpful, but one can never be sure that the Israelites were always using the same kind of weapon as their enemies.

I. *Offensive weapons*

The main offensive weapon was the *ḥereb*, which became the symbol of war (Is 51: 19; Jr 14: 15; 24: 10; Ez 7: 15; 33: 6, etc.). The word is used for both dagger and sword, since the two weapons have the same shape and are distinguished—quite arbitrarily—merely by their length. The *ḥereb* of Ehud (Jg 3: 16, 21-22) was obviously a dagger, whatever the precise meaning of *gomed*, which gives its length.[1] In all military texts, the word may be translated as 'sword', but we must remember that it was a short sword, about 20 inches long, or perhaps a little more, like the Assyrian sword. Illustrations in Egyptian monuments portray a long sword, which was used by the Peoples of the Sea; specimens of this type have been discovered in Greece and in the Aegean, but it was never used by the Israelites. The Philistine Goliath, however, may have had one, which was later wrapped up in a cloak and was quite unique (cf. 1 S 21: 9-10). The sword was carried in a sheath (*nadan* or *ta'ar*, 1 S 17: 51; 1 Ch 21: 27; Jr 47: 6; Ez 21: 8-10) attached to the belt (2 S 20: 8).

Goliath also carried 'between his shoulders' a *kîdôn* of bronze (1 S 17: 6, 45). Josue wielded the same weapon at the battle of Ai (Jos 8: 18-26), and Jeremias said the invaders from the north would use it (Jr 6: 23 = 50: 42). It is usually translated 'javelin', but the Order of the War discovered at Qumran[2] seems to describe the *kîdôn* as a sword one and a half cubits long and four finger-breadths wide. It has been suggested that the late text of Qumran drew its inspiration from the Roman *gladius*, but the meaning would fit the biblical texts also: a type of sword longer and broader than the *ḥereb*, and hung from

1. Cf. p. 196.　　　2. Cf. p. 266.

a cross-belt slung 'between the shoulders'. More probably, however, the *kîdôn* was a scimitar, a *harpe*, like those shown on monuments and discovered in excavations. Certain details of the Order of the War seem to refer to precisely such a weapon. In the biblical texts, the *kîdôn* seems to be an unusual weapon which (except in Jos 8) is never found in the hands of an Israelite. A recent writer has suggested that the Philistine name for a scimitar, the *harpe* in Greek, may be preserved in the expression 'the sons of *hrph*' (2 S 21 : 16, 18, 20, 22): the phrase would then denote a corps whose emblem was a scimitar, whereas the Massoretic vocalization and the ancient versions have all taken it to mean 'sons of Rapha' (as if it were a proper name with the article).

The word *romah* (pike) is often mentioned, but the weapon is never described in detail. Originally, it was simply a pointed stave, but at a very early date a metal head was fixed on by a pin or socket. It was a weapon for hand-to-hand fighting (cf. Nb 25 : 7-8). It is mentioned in the lists of weapons given in 2 Ch 11 : 12; 14: 7; 25: 5; 26: 14; Ne 4: 10; Ez 39: 9 and even in the very old Song of Deborah, Jg 5: 8. According to the Order of the War, it was about seven or eight cubits long, but in biblical times it cannot have been much longer than the height of an average man; this was its length in Egypt and Assyria. In the Order of the War, the socket which held the iron in place is called the *seger*; the term is also found, alongside *ḥanîth*, in Ps 35: 3, where it may well stand (*pars pro toto*) for the pike itself.

The *ḥanîth*, which is usually mentioned in old texts, is not the same as the *romah*. It seems to be a shorter and lighter lance, which could also be thrown like a javelin (cf. 1 S 18: 11; 20: 33, where there is no need to correct the Hebrew text). To balance the weight of the head and to make the throw more accurate, the lower end was iron-shod; the lance could then be stuck in the ground (1 S 26: 7) and its butt could be used as a weapon (cf. perhaps 2 S 2: 23). Specimens have been found in excavations. It was Saul's personal weapon (cf. once more 1 S 19: 9; 22: 6; 26: 7f.; 2 S 1: 6). According to 2 Ch 23: 9, the Temple guards were equipped with it (and 2 K 11: 10 depends, no doubt, on this reference), but it is never mentioned among lists of weapons and, in accounts of wars, it is only once mentioned in the hands of an Israelite (2 S 2: 23). On the other hand, an 'Egyptian' was armed with it (2 S 23: 21), and Goliath carried one (1 S 17: 7; 2 S 21: 19). The wood of this giant's lance was 'like a weaver's *manôr*'. Until recently, this was taken to refer to the size of the lance, as if it were as big as a yarn-beam, that part of a weaving-loom around which the threads are wound. A better explanation has recently been put forward: the *manôr* is the heddle-bar, the wooden rod which supports the heddle by a series of kinks or snarls. Goliath's *ḥanîth* also had a leather thong, rolled round the shaft, with a loop at the end; it made it easier to throw, and increased its range. This method of throwing was known at a very early date in Greece and in Egypt, but the other peoples of the Near East did not know of it; the Israelites therefore described this strange weapon by comparing it with an instrument they knew well. This explanation confirms the view that the *ḥanîth* was used as a projectile.

The *shelaḥ*, by etymology, is also a projectile, and the meaning dart or javelin would suit in 2 S 18: 14 (corrected in the light of the Greek; cf. Jl 2: 8); but in other texts it bears only the general meaning of a weapon carried in the hand (2 Ch 23: 10; 32: 5; Ne 4: 11, 17).

The bow (*qesheth*) is one of the most primitive weapons, both for hunting and for war, but in the Near East it passed through an evolution which we can trace with the help of texts and monuments. To begin with, the bow was simply a piece of pliable wood held bent by a taut string; the wood was later reinforced by ligaments; finally, a bow was invented which was a clever combination of wood and horn, and this had a considerably longer range. It was a splendid weapon, and came into widespread use in the middle of the second millennium B.C., through the influence of the Hyksos; in fact it became the normal weapon in Egypt. Among the Israelites, however, bows were at first used only on a small scale in war. It was Jonathan's weapon (1 S 20: 20; 2 S 1: 22), and it remained the weapon of leaders and kings (2 K 9: 24; 13: 15; Ps 18: 35; 45: 6). Yet neither Saul's army nor David's household guard used bows; at least, there is no mention of it in the Books of Samuel, though 1 Ch 12: 2 mentions some archers of Benjamin among the picked troops of David, and this information should not be lightly disregarded. To keep a balanced view, one should remember that arrow-heads inscribed with the names of their owners and dating from 1300–900 B.C. have been discovered in Phoenicia and in Palestine; this proves that there was a class of professional archers at the time, as there had been two centuries earlier at Ugarit.

The bow probably came into general use in Israel when the chariot force was introduced, for chariot tactics cut out hand-to-hand fighting and demanded the use of long-range weapons (1 S 31: 3 compared with 2 S 1: 6; 1 K 22: 32-34; 2 K 9: 24). The infantry would have been provided with bows as a result of this change, in imitation no doubt of the pattern set by the Assyrian infantry. In the relief of the capture of Lakish by Sennacherib, the ramparts are manned by archers. The statistics of Chronicles record archers on the general strength of the army of Judah only from the time of Ozias (2 Ch 26: 14; cf. Ne 4: 7, 10), but the archers of Benjamin had been famous long before that (1 Ch 8: 40; 12: 2; 2 Ch 14: 7; 17: 17). In a whole series of texts, the sword and bow symbolize every kind of weapon, and, indeed, war itself (Gn 48: 22; Jos 24: 12; 2 K 6: 22; Os 1: 7; 2: 20). David's elegy on Jonathan was used 'to instruct the Judahites in the use of the bow' (2 S 1: 18), *i.e.* for their general military training (cf. the same word in Jg 3: 2 and 2 S 22: 35).

In spite of 2 S 22: 25 = Ps 18: 35 and Jb 20: 24, there was never such a thing as a 'bronze bow': the term refers to the metal coverings of certain bows. The bowstring is called *yether* (Ps 11: 2) or *mêthar* (Ps 21: 13); the same words are also used for tent-ropes, but this does not prove that the same material was used for both purposes, since the primary meaning of the root is simply 'to stretch'. Israel's neighbours used flax cords or plaited hair for bowstrings; they were also made of catgut or, more often, from the nerve-strings of animals. The bow was bent only when action was imminent, by resting the lower part of the wood on the ground, and then pressing it down with the foot: Egyptian illustrations portray the technique, which is called in Hebrew 'stepping on the bow' (*darak qesheth*, Is 5: 28; 21: 15; Jr 46: 9; 50: 14; Ps 7: 13; 11: 2, etc.).

Arrows (*heṣ*) were made of wood, or from reed stems, but in Palestine no specimens have survived from pre-Roman periods. Countless arrow-heads, however, have been preserved. The tips were at first made of bronze, but bronze tips later gave way to iron ones. The shape varied: some were shaped like spear-heads and were fastened to the shaft by a cord as far as a protuberance that is sometimes found on the metal head. This was the only type in service at the beginning of the monarchy, and it never went out of use. Secondly, there were shorter arrows, with a diamond-shaped head, fixed to the shaft by a pin or socket; some had a barb at the side, to prevent the arrow from being pulled out of the wound. At the end of the monarchy, heavy arrows came into use, triangular in shape and designed to pierce armour; at the same period, three-bladed arrow-tips were in use, a type which originated in the north and whose use became general during the Hellenistic period. The same years saw the appearance of flat, barbed arrows. Incendiary arrows were also known (Ps 7: 14), and one of them has been found at Shechem: little holes were pierced in the blades, and oil-soaked tow was packed into them. The bow was carried in the left hand, the arrows in the right (Ez 39: 3) or in a quiver (*'ashpah*: Is 22: 6; 49: 2; Jr 5: 16; Ps 127: 5; Jb 39: 23).

Last of all, the sling (*qela'*) was a thong with a wide centre (the 'palm' of the sling, 1 S 25: 29). It was a simple, primitive weapon, used by shepherds (1 S 17: 40), but it was also a weapon of war (2 K 3: 25; 2 Ch 26: 14). The men of Benjamin had crack slingers who would not miss by a hairsbreadth, with the right hand or left (Jg 20: 16; cf. 1 Ch 12: 2). The stones used in the slings were carefully picked pebbles (1 S 17: 40), except when they were specially trimmed for the purpose (2 Ch 26: 14). They were rounded to the shape of large olives; and some have been unearthed by excavations. During the Hellenistic epoch, slingers used lead balls also.

2. *Defensive arms*

The most common defensive arm was the buckler or shield. It has two names, *magen* and *ṣinnah*, and since these two names occur together in several texts, they must denote two different kinds of shields. According to 1 K 10: 16-17 = 2 Ch 9: 15-16, the *magen* was far smaller than the *ṣinnah*. This is confirmed by 1 S 17: 7, 41 (the *ṣinnah* of Goliath was carried by a servant) and by Ez 26: 8 (where the same word is used for a siege mantelet). This no doubt explains why this type of shield is most often associated with the pike (*romaḥ*) as in 1 Ch 12: 9, 25; 2 Ch 11: 12; 14: 7; 25: 5. It must have been like the enormous covering shield of the Assyrians. The *magen* is mentioned rather with swords and bows (Dt 33: 29; 1 Ch 5: 18; 2 Ch 14: 7; 17: 17; Ps 76: 4). The text of 2 Ch 14: 7 is particularly informative: the men of Judah had the *ṣinnah* and the pike, while the men of Benjamin had the *magen* and the bow. In our terms, this would represent the difference between heavy and light infantry. The *magen* was round-shaped, like the shields fixed on the walls in the bas-relief of Lakish (cf. also Ct 4: 4). The Assyrian infantry and cavalry were equipped in the same way. In Jb 15: 26, there may be a reference to a boss reinforcing the centre of the shield, corresponding to the handle on the other side.

For purposes of parade, there were bronze shields (1 K 14: 27), and shields plated with precious metals (1 K 10: 16-17; cf. 2 S 8: 7), but the shields used in battle were made of leather, coated with fat (2 S 1: 21-22; Is 21: 5) and stained red (Na 2: 4). When not in use, they were kept in housing (Is 22: 6).

Shelet is a rare word, very similar in meaning to *magen*: the two terms are parallel in Ct 4: 4, and cf. Ez 27: 11; and in 2 Ch 23: 9 *magen* is a gloss for the *shelet* of 2 K 11: 10. This last text refers to 2 S 8: 7= 1 Ch 18: 7, which in its turn is similar to 1 K 10: 17, where *magen* is used. It may therefore be translated 'rondache', *i.e.* a small circular shield or buckler; Jr 51: 11 is the only text which seems to raise any difficulty, and it has even led some people to suggest the meaning 'quiver', but the correct translation of the phrase is 'Prepare the rondaches' (cf. the same verb in Za 9: 13).

The helmet was called *koba'* or *qoba'* and this inconsistency in pronunciation reveals the foreign, non-Semitic origin of the word and of what it represented. Goliath wore a bronze helmet (1 S 17: 5), but it is questionable whether Saul had one for David to try on (1 S 17: 38). It is recorded as part of the equipment of foreign troops in Jr 46: 4; Ez 23: 24; 27: 10; 38: 5, and is said to be part of the equipment which Ozias issued to his troops (2 Ch 26: 14). This piece of information has been questioned, but the defenders of Lakish are shown with bronze helmets in the Assyrian bas-relief so often referred to. The only question is whether these helmets were of leather or metal. The crest of a bronze helmet was found during the excavations at Lakish, but there is no doubt that it belonged to an Assyrian soldier; in the same bas-relief, some of the assailants are wearing a helmet with a crest.

The breast-plate (*siryôn* or *shiryôn*) was, like the helmet, of foreign origin. It is almost certain that the Hurrites introduced it into the Near East during the first half of the second millennium B.C. It was made of small plates, first of bronze, later of iron, 'scales' which were sewn on to cloth or leather. According to documents from Nuzu, horses and chariots, as well as men, were equipped with them, and this may be the explanation of the 'iron chariots' of the Canaanites in Jos 17: 16; Jg 1: 19; 4: 3 and 13; cf. perhaps Na 2: 4. These breast-plates were adopted by the Egyptians, and later by the Assyrians, and can be recognized on their monuments; to begin with, they were worn only by charioteers, but eventually the infantry too were issued with them. Some of the assailants of Lakish are shown wearing them, but it is impossible to make out whether they are made of small metal plates or of strips of leather. In Israel, the same development took place. In the early days, Goliath wore a 'breast-plate of scales' (*shiryôn qashqashshîm*: 1 S 17: 5) but he was a foreigner and his equipment was quite unusual anyway; we have already mentioned his sword, unique of its kind, his lance with its leather thong for throwing, and v. 6 says he also wore bronze greaves (literally 'leg-fronts'). There is no evidence that greaves were known in the East at this period, though they were used in the Aegean. Saul's breast-plate is as questionable as his helmet (1 S 17: 38), but it would be normal for Achab to wear a breast-plate in his chariot (1 K 22: 34). Under Ozias, helmets and breast-plates were issued to troops under marching orders for action (2 Ch 26: 14), and they were issued to the defenders of Jerusalem under Nehemias (Ne 4: 10). Bronze or iron scales from such breast-plates have been found in Palestinian excavations. The Greeks and Romans were familiar with this armour, but they also had coats of chain-mail: the soldiers of Antiochus Epiphanes wore them (1 M 6: 35), and this is how the Septuagint translates the armour of Goliath.

CHAPTER FOUR

WAR

1. *A short military history of Israel*

THE first wars in which Israel took part were wars of conquest, and biblical tradition shows the people taking possession of the Promised Land by force of arms and with the help of God. The defeat of Sihon, king of Heshbon, and of Og, king of Bashan (Nb 21: 21-35), and the campaign against Midian (Nb 31: 1-12) secured a territory for Reuben, Gad and half the tribe of Manasseh. The Book of Josue describes the occupation of Palestine west of the Jordan as a military operation in three sweeping actions: first, the people cross the Jordan and cut their way through to the very heart of the land (Jos 1-9); next, a coalition of five Canaanite kings from the south is overthrown and the whole of southern Palestine occupied (Jos 10); finally, the northern kings are defeated at Merom and their cities fall into the hands of the Israelites (Jos 11). It is quite certain that this is an extremely simplified version of what really happened, that the actions of the tribes were less concentrated and far slower and that they did not all meet with equal success (cf. Jos 15: 13-17; Jg 1). It is also true that the Israelites infiltrated in a peaceful manner wherever they could; but they did meet opposition, which they had to overcome by force of arms.

The wars in the period of the Judges, and under Saul, were defensive wars. The Israelites first had to withstand the counter-attacks of the Canaanites and of those other peoples out of whose lands they had carved their territory; later they had to fight against the Philistines, who were making inroads from the coast. The reign of David, on the other hand, was a period of reconquest and, later, of expansion. We are not fully informed of the reasons for David's wars. He declared war on the Ammonites because they had insulted his ambassadors (2 S 10: 1-5), and on the Aramaeans for going to the help of the Ammonites (2 S 10: 6-19; cf. 8: 3-6). We do not know what provoked the wars against Moab (2 S 8: 2) and Edom (2 S 8: 13). The bravado of the Ammonites and the eagerness with which the Aramaeans went to their aid show that the neighbouring States were growing anxious about the increasing power of Israel. But they also show that they underestimated the ability of its new leader, and it could well be that their provocation and the Israelite victories led David to adopt a policy of conquest of which he had never dreamed.

The territory he conquered was badly defended by his successors. The Ammonites declared themselves independent as soon as David was dead, and Solomon took no action when part of Edom and Aram broke away from his empire (1 K 11: 14-25); indeed, Solomon did not fight a single war. On the death of Achab, the king of Moab revolted, and even a punitive expedition by the king of Israel, with assistance from the king of Judah and his Edomite vassal, did not bring Moab back to obedience (2 K 3: 4-27). Shortly afterwards, Edom shook off the domination of Judah, after a disastrous campaign by Joram (2 K 8: 20-22).

After the schism, the artificial frontier between Israel and Judah led to conflict between the brother-kingdoms under Basha and Asa (1 K 15: 16-22), under Joas and Amasias (2 K 14: 8-14), and, for the last time, under Achaz and Peqah (the Syro-Ephraimite War: 2 K 16: 5; 2 Ch 28: 5-8). And yet both kingdoms had quite enough to do defending their own territory against foreign pressure. Roboam avoided a war with the Pharaoh Sheshonq by surrendering the treasures of the Temple and palace (1 K 14: 25-26), but in later ages, until Josias, Egypt was more often a worthless ally than an enemy. On the Philistine frontier, there was fighting under Joram (2 K 8: 22; 2 Ch 21: 16), Ozias (2 Ch 26: 6), Achaz (2 Ch 28: 18), and Ezechias (2 K 18: 8); but we have little information about it, except that Judah was sometimes the victor, sometimes defeated. Judah fought against Edom for the possession of Elath (2 K 14: 7 and 22; 16: 6) in order to keep open the trade route to the Red Sea and Arabia.

The kingdom of Israel, too, had a common frontier with the Philistines in the south-west. Gibbethon, a Philistine stronghold which constituted a threat to Gezer, was besieged by Nadab and by Omri (1 K 15: 27; 16: 15). Later still, Isaias pictures Israel hemmed in by the Philistines and the Aramaeans, both equally rapacious (Is 9: 11). The Aramaeans of Damascus were for generations an enemy to be feared. Israel was at war with them for almost the whole of the ninth century B.C.; sometimes Israel gained the upper hand, but more often victory went to the Aramaeans. The main prize of these wars was the possession of what remained of David's Aramaean possessions in Transjordan (cf. the battles before Ramoth Gilead in 1 K 22: 3, 29; 2 K 8: 28; 9: 1f.) and the districts of northern Galilee (1 K 15: 20; cf. 20: 34). Twice the Aramaeans laid siege to Samaria (1 K 20: 1f.; 2 K 6: 24f.). Hazael of Damascus even tried to gain complete control of Israel and nearly succeeded (2 K 10: 32-33; 12: 18; 13: 3, 7). The situation was stabilized under Joas (2 K 13: 25) and Jeroboam II (2 K 14: 25), but only because the power of Damascus had been crushed by the Assyrians.

The Assyrians, however, were a still more formidable enemy. When Shalmaneser II made his appearance in central Syria, a coalition tried to stop him, and in 853 B.C. Achab took part in the battle of Qarqar, in the valley of the Orontes, with 2,000 chariots and 18,000 infantrymen. The strange thing is that this expedition, the only really distant one undertaken by an Israelite army, is not mentioned in the Bible and is known to us only through cuneiform documents. Only twelve years later, in 841, Jehu agreed, without making any show of resistance, to pay tribute. In the following century, during the second· great Assyrian thrust under Tiglath-Pileser III, Menahem declared himself a vassal in 738 (2 K 15: 19-20) but in 734-732 the king of Assyria occupied the greater part of the territory of Israel without meeting any serious opposition (2 K 15: 29). The end came in 724, when Shalmaneser V laid siege to Samaria; though its king had been taken prisoner, the city held out until the beginning of 721.

At the time of Tiglath-Pileser's attack, the kings of Aram and Israel tried to persuade Achaz of Judah to join them in their struggle against Assyria; when Achaz refused, they laid siege to Jerusalem: this was the 'Syro-Ephraimite' War. Achaz then appealed for help to Assyria, and Judah became, without a fight, the vassal of Assyria (2 K 16: 5-9; Is 7-8). Ezechias tried to throw off the yoke, by taking advantage of a general revolt against Assyria. He allied himself with the coastal states and with the still more distant states of Egypt and Babylon. Sennacherib's reply was terrible: in 701, every town in Judah was captured, in spite of their resistance (which Assyrian documents record); they were handed over to the king of Philistia, who had remained true to Sennacherib. Jerusalem alone was saved (2 K 18: 13-19: 37; Is 36-37). We do not know how Ezechias and his son Manasseh made good these losses, but we do know that Judah remained a vassal-state of Assyria. When the power of Assyria had declined, Josias threw off the yoke and freed not only the territory of Judah but even part of the former territory of Israel as well (cf. 2 K 23: 15-20). At that time the supremacy of Assyria was crumbling everywhere, and perhaps he did not need to resort to force to achieve this reconquest. The Bible, preoccupied with his religious policy only, does not mention any military action in this context. On the other hand, when the Pharaoh Nechao went to the help of the last king of Assyria, who had been cornered by the Babylonians and Medes, Josias tried to stop him at the pass of Megiddo, in 609: he did not want to see Assyria reprieved, or Palestine falling into the clutches of Egypt. The battle was a short one, and Josias was mortally wounded (2 Ch 35: 20-25; which is more detailed than 2 K 23: 29-30). Nechao annexed Palestine and installed a vassal king, Joiaqim. But the overlordship of Egypt did not last for long. After the defeat of the Egyptians at Charchemish in 605, all Syria-Palestine fell into the hands of the Babylonians, and Judah became one of their vassals. Joiaqim tried to break away, and thereby stung Nabuchodonosor into reprisals. The pace of events quickened: first siege of Jerusalem in 597, the installation of Sedecias as king, his revolt, second siege (interrupted for a moment as a result of Egyptian intervention), and the final ruin of Jerusalem in 587 (cf. 2 K 24: 1-25: 21, and scattered references in Jr). The biblical narratives describe only what took place in Jerusalem, but we know that operations went on elsewhere. According to Jr 34: 1 and 7, Lakish and Azeqah were still holding out during the siege of Jerusalem. Excavations at Tell ed-Duweir (Lakish) provide evidence of the destruction of the town suffered during the two Chaldean invasions, and of the rebuilding of the defences in the meantime. The ostraka found there give some idea of the activity just before the second siege: arranging liaison with Jerusalem, exchange of signals between towns, sending a mission to Egypt.

Seen as a whole, the military history of Israel under the monarchy clearly shows that the era of wars of conquest begins and ends under David. After David, all the wars were defensive wars, rarely and by way of exception to bring a vassal back to obedience or to keep a trade route open, more often to protect or to establish a frontier; in the end they were all attempts to resist expansionist policies of the great powers. Even Achab at Qarqar and Josias at Megiddo wanted only to safeguard the integrity of their country.

For several centuries the Jews were subject to foreign masters, but in the end they revolted. The rebellion broke out under Antiochus Epiphanes, who wanted to lend unity to his empire by imposing Greek culture everywhere; in contrast with all his predecessors, he refused to allow the Jews to live according to their own law. The War of Independence under the Maccabees was therefore a religious war, and we shall have to consider it later under this aspect.[1] Here we are concerned only with its peculiar military characteristics. To begin with, it was conducted as guerilla warfare, with small groups harassing the Seleucid garrisons and the reinforcements sent to them, but Judas Maccabee very soon appealed to all the people of Israel and organized the army on the old traditional lines (1 M 3: 55-56). It was a war of mobile forces, with operations extending, sometimes at one and the same time, from south of Hebron to Galilee, and from the Mediterranean coast to Transjordan. The strongholds which held out were soon reduced, thanks to the new techniques of investment which the Jews learnt from their enemies. Religious freedom was once more achieved (1 M 6: 57-60), but Judas knew it would never be secure unless the nation became independent, and he went on with the fight. Under his brother Simon, the Jews finally achieved national independence, and 'the yoke of the nations was lifted off Israel' (1 M 13: 41).

2. The conduct of war

We said above that, before the time of David, war was conducted by the people's taking up arms.[2] Our present task is to see (as far as the documents will allow us) what strategy and tactics were followed by the organized army of monarchical times.

There was no declaration of war. The nearest approach to one is the challenge flung down by Amasias of Judah to Joas of Israel: 'Come and let us

1. Cf. p. 265.   2. Cf. pp. 215-218.

test our strength!' (2 K 14: 8), but it is unusual. The customs of those ages were different from ours: only when a commander had pitched his camp in enemy country and shown his power would he lay down conditions, the refusal of which would unleash hostilities (1 S 11: 1f.; 1 K 20: 1f.; cf. Dt 20: 10-12)[1]; but the war had already begun.

The accounts of wars provide no details about mobilization. They merely state that the king 'collected' the army or the people (1 K 20: 1; 2 K 6: 24), that he 'made a census' of them or 'reviewed' them (1 K 20: 27; 2 K 3: 6). This was simple enough with the professional army, but not so easy with the conscripts. In the days when the whole people took up arms, they used to send round messengers or to blow a trumpet.[2] In the next period certain texts presume that a trumpet was blown and a signal (the *nes*[3]) set up. In Jr 51: 27, the mobilization of the nations against Babylon is described thus:

> Raise a signal throughout the world,
> blow the trumpet among the nations!
> Consecrate nations against her,
> Gather kingdoms against her...
> Appoint a recruiting sergeant against her!

Most of Israel's wars, however, were defensive, not aggressive, and so when the prophets speak of the trumpet-sound or the setting up of a signal, they are predicting an invasion, and warning their countrymen of imminent danger: it is an alarm signal in the strict sense, a call to arms or to flight (Jr 4: 5-6; 6: 1; Os 5: 8; Am 3: 6; cf. Jl 2: 1). In the quotation from Jr 51: 27 'recruiting sergeant' is a translation of the word *ṭipsar*, which is simply a Hebrew naturalization of the Akkadian *ṭupsharru*, meaning 'scribe'. In this text it refers to the official in charge of conscription, usually called in Hebrew the *sôpher*, 'the secretary who enlists the people of the country (2 K 25: 19) or the *shôṭer*, the 'clerk' who, according to Dt 20: 5-8, gave public notice of exemptions from service.[4]

According to 2 S 11: 1 and its parallel (1 Ch 20: 1), 'the time when kings begin their campaigns' is 'the turn of the year', that is, spring.[5] In fact, almost all the Assyrian campaigns whose dates are known with precision began between April and June; in the Neo-Babylonian period, the dates stretch on to autumn and sometimes even into the winter, according to the needs of the operations. It was natural enough to choose the beginning of the good weather, whenever possible, for the roads were then in good condition; hence there were no complications over transport or camping. Supplies, too, were easily arranged, for the army would arrive in enemy territory just after the cereal harvests. All this, of course, is true of a professional army, but it must have been much harder to mobilize peasants just at the heaviest period of work in the fields, from the harvest to seed-time.

1. Cf. p. 236.   2. Cf. p. 215.   3. Cf. p. 227.   4. Cf. p. 225.   5. Cf. p. 190.

We have little information on strategy. The Hittites and the Canaanites, it seems, generally tried to draw the enemy far away from his bases and to come to grips near a strong position where their chariots could launch a surprise attack; the bulk of the army was held in reserve to exploit the success or to retreat in good order. This was how the battles of Megiddo (against Thutmoses III) and of Qadesh (against Ramses II) developed. Perhaps Josias was trying to put this old strategy into practice when he allowed Nechao to advance as far as Megiddo; when the first attack, led by the king in person, was repulsed, the Israelite army withdrew (2 K 23: 29-30; 2 Ch 35 20-24).

2 S 11: 11 tells us that during David's war against the Ammonites, the national army was *bassukkôth* with the Ark, while the professional army was encamped before Rabbah. According to 1 K 20: 12, 16, Ben-hadad and the kings allied with him got drunk *bassukkôth* while the envoys were negotiating with Achab in Samaria and the young cadets making their successful sortie. The usual translation is 'in the huts', *i.e.* in the camp pitched before Rabbah or Samaria. One writer has recently suggested the translation 'at Sukkoth', on the supposition that Ben-hadad or David had established a 'strategic advanced base' in the Jordan valley, where the bulk of the army was held in reserve. It is an interesting hypothesis, but it seems unlikely that these old stories reflect such a modern concept of strategy. The text of 1 K 20: 1, 12-13, 20 takes it for granted that Ben-hadad and his army are camped very near Samaria. And the immediate context of 2 S 11: 11 favours the ordinary translation: Uriah refuses to go home as long as the Ark and the people are living in huts, and while his comrades in the household guard are camping in the open air.

The war against Moab (2 K 3: 4-27) gives a fine example of an indirect attack: the king of Israel, instead of attacking Mesha on their common frontier north of the Arnon, persuades the king of Judah to make an alliance with him. Then by a long turning movement across Judah and Edom, he invades the territory of Moab from the south and marches on to the capital, systematically destroying everything in his path. David had used the same strategy against the Philistines, though on a smaller scale (2 S 5: 23).

Our information about combat tactics is equally incomplete. Clearly, tactics would vary with the arms and the troops employed: it depended on whether chariots were used or not, whether the professional troops were engaged alone, or the conscripts alone, or both together. If both were used together, the professional soldiers fought in the front line and led the attack, while the conscripts were held as uncommitted reserves: these tactics were employed in the Ammonite war under David and in the Aramaean wars under Achab.[1] In mobile warfare, or when a surprise attack was to be made on a camp, the commander divided his force into three assault corps (Jg 7: 16; 9: 43; 1 S 11: 11; 2 S 18: 2; cf. the Philistines also in 1 S 13: 17). Alternatively,

1. Cf. p. 221.

instead of this encircling manœuvre, a detachment might be despatched to attack the enemy from the rear (2 Ch 13: 13-15). If a good general were thus attacked from behind, he would continue to fight on both fronts while keeping his two combat forces in close liaison to give each other support (2 S 10: 8-11).

The baggage was left with guards or reserves behind the fighting line or at the departure point (1 S 17: 22; 25: 13; 30: 24; cf. vv. 9-10). According to the Hebrew text of 1 K 20: 27 (missing in the Greek and often suppressed by critics), the army was equipped with supplies before its departure; the supplies were taken from depots (*misk°nôth*), which are mentioned alongside chariot garrisons under Solomon (1 K 9: 19) and alongside citadels under Josaphat (2 Ch 17: 12). We do not know how the army in the field received its supplies. David, as a young boy, brought parched corn and loaves to his brothers at the battle front (1 S 17: 17), but as a rule the troops had to live off the land as they went. Sometimes the inhabitants would bring victuals (2 S 16: 1f.; 17: 27-29; 19: 33), and sometimes the army would requisition them (Jg 8: 4f.; 1 S 25: 7-18). An Egyptian papyrus gives a vivid description of these same methods, which the Egyptian army used in Canaan; but it would be rash to use this text, combined with 1 S 25: 18, to estimate the daily ration of an Israelite soldier.

Liaison was maintained by orderlies, on foot (Jg 9: 31; 2 S 11: 19; 18: 19) or mounted (2 K 9: 17f.). But they also used signals: the *mas°°eth* was a fire kindled on a height, whose smoke or light could be seen far away and which gave a signal agreed on beforehand (Jg 20: 38) or a simple warning (Jr 6: 1). An ostrakon found at Lakish is most explicit: 'We are watching the signals (*ms't*) of Lakish according to my Lord's orders, for we cannot see Azeqah': there must have been a code, then, to interpret these signals. In the tradition about the Exodus and the stay in the desert, the cloud of light which revealed the presence of Yahweh gave the people the signals for marching and camping, and they are represented as an army in the field (Ex 13: 21-22; Nb 9: 15-23). 'They camped on Yahweh's orders and struck camp on Yahweh's orders' (Nb 9: 20, 23).

Trumpets were also used for signalling. Immediately after the passage about the cloud of light, Nb 10: 1-10 mentions the two silver trumpets (*ḥaṣoṣ°rah*), which were used to call the assembly together and to accompany worship; but they were also used to give the order to break camp, and they were to be used for departure for battle. They were in fact carried by the priest Phinehas when Israel opened its campaign against Midian (Nb 31: 6). Similarly, according to 2 Ch 13: 12-15, the priests sounded the trumpet in the war between Abiyyah and Jeroboam. In Os 5: 8, the trumpet stands in a parallel with the horn (*shôpar*, strictly, a ram's horn); in another ancient text, the *shôpar* alone is mentioned, playing the part which the late passages just cited ascribe to the trumpet. The horn was a signal for mobilization or rallying (Jg 3: 27; 6: 34; 1 S 13: 3; 2 S 20: 1). Not to hear the sound of the horn is a synonym for being threatened with war no longer (Jr 42: 14). But the horn was also used to order the cessation of hostilities (2 S 18: 16; 20: 22).

When the battle was about to commence, the *shôpar* gave the signal to shout the battle-cry (Jos 6: 5f.; Jg 7: 16f.); the *ḥaṣoṣ'rah* also is said to be used for this (Nb 10: 9; 2 Ch 13: 12-15). This battle-cry (*t'rû'ah*: cf. also the corresponding noun and verb in 1 S 17: 20, 52; Jr 4: 19; 20: 16; 49: 2; Ez 21: 27; Os 5: 8; Am 1: 14; 2: 2) was originally a savage shout meant to inspire the ranks and to strike fear into the enemy. But it was also a religious cry, closely bound up with the rôle of the Ark in fighting (cf. 1 S 4: 5f.[1]); it then became part of the ritual surrounding the Ark (2 S 6: 15), and finally passed into the Temple liturgy (Lv 23: 24; Nb 29: 1) and certain Psalms.

3. The consequences of war

There is 'a time for war and a time for peace' (Qo 3: 8). The word *shalôm*, peace, used in a political sense, means not only the absence of war, in a purely negative sense, but includes the idea of friendly relations between two peoples, just as, in other contexts, it means friendly relations between two individuals (Jg 4: 17; 1 S 7: 14; 1 K 5: 4, 26; 22: 45; cf. Gn 34: 21; 1 Ch 12: 18). These relations would be guaranteed by a pact or treaty (*b'rîth*: 1 K 5: 26), and breaking the treaty is the equivalent of going to war (1 K 15: 19-20; cf. Is 33: 7-8).

Conversely, war ends by the establishment of peace, and this peace is the fruit of victory; to return 'in peace' from a campaign is a synonym for 'to return victorious' (Jg 8: 9; 2 S 19: 25, 31; 1 K 22: 27-28; Jr 43: 12). The peace was sealed by the conclusion, or the renewal of a treaty. For example, when Ben-hadad had been defeated at Apheq, he sued for peace, offering to return to Achab the Israelite towns occupied by his forces, and to allow the Israelites to open bazaars at Damascus like those the Aramaeans had at Samaria: Achab then signed a treaty with him (1 K 20: 34). Ben-hadad had first sent messengers (1 K 20: 32); they are the 'messengers of peace' (Is 33: 7). The victor too could propose peace (Jg 21: 13). These offers of, or requests for, peace could be made even before the commencement of hostilities, if the superior power of one party made the issue virtually certain: thus the Gibeonites sought to make a treaty with Josue, and the latter granted them peace and a treaty (Jos 9: 6, 15). The inhabitants of Yabesh asked Nahash for a treaty when he pitched camp before their town (1 S 11: 1); and Deuteronomy lays down that peace terms must be offered to a foreign city before it is attacked (Dt 20: 10).

In these three instances, the weaker party, if it accepted the peace-terms, was reduced to slavery. The outcome of a victorious war was always conquest by one side and vassaldom for the other: *e.g.* David against Aram,

1. Cf. p. 259.

Edom, Moab and Ammon, or the Assyrians against Israel, or Sennacherib, Nechao and Nabuchodonosor against Judah. In their accounts of these wars, the historical books of the Bible never mention a treaty imposed by the victor, but Ez 17: 13-21 states it clearly of Sedecias: Nabuchodonosor had made a treaty (*b'rîth*) with him, which Sedecias had confirmed with an imprecatory oath; later, Sedecias had broken the treaty, and his oath (cf. 2 K 24: 17, 20*b*). Similarly, Os 12: 2: 'They have made a *b'rîth* with Assyria, but they are taking oil to Egypt', refers to the policy of the last king of Samaria, a vassal of Shalmaneser, who turned to Egypt for help (cf. 2 K 17: 3-4). Lastly, Is 33: 8: 'They broke the *b'rîth*', refers, according to some exegetes, to the pact between Sennacherib and Ezechias. Such treaties existed even when victory was not overwhelming, *e.g.* those between Hittite and Assyrian kings and their vassals in Syria, copies of which have survived. The obligations of a defeated enemy who accepted vassaldom had to be fixed, and among these was the tribute he had to pay. The usual term for tribute is *minḥah*, a 'present', but the amount was fixed by the suzerain (2 K 18: 14; 23: 33; 2 Ch 27: 5), and withholding payment was equivalent to revolt (2 K 3: 4-5; 17: 4).

The laws of war were crude. The Annals of the kings of Assyria have a constant refrain of towns destroyed, dismantled or burnt, levelled as if by a hurricane, or reduced to a heap of rubble. It was the usual custom also in biblical wars, from a period of the Judges to the time of the Maccabees; it made no difference whether the Israelites were attacking other towns or Israelite towns were being captured by invaders (Jg 9: 45; 20: 48; 2 S 17: 13; 1 K 20: 10; 2 K 3: 25; 8: 12; 25: 9-10; 1 M 5: 35; 11: 48; 16: 10). At the very least, the fortifications were dismantled (2 K 14: 13).

Yet war had to bring profit to someone. Before being burnt, conquered towns were pillaged (2 S 8: 8; 12: 30; 2 K 14: 14; 25: 13f.; 1 M 5: 28, 35, etc.); a camp abandoned by the enemy would be pillaged (2 K 7: 16; 1 M 4: 23); flocks were carried off as booty (1 S 14: 32; 27: 9; 30: 20); even the dead were stripped of everything worth while on the very field of battle (1 S 31: 8); the victors took away everything they could carry (2 Ch 20: 25; cf. Dt 20: 14). The appetite for plunder and for the joy it brought (1 S 30: 16) was a spur to the combatants (2 K 3: 23), but there was a danger that the soldiers might take to plundering instead of exploiting their victory (1 S 14: 24; 1 M 4: 17-18). Few pleasures were accounted comparable to that of sharing in the distribution of booty (Is 9: 2; Ps 119: 162). This was how the fighting men made themselves rich, for they had no other way: Yahweh promised Nabuchodonosor the riches of Egypt as wages for his army (Ez 29: 19).

The story of 1 K 20: 39-40 could mean that every man had a right to what he himself laid hands on: a man had captured a prisoner whom he had left a comrade to guard: if the latter let him escape, he had either to take his place or to pay a large fine (cf. Jos 7: 21; 2 K 7: 8, though in these two texts, for different reasons, such behaviour is frowned on). From very ancient times, the custom was to collect and then to share out the booty (Jg 5: 30; cf. Is 9: 2; Pr 16: 19). A law is ascribed to Moses according to which the booty had to be divided equally, one half for the fighting men and the other half for the rest of the community, after both parts had been subjected to a tax for the Levites (Nb 31: 26-47). David introduced the rule that the men left behind to guard the baggage should share the spoil along with the fighting men (1 S 30: 24-25). In the early wars of Israel, the leader had a special portion which his men left him of their own free will (Jg 8: 24-25; perhaps 1 S 30: 20). Later on the king reserved the most valuable articles for himself or for the treasury of the sanctuary (2 S 8: 7-8, 11; 12: 30). In a confederate army, the allies had a right to share the booty (cf. Gn 14: 24), the amount of which was probably agreed upon beforehand, as it was among other ancient peoples.

People, as well as things, fell into the hands of the victor. The historical books of the Bible record instances of barbarous treatment meted out to defeated enemies: under Josue, five Canaanite kings were trampled under-foot and put to death (Jos 10: 24-26); Adoni-Sedeq had his thumbs and big toes cut off (Jg 1: 6); under Gideon, the Midianite leaders were beheaded (Jg 7: 25). When David went raiding in the Negeb, he killed every single man and woman (1 S 27: 9, 11); he massacred all the Amalekites who fell into his hands (1 S 30: 17), and put to death two-thirds of the population of Moab (2 S 8: 2). Amasias executed 10,000 Edomite prisoners of war (2 Ch 25: 12), and the law of Dt 20: 12-13 lays down that if a city refuses to surrender, every male in it shall be put to death. But these instances are exceptional, and the law of Dt was purely theoretical.[1] Apart from the *herem* in a holy war which involved all living beings,[2] the massacre of prisoners was never a general rule, nor were the tortures of which Assyrian texts and monuments offer only too many examples. Even Gideon, in his day, would have spared Zebah and Salmunna if he had not been bound by the law of blood-vengeance (Jg 8: 18-21), and the kings of Israel had a reputation for mercy (1 K 20: 31): they did not kill their prisoners of war (2 K 6: 22—which need not be corrected).

The reasons for this conduct were not purely humanitarian. The last two texts do not clearly state that this was the motive, and Dt 20: 19 seems to exclude the idea, when it says that trees should be spared because they are not men. Self-interest would counsel moderation, for both the community and the individual stood to gain by keeping enemy prisoners alive. They would pay tribute, could be used for forced labour, or as public slaves, or as Temple slaves; they could even be sold as slaves to private individuals. We said above that in Israel, as among other ancient peoples, war was one of the sources of the slave-supply,[3] and that, in all probability, prisoners of war became public slaves in the service of the king or the sanctuary.[4]

---

1. Cf. p. 81.   2. It will be studied in the next chapter, cf. pp. 260-261.
3. Cf. pp. 80-81.   4. Cf. pp. 88-90.

The short story in 1 K 20: 39 states that the soldier really meant to keep the prisoner as his own slave. According to Jl 4: 3, the nations drew lots for the people of Yahweh and sold the boys and girls. We are better informed about women captured in war. The soldiers of Sisera, if they had won the battle, could have had 'a young girl, or two young girls, for each warrior' (Jg 5: 30). According to Nb 31: 18, 27 after the campaign against Midian the women who were virgins were divided between the fighting men and the rest of the people. The law of Dt 21: 10-14 authorizes an Israelite to marry a woman captured in war,[1] but she thereby ceases to be a slave, 'puts off her captive's robes' and (though she may be divorced) may never be sold. This presumes that if a female prisoner is not taken to wife by her master, she remains a slave.

Lastly, political reasons led first the Assyrians and then the Babylonians to substitute deportation for enslavement, and whole populations were deported, as they had previously been enslaved. The Israelites never had an opportunity to copy this practice, but they suffered from it: the inhabitants of the northern kingdom were deported *en masse* after the conquests of Tiglath-Pilesar (2 K 15: 29) and after the fall of Samaria (2 K 17: 6). Part of the population of Judah was deported after each of the two sieges of Jerusalem by Nabuchodonosor (2 K 24: 14f.; 25: 11; Jr 52: 27-30). At the beginning of the Exile, their lot was an unenviable one, but at least they were not slaves.

1. Cf. p. 81.

CHAPTER FIVE

THE HOLY WAR

AMONG all the peoples of antiquity, war was linked with religion. It was begun at the command of the gods, or at least with their approval, manifested by omens; it was accompanied by sacrifices, and conducted with the help of the gods who ensured victory, for which they were thanked by an offering of part of the booty. In antiquity, then, every war was a holy war, in a broad sense. More strictly, the Greeks gave the name of 'holy wars' (ἱεροὶ πόλεμοι) to those which the amphictyony of Delphi conducted against any of its members who had violated the sacred rights of Apollo. More strictly still, the holy war of Islam, the *jihad*, is the duty incumbent upon every Moslem to spread his faith by force of arms.

This last notion of a holy war is utterly foreign to Israel. It is incompatible with the idea of Yahwism as the particular religion and the peculiar possession of the chosen people. But, precisely because of this essential relation between the people and its God, all the institutions of Israel were invested with a sacred character, war just as much as kingship or legislation. This does not mean that every war was a religious war—a concept which does not appear until very late, under the Maccabees: Israel did not fight for its faith, but for its existence. This means that war is a sacred action, with its own particular ideology and rites; this ideology, these rites, give it a specific character of its own, and single it out among the other wars of antiquity, where the religious aspect was something accessory. Such was the primitive concept of war in Israel but (as with kingship), this sacral character faded into the background and war became a 'profane' thing. Nevertheless, it did retain a religious character for a long time; the old ideal survived, sometimes modified, sometimes taking on a new lease of life in particular surroundings or at particular times. We shall attempt to trace the evolution of this process.

1. *The concept of the holy war, and its rites*

When the people took up arms they were called the people of Yahweh or the people of God (Jg 5: 13; 20: 2), the troops of God (1 S 17: 26), or the armies of Yahweh (Ex 12: 41; cf. 7: 4). The combatants had to be in a state of ritual cleanliness, *i.e.* 'made holy' (Jos 3: 5; cf. Jr 6: 4; 22: 7; Jl 4: 9). They were bound to remain continent (1 S 21: 6; 2 S 11: 11), and this obligation of cleanliness extended to the camp, which had to be kept 'holy' if Yahweh was to encamp with his troops (Dt 23: 10-15).

The reason is that the wars of Israel were the wars of Yahweh (1 S 18: 17; 25: 28), and the national epic was sung of in the 'Book of the Wars of Yahweh' (Nb 21: 14), a book no longer extant. The enemies of Israel were the enemies of Yahweh (Jg 5: 31; 1 S 30: 26; cf. Ex 17: 16). Before marching out to battle a sacrifice was offered to Yahweh (1 S 7: 9; 13: 9, 12); most important of all, Yahweh was consulted (Jg 20: 23, 28; 1 S 14: 37; 23: 2, 4) by means of the ephod and sacred lots (1 S 23: 9f.; 30: 7f.) and he decided when to go to war. He himself marched in the van of the army (Jg 4: 14; 2 S 5: 24; cf. Dt 20: 4).

The visible sign of this presence of Yahweh was the Ark. Tradition told how it had been with the people during their many wanderings in the desert, wanderings which are represented as the marches of an army on the move, and Nb 10: 35-36 has preserved some ancient battle-cries. When the Ark was leaving, they shouted: 'Arise, Yahweh, and let thy enemies be scattered . . .', and when it came to rest: 'Return, Yahweh, to the countless thousands of Israel.' It had led the Israelites across the Jordan, when they themselves had been 'sanctified' for the war of conquest (Jos 3: 6), and had been carried in solemn procession around the walls of Jericho (Jos 6: 6f.). Even under David, the Ark was in the camp with all Israel in front of Rabbath Ammon (2 S 11: 11). The history of the battle of Apheq is particularly instructive (1 S 4). The success of the Philistines is attributed to the absence of the Ark; so it is brought from Shiloh and the Philistines deduce that 'God has come into the camp'. This time, however, the Ark does not bring victory; worse, it is itself captured by the enemy, and this capture is felt as an inexplicable disaster, more painful than the massacre of the army itself.

When the Ark arrived at Apheq, the Israelites had raised the battle-cry, the t'rû'ah (1 S 4: 5f.), which was the signal for battle,[1] but this cry was also part of the ritual surrounding the Ark (2 S 6: 15) and was a religious cry. It is not quite so certain that the title Yahweh Sabaoth should be connected with the Ark and its rôle as a *palladium* in the wars of Israel, though the assertion is often made. This title seems to stem originally from the sanctuary of Shiloh,[2] but not strictly with reference to the Ark which was kept there; besides, it is not certain that Yhwh S'ba'ôth means 'Yahweh of the armies' (of Israel), or that the title had any connection whatever with the military institutions of Israel or with their religious aspect.

The combatants in a holy war left home with the certainty of victory, for 'Yahweh had' already 'given the enemy into their hands' (Jos 6: 2; 8: 1, 18; Jg 3: 28; 4: 7; 7: 9, 15; 1 S 23: 4; 24: 5, etc.). Faith was an indispensable condition: they had to have faith and to be without fear (Jos 8: 1; 10: 8, 25). Those who were afraid did not have the necessary religious dispositions and

1. Cf. p. 254.   2. Cf. p. 304.

were to be sent away (Jg 7: 3; cf. Dt 20: 8, where the dismissal of such men is explained by a psychological reason, which was not the original reason for the custom).

During battle, it was Yahweh who fought for Israel (Jos 10: 14, 42; Jg 20: 35). He called into service the elements of nature (Jos 10: 11; 24: 7; Jg 5: 20; 1 S 7: 10) and threw the enemy into confusion (Jg 4: 15; 7: 22; 1 S 7: 10; 14: 20), striking a 'divine terror' into them (1 S 14: 15).

But victory was neither the last act of the holy war nor its culmination. This occurs in the *ḥerem*, the anathema carried out on the vanquished enemy and his goods. The meaning of the root and the usage of the cognate verb show that the word *ḥerem* denotes the fact of 'separating' something, of taking it out of profane use and reserving it for a sacred use; alternatively, it may stand for the thing which is 'separated' in this way, forbidden to man and consecretated to God. The term found its way into the general vocabulary of worship (Nb 18: 14; Lv 27: 21, 28; Ez 44: 29), but originally it belonged to the ritual of the holy war: it meant leaving to God the fruits of victory. The precise form of this varies in different texts. As a general rule, the *ḥerem* originates from an order of Yahweh (Dt 7: 2; 20: 17; Jos 8: 2; 1 S 15: 3); by way of exception, it may be the result of a vow by the people (Nb 21: 2). In theory, it admits of no exception whatsoever: at Jericho, all living things, men and beasts, had to be put to death, the town and all its movables were burnt, the metal objects consecrated to Yahweh (Jos 6: 18-24). Akan, by transgressing the *ḥerem*, brought down a curse upon the people; he was therefore punished and the goods he had stolen were destroyed (Jos 7). In Saul's war against the Amalekites (1 S 15), too, the anathema was to admit of no exception and Saul was condemned for not having interpreted it strictly. The destruction of cultic objects in the towns of Canaan is explicitly prescribed in Dt 7: 5, 25. The *ḥerem* was to be applied with the utmost rigour against any Israelite town which had denied Yahweh (Dt 13: 13-18). Elsewhere, however, the *ḥerem* was more or less restricted: it applied to all human beings, but the cattle and movable goods could be kept as booty (Dt 2: 34-35; 3: 6-7 and probably 20: 16; Jos 8: 2, 27; 11: 14 and probably 10: 28f.); sometimes women who were virgins might be excepted (Nb 31: 14-18; Jg 21: 11, though in these two references a special reason is given). When a foreign town was captured, only the male population was put to death (Dt 20: 14, but here the word *ḥerem* is not found and the text does not refer to a holy war, in contrast with the reference to towns in the Holy Land, Dt 20: 16-17).

It is hard to say to what extent these prescriptions were in fact applied. It is remarkable that they should be laid down in Deuteronomy, published at a period when the holy war was little more than a memory, and that the concrete examples should be found in the Book of Josue, the final redaction of which is equally late. On the other hand, neither the word nor the custom is found in the stories of the Judges, who really did conduct holy wars. Yet there is no doubt that both the notion and the practice of the *ḥerem* are of great antiquity. They are found in the old story of the war of the tribes against Benjamin (Jg 21: 11), and in the prophetical tradition about Saul's war against the Amalekites (1 S 15). In addition, we have one parallel from outside the Bible: Mesha, king of Moab in the ninth century B.C., boasts in his inscription that he had massacred the entire Israelite population of Nebo, which he had vowed to anathema (verb: *ḥrm*) in honour of his god Ashtar-Kemosh.

2. *The holy wars at the beginning of Israel's history*

What we have just said about the *ḥerem* applies also, in a more general way, to the whole picture of the holy war sketched out in the preceding paragraph. The features which go to its making are borrowed from various books, and among all the accounts of the early wars of Israel, there is not one where all the several elements are found. Yet the way in which some of the stories are grouped, the recurrence of the same formulas, and the common spirit which pervades these texts all stamp these wars as genuine holy wars. Let us take a few examples.

The character is clearly seen in the war of Deborah and Baraq against Sisera, both in the prose account (Jg 4) and in the Song of Deborah (Jg 5). Yahweh gave Baraq the order to march and promised to deliver Sisera into his hands (4: 6-7); even before the fighting starts, Yahweh has already handed over Sisera, is marching ahead of Baraq, striking panic into the enemy, so that not a man will escape (4: 14-16). The poem sings the praises of those who freely answered the call, *i.e.* of those who had faith in their victory (5: 2, 9): the fighting men were, then, God's champions (5: 8), the people of Yahweh (5: 13) come to Yahweh's aid (5: 23). It was Yahweh himself who went forward in the earthquake and in the rending of the skies (5: 4); the stars themselves fought on his side (5: 20) and the enemies of Yahweh were annihilated (5: 31). Both the prose account and the song are close enough to the events to have given us a faithful version of what the participants thought of this war: for them, it was a sacred action.

We discussed above[1] the strategy of Gideon against the Midianites, but that examination did not take into account the religious element, which is an essential factor in Jg 6-8. Gideon had received the spirit of Yahweh (6: 34), who had intervened twice to assure him of success (6: 36-40; 7: 9f.). It was Yahweh who delivered Midian into the hands of Israel (7: 2, 7, 14-15; 8: 3, 7). It was Yahweh and not Israel who emerged victorious (7: 2); the timid, who had no faith to support them, had been sent away (7: 3), and the army itself had then been reduced to a tiny group, in order to make the divine intervention even more striking (7: 7). The battle-cry (*t'rûah*) was: 'The

1. Cf. pp. 217-218.

sword for Yahweh and for Gideon!' (7: 20). Yahweh threw the enemy camp into confusion (7: 21). This too was a war of Yahweh.

The wars against the Philistines will provide a last example. Jonathan and his armour-bearer went unescorted to attack the Philistine post at Mikmas, for Yahweh would give them victory, whether they were many or few (1 S 14: 6f.); a sign assures Jonathan that Yahweh had delivered the enemy into his hands (14: 10, 12); the earth quaked, and a panic sent by God fell upon the camp (14: 15). Saul consulted the oracles (14: 18), and the panic among the Philistines increased until they took to flight: 'that day, Yahweh gave the victory to Israel' (14: 18-23). A fast had been ordered for all combatants.

During the period of the Judges and under the reign of Saul, the Israelites fought only defensive wars, and it has recently been suggested that the holy wars of Israel were always defensive wars. But the conquest of the Promised Land is certainly described as a holy war, as *the* holy war, in the Book of Josue, and whatever the date of its redaction or the part to be attributed to its redactors, they certainly did not invent this tradition. It is represented also by the quite independent account in Jg 1: Judah and Simeon undertake the conquest of their territory after consulting Yahweh, who gives them the land (Jg 1: 1-2, 4). In addition, we must admit that arms played at least some part in the settlement in Canaan, and that this conquest created a climate of opinion particularly favourable to the idea of the holy war: then above all Yahweh the Warrior (Ex 15: 3), the Master of War (1 S 17: 47), had to fight for his people.

This is the principal fact: it was Yahweh who fought for Israel, not Israel which fought for its God. The holy war, in Israel, was not a war of religion. According to the ancient texts, the wars in the time of Josue and the Judges were not undertaken in order to spread belief in Yahweh, as the *jihad* is undertaken to spread the Moslem faith; nor was their object to defend a faith against a foreign religion. It is worthy of note that, in the Book of Josue, the accounts of the conquest do not contain a single allusion to the gods or the worship of Canaanites. Similarly, in the Book of Judges, Israel is not fighting (directly) for its religious freedom, but for its existence as a people. The Song of Deborah contrasts Yahweh and his champions with Sisera and his chariots, but not with Sisera and his gods; Gideon destroys an altar to Baal, but the episode has no connection whatever with his holy war against the Midianites. Religious preoccupations appear only in texts which are of late redaction, in the prescriptions of Deuteronomy on the *ḥerem* (Dt 7: 2-5, 25; 20: 17-18), in the Deuteronomic framework of the Book of Judges (Jg 2: 2-3), and in the still later redaction of the war of Moses against Midian (Nb 25: 17-18; 31: 15-16). But everything we have so far said shows that, even if these holy wars were not wars of religion, they were essentially religious: in these wars, Yahweh was fighting for the life of his people, and the people associated themselves with this action by an act of faith and by conforming to a definite ritual.

3. Religion and the wars under the monarchy

One could say that this strictly sacred character of war disappeared with the advent of the monarchy and the establishment of a professional army. It is no longer Yahweh who marches ahead of his people to fight the Wars of Yahweh, but the king who leads his people out and fights its wars (1 S 8: 20). The combatants are no longer warriors who volunteer to fight, but professionals in the pay of the king, or conscripts recruited by his officials. This transformation was obviously going to precipitate a crisis: the ground was prepared for it under Saul, who transgressed the ritual laid down for a holy war (1 S 15), and it happened under David, who engaged a large number of foreign mercenaries, and ordered a census of the people for military purposes (2 S 24: 1-9). War became, of necessity, the state's concern; it was 'profaned'.

To begin with, however, certain rites of the holy war were retained. In the Ammonite war, the Ark accompanied the troops, and Uriah (a Hittite mercenary!) kept strict continence (2 S 11: 11). David 'consecrated' to Yahweh the silver and gold of his conquests (2 S 8: 11). But these rites became accessory things, mere trappings, and even if the saying 'Yahweh gives the victory' (2 S 8: 6, 14) was still heard, it was certainly David who secured it by human means and who received the glory which ensued (2 S 12: 28).

Yahweh was no longer consulted, by drawing lots, about the opportuneness of war or about the manner in which it should be waged, but prophets did intervene with the king (1 K 20: 13-14, 22, 28); sometimes the king would even ask them for an oracle (1 K 22: 5-12). Eliseus accompanied the kings of Israel and of Judah in their expedition against Moab and passed on to them the word of Yahweh (2 K 3: 11-19; cf. also 2 K 13: 15f.). These prophets still used the time-honoured vocabulary of the holy war: Yahweh would deliver the enemy into the hands of Israel (1 K 20: 13, 28; 22: 6, 12; 2 K 3: 18), but whereas in olden times it had been the leader in war who was inspired by God, the prophets were no longer anything more than the religious auxiliaries of the king. In the first prophetical schools the idea of the holy war lived on, but precisely because the wars were no longer holy, the prophets often stood opposed to the king. In opposition to a false prophet who foretells that Yahweh will deliver Ramoth of Gilead into the hands of Achab, a true prophet predicts disaster (1 K 22: 19-28), and Eliseus refused to consult Yahweh on behalf of the king of Israel, who is nevertheless leader of an expedition against Moab (2 K 3: 13-14).

In the following century, Isaias stood out as the defender of the ancient concept of the holy war, against those who would appeal to political motives. When Aram and Ephraim launched their attack on Judah, he foretold disaster for them; if only Achaz would have faith in Yahweh (Is 7: 4-9), and when Sennacherib was threatening Jerusalem, Isaias assured the people that God would save the city (37: 33-35). He condemned military preparations (22: 9-11) and the seeking of help from abroad (31: 1-3), for 'Yahweh Sabaoth would come down to fight on mount Sion and on its hill' (31: 4). Against Assur, Yahweh would come from afar 'in the heat of his anger, in the heart of a consuming fire, in a storm of rain and hail' (30: 27-30). Against Egypt, he would come on a cloud, and the Egyptians would lose heart and turn against one another (19: 1-2). Characteristics of the holy war recur in these passages: there is a certitude of victory, faith in Yahweh, a warrior action on the part of God, who unleashes the elements and strikes his enemies with terror: we can still hear an echo of the Song of Deborah, of the conquest stories and of the period of the Judges. Isaias and other prophets probably borrowed their concept of the 'day of Yahweh' from this ancient ideology; it would be a day when Yahweh would come for a victorious battle. But these new 'wars of Yahweh' take place only in the visions of the prophets and are no longer the wars of Israel: the latter have become utterly profane. Isaias tells his contemporaries: you counted on human means 'but you have not looked at their Author nor seen him who made all things long ago' (22: 11), or: 'Salvation lay in conversion and calm, your power lay in perfect confidence, and you did not want them' (30: 15).

What is even more remarkable is that the rules of the holy war should have received their clearest and most complete expression at the end of the monarchy in the redaction of Deuteronomy. The book contains many very ancient elements, and this justifies the use made of it above to describe the practices of the holy war. But our particular interest at present is to study the new spirit which animates these laws, and which dominates the speeches at the beginning and end of the book. The entire history of Israel is presented as a holy war. And the past is a pledge against the future: 'Yahweh your God, who marches in front of you, will fight for you, just as you have seen him do in Egypt' (Dt 1: 30). Again, 'Remember what Yahweh your God did to Pharaoh and to all Egypt . . . so Yahweh your God will deal with all the peoples you are afraid to face' (7: 18-19). 'It is not the uprightness of your behaviour nor the rightness of your heart which will win you possession of their country; it is because of their perversity that Yahweh your God will dispossess these nations to your advantage' (9: 5). 'No one will hold his ground before you; Yahweh your God will make you feared and formidable throughout the length of the land your feet shall tread' (11: 25). 'Be strong and hold fast, do not be afraid, for it is Yahweh your God who is marching with you' (31: 6). And the book closes with the Blessings of Moses, an old song breathing a warlike spirit, which ends (Dt 33: 29):

> Happy art thou, O Israel—who is like thee?
> People victorious through Yahweh,

> whose shield is thy help,
> whose sword is thy victory.
> Thy enemies will stoop low to worst thee,
> but thou shalt trample on their backs.

When Deuteronomy was edited, under Josias, the age of conquests and military triumphs was long past, and there was no longer any occasion to apply its prescriptions about the siege of foreign towns (Dt 20: 10-20) or the execution of an anathema (Dt 2: 34-35; 3: 6-7; 7: 2, 5). Yet this new reflection on the idea of the holy war, though transformed by the progress in theology, does fit in with a concrete historical situation. Under Josias, the revival of the national spirit and the overthrow of the Assyrian yoke gave new and lively hope to the people, and it is by no means impossible that these texts of Deuteronomy inspired the king when he tried to halt the march of Nechao (2 K 23: 29; 2 Ch 35: 20f.). But it was only a momentary blaze, which the disaster of Megiddo quenched utterly. Jeremias lived through these events, and he has no place for the holy war in his preaching: the contrast with Isaias is striking. The last wars of Judah and the desperate resistance against the Chaldeans, recorded in the books of Jeremias and Kings, had no religious character. The reason was that Yahweh had deserted the camp of Israel, and decided, in anger, to chastise his people (2 K 23: 27; 24: 3, 20); he even fought against them (Jr 21: 5) and issued orders to the Chaldeans 'to attack, to capture and burn Jerusalem' (Jr 34: 22). It is impossible to imagine anything more opposed to the ancient ideology of the holy war.

4. The religious wars of the Maccabees

During the Jewish period, in the books of Maccabees, we meet once more some of the characteristics of the holy war. Judas and his brothers conduct 'the fight of Israel' (1 M 3: 2). The raising of the liberation army recalls many ancient memories (1 M 3: 46-60): the assembly met at Mispah, as it had once done for the holy war against Benjamin (Jg 20: 1); they fasted, and sought to know the will of God by opening the book of the law, since there was no longer any ephod or prophet; they sounded the trumpet, shouted the battle-cry (cf. Nb 10: 9 and the *t'rûah*), and mobilized the army according to the rules set down in Dt 20: 5-8. Before the battle of Emmaus, Judas exhorted the people not to fear and to call upon God: 'All the nations shall acknowledge that there is someone who saves Israel' (1 M 4: 8-11; cf. 1 S 17: 46), and after the victory they blessed God for the 'great salvation' he had wrought in Israel (1 M 4: 24-25; cf. 1 S 14: 45). Judas overthrew altars in Philistine territory, burnt their idols and sacked the towns (1 M 5: 68; cf. Dt 7: 5, 25). In the second book, the echo of ancient texts rings fainter, but the same ideas are found: they prepare for battle by prayer and fasting (2 M 13: 10-12), and Iudas' exhortation to the troops runs: 'The enemy trusts his arms and his boldness, but we—we have placed our trust in God, master of all things' (2 M 8: 18). 'Help from God' (2 M 8: 23) or 'Victory from God' (2 M 13: 15) are the passwords. Judas asks the Lord 'to send a good angel before us to sow fear and fright' among the enemy (2 M 15: 23).

But in spite of these resemblances, the spirit is no longer that of the holy war. The Maccabees and their men are not inspired by God; God did not order the war and he does not intervene directly in it. The most one dare ask is that he should send an angel (2 M 15: 23), and God answers this prayer when an armed rider appears on the road to Bethsur (2 M 11: 6-8). But this heavenly envoy plays only a symbolic part: this fight, like all the others, is undertaken and won by merely human means. It is significant that the allusions to the help God gave his people in ancient times refer to the crossing of the Red Sea (1 M 4: 9), and to the deliverance of Jerusalem from Sennacherib (1 M 7: 40-42; 2 M 8: 19; 15: 22), but never to the holy wars of the conquest and the period of the Judges.

All this prevents us from taking the Maccabean war as a holy war. But it is a war of religion. Mattathias calls upon 'everyone who is zealous for the law and who observes the Covenant' to follow him (1 M 2: 27); Judas fights for the people and the holy place (1 M 3: 43, 59), for 'the town, religion and the Temple' (2 M 15: 17). The combatants fight for religious freedom, not only against foreign masters who proscribe the observance of the law, but also against their perjured brethren 'who abandon the holy Covenant' (Dn 11: 30), and 'who have abandoned the law' (1 M 10: 14; cf. 1: 52). The rebellion began when Mattathias cut the throat of a Jew who had agreed to offer sacrifice on the altar at Modin (1 M 2: 24). Always and everywhere, the Maccabees vow to fight against the 'wicked', the 'miscreants', the 'sinners' (1 M 2: 44, 48; 3: 5-6; 6: 21; 7: 23-24), who were allying themselves with pagans (1 M 3: 15; 4: 2; 7: 5; 9: 25; 11: 21-25). It was a war of religion which set the faithful Jews fighting against their fellow-Jews who had rallied to the cause of Hellenism and against their foreign protectors. It was inevitable that both sides should soon introduce into it political interests, as happened in the French wars of religion during the sixteenth century, and in Holland during the seventeenth century.

5. The 'Order of the War' from Qumran

An astonishing document has recently been found which shows that the ideas of the holy war gained a new lease of life among a group of Jews: it is the 'Order of the War' found in the caves of Qumran. The book dates, in all probability, from the first century B.C., and gives rules for the war which will take place at the end of time between the 'Sons of Light' and the 'Sons of Darkness', *i.e.* between the faithful Jews, those of the Qumran community, on the one hand, and all the pagan nations on the other. One can, of course, point to external similarities with the Books of Maccabees, but in the Qumran writing the struggle is evidently regarded as a holy war. It is worthy of note that of the five explicit citations of the Old Testament, three refer to texts used above (Nb 10: 9; Dt 7: 21-22; 20: 2-5), and there are in addition many expressions which recall the ancient ideology. This 'war', like the holy war of bygone ages, had its own rites; it even turns into a ceremony in which priests and Levites have an essential part to play. The army is 'the people of God', and the soldiers are volunteers called to fight the battles of God. In battle the standards are inscribed 'Right hand of God', 'God's moment', 'God's slaughter', and God himself, who is called 'The Hero of the Fight', marches along with his faithful, accompanied by the army of angels. It is the Hand of God which is raised against Belial and his empire. Victory is certain: there may be moments of distress, but the enemies of God and Israel will finally be annihilated, and the eternal reign of Light will begin.

The vision is not of a religious conquest of the world, of a conversion imposed by force of arms; there is nothing resembling the Moslem *jihad*. The world is at the moment divided between Light and Darkness, between Good and Evil, and order can only be established by the total destruction of the forces of Darkness and of Evil, by the total victory of God and the Sons of Light. Against the background of this dualist thought, the old notion of the holy war takes on a particularly violent character, expands to cosmic dimensions, and yet is referred to the end of the present era of time: it is an apocalyptic war.

In this curious text, visionary dreams are mingled with practical arrangements that could be taken straight from a Roman military text-book; yet the authors of the work were apparently convinced that this war was certainly coming, and were waiting for it. The text was copied time and time again, and fragments of many copies have been found. In its pages, the readers could feed their hatred for the Sons of Belial, whom they recognized in the pagan occupants of the Holy Land. Possibly it was inspired by the fanaticism of those Zealots who took part in the revolts against the Romans, and who may have thought that the time was come for the final struggle between the Sons of Darkness and the Sons of Light.

BIBLIOGRAPHY

ABBREVIATIONS

AASOR	Annual of the American Schools of Oriental Research.
AfO	Archiv für Orientforschung.
AJSL	American Journal of Semitic Languages and Literatures.
BASOR	Bulletin of the American Schools of Oriental Research.
BIFAO	Bulletin de l'Institut Français d'Archéologie Orientale (Cairo).
BJPES	Bulletin of the Jewish Palestine Exploration Society.
BJRL	Bulletin of the John Rylands Library (Manchester).
HTR	Harvard Theological Review.
HUCA	Hebrew Union College Annual.
IEJ	Israel Exploration Journal.
JAOS	Journal of the American Oriental Society.
JBL	Journal of Biblical Literature.
JNES	Journal of Near Eastern Studies.
JPOS	Journal of the Palestine Oriental Society.
JQR	Jewish Quarterly Review.
JTS	Journal of Theological Studies.
PEQ	Palestine Exploration Quarterly.
PJB	Palästinajahrbuch.
RB	Revue Biblique.
RHPR	Revue d'Histoire et de Philosophie Religieuses.
TLZ	Theologische Literaturzeitung.
VT	Vetus Testamentum.
ZA	Zeitschrift für Assyriologie und verwandte Gebiete.
ZAW	Zeitschrift für die Alttestamentliche Wissenschaft.
ZDMG	Zeitschrift der Deutschen Morgenländischen Gesellschaft.
ZDPV	Zeitschrift der Deutschen Palästina-Vereins.

INTRODUCTION

NOMADISM AND ITS SURVIVAL

On the tribal organization of the Arabs:

F. WÜSTENFELD, Genealogische Tabellen der Arabischen Stämme und Familien, Göttingen, 1852.

W. ROBERTSON SMITH, Kinship and Marriage in Early Arabia, London, 1885; 3rd edition, 1903. Very important review by TH. NOLDEKE, in ZDMG, XL, 1886, 148-87.

I. GOLDZIHER, 'Das Arabische Stämmewesen und der Islam', in his Muhammedanische Studien, I, Halle, 1889, 40-100.

A. JAUSSEN, Coutumes Arabes au pays de Moab, Paris, 1908; re-ed. 1948.

A. JAUSSEN, 'Coutumes des Fuqara', in A. JAUSSEN and R. SAVIGNAC, Mission Archéologique en Arabie, III, Paris, 1920.

A. MUSIL, The Manners and Customs of the Rwala Beduins, New York, 1928.

T. ASHKENAZI, Tribus semi-nomades de la Palestine du Nord, Paris, 1938.

H. CHARLES, Tribus moutonnières du Moyen-Euphrate, Damascus, 1939.

H. CHARLES, La sédentarisation entre Euphrate et Balik, Beyrouth, 1942.

M. VON OPPENHEIM, Die Beduinen, Leipzig-Wiesbaden. Three volumes have appeared; vol. V is to give a general résumé, but the author has already summarized his views in vol. I, 1939, 22-36. With this one should read the article by his collaborator E. BRAUNLICH, 'Beiträge zur Gesellschaftsordnung der arabischen Beduinenstämme', published in Islamica, VI, 1934, 68-111; 182-229.

R. MONTAGNE, La civilisation du désert, Paris, 1947.

B. COUROYER, 'Histoire d'une tribu semi-nomade de Palestine', in RB, LVIII, 1951, 75-91.

J. SONNEN, Die Beduinen am See Genesareth, Cologne, 1952.

J. R. KUPPER, Les nomades en Mésopotamie au temps des rois de Mari, Paris, 1957.

F. GABRIELI and others, L'antica società beduina, Roma, 1959.

H. CHARLES, art. 'Nomadisme', in Dictionnaire de la Bible, Supplément, VI, 1959, 541-50.

On the tribal organization of Israel:

A. CAUSSE, *Du groupe ethnique à la communauté religieuse*, Strasbourg, 1937, ch. 1: 'La solidarité familiale et tribale'.

J. VAN DER PLOEG, 'Sociale groepeeringen in het oude Israel', in *Jaarbericht Ex Oriente Lux*, VIII, 1942, 646-50.

C. UMHAU WOLF, 'Terminology of Israel's Tribal Organization', in *JBL*, LXV, 1946, 45-9.

S. NYSTRÖM, *Beduinentum und Jahwismus*, Lund, 1946.

R. DE VAUX, 'Les Patriarches hébreux et les découvertes modernes', in *RB*, LVI, 1949, 5-19.

On the system of the Twelve Tribes of Israel:

B. LUTHER, 'Die Israelitischen Stämme', in *ZAW*, XXII, 1901, 1-76.

ED. MEYER and B. LUTHER, *Die Israeliten und ihre Nachbarstämme*, Halle, 1906.

M. NOTH, *Das System der Zwölf Stämme Israels*, Stuttgart, 1930. (Specially valuable.)

On war:

P. HUMBERT, *La Terou'ah. Analyse d'un rite biblique*, Neuchâtel, 1946.

G. VON RAD, *Der Heilige Krieg im Alten Israel*, Zürich, 1951.

On the right of asylum:

QUATREMÈRE, 'Mémoire sur les asiles chez les Arabes', in *Mémoires de l'Institut Royal, Académie des Inscriptions et Belles-Lettres*, XV, 2, Paris, 1845, 307-48.

M. LÖHR, *Das Asylwesen im Alten Testament*, Halle, 1930.

N. M. NIKOLSKY, 'Das Asylrecht in Israel', in *ZAW*, XLVIII, 1930, 146-75.

On blood-vengeance:

O. PROCKSCH, *Ueber die Blutrache bei den vorislamischen Arabern*, Leipzig, 1899.

H. LAMMENS, 'Le caractère religieux du târ ou vendetta chez les Arabes préislamiques', in *BIFAO*, XXVI, 1926, 83-127.

E. MERZ, *Die Blutrache bei den Israeliten*, Leipzig, 1916.

On the 'nomadic ideal' of the Old Testament:

The expression is derived from K. BUDDE, 'Das nomadische Ideal im Alten Testament', in *Preussische Jahrbücher*, 1896; and his *Die Religion des Volkes Israel*, Giessen, 1899, 112f. The idea has often been repeated:

P. HUMBERT, 'Osée le prophète bédouin, in *RHPR*, I, 1921, 97-118.

P. HUMBERT, 'La logique de la perspective nomade chez Osée', in *Festschrift Marti*, Giessen, 1925, 158-66.

A. CAUSSE, *Les 'pauvres d'Israël'*, Strasbourg, 1922, ch. V: 'Les Prophètes du VIIIᵉ siècle et l'idéal patriarcal'.

J. W. FLIGHT, 'The Nomadic Idea and Ideal in the Old Testament', in *JBL*, XLIII, 1923, 158-226.

S. NYSTRÖM, *Beduinentum und Jahwismus*, Lund, 1946.

On the Rekabites:

Apart from dictionary articles there are only:

L. GAUTIER, 'À propos des Rékabites', in *Études sur la religion d'Israël*, Lausanne, 1927, 104-29.

S. TALMON, '1 Ch 2: 55', in *Eretz-Israel*, V, 1958 (Volume Mazar), 111-13 (in Hebrew with a summary in English).

I

FAMILY INSTITUTIONS

1

THE FAMILY

On the typical Israelite family, and general points:

W. ROBERTSON SMITH, *Kinship and Marriage*, London, 1885: 2nd ed. 1903.

V. APTOWITZER, 'Spuren des Matriarchats im jüdischen Schrifttum', in *HUCA*, IV, 1927, 207-405; V, 1928, 261-97.

P. KOSCHAKER, 'Fratriarchat, Hausgemeinschaft und Mutterrecht in Keilschriftrecten', in *ZA*, XLI, 1933, 1-89.

C. H. GORDON, 'Fratriarchy in the Old Testament', in *JBL*, LIV, 1935, 223-31.

J. Henninger, 'Die Familie bei den heutigen Beduinen Arabiens und seiner Randgebiete', in *Internationales Archiv für Ethnologie*, XLII, 1943, 1-188.
J. Pedersen, *Israel, its Life and Culture*, I-II, London, re-ed. 1946, 46-60.
I. Mendelsohn, 'The Family in the Ancient Near East', in *Biblical Archaeologist*, XI, 1948, 24-40.
R. Patai, *Sex and Family in the Bible and the Middle East*, Garden City, New York, 1959.

On the development of family customs:

A. Causse, 'La crise de la solidarité de famille et de clan dans l'Ancien Israël', in *RHPR*, X, 1930, 24-60.
A. Causse, *Du groupe ethnique à la communauté religieuse*, Strasbourg, 1937, ch. II: 'L'évolution politique et culturelle et la désintégration des anciens groupes'.

2

MARRIAGE

On marriage in general:

J. Neubauer, *Beiträge zur Geschichte des bibl-talmudischen Eheschliessungsrechts* (*Mitteilungen der vorderasiatisch-ägyptischen Gesellschaft*), XXIV-XXV, Leipzig, 1919-20.
S. Bialoblocki, *Materialen zum islamischen und jüdischen Eherecht*, Giessen, 1928.
H. Granquist, *Marriage Conditions in a Palestine Village*, I-II, Helsingfors, 1931-5.
R. Dussaud, 'Le "mohar" Israëlite', in *Comptes Rendus de l'Académie des Inscriptions et Belles-Lettres*, 1935, 142-51.
G. R. Driver and J. C. Miles, *The Assyrian Laws*, Oxford, 1935, 126-271.
M. Burrows, *The Basis of Israelite Marriage*, New Haven, 1938.
L. M. Epstein, *Marriage Laws in the Bible and the Talmud*, Cambridge, Mass., 1942.
E. Neufeld, *Ancient Hebrew Marriage Laws*, London, 1944.
A. Gelin, 'Le passage de la polygamie à la monogamie', in *Mélanges Podechard*, Lyons, 1945, 135-46.
W. Kornfeld, 'L'adultère dans l'Orient antique', in *RB*, LVII, 1950, 92-109.
P. Koschaker, 'Ehesschliessung und Kauf nach alten Rechten', in *Archiv Orientální*, XVIII, III, 1950 (Festschrift Hrozný), 210-96.
G. R. Driver and J. C. Miles, *The Babylonian Laws*, III, Oxford, 1952, 245-324.
D. R. Mace, *Hebrew Marriage*, London, 1953.
J. J. Rabinowitz, 'Marriage Contracts in Ancient Egypt in the Light of Jewish Sources', in *HTR*, XLVI, 1933, 91-7.
W. Kornfeld, 'Mariage dans l'Ancien Testament', in *Supplément au Dictionnaire de la Bible*, Paris, V, 1954, 905-26.
A. van Selms, *Marriage and Family Life in Ugaritic Literature*, London, 1954.
C. Wiener, 'Jérémie II, 2, "Fiançailles" ou "épousailles"?', in *Recherches de Science Religieuse*, XLIV, 1956, 403-7.
E. Volterra, 'Osservazioni sul divorzio nei documenti aramaici', in *Studi Orientalistici in onore di Giorgio Levi della Vida*, Rome, 1956, 586-600.
R. Yaron, 'On Divorce in Old Testament Times', in *Revue Internationale des Droits de l'Antiquité*, VI, 1957, 77f.
R. Yaron, 'Aramaic Marriage Contracts from Elephantine', in *Journal of Semitic Studies*, III, 1958, 1-39.
S. Lowy, 'The Extent of Jewish Polygamy in Talmudic Times', in *Journal of Jewish Studies*, IX, 1958, 115-38.
J. J. Rabinowitz, 'The "Great Sin" in Ancient Egyptian Marriage Contracts', in *JNES*, XVIII, 1959, 73.
R. Yaron, 'Aramaic Marriage Contracts: Corrigenda and Addenda', in *Journal of Semitic Studies*, V, 1960, 66-70.
W. L. Moran, 'The Scandal of the "Great Sin" at Ugarit', in *JNES*, XVIII, 1959, 280-1.

On the Assyro-Babylonian *tirḫatu*:

E. A. Speiser, 'New Kirkuk Documents relating to Family Laws', in *AASOR*, X, 1930, especially 23f.
P. van der Meer, 'Tirḫātu', in *Revue d'Assyriologie*, XXXI, 1934, 121-3.
C. H. Gordon, 'The Status of Women as reflected in the Nuzi Tablets', in *ZA*, XLIII, 1936, 146-69, especially 157-8.

On *beena* marriage:

J. Morgenstern, 'Beena Marriage (Matriarchate) and its Historical Implications', in *ZAW*, N.F. VI, 1929, 91-110; VIII, 1931, 46-58.

On Samson's marriage:

A. Jaussen, 'Le ğôz musarrib', in *RB*, XIX, 1910, 237-49.
A. van Selms, 'The Best Man and Bride', in *JNES*, IX, 1950, 65-75.

On Jacob's marriages:

C. H. GORDON, 'The Story of Jacob and Laban in the Light of the Nuzi Tablets', in *BASOR*, **66**, 1937, 25-7.
M. BURROWS, 'The Complaint of Laban's Daughters', in *JAOS*, LVII, 1937, 259-76.

On the levirate:

J. SCHEFTELOWITZ, 'Die Leviratsehe', in *Archiv für Religionswissenschaft*, XVIII, 1915, 250-6.
P. CRUVEILHIER, 'Le lévirat chez les hébreux et chez les assyriens', in *RB*, XXXIV, 1925, 524-46.
K. H. RENGSTORF, *Die Mischna, Traktat Jebamot*, Giessen, 1929, with historical introduction and commentary.
P. KOSCHAKER, 'Zum levirat nach hethitischem Recht', in *Revue hittite et asianique*, II, 1933, 77-89.
J. MITTELMANN, *Der altisraelitische Levirat*, Leipzig, 1934.
G. R. DRIVER and J. C. MILES, *The Assyrian Laws*, Oxford, 1935, 240-50.
M. BURROWS, 'Levirate Marriage in Israel', in *JBL*, LIX, 1940, 23-33.
M. BURROWS, 'The Ancient Oriental Background of Hebrew Levirate Marriage', in *BASOR*, **77**, 1940, 2-15.
M. BURROWS, 'The Marriage of Boaz and Ruth', in *JBL*, LIX, 1940, 445-54.
H. H. ROWLEY, 'The Marriage of Ruth', in *HTR*, XL, 1947, 77-99, reproduced in *The Servant of the Lord and Other Essays on the Old Testament*, London, 1952, 161-86.
A. F. PUUKKO, 'Die Leviratsehe in den altorientalischen Gesetze', in *Archiv Orientální*, XVII, II, 1949 (Festschrift Hrozný), 296-9.
M. TSEVAT, 'Marriage and Monarchical Legitimacy in Ugarit and in Israel', in *Journal of Semitic Studies*, III, 1958, 237-43.

On the impediments to marriage:

W. KORNFELD, *Studien zum Heligkeitsgesetz*, Vienna, 1952, 89-134.
K. ELLIGER, 'Das Gesetz Leviticus 18', in *ZAW*, LXVII, 1955, 1-25.

3

THE POSITION OF WOMEN

M. LÖHR, *Die Stellung des Weibes zu Yahve-Religion und Kult*, Leipzig, 1918.
G. BEER, *Die soziale und religiöse Stellung der Frau im israelitischen Altertum*, Tübingen, 1919.
J. DOLLER, *Das Weib in Alten Testament*, Münster i.W., 1920.
P. CRUVEILHIER, 'La droit de la femme dans la Genèse et dans le recueil de lois assyriennes', in *RB*, XXXVI, 1927, 350-76.
E. M. MACDONALD, *The Position of Women as reflected in Semitic Codes*, Toronto, 1931.
J. LEIPOLDT, *Die Frau in der antiken Welt und im Urchristentum*, Leipzig, 1954, 69-114.

4

CHILDREN

On the attitude to children, and general points:

A. MARGOLIUS, *Mutter und Kind im altbiblischen Schrifttum*, Berlin, 1936.
H. GRANQUIST, *Child Problems among the Arabs*, Helsingfors, 1950.

On birth:

H. GRANQUIST, *Birth and Childhood among the Arabs*, Helsingfors, 1947.

On the name:

G. B. GRAY, *Studies in Hebrew Proper Names*, London, 1896.
M. NOTH, *Die israelitischen Personennamen im Rahmen der gemeinsemitischen Namengebung*, Stuttgart, 1928.

On circumcision:

Nothing useful apart from dictionary articles. The latest, with bibliography, are: *Reallexicon für Antike und Christentum*, II, Stuttgart, 1954, 159-69; *Theologisches Wörterbuch zum Neuen Testament*, VI, Stuttgart, 1955, 72-80. The study by F. SIERKSMA, 'Quelques remarques sur la circoncision en Israël', in *Oudtestamentische Studiën*, IX, 1951, 136-69, is not very trustworthy.

On education:

The essential work is L. DÜRR, *Das Erziehungswesen im Alten Testament und im Antiken Orient* (*Mitteilungen der vorderasiatisch-ägyptischen Gesellschaft*, XXXVI, 2), Leipzig, 1932.
J. HEMPEL, '*Pathos und Humor in der israelitischen Erziehung*' in *Von Ugarit nach Qumran*, Festschrift Eissfeldt, Berlin, 1958, 63-81.

On the rights of the eldest son:

I. MENDELSOHN, 'On the Preferential Status of the Eldest Son' in *BASOR*, 156, Dec. 1959, 38-40.

On adoption:

L. KÖHLER, 'Die Adoptionsform von Rt 4, 16', in *ZAW*, XXIX, 1909, 312-14.
M. DAVID, *Die Adoption im altbabylonischen Recht*, Leipzig, 1927.
S. FEIGIN, 'Some Cases of Adoption in Israel', in *JBL*, L, 1931, 186-200.
E. M. CASSIN, *L'adoption à Nuzi*, Paris, 1938.
W. H. RUSSELL, 'New Testament Adoption—Graeco-Roman or Semitic?', in *JBL*, LXXI, 1952, 233-4.
M. DAVID, 'Adoptie in het oude Israel', in *Mededeelingen d. kon. Nederl. Akad. v. Wetensch., Afd. Letterek.*, **18**, 4, 1955.
S. KARDIMON, 'Adoption as a Remedy for Infertility in the Period of the Patriarchs', in *Journal of Semitic Studies*, III, 1958, 123-6.

5

SUCCESSION AND INHERITANCE

M. TSCHERNOWITZ, 'The Inheritance of Illegitimate Children according to Jewish Law', in *Jewish Studies in Memory of Isaac Abrahams*, New York, 1927, 402-15.
E. NEUFELD, *Ancient Hebrew Marriage Laws*, London, 1944, 259-65.
J. PEDERSEN, *Israel, its Life and Culture*, I-II, 2nd ed., London, 1946, 89-96.

6

DEATH AND FUNERAL RITES

H. J. ELHORTS, *Die israelitischen Trauerriten*, Giessen, 1914.
S. H. JAHNOW, *Das hebräische Leichenlied im Rahmen der Völkerdichtung*, Giessen, 1923.
G. QUELL, *Die Auffassung des Todes im Israel*, Leipzig, 1925.
P. HEINISCH, *Die Trauergebrauche bei den Israeliten*, Munster i.W., 1931.
P. HEINISCH, *Die Totenklage im Alten Testament*, Munster i.W., 1931.
B. ALFRINK, 'L'expression shâkab 'im ãbôtâw, in *Oudtestamentische Studiën*, II, 1943, 106-18.
B. ALFRINK, 'L'expression neĕŝap el-'ammâw', in *Oudtestamentische Studiën*, V, 1948, 118-31.
W. F. ALBRIGHT, 'The High Place in Ancient Palestine', in *Volume du Congrès, Strasbourg, 1956* (Supplement to *VT*, IV), Leiden, 1957, 242-58.

II

CIVIL INSTITUTIONS

1

POPULATION

These questions have hardly ever been studied, for lack of evidence. Some incidental information and solutions will be found in the following works:

F. BUHL, *La société israélite d'après l'Ancien Testament*, Paris, 1904, 83-9.
W. F. ALBRIGHT, in *JPOS*, V, 1925, 20-5.
M. LURJE, *Studien zur Geschichte der wirtschaftlichen und sozialen Verhältnisse im israelitisch-jüdischen Reiche*, Giessen, 1927, 35-41.
R. ZIMMERMAN, 'Bevölkerungsdichte und Heereszahlen im Alt-Palästina', in *Klio*, XXI, 1927, 340-3.
S. W. BARON, 'La population israélite sous les rois' (in Hebrew), in *Abhandlungen zur Erinnerung an H. P. Chajes*, 1932, 76-136.
J. W. CROWFOOT, *The Buildings of Samaria*, London, 1942, 2 and 4.
W. F. ALBRIGHT, *The Excavations of Tell Beit Mirsim*, II (*AASOR*, XXI-XXII, 1941-3), 39.
A. UNGNAD, 'Die Zahl der von Sanherib deportierten Judäer', in *ZAW*, LIX, 1942-3, 199-202.
J. JEREMIAS, 'Die Einwohnerzahl zur Zeit Jesu', in *ZDPV*, LXVI, 1943, 24-31.

A. Lucas, 'The Number of Israelites at the Exodus', in *PEQ*, 1944, 164-8.
W. F. Albright, *The Biblical Period*, Pittsburgh, 1950, 2nd ed., 1955, 59-60, n. 75.
S. W. Baron, *A Social and Religious History of the Jews*, I, 1, 2nd ed., New York, 1952, 64 and 320-1, n. 2.
G. E. Mendenhall, 'The Census Lists of Numbers 1 and 26', in *JBL*, LXXVII, 1958, 52-66.

2

The Free Populations: Its Divisions

On the dignitaries:

J. van der Ploeg, 'Le sens de gibbôr hail in *RB*, L 1941 (= *Vivre et Penser*, I) 120-5.
C. U. Wolf, 'Traces of Primitive Democracy in Israel', in *JNES*, VI, 1947, 98-108.
J. van der Ploeg, 'Les chefs du people d'Israël et leurs noms', in *RB*, LVII, 1950, 40-61.
J. van der Ploeg, 'Les "nobles israélites"', in *Oudtestamentische Studiën*, IX, 1955, 49-64.
W. McKane, 'The *gibbor hayil* in the Israelite Community', in *Transactions of the Glasgow University Oriental Society*, XVII, 1957-8 (1959), 28-37.
E. Neufeld, 'The Emergence of a Royal-Urban Society in Ancient Israel', in *HUCA*, XXXI, 1960. 31-53.

On the 'people of the land':

M. Sulzberger, *Am ha-aretz, the Ancient Hebrew Parliament*, Philadelphia, 1909.
E. Klamroth, *Die jüdischen Exulanten in Babylonien*, Leipzig, 1912, Excursus, 99-101.
M. Sulzberger, 'The Polity of the Ancient Hebrews', in *JQR*, n.s. III, 1912-13, 1-81.
N. Slousch, 'Representative Government among the Hebrews and Phoenicians', in *JQR*, n.s. IV, 1913-14, 303-10.
E. Gillischewski, 'Der Ausdruck 'am haares im Alten Testament', in *ZAW*, XL, 1922, 137-42.
S. Daiches, 'The Meaning of am ha-aretz in the Old Testament', in *JTS*, XXX, 1929, 245-9.
S. Zeitlin, 'The Am haarez', in *JQR*, n.s. XXIII, 1932-3, 45-61.
L. Rost, 'Die Bezeichnungen für Land und Volk im Alten Testament', in *Festschrift Procksch*, Leipzig, 1934, 125-48.
R. Gordis, 'Sectional Rivalry in the Kingdom of Judah', in *JQR*, n.s. XXV, 1934-5, 237-59.
P. Lemaire, 'Crise et effondrement de la monarchie davidique', in *RB*, XLV, 1936, 161-83.
E. Würthwein, *Der 'am ha'arez im Alten Testament*, Stuttgart, 1936.
I. D. Amussin, 'Le "Peuple du Pays"' (in Russian) in *Vestnik Drevnej Istorii*, 1955, 2, 14-36. A German summary in *Bibliotheca Classica Orientalis* (Berlin), I, 1956, 73-5.
L. A. Snijders, 'Het "Volk des Lands" in Juda', in *Nederlands Theologisch Tijdschift*, XII, 1957-8, 241-56.

On the rich and the poor: the question has been studied chiefly from the religious angle. See in particular:

A. Kuschke, 'Arm und Reich im Alten Testament, mit besonderer Berücksichtung der nachexilischen Zeit', in *ZAW*, LVII, 1939, 31-57.
J. van der Ploeg, 'Les pauvres d'Israël et leur piété', in *Oudtestamentische Studiën*, VII, 1950, 236-70.
A. Gelin, *Les pauvres de Yahvé*, Paris, 1953, with critical bibliography.
C. van Leeuwen, *Le développement du sens social en Israël avant l'ère chrétienne*, Assen, 1955.

On the resident foreigners:

A. Bertholet, *Die Stellung der Israeliten und der Juden zu den Fremden*, Leipzig, 1896, 27-50.
M. Sulzberger, 'Status of Labor in Ancient Israel', in *JQR*, n.s. XIII, 1922-3, 397-459.
M. Weber, *Das Antike Judentum*, 2nd ed., Tübingen, 1923, 38-42.
J. van der Ploeg, 'Sociale groepeeringen in het Oude Israël', in *Jaarbericht van het Vooraziatisch-Egyptisch Gezelshap*, VII, 1942, 642-6.
J. Pedersen, *Israel, its Life and Culture*, I-II, London, 2nd ed., 1946, 39-43.
E. Marmorstein, 'The Origins of Agricultural Feudalism in the Holy Land', in *PEQ*, 1953, 111-17.

On the wage-earners:

K. Fuchs, *Die alttestamentliche Arbeitergesetzgebung im Vergleich zu CH, zum altassyrischen und hettitischen Recht*, Dissertation Heidelberg, 1935.
W. Lauterbach, *Der Arbeiter in Recht und Rechtspraxis des Alten Testament und des Alten Orients*, Dissertation Heidelberg, 1935.
W. Bienert, *Die Arbeit nach der Lehre der Bibel*, Stuttgart, 2nd ed., 1956, 88-96.

On the artisans:

I. Mendelsohn, 'Guilds in Babylonia and Assyria', in *JPOS*, LX, 1940, 68-72.
I. Mendelsohn, 'Guilds in Ancient Palestine', in *BASOR*, 80, 1940, 17-21.

On the merchants:

W. F. LEEMANS, *The Old Babylonian Merchant* (*Studia et Documenta ad jura Orientis pertinentia*, III), Leyde, 1950.
C. H. GORDON, 'Abraham and the Merchants of Ura', in *JNES*, XVII, 1958, 28-31.

3

SLAVES

General points:

P. HEINISCH, 'Das Sklavenrecht in Israel und im Alten Orient', in *Studia Catholica*, XI, 1934-5, 201-18.
I. MENDELSOHN, *Slavery in the Ancient Near East*, New York, 1949.
R. NORTH, *Sociology of the Biblical Jubilee*, Rome, 1954, with bibliography of older works, pp. xix-xxi; summary, pp. 135-57.

On slavery in the neighbouring countries:

A. BAKIR, *Slavery in Pharaonic Egypt*, Cairo, 1952.
G. R. DRIVER and J. C. MILES, *The Babylonian Laws*, I, Oxford, 1952, especially 105-8, 221-30, 478-90.
J. KLIMA, 'Einige Bemerkungen zum Sklavenrecht nach den vorhammurapischen Gesetzefragmenten', in *Archiv Orientdlní*, XXI, 1933, 143-51.
I. MENDELSOHN, 'On Slavery in Alakakh', in *IEJ*, V, 1955, 65-72.

On Israelite slaves:

I. MENDELSOHN, 'The Conditional Sale into Slavery of Free-Born Daughters in Nuzi and in the Law of Ex 21, 7-11', in *JAOS*, LV, 1935, 190-5.
H. M. WEIL, 'Gage et cautionnement dans la Bible', in *Archives de l'Histoire du Droit Oriental*, II, 1938, 68 pp.
R. SUGRANYES DE FRANCH, *Études sur le droit palestinien à l'époque évangélique*, Fribourg (Switzerland), 1946, 68-106.

On the 'Hebrew' slave:

A. ALT, *Die Ursprünge des israelitischen Rechts*, Leipzig, 1934, 19-23=*Kleine Schriften*, I, Munich, 1953, 291-4.
A. JEPSEN, 'Die "Hebräer" und ihr Recht', in *AfO*, XV, 1945-51, 55-68.

On capture:

A. ALT, 'Das Verbot des Diebstahls im Dekalog', in *Kleine Schriften*, I, Munich, 1953, 333-40.

On the *yᵉlid bayt*:

F. WILLESEN, 'The Yalid in Hebrew Society', in *Studia Theologica*, XII, 1958, 192-210.

On emancipation:

M. DAVID, 'The Manumission of Slaves under Zedekiah', in *Oudtestamentische Studiën*, V, 1948, 63-79.
Z. W. FALK, 'The Deeds of Manumission in Elephantine', in *Journal of Jewish Studies*, V, 1954, 114-17.
Z. W. FALK, 'Manumission by Sale', in *Journal of Semitic Studies*, III, 1958, 127-8.

On the *ḥofŝi*:

I. MENDELSOHN, 'The Canaanite term for "Free Proletarian"', in *BASOR*, **83**, 1941, 36-9.
E. R. LACHEMAN, 'Note on the Word ḫupšu at Nuzi', in *BASOR*, **86**, 1942, 36-7.
J. GRAY, 'Feudalism in Ugarit and Early Israel', in *ZAW*, LXIV, 1952, 49-55.
I. MENDELSOHN, 'New Light on the ḫupšu', in *BASOR*, **139**, 1955, 9-11.

On public slaves:

A. BERTHOLET, *Die Stellung der Israeliten und der Juden zu den Fremden*, Leipzig, 1896, 50-3.
I. MENDELSOHN, 'State Slavery in Ancient Israel', in *BASOR*, **85**, 1942, 14-17. Revised and developed in *Slavery in the Ancient Near East*, New York, 1949, 92-106.
M. HARAN, 'The Gibeonites, the Nethinim and the Servants of Solomon', in *Judah and Jerusalem*, 1957, 37-45.

4

THE ISRAELITE CONCEPT OF THE STATE

K. GALLING, *Die israelitische Staatsverfassung in ihrer vorder-orientalischen Umwelt* (*Der Alte Orient*, XXVIII, 3 4), Leipzig, 1929.

A. ALT, *Die Staatbildung der Israeliten in Palästina*, Reformations-program der Universität Leipzig 1930= *Kleine Schriften*, II, Munich, 1953, 1-65.

M. NOTH, *Das System der Zwölf Stämme Israels*, Stuttgart, 1930.

C. R. NORTH, 'The Old Testament Estimate of the Monarchy', in *AJSL*, XLVIII, 1931-2, 1-19.

A. ALT, 'Das Grossreich Davids', in *TLZ*, LXXV, 1950, 213-20= *Kleine Schriften*, II, 66-67.

M. NOTH, 'Gott, König, Volk im Alten Testament', in *Zeitschrift für Theologie und Kirche*, XLVII, 1950, 157-91.

A. ALT, 'Das Königtum in den Reichen Israel und Juda', in *VT*, I, 1951, 2-22= *Kleine Schriften*, II, 116-34.

K. GALLING, 'Das Königsgesetz im Deuteronomium', in *TLZ*, LXXVI, 1951, 133-8.

H. J. KRAUS, *Prophetie und Politik*, Munich, 1952.

A. ALT, *Der Stadtstaat Samaria* (Berichte über die Verhandlungen der sachsischen Akademie der Wissenschaften zu Leipzig, Phil.-hist. Klasse, 101, 5), Berlin, 1954= *Kleine Schriften*, III, 258-302.

I. MENDELSOHN, 'Samuel's Denunciation of Kingship in the Light of the Akkadian Documents from Ugarit', in *BASOR*, **143**, 1956, 17-22.

5

THE PERSON OF THE KING

On Eastern parallels, in general:

K. F. EULER, 'Königtum und Götterwelt in den altaramäischen Inschriften Nordsyriens', in *ZAW*, LVI, 1938, 272-313.

R. LABAT, *Le caractère religieux de la royauté assyro-babylonienne*, Paris, 1939.

I. ENGNELL, *Studies in Divine Kingship in the Ancient Near East*, Uppsala, 1943.

H. FRANKFORT, *Kingship and the Gods*, Chicago, 1948.

T. FISH, 'Some Aspects of Kingship in the Sumerian City and Kingdom of Ur', in *BJRL*, XXXIV, 1951-2, 37-43.

J. RYCKMANS, *L'institution monarchique en Arabie méridionale avant l'Islam*, Louvain, 1951.

J. GRAY, 'Canaanite Kingship in Theory and Practice', in *VT*, II, 1952, 193-220.

'Authority and Law in the Ancient Orient', Supplement 17 to *JAOS*, 1954: J. A. WILSON (Egypt); E. A. SPEISER (Mesopotamia); H. G. GÜTERBOCK (Hittites); I. MENDELSOHN (Canaan and Israel).

On the religious character of the king, in general:

S. MOWINCKEL, *Psalmenstudien*, II, *Das Thronbesteigungsfest Jahwäs und der Ursprung der Eschatologie*, Christiania, 1922.

C. R. NORTH, 'The Religious Aspects of Hebrew Kingship', in *ZAW*, L, 1932, 8-38.

S. H. HOOKE (Ed.), *Myth and Ritual. Essays on the Myth and Ritual of the Hebrews in Relation to the Culture Pattern of the Ancient East*, London, 1933.

S. MOWINCKEL, 'Urmensch und "Königsideologie"', in *Studia Theologica* (Lund), II, 1948, 71-89.

A. BENTZEN, 'King Ideology—"Urmensch"—"Troonsbestijgingsfeest"', in *Studia Theologica* (Lund), III, 1950, 143-57.

A. R. JOHNSON, 'Divine Kingship and the Old Testament', in *Expository Times*, LXII, 1950, 36-42.

M. NOTH, 'Gott, König, Volk im Alten Testament', in *Zeitschrift für Theologie und Kirche*, XLVII, 1950, 157-91= *Gesammelte Studien zum Alten Testament*, Munich, 1956, 188-229.

J. DE FRAINE, *L'aspect religeux de la royauté israélite. L'institution monarchique dans l'Ancien Testament et dans les textes mésopotamiens*, Rome, 1954.

G. WIDENGREN, *Sakrales Königtum im Alten Testament und in Judentum*, Stuttgart, 1955.

A. R. JOHNSON, *Sacral Kingship in Ancient Israel*, Cardiff, 1955.

S. MOWINCKEL, *He that Cometh* (English translation), Oxford, 1956, esp. pp. 21-95.

G. FOHRER, 'Der Vertrag zwischen König und Volk in Israel', in *ZAW*, LXXI, 1959, 1-22.

E. I. J. ROSENTHAL, 'Some Aspects of the Hebrew Monarchy', in *Journal of Jewish Studies*, IX, 1958, 1-18.

S. H. HOOKE (Editor), *Myth, Ritual and Kingship. Essays on the Theory and Practice of Kingship in the Ancient Near East, and in Israel*, 1958.

G. W. AHLSTRÖM, 'Psalm 89. Eine Liturgie ans', in *Ritual des Leidenden Königs*, Lund, 1959.

A. GARDINER, 'The Baptism of Pharao', in *Journal of Egyptian Archaeology*, XXXVI, 1950, 3-12.

S. MOWINCKEL, 'General Oriental and Specific Israelite Elements in the Israelite Conception of the Sacral Kingdom', in *The Sacral Kingship* (Supplement IV to *Numen*), Leiden, 1959, 285-93.

On the coronation rites:

K. SETHE, *Dramatische Texte zu altägyptischen Mysterienspielen*, Leipzig, 1928.

K. F. MULLER, *Das assyrische Ritual. I. Texte zum assyrischen Königsritual* (Mitteilungen der vorderasiatisch-ägyptischen Gesellschaft, XLI, 3), Leipzig, 1937.

G. VON RAD, 'Das judaische Königsritual', in *TLZ*, LXXII, 1947, 211-16.

P. A. H. DE BOER, 'Vive le roi', in *VT*, V, 1955, 225-31.
M. NOTH, *Amt und Berufung im Alten Testament*, Bonn, 1958.
E. COTHENET, art. 'Onction', in *Dictionnaire de la Bible, Supplément*, VI, 1959, 701-32.
J. MORGENSTERN, 'David and Jonathan', in *JBL*, LXXVIII, 1959, 322-5.
Z. W. FALK, 'Forms of Testimony', in *VT*, XI, 1961, 88-91 (on 'edûth).

On the coronation names:

A. M. HONEYMAN, 'The Evidence for Royal Names among the Hebrews', in *JBL*, LXVII, 1948, 13-26.
A. ALT, 'Jesaja 8, 23-9, 6. Befreiungsnacht und Krönungstag', in *Festschrift Bertholet*, Tübingen, 1950, 29-49.=*Kleine Schriften*, II, 206-25.
I. GELB, 'The Double Name of Hittite Kings', in *Rocznyk Orientalistyczny*, Cracow, XVII, 1953 (*Memorial T. Kowalsky*), 146-54.
S. MORENZ, 'Aegyptische und davidische Königstitulatur', in *Zeitschrift für ägyptische Sprache und Altertumskunde*, LXXIX, 1954, 73-4.
H. CAZELLES, 'La titulature du roi David', in *Mélanges A. Robert*, 1957, 131-6.
L. M. VON PAKOZDY, "Elḫanan, der frühere Name Davids?', in *ZAW*, LXVIII, 1956, 257-9.
R. BORGER, 'Mesopotamien in den Jahren 629-621 v. Chr.', in *Wiener Zeitschrift für die Kunde des Morgenlandes*, LV, 1959, 62-76 (Assurbanipal=Kandalanu).

On the enthronement psalms:

L. DÜRR, *Psalm 110 im Lichte der neueren alttestamentlischen Forschung*, Münster i.W., 1929.
G. VON RAD, 'Erwägungen zu den Königpsalmen', in *ZAW*, LXVIII, 1940-1, 216-22.
G. WIDENGREN, *Psalm 110 och det sakrale Kungedömet i Israel*, Uppsala, 1941.
A. BENTZEN, *Messias, Moses redivivus, Menschensohn*, Zurich, 1948, esp. pp. 11-32.
R. MURPHY, *A Study of Psalm 72*, Washington, 1948.
A. ROBERT, 'Considérations sur le messianisme du Ps 2', in *Recherches de Science Religieuse*, XXXIX, 1951-2, 88-98.
J. DE FRAINE, 'Quel est le sens exact de la filiation divine dans Ps 2, 7?', in *Bijdragen, Tijdschrift voor Philosophie en Theologie* (Louvain and Maastricht), XVI, 1955, 349-56.
J. COPPENS, 'La portée messianique du Ps CX', in *Ephemerides Theologicae Lovanienses*, XXXII, 1956, 5-23.
J. DE SAVIGNAC, 'Théologie Pharaonique et messianisme d'Israël', in *VT*, VII, 1957, 82-90.
R. PRESS, 'Jahwe und seine Gesalbten (Ps. 2)', in *Theologische Zeitschrift*, XIII, 1957, 321-34.
H. J. STOEBE, 'Erwägungen zu Psalm 110 auf dem Hintergrund von 1. Sam. 21', in *Festschrift. F. Baumgärtel*, Erlangen, 1959, 175-91.
M. BIČ, 'Das erste Buch des Psalters, eine Thronbesteigungsfestliturgie', in *The Sacral Kingship* (Supplement IV to *Numen*), Leiden, 1959, 316-32.
J. COPPENS, 'Les apports du Psaume cx (Vulgate cix) à l'idéologie royale israélite', ibid., 333-48.

On the king as saviour:

G. WIDENGREN, *The King and the Tree of Life in Ancient Near Eastern Religion (King and Saviour IV)*, Uppsala, 1951.
R. MEYER, 'Der Erlöserkönig des Alten Testaments', in *Münchener Theologische Zeitschrift*, III, 1952, 221-43, 367-84.
J. L. MCKENZIE, 'Royal Messianism', in *Catholic Biblical Quarterly*, XIX, 1957, 27-52.

On the priesthood of the king:

A. R. JOHNSON, 'The Role of the King in the Jerusalem Cultus', in S. H. Hooke, *The Labyrinth*, London, 1935, 73-111.
J. MORGENSTERN, 'A Chapter in the History of the High Priesthood', in *AJSL*, LV, 1938, 5-13.
H. H. ROWLEY, 'Melchizedek and Zadok', in *Festschrift Bertholet*, Tübingen, 1950, 461-72.
J. DE FRAINE, 'Peut-on parler d'un véritable sacerdoce du roi en Israël?', in *Sacra Pagina*, I, Gembloux, 1959, 537-47.
H. J. KRAUS, 'Königtum und Kultus in Jerusalem, Excursus 6' in the author's *Psalmen*, II, Neukirche Kreis Moer, 1960, 879-83.

6

THE ROYAL HOUSEHOLD

Nothing exists except some special studies on particular questions.

On the harem:

E. WEIDNER, 'Hof- und Harems-Erlasse assyrischen Könige', in *AfO*, XVII, 1956, 257-93.
M. TSEVAT, 'Marriage and Monarchical Legitimacy in Ugarit and Israel', in *Journal of Semitic Studies*, III, 1958, 237-43.

On the Great Lady:

A. KAMPMANN, 'Tawannanaš, de Titel der hethietische Köningin', in *Jaarbericht Ex Oriente Lux*, II (numbers 6-8), 1940, 432-42.
A. CAQUOT, 'La déesse Shegal', in *Semitica*, IV, 1951-2, 55-8.
H. LEWY, 'Nitokris-Naqî'a', in *JNES*, XI, 1952, 264-86.
G. MOLIN, 'Die Stellung der Gebira im Staate Juda', in *Theologische Zeitschrift*, X, 1954, 161-75.
C. J. GADD, 'The Harran Inscriptions of Nabonidus', in *Anatolian Studies*, VIII, 1958, 35-92.
H. DONNER, 'Art und Herkunft des Amtes der Königinmutter im Alten Testament', in *Festschrift J. Friedrich*, 1959.

On the 'king's son':

H. GAUTHIER, 'Les "Fils royaux de Koush"', in *Recueil de Travaux relatifs à la philologie et à l'archéologie égyptiennes et assyriennes*, XXXIX, 1920, 178-237.
S. YEIVIN, art. 'ben hammèlèk', in *Encyclopaedia Biblica* (in Hebrew), Jerusalem, III, 1954, 160.

On the king's 'servants':

W. F. ALBRIGHT, 'The Seal of Eliakim and the Latest Pre-exilic History of Judah', in *JBL*, LI, 1932, 77-106, esp. 79-80.
A. BERGMAN, 'Two Hebrew Seals of the 'Ebed Class', in *JBL*, LV, 1936, 221-6.

On armour-bearers:

E. KLAUBER, *Assyrisches Beamtentum nach den Briefen aus der Sargonidenzeit (Leipziger Semitische Studien, V, 3)*, Leipzig, 1910, 111-15: *Der šalšu*.
A. GOETZE, 'Hittite Courtiers and their Titles', in *Revue Hittite et asianique*, XII, fasc, 54, 1952, 1-7.

On the *saris*:

E. VON SCHULER, *Hethitische Dienstanweisungen für höhere Hof- und Staatsbeamte (AfO, Beihefte 10)*, 1957.

On the 'king's friend':

R. DE VAUX, 'Titres et fonctionnaires égyptiens à la cour de David et de Salomon', in *RB*, XLVIII, 1939, 403-5.
A. VAN SELMS, 'The Origin of the Title "the King's Friend"', in *JNES*, XVI, 1957, 118-23.

On the royal estate:

M. NOTH, 'Das Krongut der israelitischen Könige und seine Verwaltung', in *ZDPV*, L, 1927, 211-44; cf. *PJB*, XXVIII, 1932, 60-1.
A. ALT, 'Der Anteil des Königstum an der sozialen Entwicklung in den Reichen Israel und Juda', in *Kleine Schriften*, III, Munich, 1959, 348-72.
W. F. ALBRIGHT, incidentally in *JPOS*, XI, 1931, 249; *JBL*, LI, 1932, 82-4.
E. SELLIN, 'Die palästinischen Krughenkel mit den Konigsstempeln', in *ZDPV*, LXVI, 1943, 216-32.

7

THE PRINCIPAL OFFICIALS OF THE KING

E. KLAUBER, *Assyrisches Beamtentum nach den Briefen aus der Sargonidenzeit (Leipziger Semitische Studien, V, 3)*, Leipzig, 1910.
K. GALLING, 'Die Halle des Schreibers', in *PJB*, XXVII, 1931, 51-7.
H. KEES, *Kulturgeschichte des Alten Orients*, I, *Aegypten (Handbuch der Altertumswissenschaft)*, Munich, 1933, 185-218.
R. DE VAUX, 'Le sceau de Godolias, maitre du palais', in *RB*, XLV, 1936, 96-102.
R. DE VAUX, 'Titres et fonctionnaires égyptiens à la cour de David et de Salomon', in *RB*, XLVIII, 1939, 394-405
J. BEGRICH, 'Sopher und Mazkir. Ein Beitrag zur inneren Geschichte des davidisch-salomonischen Grossreiches und der Königreiches Juda', in *ZAW*, LVIII, 1940-1, 1-29.
B. MAISLER, 'Le scribe de David et le problème des grands officiers dans l'ancien royaume d'Israël' (in Hebrew), in *BJPES*, XIII, 1946-7, 105-14.
N. AVIGARD, 'The Epitaph of a Royal Steward from Siloam Village', in *IEJ*, III, 1953, 137-52.
A. ALT, 'Hohe Beamten in Ugarit', in *Studia Orientalia Ioanni Pedersen . . . dedicata*, Copenhagen, 1953, 1-11 = *Kleine Schriften*, III, 186-97.
J. R. KUPPER, 'Baḫdi-lim, préfet du Palais du Mari', in *Bulletin de la Classe des Lettres et des Sciences Morale et Politique de l'Académie Royale de Belgique*, 5th series, XL, 1954, 572-87.
H. J. KATSENSTEIN, 'The House of Eliakim, a Family of Royal Stewards', in *Eretz-Israel*, V, 1958 (Volume Mazar), 108-10 (in Hebrew, with a summary in English).

8

THE ADMINISTRATION OF THE KINGDOM

On Solomon's prefectures:

A. ALT, 'Israels Gaue unter Salomo', in *Alttestamentliche Studien R. Kittel . . . dargebracht*, Leipzig, 1913, 1–19= *Kleine Schriften*, II, Munich, 1953, 76–89.
W. F. ALBRIGHT, 'The Administrative Divisions of Israel and Juda', in *JPOS*, V, 1925, 17–54.
R. P. DOUGHERTY, 'Cuneiform Parallels to Solomon's Provisioning System', in *AASOR*, V, 1925, 23–46.
F. M. ABEL, *Géographie de la Palestine*, II, Paris, 1938, 79–83.
F. PUZO, 'La segunda prefectura salomónica', in *Estudios Biblicos*, VII, 1949, 43–73.
A. ALT, 'Menschen ohne Namen', in *Archiv Orientální*, XVIII, 1-2, 1950, 9–24= *Kleine Schriften*, III, 198–213.

On the districts of Judah:

A. ALT, 'Judas Gaue unter Josia', in *PJB*, XXI, 1925, 100–16= *Kleine Schriften*, II, Munich, 1953, 276–88.
S. MOWINCKEL, *Zur Frage nach dokumentarischen Quellen in Josua 13–19*, Oslo, 1946.
F. M. CROSS and G. E. WRIGHT, 'The Boundary and Province Lists of the Kingdom of Judah', in *JBL*, LXXV, 1956, 202–26.
Z. KALLAI-KLEINMANN, 'The Town Lists of Judah, Simeon, Benjamin and Dan', in *VT*, VIII, 1958, 134–60.
Y. AHARONI, 'The Province-List of Judah', in *VT*, IX, 1959, 225–46.

On the districts of Israel:

A. ALT, 'Eine galiläische Ortsliste in Josua 19', in *ZAW*, XLV, 1927, 59–81.
M. NOTH, 'Studien zur Geschichte der historisch-geographischen Dokumente des Josuabuches', in *ZDPV*, LVIII, 1935, 185–255, esp. 215–30.

On the cantons of Samaria:

W. F. ALBRIGHT, 'The Administrative Divisions of Israel and Judah', in *JPOS*, V, 1925, 17–54, esp. 38–43.
M. NOTH, 'Das Krongut der israelitischen Könige und seine Verwaltung', in *ZDPV*, L, 1927, 211–44, esp. 230–40.
M. NOTH, 'Der Beitrag der samaritischen Ostraka zur Lösung topographischen Fragen', in *PJB*, XXVIII 1932, 54–67.
F. M. ABEL, *Géographie de la Palestine*, II, Paris, 1938, 95–7.
B. MAISLER, 'The Historical Background of the Samaria Ostraka', in *JPOS*, XXI, 1948, 117–33.
S. MOSCATI, *L'epigrafia ebraica antica 1935–1950*, Rome, 1951, 27–31.

On the local administration, for comparison:

F. CHARLES JEAN, *Les lettres de Ḫammurapi à Sin-Idinnam*, Paris, 1913.
J. R. KUPPER, 'Un gouvernement provincial dans le royaume de Mari', in *Revue d'Assyriologie*, XLI, 1947, 149–83.
J. R. KUPPER, *Correspondance de Kibri-Dagan, gouverneur de Tirqa* (*Archives Royales de Mari*, III), Paris, 1950.

9

FINANCE AND PUBLIC WORKS

No special work. Material will be found in the following:

F. BUHL, *La société israélite d'après l'Ancien Testament*, Paris, 1904, 185–94.
A. BERTHOLET, *Kulturgeschichte Israels*, Göttingen, 1919, 181–4.
J. PEDERSEN, *Israel, its Life and Culture*, III–IV², London, 1947, 66–71.
I. MENDELSOHN, *Slavery in the Ancient Near East*, New York, 1949, 97–9, and the long note, pp. 149–50.
H. CAZELLES, 'La dîme israélite et les texts de Ras-Shamra', in *VT*, I, 1951, 131–4.
J. NOUGAYROL, *Le palais royal d'Ugarit*, III, *Textes accadiens et hourrites . . .* , Paris, 1955, Index s.v. 'Franchises et Exemptions', 'Recettes fiscales', 'Services et corvées'.
I. MENDELSOHN, 'Samuel's Denunciation of Kingship in the Light of the Akkadian Documents from Ugarit', in *BASOR*, **143**, 1956, 17–22.
Y. AHARONI, 'Hebrew Jar-Stamps from Ramat Rachel', in *Eretz-Israel*, VI, 1960 (in Hebrew, with a summary in English).

10

LAW AND JUSTICE

General:

M. NOTH, *Die Gesetze im Pentateuch. Ihre Voraussetzungen und ihr Sinn.* (Schriften der Königsberger Gelehrten Gesellschaft), Halle, 1940 = *Gesammelte Studien zum Alten Testament*, Munich, 1957, 9-141.
G. OSTBORN, *Tôrah in Old Testament*, Lund, 1945.
D. DAUBE, *Studies in Biblical Law*, Cambridge, 1947.
J. VAN DER PLOEG, 'Studies in Biblical Law', in *Catholic Biblical Quarterly*, XII, 1950, 248-59; 416-27; XIII, 1951, 28-43; 164-71; 296-307.
H. CAZELLES, 'Loi Israélite', in *Supplément au Dictionnaire de la Bible*, Paris, V, 1952-3, 497-530.

On the laws of the ancient East:

G. LANDSBERGER, 'Die babylonischen Termini für Gesetz und Recht', in *Symbolae . . . P. Koschaker dedicatae*, Leyden, 1939, 219-34.
'Authority and Law in the Ancient Orient', Supplement 17 to *JAOS*, 1954: J. A. WILSON (Egypt); E. A. SPEISER (Mesopotamia); H. G. GUTERBOCK (Hittites); I. MENDELSOHN (Canaan and Israel).
G. BOYER, 'La place des textes d'Ugarit dans l'histoire de l'ancien droit oriental', in J. NOUGAYROL, *Le Palais Royal d'Ugarit*, III, Paris, 1955, 283-308.
E. SZLECHTER, 'Les anciennes codifications en Mésopotamie', in *Revue Internationale des Droits de l'Antiquité*, IV, 1957, 73-92.
The most important texts. well translated and with a bibliography, are collected in J. B. PRITCHARD, *Ancient Near Eastern Texts relating to the Old Testament*, 2nd ed., Princeton, 1955, 159-98.

Other recent translations, with commentary:

E. SZLECHTER, 'Le code d'Ur-Nammu', in *Revue d'Assyriologie*, XLIX, 1955, 169-77.
J. P. LETTINGA, 'Het sumerische wetboek van Lipitištar, koning van Isin', in *Jaarbericht Ex Oriente Lux* XII, 1951-2, 249-63.
E. SZLECHTER, 'Le code de Lipit-Ištar', in *Revue d'Assyriologie*, LI, 1957, 57-82.
A. GOETZE, *The Laws of Eshnunna* (*AASOR*, XXXI, 1951-2), 1956.
G. R. DRIVER and J. C. MILES, *The Babylonian Laws*, Oxford, I, 1952; II, 1955.
G. R. DRIVER and J. C. MILES, *The Assyrian Laws*, Oxford, 1935.
E. NEUFELD, *The Hittite Laws*, London, 1951.
J. FRIEDRICH, *Die hethitischen Gesetze*, Leiden, 1959.

On the sources of Israelite law:

A. JIRKU, *Das weltliche Recht im Alten Testament*, Gütersloh, 1927.
H. SCHMÖKEL, *Das angewandte Recht im Alten Testament*, Leipzig, 1930.
V. KOROŠEC, *Hethitische Staatsverträge. Ein Beitrag zu ihrer juristichen Wertung*, Leipzig, 1931.
E. F. WEIDNER, 'Der Staatsvertrag Aššurnirâris VI. von Assyrien mit Mati'ilu von Sît-Agusi', in *AfO*, VIII, 1932-3, 17-34.
M. DAVID, 'The Codex Hammurabi and its relations to the Provisions of Law in Exodus', in *Oudtestamentische Studiën*, VII, 1950, 149-78.
A. ALT, *Die Ursprünge des israelitischen Rechts*, Leipzig, 1934 = *Kleine Schriften*, I, Munich, 1953, 278-332.
A. DUPONT-SOMMER, 'Une inscription araméenne inédite de Sfiré (stèle III)', in *Bulletin du Musée de Beyrouth*, XII, 1956, 23-41.
J. NOUGAYROL, *Le Palais d'Ugarit*, IV, Paris, 1956.
D. J. WISEMAN, 'The Vassal-Treaties of Esarhaddon', in *Iraq*, XX, 1958, 1-99.
A. DUPONT-SOMMER, 'Les inscriptions araméennes de Sfiré (stèles I et II)', in *Mémoires présentés par divers savants à l'Académie des Inscriptions et Belles-Lettres*, XV, 1958.

On the characteristics of Israelite law:

A. ALT, 'Zur Talionsformel', in *ZAW*, III, 1934, 303-5 = *Kleine Schriften*, I, Munich, 1953, 341-4.
J. BEGRICH, 'Berit. Ein Beitrag zur Erfassung einer alttestamentlichen Denkform', in *ZAW*, LX, 1944, 1-11.
B. GEMSER, 'The Importance of the Motive Clause in Old Testament Law', in *Congress Volume Copenhagen*, Supplement I to *VT*, 1953, 50-66.
M. NOTH, 'Das alttestamentliche Bundschliessen im Lichte eines Mari-Textes', in *Mélanges Isidore Lévy* (*Annuaire de l'Institut de Philologie et d'Histoire Orientales et Slaves*), XIII, 1953, 433-44 = *Gesammelte Studien zum Alten Testament*, Munich, 1957, 142-54.
G. E. MENDENHALL, *Law and Covenant in Israel and the Ancient Near East*, Pittsburgh, 1955, Reprinted from *Biblical Archaeologist*, XVII, 1954, 26-46; 49-76.
F. HORST, 'Recht und Religion im Bereich des Alten Testaments', in *Evangelische Theologie*, XVI, 1956, 49-74.
A. S. DIAMOND, 'An Eye for an Eye', in *Iraq*, XIX, 1957, 151-5.

E. Würthwein, 'Der Sinn des Gesetzes im Alten Testament', in *Zeitschrift für Theologie und Kirche*, LV, 1958, 255-70.
W. Zimmerli, 'Das Gesetz im Alten Testament', in *TLZ*, LXXXV, 1960, 481-98.

On the legislative and judicial power of the king:

M. Noth, *Die Gesetze im Pentateuch, op. cit.*, pp. 9-22; 33-29=*Gesammelte Studien* . . . , pp. 23-42; 58-67.
M. Noth, 'Das Amt des "Richters Israels"', in *Festschrift A. Bertholet*, Tübingen, 1950, 404-17.
H. W. Hertzberg, 'Die Kleinen Richter', in *TLZ*, LXXIX, 1954, 285-90.
G. Widengren, 'King and Covenant', in *Journal of Semitic Studies* (Manchester), II, 1957, 1-32.

On the courts of justice:

A. Walther, *Das altbabylonische Gerichtswesen* (*Leipziger Semitische Studien*, VI, 4-6), Leipzig, 1917.
J. van der Ploeg, 'Shapaṭ et Mishpaṭ', in *Oudtestamentische Studiën*, II, 1943, 144-55.
H. Liebesny, 'The Administration of Justice in Nuzi', in *JAOS*, LXIII, 1943, 128-44.
K. Pfluger, 'The Edict of King Haremhab', in *JNES*, V, 1946, 260-8.
W. F. Albright, 'The Reform of Jehoshaphat', in *Alexander Mark Jubilee Volume*, New York, 1950, 61-82.
E. Seidl, *Einführung in die ägyptische Rechtsgeschichte bis zum Ende des Neun Reiches*, I, *Juristischer Teil*, Gluckstadt-Hamburg, 2nd ed., 1951.
L. Köhler, *Der hebräische Mensch*, Tübingen, 1953. Appendix, pp. 143-71; 'Die hebräische Rechtsgemeinde'.
J. van der Ploeg, 'Les šôṭerim d'Israél, in *Oudtestamentische Studiën*, X, 1954, 185-96.
W. Helck,'Das Dekret des Königs Haremhab',in *Zeitschrift für Aegyptische Sprache und Altertumskunde*, LXXX, 1955, 109-36.
A. Falkenstein, *Die neusumerischen Gerichtsurkunden* (Bayerische Akademie der Wissenschaften, Phil.-Hist. Klasse, Abhandlungen, N.F. 39), Munich, 1956.
E. Seidl, *Aegyptische Rechtsgeschichte der Saiten- und Perserzeit*, Gluckstadt-Hamburg, 1956.
H. Klengel, 'Zu den šibūtum in alt-babylonischer Zeit', in *Orientalia*, XXIX, 1960, 357-75.

On procedure:

L. Köhler, *Deuterojesaja stilkritisch untersucht* (Supplement to *ZAW*, 37), Giessen, 1923, 110-20.
H. Liesbesny, 'Evidence in Nuzi Legal Procedure', in *JAOS*, LXI, 1941, 130-42.
B. Gemser, 'The Rîb-Pattern in Hebrew Mentality', in *Wisdom in Israel and in the Ancient Near East—Rowley Volume* (Supplement III to *VT*, 1955, 120-37).
D. Daube, 'Rechtsgedanken in der Erzählungen des Pentateuchs', in *Von Ugarit nach Qumran* (*Festschrift Eissfeldt*), Berlin, 1958, 32-41.
H. B. Huffman, 'The Covenant Lawsuit in the Prophets', in *JBL*, LXXVIII, 1959, 285-95.

On the judgment of God:

R. Press, 'Ordal im alten Israel', in *ZAW*, LI, 1933, 121-40; 227-55.
C. H. Gordon, 'Elohim in its Reputed Meaning of Rulers, Judges', in *JBL*, LIV, 1935, 139-44.
G. R. Driver and J. C. Miles, 'The Assyrian Laws', Oxford, 1935, 86-106.
G. Dossin, 'Un cas d'ordalie par le dieu Fleuve d'après une lettre de Mari', in *Symbolae . . . P. Koschaker dedicatae*, Leyden, 1939, 112-18.
G. R. Driver and J. C. Miles, *The Babylonian Laws*, I, Oxford, 1952, 63-5.
G. R. Driver and J. C. Miles, 'Ordeal by Oath at Nuzi', in *Iraq*, VII, 1940, 132-8.
A. Speiser, 'Nuzi Marginalia', in *Orientalia*, XXV, 1956, 15-23.
A. E. Draffkorn, 'Ilâni Elohim', in *JBL*, LXXVI, 1957, 216-24.
F. C. Fensham, 'New Light on Ex 21: 6 and 22: 7 from the Laws of Eshnunna', in *JBL*, LXXVIII, 1959, 160-1.
G. Dossin, 'L'ordalie à Mari', in *Comptes-rendus de l'Académie des Inscriptions et Belles Lettres* (Paris) 1958, 387-92.

On penalties:

Little exists apart from dictionaries and general works:

R. Sugranyes de Franch, *Etudes sur le droit palestinien à l'époque évangelique. La contrainte par corps*, Fribourg (Switzerland), 1946.
J. Gabriel, 'Die Todesstrafe im Licht des Alten Testaments', in *Theologische Fragen der Gegenwart*, Vienna, 1952, 69-79.

On the cities of refuge:

N. H. Nicolsky, 'Das Asylrecht in Israel', in *ZAW*, XLVIII, 1930, 146-75.
M. Löhr, *Das Asylwesen im Alten Testament*, Halle, 1930.
M. David, 'Die Bestimmungen über die Asylstädte in Josue XX', in *Oudtestamentische Studiën*, IX, 1951, 30-48.

B. DINUR, 'The Religious Character of the Cities of Refuge and the Ceremony of Admission into them', in *Eretz-Israel*, III, 1954, 135-46 (in Hebrew, with English summary).

M. GREENBERG, 'The Biblical Conception of Asylum', in *JBL*, LXXVIII, 1959, 125-32.

11

ECONOMIC LIFE

On landed property:

G. DALMAN, *Arbeit und Sitte in Palästina*, II, *Der Ackerbau*, Gütersloh, 1932, 36-46.

R. CLAY, *The Tenure of Land in Babylonia and Assyria*, London, 1938.

H. LEWY, 'The Nuzian Feudal System', in *Orientalia*, XI, 1942, 1-40; 209-50; 297-349.

F. R. STEELE, *Nuzi Real Estate Transactions*, New Haven, 1943.

H. BUCKERS, *Die Biblische Lehre von Eigentum*, Bonn, 1947.

E. MARMORSTEIN, 'The Origin of Agricultural Feudalism in the Holy Land', in *PEQ*, 1953, 111-17.

K. H. HENRY, 'Land Tenure in the Old Testament', in *PEQ*, 1954, 5-15.

A. ALT, 'Der Anteil des Königstums an der sozialen Entwicklung in den Reichen Israel und Juda', in *Kleine Schriften*, III, Munich, 1959, 348-72.

On the formalities of transfer:

L. FISCHER, 'Die Urkunden in Jer. 32, 11-14 nach den Ausgrabungen und dem Talmud', in *ZAW*, XXX, 1910, 136-42.

L. WENGER, 'Signum (Doppelurkunden)', in PAULY-WISSOWA, *Real-Encyclopädie der classischen Altertumswissenschaft*, II, 11, 1923, col. 2408-30.

E. R. LACHMAN, 'Note on Ruth 4, 7-8', in *JBL*, LVI, 1937, 53-6.

E. A. SPEISER, 'Of Shoes and Shekels', in *BASOR*, **77**, February 1940, 15-18.

On interest:

J. HEJCL, *Das alttestamentliche Zinsverbot (Biblische Studien*, XII, 4), Freiburg i.Br., 1907.

S. STEIN, 'The Laws of Interest in the Old Testament', in *JTS*, n.s. IV, 1953, 161-70.

E. NEUFELD, 'The Rate of Interest and the Text of Nehemiah 5. 11', in *JQR*, n.s. XLIV, 1953-4, 194-204.

E. SZLECHTER, 'Le prêt dans l'Ancien Testament et dans les codes mésopotamiens d'avant Hammourabi', in *RHPR*, XXXV, 1955, 16-25.

On pledges and sureties:

P. KOSCHAKER, *Babylonisch-assyrisches Bürgschaftsrecht*, Leipzig, 1911.

A. ABELES, 'Der Bürge nach Biblischen Recht', in *Monatsschrift für Geschichte und Wissenschaft das Judentums*, LXVI, 1922, 279-94; LXVII, 1923, 35-53.

E. M. CASSIN, 'La caution à Nuzi', in *Revue d'Assyriologie*, XXXIV, 1937, 154-68.

H. M. WEIL, 'Gage et cautionnement dans la Bible', in *Archives d'Histoire du Droit Oriental*, II, 1938, 171-240.

H. M. WEIL, 'Exégèse de Jérémie 23, 33-40 et de Job 34, 28-33', in *Revue de l'Histoire des Religions*, CXVIII, 1938, 201-8.

M. DAVID, 'Deux anciens termes bibliques pour le gage', in *Oudtestamentische Studiën*, II, 1943, 79-86.

On the sabbatical and jubilee years:

C. H. GORDON, 'Parallèles nouziens aux lois et coutumes de l'Ancien Testament', in *RB*, XLIV, 1935, 38-41.

J. B. ALEXANDER, 'A Babylonian Year of Jubilee?' in *JBL*, LVII, 1938, 75-9.

V. TSCHERIKOWER and F. M. HEICHELHEIM, 'Jewish Religious Influence in the Adler Papyri', in *HTR*, XXV, 1942, 25-44.

M. DAVID, 'The Manumission of Slaves under Zedekiah', in *Oudtestamentische Studiën*, V, 1948, 63-79.

F. M. LEMOINE, 'Le jubilé dans la Bible', in *Vie Spirituelle*, LXXXI, 1949, 262-88.

G. LAMBERT, 'Jubilé biblique et jubilé chrétien', in *Nouvelle Revue Théologique*, LXXII, 1950, 234-51.

J. T. MILIK, 'De vicissitudinibus notionis et vocabuli jubilaei', in *Verbum Domini*, XXVIII, 1950, 162-7.

R. NORTH, 'Maccabean Sabbath Years', in *Biblica*, XXXIV, 1953, 505-15.

R. NORTH, 'Yad in the Shemittah Law', in *VT*, IV, 1954, 196-9.

R. NORTH, *Sociology of the Biblical Jubilee*, Rome, 1954.

J. LEWY, 'The Biblical Institution of Deror in the Light of Akkadian Documents', in *Eretz-Israel*, V (Volume Mazar), 1958, 21-31.

J. J. RABINOWITZ, 'A Biblical Parallel to a Legal Formula from Ugarit', in *VT*, VIII, 1958, 95.

E. NEUFELD, 'Socio-Economic Background of Yobel and Semiṭṭa', in *Rivista degli Studi Orientali*, XXXIII, 1958, 53-124.

D. CORRENS, *Die Mischna . . .* , I, 5, Schebiit (Vom Sabbatjahr), Berlin, 1960.

12

DIVISIONS OF TIME

On the ancient Eastern calendars:

B. LANDSBERGER, *Der kultischer Kalender der Babylonier und Assyrer* (*Leipziger Semitische Studien*, VI, 1-2), Leipzig, 1915.

L. BORCHARDT, *Die altägyptische Zeitmessung*, Berlin, 1920.

R. W. SLOLEY, 'Primitive Methods of Measuring Time, with Special Reference to Egypt', in *Journal of Egyptian Archaeology*, XVII, 1931, 166-78.

S. LANGDON, *Babylonian Menologies and the Semitic Calendars*, London, 1935.

L. BORCHARDT, *Das Mittel zur zeitlichen Festlegung von Punkten der ägyptischen Geschichte und ihre Anwendung*, Cairo, 1935.

C. H. GORDON and E. R. LACHEMAN, 'The Nuzu Menology', in *Archiv Orientální*, X, 1938, 51-64.

H. and J. LEWY, 'The Origin of the Week and the Oldest Asiatic Calendar', in *HUCA*, XVII, 1942-3, 1-155.

R. A. PARKER and W. H. DUBBERSTEIN, *Babylonian Chronology, 626 B.C.-A.D. 45*, Chicago, 2nd ed., 1946.

S. SCHOTT, *Altagyptische Festdaten* (Abhandlungen der Akademie der Wissenschaften und der Literatur in Mainz), Wiesbaden, 1950.

R. A. PARKER, *The Calendars of Ancient Egypt*, Chicago, 1950.

A. GARDINER, 'The Problems of the Month-Names', in *Revue d'Égyptologie*, X, 1955, 9-31.

M. HÖFNER, 'Die altsüdarabischen Monatsnamen', in *Festschrift V. Christian*, Vienna, 1956, 46-54.

On the Israelite day:

J. MORGENSTERN, 'Supplementary Studies in the Calendars of Ancient Israel', in *HUCA*, X, 1935, 15-28.

P. J. HEADWOOD, 'The Beginning of the Jewish Day', in *JQR*, n.s. XXXVI, 1945-6, 393-401.

S. ZEITLIN, 'The Beginning of the Jewish Day during the Second Commonwealth', in *JQR*, n.s. XXXVI, 1945-6, 403-14.

S. IWRY, 'The Qumran Isaiah and the End of the Dial of Achaz', in *BASOR*, 147, October 1957, 27-33.

Y. YADIN, 'The Dial of Achaz', in *Eretz-Israel*, V (Volume Mazar), 1958, 83-90 (in Hebrew with a summary in English).

J. M. BAUMGARTEN, 'The Beginning of the Day in the Calendar of Jubilees', in *JBL*, LXXVII, 1958, 355-60.

S. ZEITLIN, 'The Beginning of the Day in the Calendar of Jubilees', in *JBL*, LXXVIII, 1959, 153-6 (with a reply by Baumgarten, 157).

On the month and the week:

S. GANDZ, 'Studies in the Hebrew Calendar', in *JQR*, n.s. XXXIX, 1948-9, 259-80; LX, 1949-50, 157-72, 251-77.

N. H. TUR-SINAI, 'Sabbat und Woche', in *Bibliotheca Orientalis*, VIII, 1951, 14-24.

E. AUERBACH, 'Die babylonische Datierung im Pentateuch und das Alter des Priester-Kodex', in *VT*, II, 1952, 334-42.

A. JAUBERT, 'Le calendrier des Jubilés et de la secte de Qumrân. Ses origines bibliques', in *VT*, III, 1953, 250-64.

Y. KAUFMAN, 'Der Kalendar und das Alter des Priester-Kodex', in *VT*, IV, 1954, 307-13.

J. MORGANSTERN, 'The Calendar of the Book of Jubilees, its Origin and its Character', in *VT*, V, 1955, 34-76.

A. JAUBERT, 'Le calendrier des Jubilés et les jours liturgiques de la semaine', in *VT*, VII, 1957, 35-61.

J. B. SEGAL, 'Intercalation and the Hebrew Calendar', in *VT*, VII, 1957, 250-307.

A. JAUBERT, *Le date de la Cène. Calendrier biblique et liturgie chrétienne*, Paris, 1957.

E. R. LEACH, 'A Possible Method of Intercalation in the Calendar of the Book of Jubilees', in *VT*, VII, 1957, 392-9.

S. TALMON, 'Divergences in Calendar Reckoning in Ephraim and Juda', in *VT*, VIII, 1958, 48-74.

S. TALMON, 'The Calendar Reckoning of the Sect from the Judaean Desert', in *Aspects of the Dead Sea Scrolls* (*Scripta Hierosolymitana*, IV), Jerusalem, 1958, 161-99.

A. JAUBERT, 'Jésus et le calendrier de Qumrân', in *New Testament Studies*, VII, 1960-1, 1-30.

E. KUTSCH, 'Der Kalendar des Jubiläenbuches und das Alte und das Neue Testament', in *VT*, XI, 1961, 39-47.

On the year and its beginning: the eras:

J. BEGRICH, *Die Chronologie der Könige von Israel und Juda*, Tübingen, 1929, 66-94.

J. A. MONTGOMERY, 'The Year-Eponymate in the Hebrew Monarchy', in *JBL*, XLIX, 1930, 311-19.

J. MORGENSTERN, 'The New Year for Kings', in *Gaster Anniversary Volume*, London, 1936, 439-56.

N. H. SNAITH, *The Jewish New Year Festival, its Origin and Development*, London, 1947.

J. Morgenstern, 'The Chanukkah Festival and the Calendar of Ancient Israel.—The History of the Calendar of Israel during the Biblical Period', in *HUCA*, XXI, 1948, 365-496, with references to many of the author's previous works.

E. R. Thiele, *The Mysterious Numbers of the Hebrew Kings*, Chicago, 1951, 14-41.

S. Mowinckel, *Zum israelitischen Neujahr und zur Deutung der Thronbesteigungspsalmen*, Oslo, 1952, 5-38.

S. H. Horn and L. H. Wood, 'The Fifth Century Jewish Calendar in Elephantine', in *JNES*, XIII, 1954, 623-46.

S. Gandz, 'The Calendar of Ancient Israel', in *Homenaje Millás Vallícroza*, I, 1954, 1-20.

J. Schaumberger, 'Die neue Seleukidenliste BM 35603 und die makkabäische Chronologie', in *Biblica*, XXXVI, 1955, 423-5.

E. R. Thiele, 'New Evidence on the Chronology of the Last Kings of Judah', in *BASOR*, **143**, 1956, 22-7.

E. Auerbach, 'Der Wechsel des Jahres-Anfangs in Juda', in *VT*, IX, 1959, 113-21.

E. Auerbach, 'Die Umschaltung vom judäischen auf den babylonischen Kalendar', in *VT*, X, 1960, 69-70.

13

Weights and Measures

On metrology:

A. G. Barrois, 'La métrologie dans la Bible', in *RB*, XL, 1931, 185-213; XLI, 1932, 50-76. Summarized with some modifications in *The Interpreter's Bible*, I, New York, 1952, 152-7, and in *Manuel d'Archéologie Biblique*, II, Paris, 1953, 243-58.

H. Lewy, 'Assyro-Babylonian and Israelite Measures of Capacity and Rates of Seeding', in *JAOS*, LXIV, 1944, 65-73.

A. Segrè, 'A Documentary Analysis of Ancient Palestine Units of Measure', in *JBL*, LXIV, 1945, 357-75.

C. C. Wylie, 'On King Solomon's Molten Sea', in *Biblical Archaeologist*, XII, 1949, 86-90.

O. Eissfeldt, 'Die Menetekel-Inschrift und ihre Deutung (Dn 5 25)', in *ZAW*, LXIII, 1951, 105-14.

B. N. Wambacq, 'De 'ponderibus in S. Scriptura', in *Verbum Domini*, XXIX, 1951, 341-50.

O. Tufnell, *Lachish III, The Iron Age*, London, 1953, 313-15 and 340-57.

N. Avigad, 'Another bath le-melekh Inscription', in *IEJ*, III, 1953, 121-2.

B. N. Wambacq, 'De mensuris in S. Scriptura', in *Verbum Domini*, XXXII, 1954, 266-74; 325-34.

H. Otten, 'Zum Hethitischen Gewichtsystem', in *AfO*, XVII, 1954-6, 128-31.

J. Trinquet, 'Métrologie biblique', in *Supplément au Dictionnaire de la Bible*, V, Paris, 1957, col. 1212-50, with detailed bibliography.

R. B. Y. Scott, 'The Hebrew Cubit', in *JBL*, LXXVII, 1958, 295-14.

A. I. Lebowitz, 'A Note on R. B. Y. Scott's "The Hebrew Cubit"', in *JBL*, LXXVIII, 1959, 75-7.

R. B. Y. Scott, 'The Shekel Sign on Stone Weights', in *BASOR*, **153**, February 1959, 32-5.

N. Glueck, 'A Seal Weight from Nebi Rubin', in *BASOR*, **153**, February, 1959, 35-8.

R. B. Y. Scott, 'Weights and Measures of the Bible', in *Biblical Archaeologist*, XXII, 1959, 22-40.

J. T. Milik, 'Deux jarres inscrites provenant d'une grotte de Qumrân', in *Biblica*, XL, 1959, 985-91.

R. B. Y. Scott, 'Postscript on the Cubit', in *JBL*, LXXIX, 1960, 368.

Y. Yadin, 'Ancient Judaean Weights and the Date of the Samaria Ostraca', in *Studies in the Bible* (Studia Hierosolymitana, VIII), 1960, 1-17.

On coinage:

J. Babelon, 'Monnaie', in *Supplément au Dictionnaire de la Bible*, V, Paris, 1957, col. 1346-75, with long bibliography.

Consult also:

A. Reifenberg, *Ancient Jewish Coins*, Jerusalem, 2nd ed., 1947.

B. Kanael, 'The Beginning of Maccabean Coinage', in *IEJ*, I, 1950-1, 170-5.

A. Reifenberg, *Israel's History in Coins from the Maccabees to the Roman Conquest*.

D. Schlumberger, *L'argent grec dans l'empire achéménide*, Paris, 1953.

L. Kadman, 'A Coin Find at Masada', in *IEJ*, VII, 1957, 61-5.

Publications of the Israel Numismatic Society, I. Recent Studies and Discoveries in Ancient Jewish and Syrian Coins, Jerusalem, 1954.

Publications of the Israel Numismatic Society, II. The Dating and Meaning of Ancient Jewish Coins and Symbols, Jerusalem, 1958.

B. N. Wambacq, 'De Nummis in Sacra Scriptura', in *Verbum Domini*, XXXVIII, 1960, 156-72.

L. Kadman, *The Coins of the Jewish War of 66-73 (Corpus Nummorum Palestinensium, III)*, Jerusalem 1960.

III

MILITARY INSTITUTIONS

I

THE ARMIES OF ISRAEL

On armies in the Ancient Near East:

B. MEISSNER, *Babylonien und Assyrien*, I, Heidelberg, 1920, 80-114.
O. R. GURNEY, *The Hittites*, London, 1952, 104-16.
R. O. FAULKNER, 'Egyptian Military Organization', in *Journal of Egyptian Archaeology*, XXXIX, 1953, 32-47.

On the people under arms:

S. TOLKOWSKY, 'Gideon's 300', in *JPOS*, V, 1925, 69-74.
Y. SUKENIK (YADIN), 'Let the young men, I pray thee, arise and play before us', in *JPOS*, XXI, 1948, 110-16.
F. M. ABEL, 'Stratagèmes dans le livre de Josué', in *RB*, LVI, 1949, 321-39.
A. MALAMAT, 'The War of Gideon and Midian. A Military Approach', in *PEQ*, 1953, 61-5.
G. E. MENDENHALL, 'The Census Lists of Numbers 1 and 26', in *JBL*, LXXVII, 1958, 52-66.
R. DE VAUX, 'Les combats singuliers dans l'Ancien Testament', in *Studia Biblica et Orientalia, I. Vetus Testamentum*, Rome, 1959, 361-74=*Biblica*, XL, 1959, 495-508.

On the professional army:

(a) Mercenary troops:
K. ELLIGER, 'Die dreissig Helden Davids', in *PJB*, XXXI, 1935, 29-75.
J. VAN DER PLOEG, 'Le sens de *gibbôr hail*', in *Vivre et Penser*, I (*Revue Biblique*, L), 1941, 120-5.
F. WILLESEN, 'The *Yālîd* in Hebrew Society', in *Studia Theologica*, XII, 1958, 192-210.

(b) The chariot force:
M. LÖHR, 'Aegyptische Reiterei im Alten Testament?', in *Orientalistische Literaturzeitung*, XXXI, 1928, 923-8.
A. MOORTGAT, 'Der Kampf zu Wagen in der Kunst des alten Orients', in *Orientalistische Literaturzeitung*, XXXIII, 1930, 842-54.
W. F. ALBRIGHT, 'Mitannian maryannu "Charriot-Warrior" and the Canaanite and Egyptian Equivalents', in *AfO*, VI, 1930-1, 217-22.
J. WIESNER, 'Fahren und Reiten in Alteuropa und im Alten Orient' (*Der Alte Orient*, XXXVIII, 2-4), Leipzig, 1939.
R. T. O'CALLAGHAN, 'New Light on the Maryannu as "Charriot-Warrior"', in *Jahrbuch für kleinasiatische Forschung*, I, 1950-1, 309-21.
A. SALONEN, 'Die Landsfahrzeuge des alten Mesopotamien' (*Annales Acad. Scient. Fennicae*, ser. B, 72/73), Helsinki, 1951.
H. VON DEINES, 'Die Nachrichten über das Pferd und den Wagen in den ägyptischen Texten', in *Mitteilungen des Instituts für Orientforschung* (Berlin), I, 1953, 3-15.
A. ALT, 'Bemerkungen zu den Verwaltungs- und Rechtsurkunden von Ugarit und Alalakh', in *Die Welt des Orients*, II, 1, 1954, 10-15; II, 4, 1956, 234-7.
F. HANČAR, *Das Pferd in prähistorischer und früher historischer Zeit*, Vienna, 1956, 472-535.
A. SALONEN, 'Hippologica Akkadica' (*Annales Acad. Scient. Fennicae*, ser B, 100), Helsinki, 1956.
A. R. SCHULMAN, 'Egyptian Representations of Horsemen and Riding in the New Kingdom', in *JNES*, XVI, 1957, 263-71.

On the conscript army:

B. GRAY, 'The meaning of the Hebrew Word *dègèl*', in *JQR*, XI, 1899, 92-101.
E. JUNGE, *Der Wiederaufbau des Heerwesens des Reiches Juda unter Josia*, Stuttgart, 1937.
R. O. FAULKNER, 'Egyptian Military Standards', in *Journal of Egyptian Archaeology*, XXVII, 1941, 12-18.
Y. YADIN, 'The reorganization of the Army of Judah under Josiah', in *BJPES*, XV, 1949-50, 86-98 (in Hebrew).
J. R. KUPPER, 'Le recensement dans les textes de Mari', in A. PARROT, *Studia Mariana*, Leiden, 1950, 99-110.
J. VAN DER PLOEG, 'Les *šoterim* d'Israël', in *Oudtestamentische Studiën*, X, 1954, 185-96.
E. A. SPEISER, 'Census and Ritual Expiation in Mari and Israel', in *BASOR*, 149, 1958, 17-25.

2

Fortified Cities and Siege Warfare

On the fortified cities of Israel:

G. BEYER, 'Das Festungssystem Rehabeams', in *ZDPV*, LIV, 1931, 113-34.
E. JUNGE, *Der Wiederaufbau des Heerwesens des Reiches Juda unter Josia*, Stuttgart, 1937, 60-73.
A. ALT, 'Festungen und Levitenorte im Lande Juda', in *Kleine Schriften*, II, Munich, 1953, 306-15.

On fortifications:

The main source of information is archaeology, cf. A. G. BARROIS, *Manuel d'Archéologie Biblique*, I, Paris, 1939, ch. IV: 'La fortification'.

In addition, recent reports:

R. S. LAMON and G. M. SHIPTON, *Megiddo I*, Chicago, 1939, 28-32; 74-83.
W. F. ALBRIGHT, 'The Excavations of Tell Beit Mirsim', III (*Annual of the American Schools of Oriental Research*, XXI-XXII), New Haven, 1943, §§ 5-8; 26-31.
C. C. McCOWN, *Tell en-Naṣbeh*, I, Berkeley, 1947, 182-205.
G. LOUD, *Megiddo II*, Chicago, 1948, 46-57.
B. MAISLER, *The Excavations at Tell Qasîle. Preliminary Report*, Jerusalem, 1951, 39-41 = *IEJ*, I, 1950-1, 200-2.
O. TUFNELL, *Lachish III. The Iron Age*, London, 1953, 87-102.
Y. AHARONI, 'Excavations at Rameth Raḥel', in *IEJ*, VI, 1956, 138-41.
Y. YADIN, 'Solomon's City Wall and Gate at Gezer', in *IEJ*, VIII, 1958, 80-6.

In addition:

J. SIMONS, 'Topographical and Archaeological Elements in the Story of Abimelech', in *Oudtestamentische Studiën*, II, 1943, 35-78.
L. KÖHLER, *Kleine Lichter*, Zürich, 1945, 6. 'Wohnturm statt Palast', 30-32.
Y. AHARONI, 'The Date of the Casemate Walls in Judah and Israel and their Purpose', in *BASOR*, **154**, 1959, 35-9.
Y. YADIN, *Hazor, I: An Account of the First Season of Excavations*, 1955, Jerusalem, 1958.
L. A. SINCLAIR, 'An Archaeological Study of Gibeah (Tell el-Ful)', in *AASOR*, XXXIV-XXXV, 1954-6 (1960), 1-52.

On siege warfare:

R. P. DOUGHERTY, 'Sennacherib and the Walled Cities of Palestine', in *JBL*, XLIX, 1930, 160-71.
Y. SUKENIK (YADIN), '"Engines invented by Skilful Men" (2 Ch 26: 15)', in *BJPES*, XIII, 1946-7, 19-24 (in Hebrew).

On the water supply:

The archaeological information and bibliographical references can be found in A. G. BARROIS, *Manuel d'Archéologie Biblique*, I, Paris, 1939, ch. V: 'Installations hydrauliques'.

In addition:

O. TUFNELL, *Lachish III. The Iron Age*, London, 1953, 92-3 and 158-63.
J. B. PRITCHARD, 'The Water System at Gibeon', in *The Biblical Archaeologist*, XIX, 1956, 66-75.

3

Armaments

H. BONNET, *Die Waffen der Völker des Alten Orients*, Leipzig, 1926.
E. A. SPEISER, 'On Some Articles of Armor and their Names', in *JAOS*, LXX, 1950, 47-9.
J. T. MILIK and F. M. CROSS, 'Inscribed Javelin-Heads from the Period of the Judges', in *BASOR*, **134**, 1954, 5-15.
O. EISSFELDT, 'Zwei verkannte militär-technische Termini', in *VT*, V, 1955, 232-8.
Y. YADIN, 'Goliath's Javelin and the *menôr 'orgîm*', in *PEQ*, 1955, 58-69.
Y. YADIN, *The Scroll of the War of the Sons of Light against the Sons of Darkness*, Jerusalem 1956 (in Hebrew; Engl. tr., Oxford 1962).
J. T. MILIK, 'An Unpublished Arrow-Head with Phoenician Inscription of the 11th-10th Century B.C.', in *BASOR*, **143**, 3-6.
F. M. CROSS and J. T. MILIK, 'A Typological Study of the El Khadr Javelin- and Arrow-Heads', in *Annual of the Department of Antiquities of Jordan*, III, 1956, 15-23.
G. MOLIN, 'What is a Kidon?', in *Journal of Semitic Studies*, I, 1956, 334-7.
F. WILLESEN, 'The Philistine Corps of the Scimitar of Gath', in *Journal of Semitic Studies*, III, 1958, 327-35.

4
WAR

On the wars of Israel:

See the various histories of Israel, and add:

F. M. ABEL, 'Topographie des campagnes maccabéennes', in *RB*, XXXII, 1923, 495-521; XXXIII, 1924, 201-17, 371-87; XXXIV, 1925, 194-216; XXXV, 1926, 206-22, 510-33.

G. E. WRIGHT, 'The Literary and Historical Problem of Joshua 10 and Judges 1', in *JNES*, V, 1946, 105-14.

A. MALAMAT, 'The Last Wars of the Kingdom of Juda', in *JNES*, IX, 1950, 105-14.

A. MALAMAT, 'Introduction à l'histoire militaire d'Israël', in '*Athidôt*, IV, 12, 1951, 1-11 (in Hebrew).

On the conduct of war:

S. B. FINESINGER, 'The Shofar', in *HUCA*, VIII-IX, 1931-2, 193-228.

G. DOSSIN, 'Signaux lumineux au pays de Mari', in *Revue d'Assyriologie*, XXXV, 1938, 174-86.

P. HUMBERT, *La 'terou'a'. Analyse d'un rite biblique*, Neuchâtel, 1946.

S. YEIVIN, 'Canaanite and Hittite Strategy in the Second Half of the Second Millenary B.C.', in *JNES*, IX, 1950, 101-7.

Y. YADIN, 'Some Aspects of the Strategy of Achab and David', in *Biblica*, XXXVI, 1955, 322-51.

A. MALAMAT, 'Military Rationing in Papyrus Anastasi I and the Bible', in *Mélanges Bibliques rédigés en l'honneur de André Robert*, Paris, 1957, 114-21.

On the consequences of war:

W. J. MARTIN, 'Tribut und Tributleistungen bei den Assyrern' (*Studia Orientalia*, VIII, 1), Helsinki, 1936.

H. KRUSE, 'Ethos Victoriae in Vetere Testamento', in *Verbum Domini*, XXX, 1952, 3-13, 65-80, 143-53.

A. AYMARD, 'Le partage des profits de la guerre dans les traités d'alliance antiques', in *Revue Historique*, CCXVII, 1957, 233-49.

M. NOTH, 'Das alttestamentliche Bundschliessen im Lichte eines Mari-Textes', in *Mélanges Isidore Lévy*, Brussels, 1955, 433-44 = *Gesammelte Studien zum Alten Testament*, Munich, 1957, 142-54.

5
THE HOLY WAR

F. SCHWALLY, *Semitische Kriegsaltertümer*. I, *Der heilige Kreig im alten Israel*, Leipzig, 1901.

E. BICKERMANN, *Der Gott der Makkabäer*, Berlin, 1937.

H. FREDRIKSSON, *Jahwe als Krieger*, Lund, 1945.

P. HUMBERT, *La 'terou'a'. Analyse d'un rite biblique*, Neuchâtel, 1946.

B. N. WAMBACO, *L'épithète divine Jahvé Sᵉba'ot*, Bruges, 1948.

O. EISSFELDT, 'Jahwe Zebaoth', in *Miscellanea Academica Berolinensia*, Berlin, 1950, 128-50.

H. KRUSE, 'Conceptus interdicti in Levitico 27: 28-29', in *Verbum Domini*, XXVIII, 1950, 43-50.

G. VON RAD, *Der Heilige Krieg im alten Israel*, Zürich, 1951.

Y. YADIN, *The Scroll of the War of the Sons of Light against the Sons of Darkness*, Jerusalem, 1955 (in Hebrew).

A. DUPONT-SOMMER, '"Règlement de la Guerre des Fils de Lumière", traduction et notes', in *Revue de l'Histoire des Religions*, CXLVIII, 1955-II, 25-43, 141-80.

G. VON RAD, 'The Origin of the Concept of the Day of Yahweh', in *Journal of Semitic Studies*, IV, 1956, 97-108.

J. VAN DER PLOEG, 'La guerre sainte dans la "Règle de la Guerre" de Qumrân', in *Mélanges Bibliques rédigés en l'honneur de André Robert*, Paris, 1957, 326-33.

J. CARMIGNAC, *La Règle de la Guerre des Fils de Lumière contre les Fils de Ténèbres*, Paris, 1958.

J. VAN DER PLOEG, 'Le Rouleau de la Guerre', translated and annotated with an introduction (*Studies on the Texts of the Desert of Judah*, II), Leiden, 1959.

C. H. W. BREKELMANN, *De herem in het Oude Testament*, Nijmegen, 1959.

GENERAL INDEX

In this first index, the most important page-references are given first, and the sub-headings are arranged, as far as possible, in a logical order (e.g. historically).

INDEX TO PROPER NAMES

liii

Deuteronomy: see General Index
Dinah, 19, 30, 368
Dionysus, 513, 514
Dioscorus (month), 186, 189
Dod of Beersheba, 293
Doeg, 94, 219, 221
Dor, 134
Dusares, 513
Duweir, Tell ed-: see Lakish
Dystros (month), 186

Ea, 110
Ebal, 143, 290, 408
Ebyathar, 127, 128, 359–360, 376, 387, 388, 396, and especially, 372–374
Ecbatane, 235
Edom(ites), 'sons of', 5; clans, 8; not dynastic, 94; David's conquest, 96, 247, 255; their revolt, 248; Solomon marries, 31; defeat Joram, 223; Moab invaded through, 252; enforced circumcision, 47; Baalhanan=David?, 108
'Eglah, 44
Eglon, 235
Ehud, 196, 215, 241
Ekron: see Eqron
El, 294, 310; =Yahweh, 45, 413; beth-El, 291; at Ugarit, 286, 410
El-berith, 294
El-Bethel, 292, 294, 310
El-'Elyon, 113, 310, 374
El-Kunirsha, 310
El 'Obeid, 274, 281
El-'Olam, 293, 294, 310
El-Shaddai, 294, 310
'Ela (El-), 369
Elah, 129, 224
Elath, 248
Elath-'Olam, 293
Eleazar, son of Aaron, 54, 347, 352, 360, 373, 388, 396, 397, 399
Eleazar of Qiryath-Yearim, 346, 361
Elephantine: see especially, 340–341; marriage contracts, 27, 33, 36; writs of divorce, 35, 36; wife's civil rights, 40, 54; patronymic names 45; judicial oaths, 157; interest on loans, 170, 171; calendar, 185 fn., 192; meaning of degel, 226; El and Bethel, 292; Temple, 340–341, 342, 431; and high priests, 397, 401; Passover, 484, 485, 490
Eleusis, 292
Elhanan, 108
Eli, 50, 349, 355, 359, 373, 374, 376, 377, 379, 396, 453, 496
Eliab, 128
Eliakim (king): see Elyaqim
Eliakim, seal of, 126
Elias, 'leaders of fifty', 226; 'Gilgal', 304; Golden Calves, 334; Carmel, 198, 280, 306, 19—A.I.

408, 426, 438, 469; Sinai= Horeb, 281; Hazael, 104
Elijah: see preceding
Elihaph, Elihoreph, 128, 129, 193
Elimelek, 167
Eliphaz, 24
Eliseus, widow, 83, 172; accompanies army, 263; Naaman, 85; Jehu, 97, 104; not anointed, 105; prophets, 384
Elisha: see preceding
Elishama, 131
Eliun, 310
Elkanah: see Elqanah
Elôn, 44
Elqanah, 304, 355, 495
Elul, 186, 189, 193
Elyaqim, 46, .107, 129, 130
Elyashib, 397
Emmanuel, 107
Encaenia: see General Index, s.v. Hanukkah
Endor, 181
Engaddi, 136
Engedi: see preceding
En-ha-Tannîn, 278
Eninnu, 277
Enlil, 148
En-Mishpat, 278
En-Shemesh, 278
Ephraim, adopted by Jacob, 51; clans of, 8; richness of, 73; territory, 134; slaughter Midianites, 218; Levites in, 71, 181, 215, 368, 359–360; pursue Philistines, 217; Gilgal?, 302–303; Syro-Ephraimite war, 263; calendar of?, 487, 499
Ephron, 167, 207
Eqron, 298
Er, 36, 37
Esau, 24, 29, 30, 31, 42, 92, 345
Esdraelon, 134
Esdras, caravan, 21, 339, 366, 383, 388–390, 391; 'sons of Aaron', 396; letter, 403; 'people of the land', 72; mixed marriages, 31; and Law, 148, 151, 497, 500, 503; and Pentateuch, 473; calendar, 473; synagogues?, 343
Eshnunna, Law of, 145, 169
Eshtaol, 21
Essenes, 455, 456, 483; cf. Qumran
Esther, 514–517, 39, 51, 117, 181
Esyon Geber, 77, 78, 89, 141, 234
Etham, 230, 239
Ethan, 382, 392
Ethanim, 183, 499
Etemenanki, 274, 277, 282
Eusebius, 445
Eve, 43
Expiation, Day of: see General Index, s.v. Atonement

Ezechias, king, royal estate, 125; cubit, 197; war with Philistines, 248; defences of Jerusalem, 230, 239; religious reform, 288, 322, 326–327, 336, 339, 364, 375, 379, 391, 472, 484, 487; Deuteronomy, 144, 339; Sennacherib, 66, 115, 122, 129, 132, 222, 224, 249, 255, 326–327
Ezechias, priest, 208
Ezechiel: see Index of Biblical References
Ezra: see Esdras
Ezrahite, 382

Far'ah, Tell el- (S.), 186
Far'ah, Tell el- (N., near Nablus), 72, 137, 234, 283, 314; cf. Tirsah
Farvadin, 517
Fûl, Tell el-, 235
Fuller's Field, 70

Gabael, 169
Gad, 133, 139, 163, 214, 219, 247
Galilee, 66
Gamaliel II, 189
Garizim, 143, 290, 342
Gate of the Potsherds, 77
Gath, 87, 164, 219, 230, 298
Gaumata, 516
Gaza, 81
Gé, 310
Geba, 142, 230, 237, 367, 389
Gedaliah: see Godolias
Gedera, 77
Gehazi, 85
Genubat, 51
Gerar, 9, 37
Gerizim: see Garizim
Gershom, 44, 362, 391, 392
Gershonites, 370
Geshur, 116
Gezer, Canaanite enclave, 95; Pharaoh's harem, 26, 28, 116; given to Solomon, 125; a chariot town, 223, 248; its fortifications, 231–234 passim; water supply, 240; cuneiform contracts, 168, 185, 192; its calendar, 184, 185, 189, 190, 192, 493, 498; weight from, 205; high place, 287; altar, 407
Ghazza, Khirbet, 235
Gibbethon, 248
Gibeah, 10, 74, 92, 215, 236, 304, 306, 360, 370
Gibeon, 305–306; combat at 220; its high place, 113, 287, 288, 297, 331–332, 442; Sadoq a priest of, 373; Tent at?, 297, 391; administrative centre, 136; water supply, 239, 240
Gibeonites and Josue, 90, 254, 303, 383; their towns, 91, 95; mercenaries, 94; execute Saul's descendants, 442, 491; Temple slaves, 90, 383

INDEX OF SEMITIC FORMS

(including a few Egyptian words)

INDEX OF BIBLICAL REFERENCES

INDEX OF BIBLICAL REFERENCES

INDEX OF BIBLICAL REFERENCES

LIST OF ABBREVIATIONS OF BIBLICAL REFERENCES